Jonathan Swift

Longman Critical Readers

General Editor:
STAN SMITH, Research Professor in Literary Studies, Nottingham Trent University

JONATHAN SWIFT

Edited and Introduced by

NIGEL WOOD

LONGMAN

LONDON AND NEW YORK

Addison Wesley Longman Limited
Edinburgh Gate
Harlow
Essex CM20 2JE
United Kingdom
and Associated Companies throughout the world.

*Published in the United States of America
by Addison Wesley Longman Inc., New York*

First published 1999

ISBN 0–582–22573–6 CSD
ISBN 0–582–22572–8 PPR

Visit Addison Wesley Longman on the world wide web at
http://www.awl-he.com

British Library Cataloguing-in-Publication Data

A catalogue record for this book is available from the British Library

Library of Congress Cataloging-in-Publication Data

Jonathan Swift / edited and introduced by Nigel Wood.
    p.   cm. — (Longman critical readers)
    Includes bibliographical references and index.
    ISBN 0–582–22573–6 (CSD). — ISBN 0–582–22572–8 (PPR)
    1. Swift, Jonathan, 1667–1745—Criticism and interpretation.
    2. Satire, English—Ireland—History and criticism.   I. Wood,
    Nigel, 1953–   .   II. Series.
    PR3727.J627   1999
    828′.509—dc21   98–30635
                                                       CIP

Set by 35 in $9\frac{1}{2}$/$11\frac{1}{2}$pt Palatino
Produced by Addison Wesley Longman Singapore (Pte) Ltd
Printed in Singapore

Contents

Contents

General Editors' Preface

The outlines of contemporary critical theory are now often taught as a standard feature of a degree in literary studies. The development of particular theories has seen a thorough transformation of literary criticism. For example, Marxist and Foucauldian theories have revolutionised Shakespeare studies, and 'deconstruction' has led to a complete reassessment of Romantic poetry. Feminist criticism has left scarcely any period of literature unaffected by its searching critiques. Teachers of literary studies can no longer fall back on a standardised, received methodology.

Lecturers and teachers are now urgently looking for guidance in a rapidly changing critical environment. They need help in understanding the latest revisions in literary theory, and especially in grasping the practical effects of the new theories in the form of theoretically sensitised new readings. A number of volumes in the series anthologise important essays on particular theories. However, in order to grasp the full implications and possible uses of particular theories it is essential to see them put to work. This series provides substantial volumes of new readings, presented in an accessible form and with a significant amount of editorial guidance.

Each volume includes a substantial introduction which explores the theoretical issues and conflicts embodied in the essays selected and locates areas of disagreement between positions. The pluralism of theories has to be put on the agenda of literary studies. We can no longer pretend that we all tacitly accept the same practices in literary studies. Neither is a *laissez-faire* attitude any longer tenable. Literature departments need to go beyond the mere toleration of theoretical differences: it is not enough merely to agree to differ; they need actually to 'stage' the differences openly. The volumes in this series all attempt to dramatise the differences, not necessarily with a view to resolving them but in order to foreground the choices presented by different theories or to argue for a particular route through the impasses the differences present.

The theory 'revolution' has had real effects. It has loosened the grip of traditional empiricist and romantic assumptions about language and literature. It is not always clear what is being proposed as the new agenda for literary studies, and indeed the very notion of 'literature' is questioned by the post-structuralist strain in theory. However, the uncertainties and obscurities of contemporary theories appear much less worrying when we see what the best critics have been able to do with them in practice. This series aims to disseminate the best of recent criticism and to show that it is possible to re-read the canonical texts of literature in new and challenging ways.

RAMAN SELDEN AND STAN SMITH

The Publishers and fellow Series Editor regret to record that Raman Selden died after a short illness in May 1991 at the age of fifty-three. Ray Selden was a fine scholar and a lovely man. All those he has worked with will remember him with much affection and respect.

Acknowledgements

The publishers are grateful to the following for permission to reproduce copyright material:

Associated University Presses for the essays 'Deconstructing Gulliver's Travels' by Louise K. Barnett in THE GENRES OF GULLIVER'S TRAVELS (1990) ed. Frederick N. Smith and 'Freud, Swift and Narcissism' by Thomas B. Gilmore Jr. in CONTEMPORARY STUDIES OF SWIFT'S POETRY (1981); Cambridge University Press and the author for an extract from THE BODY IN SWIFT AND DEFOE by Carol Houlihan Flynn (1990); the author, Terry Castle for her essay 'Why the Houyhnhnms Don't Write' in ESSAYS IN LITERATURE Volume 7 (1980); Cornell University Press for an extract from SWIFT'S NARRATIVE SATIRES: AUTHOR AND AUTHORITY by Everett Zimmerman, Copyright © 1983 by Cornell University Press; the author, Carole Fabricant for an extract from her SWIFT'S LANDSCAPE. pubd. Johns Hopkins University Press (1982); Harvard University Press and the author, Professor Edward Said for an extract from THE WORLD, THE TEXT AND THE CRITIC by Edward W. Said, Cambridge, Mass.: Harvard University Press, Copyright © 1983 by Edward W. Said; Modern Language Association of America for the essay 'Splendide Mendax' by Richard H. Rodino in PLMA 106 (1991) pp. 1054–77; the editor, MODERN LANGUAGE REVIEW and the author, Marcus Walsh for his essay 'Text, "Text" and Swift's A Tale of a Tub' in MODERN LANGUAGE REVIEW, vol. 85 (1990) pp. 290–303, © Modern Humanities Research Association, All rights reserved; Routledge/ Methuen & Co. for an extract from THE POLITICS AND POETICS OF TRANSGRESSION by Peter Stallybrass & Allon White pp. 100–12, published by Methuen & Co.; University Press of Kentucky for an extract from READING DECONSTRUCTION by G. Douglas Atkins pp. 105–17; University of North Carolina Press for an extract from JONATHAN SWIFT AND THE VESTED WORD by Deborah Baker Wyrick, pp. 95–108, Copyright © 1988 by The University of North Carolina Press; the author, Penelope Wilson for her essay 'Feminism and the Augustans' in FUTURES FOR ENGLISH ed. Colin MacCabe, published 1988 by Manchester University Press; the editor, YEARBOOK OF ENGLISH STUDIES and the authors, Margaret Anne Doody for her essay 'Swift among the Women' in YEARBOOK OF ENGLISH STUDIES, vol. 18 (1988) pp. 68–92, © Modern Humanities

Acknowledgements

Research Association, and Professor Brean Hammond for his essay 'Scriblerian Self-Fashioning' in *YEARBOOK OF ENGLISH STUDIES*, vol. 18, (1988) pp. 108–22, © Modern Humanities Research Association, All rights reserved.

Abbreviations

References to Swift's works include either the volume and page number of the *Prose Works* (*PW*) edited by Herbert Davis, 14 vols (Oxford, 1939–68) or, in the case of the poetry, the line numbers of the *Complete Poems* (*CP*) edited by Pat Rogers (Harmondsworth, 1983).

The following abbreviations appear in the text:

CH   *Swift: The Critical Heritage*, ed. Kathleen Williams (London, 1970).

Corr.   *The Correspondence of Jonathan Swift*, ed. Harold Williams, 5 vols (Oxford, 1963–65)

ELH   *Journal of English Literary History*

Whenever he was en route from one place to another, he was able to look at his life with a little more objectivity than usual. It was often on trips that he thought most clearly, and made the decisions that he could not reach when he was stationary.

(Paul Bowles, *The Sheltering Sky*)

Introduction

When reviewing Sir Walter Scott's edition of Swift (1814), Francis Jeffrey, the editor of *The Edinburgh Review*, accounted for the sudden decline in favour recently shown the Augustan wits by re-creating a pre-Romantic image of authorship:

> ['Almost all' of their writing was] what may be called occasional productions – not written for fame or for posterity – from the fulness of the mind, or the desire of instructing mankind – but on the spur of the occasion – for promoting some temporary and immediate object, and producing a practical effect, in the attainment of which their whole importance centred.
>
> (*ER*, vol. 27, no. 53 [September, 1816])[1]

Jeffrey discounted any pretensions to Art that embraced 'a practical effect' and an 'immediate object'. As did Scott, he also equated the savagery of Swift's satiric means with disturbed, even pathological, motives.[2] Praise might be heaped on his rhetoric, its mix of vehemence and complexity, yet it displays also a lack of the true artistic *ethos*: sagacious, sincere and all of a piece throughout – derived from a vocation, not the pretextual occasion. This distrust of Swift's work takes us to the very edge of definitions of the artistic, as his writing can often appear the very opposite of aesthetic and can now require plentiful footnotes.

Conversely, there is some point to using the adjective 'Swiftian'. Quite unlike the (syntactically) balanced inexorability of Johnson as *Rambler* or Pope's urbane couplets, the eighteenth-century canon now accommodates Swift as the anarchist and even post-modern jester, one who strikes at the root of all easy faiths and comfortable fictions. Martin Battestin found in his verse an 'arch repudiation of the Augustan idea of poetry itself', whereby the pursuit of *la belle nature* 'seemed morally irresponsible because calculated to conceal, even to deny, the truth of things as they are'.[3] Such a verdict could hardly be used of any other of his contemporaries. Pope, his life-long friend, seemed genuinely engrossed by his ventriloquilism:

> O Thou! whatever title please thine ear,
> Dean, Drapier, Bickerstaff, or Gulliver!
> Whether thou choose Cervantes' serious air,
> Or laugh and shake in Rabelais' easy chair, . . .
>
> (*The Dunciad* [1742], 1: 19–22)[4]

This does not prevent Pope using the familiar second person, and, as he stated in a letter to Swift of 6 January 1733/34, actually identifying a 'self' in the midst of these masks: 'Your method of concealing your self puts me in mind of the bird I have read of in India, who hides his head in a hole, while all his feathers and tail stick out.'[5] Jeffrey found him the puppeteer (and thus perhaps also the puppet) of contingency, yet Pope finds a 'method' in concealment and an eventual consistency in such evasiveness.

Sorely afflicted by the vicissitudes of fortune, Swift increasingly regarded himself as a protean set of selves. When imagining others' verdicts on him, he strove to gain the impersonality that did not deceive at the same time as revelling in the mystery of a split personality. In his *A Panegyric on the Dean, In the Person of a Lady in the North* (*c.* 1730; pub. 1735), the fashionable Lady Acheson simply cannot quite read Swift:

> . . . My grateful muse
> Salutes the Dean in different views;
> Dean, butler, usher, jester, tutor; . . .
>
> (ll. 37–8)[6]

There is gratitude here, but it also may be empty praise. Swift has the Lady know him as a collection of external features and servile functions. Similarly, his English friends' concern at his demise, in both *The Life and Character of Dean Swift* (1733) and its expanded and revised version, *Verses on the Death of Dr. Swift, D.S.P.D.* (1739), is composed of knowledge and also a concern that is both transient and, understandably, jostled by necessary diurnal activities. Grub Street wits cloy the town with elegies, which alternately 'curse the Dean, or bless the Drapier' (*Verses*, l. 168), but whether anybody can catch hold of the real, unified, ego is part of the anxiety, and perhaps triumph, projected by the whole performance. It is left to 'One quite indifferent in the cause' to draw his 'character impartial' (ll. 305–6), but the more the statements are convincingly judicious and lapidary, the less the imagined death is seen to provoke deep sentiment.[7] As Edward Said has noted (in this volume, p. 42), in delivering his own *ethos* to History at the poem's end, Swift is also reaching for 'the fictive element of language' to subsume 'a [future] real event'. It is as if the author cannot ignore the transitive demands of the Real, yet also has a diminished confidence that the external world supplies Truth and lasting consolation.

Assembling a collection such as this could have as its aim a form of collective biographical witness and disclosure, the location of a Swift off-stage and 'known perhaps for the first time, yet the premature reduction of his writing to some generalized consistency has its own flaws. Jeffrey is perceptive in acknowledging that works such as *Gulliver's Travels* or *The Drapier's Letters* are embedded in a precise historical moment, and that they may therefore address a particular set of audiences. Swift must be allowed to change his priorities if not his mind. 'Bickerstaff' is, after all, separated from 'Drapier' by some twenty years, and, if we are not careful, we may be led to expect the Church of Ireland Anglican in all of his work, and read accordingly. If there is a logic or bias in this Reader, then it might lie in representing how a wide variety of criticism has faced three associated and common problems in interpreting Swift's writing: (a) how to comprehend the ways in which Swift's overt Tory sympathies could give rise to such unclassical and adventurous prose; (b) how his perspective on the body, often figured in the female, could avoid being merely prurient and auto-erotic; and (c) how works so transitive and politically aligned could at the same time question some of the most perennial concepts taken to define human identity, society and the spiritual.

This collection is an attempt to represent several current ideas not only about Swift's art and literary personality but also about its wider contexts. Inevitably, it is selective, for Swift has been the occasion for not only varied and committed criticism but also radical disagreement about the fundamentals of all literary comment. In short, theoretical alignment is often sharpened in reading Swift's work, indeed, is sometimes found necessary in providing a coherent account, and I have tried to represent some of the bases for this powerful sense of engagement, without, I hope, offering comment that is too partisan.

'His Delight was in Simplicity'

In his 'Life of Swift' (*Lives of the Poets* [1779–81]), Samuel Johnson found *A Tale of a Tub* an exception to Swift's other work. Here there was exhibited 'a vehemence and rapidity of mind, a copiousness of images, and vivacity of diction', whereas more normally there was a 'delight . . . in simplicity', where 'his few metaphors [could] seem to be received rather by necessity than choice'. While he 'studied purity', however, not all of his 'structures' were 'exact'.[8] This has now something of the force of calculated euphemism, for the simplicity Johnson noted is rarely regarded now as just a matter in Swift's work of 'exact' structures and denotative lexis. Certainly, the almost forensic deployment of language, admitting of no interpretative uncertainty, was a frequently stated aim. One of the very few of his works actually to have first been published bearing his own name on the title-page was his *Proposal for Correcting, Improving and Ascertaining the English Tongue* (1712), and the validity of a serious attempt to fix the language has often been misrepresented. Swift calls on the then Prime Minister, the Earl of Oxford, for an academy to ascertain the meanings of words 'for ever': 'For I am of Opinion, that it is better a Language should not be wholly perfect, than that it should be perpetually changing; and we must give over at one Time or other, or at length infallibly change for the worse' (*PW*, 4: 14). The goal of a 'zero degree' of communication is one of the most defining aspirations of the Enlightenment,[9] yet it would be rash to enlist Swift too readily in the project on a philosophical basis. He has this academy 'most at Heart', admits that some augmentation may from time to time be necessary and hopes that 'some Method should be thought on' to bring this to pass. Quite *how* it could be brought about is never clear. Swift is precise about his aims, the principal one being stability in culture (good news to any presiding politician), yet how one prevents usage or 'Practice' adulterating this native idiom we must assume is down to a branch of government, and a most illiberal one at that. The reader also never quite gets to inspect the father's will in the *Tale* that offers the three sons such 'full Instructions' about the wearing of the new coats that it will ensure their freshness 'as long as you live . . . so as to be always fit' (*PW*, 1: 44) nor an example of the Brobdingnagian laws in Book two of *Gulliver's Travels*, which are expressed 'in the most plain and simple Terms, wherein these People are not Mercurial enough to discover above one Interpretation' (*PW*, 11: 136).[10] The truths embodied in these commandments, as Terry J. Castle is insistently aware (in this volume, pp. 239–54), are numinous and so eventually uninterpretable.

This reticence accounts for the great interest shown in Swift's 'grammophobia', that is, his steadfast distrust of textual authority (writing) in that it removes power from the vocative context (oral, direct, personal and intended) and delivers meanings to the critic. When confronted by heroes of the modern historical account in Glubbdubdrib, Gulliver is alarmed at how often we had been 'misled by prostitute Writers' to praise those whom, on meeting, we would have condemned, and also how often 'great Enterprizes and Revolutions in the World' had been precipitated by 'contemptible Accidents' (*PW*, 11: 199). This is anarchy and it is the Real for Swift.

The Houyhnhnms have no writing because they have no need of it. In the human world, on the other hand, true meaning and instinct invariably work against each other. The hope that, in 1712, the Earl of Oxford might have been able to protect the sacerdotal status of language was indeed a pious one, and, by 1726, the emphases had changed. The fallible promises of politics had provided fools' gold for the exiled Swift, for, at the same time as he feared texts, he also revered and desired the true one. When shown the Academy at Lagado, Gulliver reveals the apparently harmless diversions at the School of Languages, including a 'Scheme for entirely abolishing all Words whatsoever' on the grounds that, 'since Words are only Names for *Things*', one could simply bypass the treacherous verbal realm by carrying the objects of discourse with one and producing them when needed. The 1712 *Proposal* would appear here to have been reduced to absurdity, yet the ultimate aim of Swift's appeal to the Tory administration had been political and moral stability, a continuity with the traditional mainstream, validated by historical precedent and so found viable. From this perspective, empiricism is yet another mechanical operation of the spirit. Even the academicians yield to 'the Women in Conjunction with the Vulgar and Illiterate' who overturn such forces of modernity by claiming 'the Liberty to speak with their Tongues, after the Manner of their Forefathers' (*PW*, 11: 185). The project is risible, and the scene depicted of heavily-laden projectors savage burlesque, but it is not clear whether it is so because it depicts just amnesiac radicalism or because it shows how words should retain an history in their use, a semantic ingredient free of the particular locutionary context – or a mixture of both.

Put bluntly, what does Swift find in words that is ignored by the Projectors? What is the supplementary essence that stands distinct from exact and unambiguous mimesis? Words are not things, but they are not also the breath of mere inspiration, as the Aeolists' enthusiastic witness to God (from Section VIII in the *Tale*) renders language as on a par with belching. The semantic space between rhetoric and some basic linguistic transparency implies a questioning of denotation itself. For Derrida, this fear of textualist play is superfluous, as 'language bears within itself the necessity of its own critique'.[11] The consequent emergence of a new range of symbolic possibilities is evident in many of the canonical ironic texts for which Swift is now famous. Limiting signification depends on a tacit, but still relative, consensus as to what the discourse is about to communicate, and this pre-emptive horizon of 'agreed' rules or codes presupposes a common humanity, that bedrock of civilized rituals and distinctive spiritual aspirations that constitute humankind. Did Swift, in adopting his various meretricious and modern personae,

5

discover a kinship with them he dared not otherwise acknowledge? In the work of both Louise K. Barnett and G. Douglas Atkins (in this volume) Swift realizes (despite himself?) the inevitability of linguistic nominalism and abhors its consequences: the blurring of distinction, hybridization and interpretations so rootless that they are merely an indulgence in verbal play. This insight is also truth, however, as Swift also dramatizes the clash between the moral principle that unequivocal meanings should exist and his desperation that, in reality, he cannot be sure that he has ever found them. Perhaps the Teller of the *Tale* and Gulliver exist in all storytellers.

For deconstructive readings to be fully persuasive, however, we need to lift Swift out of his immediate literary and moral context – in short, to discover elements of the text not directly linked (and sometimes counter to) what the conscious Swift thought he was accomplishing. Marcus Walsh's understanding of the Restoration debate about orality presents a plainer picture of Swift's conscious and deliberate undertaking, which uncovers a sophisticated contemporary hermeneutical faith in immanent meanings which in no way removes an individual voice from the text. Walsh locates Swift in Martin's position in the *Tale* and certainly not in those projections of the Modern consciousness, the Teller and Peter. Certainly, there is a 'Swift' confident of a bold simplicity that might be free of contingency. One thinks of those 'simple topics told in rhyme' that would appear to encapsulate 'No thought, no fancy, no sublime' in his verse epistle 'To Mr. Delany' (ll. 11–12; 1718, pub. 1765), and those plain style Birthday Odes to Stella that derive comfort from the assumption that the body may 'thrive and grow / By food of twenty years ago' (ll. 55–6, 'Stella's Birthday [1727]' [pub. 1728]). Martin Price's seminal analysis of Swift's rhetorical strategies identified such simplicity as a carefully laboured creation, and placed it against a later, more Romantic notion of artless inspiration, akin to the transient modishness found in genteel conversation.[12]

As with all reconstructive readings, however, the view that Swift was in full control of his rhetoric amounts to no more than a belief that meaning is always validated only by reference to intention. This eventually places complex and ironic works such as the *Tale* and *An Argument Against Abolishing Christianity* (1708) on a semantic par with the relatively 'simple topics' of *The Sentiments of a Church of England Man* (1711) and his *Project for the Advancement of Religion and the Reformation of Manners* (1709). It also ignores the clear influence on Swift of sceptics such as La Rochefoucauld[13] and also the vitality of performance kindled by anarchy noted by several commentators, most eloquently by Claude Rawson.[14] Swift was fascinated as well as appalled by the loss of meaning in the process of communication.

One of the most uncomplicated rhetorical questions in *Mr. C[olli]ns's Discourse of Free-Thinking, Put into Plain English,* . . . (1713) would seem to exclude all but the most literal understanding of literary texts: 'For what Authority can a Book pretend to, where there are various Readings?' Swift proceeds, however, to offer a more sophisticated riposte to Anthony Collins's own *Discourse of Freethinking* (1713), a work he felt was a 'brief compleat Body of Atheology' (*PW*, 4: 33, 27). Where the Deist Collins had stressed a most dispersed authority – divinity discoverable by interpretation – and the openness of texts to dissenting ingenuity, Swift perceives a liberal tyranny: the encouragement of free speech and thought means the devaluation of truth and a surrender to modishness. It should not follow, indeed, must not follow, that, because there are 'various Readings', books 'become utterly useless' (*PW*, 4: 33). Always to a degree abstract, meaning, therefore, exists as beyond our power to express it totally. Simplicity should be the most plaindealing method, yet the paradox remains that Swift rarely rests content with it. Even if the same thesis can at last be deduced from them, a double negative does not always amount to the same as a positive statement.

'Whenever He Offends against Delicacy, He Teaches It'

John Hawkesworth's six-volume *Works of Jonathan Swift* (1755) provided the first conspectus of Swift's full achievement, and also the first thoroughgoing defence of his satiric 'indelicacy'. Confronted by the apparent obscenity of the Yahoos and ladies' dressing-rooms, he regarded such importunate physicality as themes rather than direct evidence of Swift's inner life. Consequently, the satiric force of his work was rendered as no more than shocking techniques to realize more orthodox ends and certainly not compulsive self-revelation. Yahoos may disgust, yet the image is always an instructive one, provoking the realization that 'virtue is the perfection of reason' (*CH*, p. 153). The iconoclasm of poems that would seem to have inherited the spirit of anti-female insult from the Restoration is no more than a pedagogical device. 'Strephon and Chloe' may have been found coarse, but 'with no better reason than a medecine would be rejected for its ill taste'. 'A Beautiful Young Nymph going to Bed' always has a reader consider the dangers of 'picking up a prostitute' (females would probably not have been allowed to read the poem), and 'The Lady's Dressing-Room' is strategically repulsive because 'whenever he offends against delicacy, he teaches it; he stimulates the mind to sensibility, to correct the faults of habitual negligence' (*CH*, pp. 154–5). This jolting of the complacent reader has, however, a savagery about it that cannot quite be erased in the service of promoting piercing moral insight. Swift knew that his tactics were divisive. He had good reason to suspect that, once his authorship of *A Tale of a Tub* were known, it would prevent necessary preferment, especially at the court of Queen Anne, even if Swift believed it helped (in its inimitable way) the Anglican cause. The depiction of the Lilliputian Empress's pique at his saving of her apartments from fire by urination in Chapter V (first voyage) of *Gulliver's Travels* is usually taken as a reflection of this undue courtly delicacy, yet, while this necessary distasteful act actually preserved the palace and thus rescued an edifice that 'had cost so many Ages in erecting', can we find her determination not to live there again so mysterious? The net effect of this action is the same as if the fire had done its own work regardless, as she becomes 'firmly resolved that those Buildings should never be repaired for her Use' (11: 56). Real christianity, in *An Argument Against Abolishing Christianity*, is only of actual benefit in a moral Utopia; otherwise, it 'would be to dig up Foundations; to destroy at one Blow *all* the Wit, and *half* the Learning of the Kingdom' (*PW*, 2: 27). It is only of Job's comfort that such Wit and Learning is presumably meretricious.

Can truth be communicated in the polite idiom that would render it acceptable? Or is it destined always to be a parlour game, wherein such honest attempts at reformation end up only as 'a *Ball* bandied to and fro, . . .', according to the *Tale*'s 'Preface' (*PW*, 1: 31). Even a commentator later friendly to Swift, Dr William King, in 1704, could, or would, not decipher the high moral purpose in the *Tale*: 'He takes the air upon dung-hills, in ditches, and common-shoars, and at my Lord Mayor's dog-kennel' (*CH*, p. 33). Sir Richard Blackmore found the main flaw to be excessive wit, whereby 'Vertue and Sobriety of Manners' were treated with 'Raillery and Ridicule' (*CH*, p. 52). Not for these commentators the sophistication of discounting the signifier for the sake of an ethical purpose. Wit, where verbal or accidental resemblance can take the place of real identity, dangerously moves between the germane and the indecorous, and, in so doing, can uncover a truth in jest. When Pope found 'True wit' to be 'nature to advantage dressed' he was at pains to dissociate it from conceitful profligacy, the 'glaring chaos and wild heap of wit' that forsakes the judicial faculty and is thus the foe of formal constraint and order (*An Essay on Criticism* [1711], ll. 297, 292). Nature is hardly ever dressed to advantage in Swift's writing.

There have been many followers of both King and Blackmore where Swift's scatology is concerned. In terms so diametrically opposed to Hawkesworth's, Swift is the misanthropist – and so is kin to Gulliver at the conclusion of his travels. It is as if the ironic fault-line between outrageous surface and moral depth running through the writing can be for many readers aggressively unstable. Swift is from this perspective actually the peeping-tom at beaux stripped and women flayed in the *Tale* (section IX), a Strephon who is surprised and thus repelled by the fact that Celia shits ('The Lady's Dressing-Room' [1732] or 'Cassinus and Peter' [1734]), and a Gulliver who would prefer to disown imperfect humankind completely in pursuit of the Utopian rationality of horses. It is not that F. R. Leavis, for example, does not discern Swift's superegoistic moral purpose in his reading of *An Argument Against Abolishing Christianity* and *A Modest Proposal*, it is just that he still finds the net effect to embrace an 'intensity [that] is purely destructive'.[15] It is a form of cruelty, as Claude Rawson has on several occasions noted, a matter rather more of 'mental atmosphere and ironic manipulation' than 'official ideological views'.[16] If so, then the very surplus of figurative energy begins to dissolve the barriers between what is stated – the only natural produce of 1720s Ireland that could sustain the people *is* human flesh – and what is implied – the immodesty of the proposal could only emerge from the econometric discourse deployed by a persona, here the Modest Proposer. When, in 1959, Norman O. Brown perceived an 'excremental vision' in Swift's work, he unflinchingly found him an analyst of 'an universal human neurosis' and not just a neurotic himself: 'we are not even disturbed by the thought that his individual neurosis may have been abnormally acute, or by the thought that his abnormality may be inseparable from his art'.[17] To be thoroughly civilized *is* to be anal and repressive. The impulse towards abstraction involves a fastidious blindness to the distractions of the erotic and the earthly – and yet, the repelled and also fascinated reader is held in an ironic double-bind: there is just enough truth in the perception that we are so ambivalent about anality because, as Freud understood in 1912, 'The excremental is all too intimately and inseparately bound up with the sexual'.[18] *A Tale of a Tub*, in its own terms, might simply signify a meaningless distraction (see the tub pitched into the sea to distract the Hobbesian Leviathan in the 'Preface' [l: 24]), but there was a less innocent meaning: an immersion in a sweating-tub was a favourite device to cure venereal disease (see John Webster's *The White Devil* [*c.* 1612], ll. i. 91).[19] In Thomas B. Gilmore, Jr.'s contribution to the volume this intersection of sexual horror and compulsive voyeurism is an indication of how relevant a reading of Swift is to any 'civilized' reader. Higher and lower are fated to meet alarmingly and, worse still, to suggest each other.

Several of the essays chosen for this collection touch on how Swift sought to explore this syndrome. In Carole Fabricant's piece, 'viewing', in its most literal sense, is both problematic and necessary. It is problematic for some of the reasons mentioned above, as perspective can often be a matter of the will, and it is necessary because it is a duty not to let distance lend enchantment to the view. Recalcitrant realities impinged upon Swift most insistently during, as he often regarded it, his later years of Irish exile, and the most effectual method to counter humankind's penchant for romantic delusion was to shock in the most visceral way. In a sense, this is to follow Hawkesworth and others and find a Swift always in control of his semiotic material, each signifier eventually anchored to its intended signified, but several of the later essays question this assumption. In Stallybrass and White's examination of references to the 'Grotesque Satiric Body' they uncover many associations of festive hybridization with the 'unnatural' incursion of the market-place and popular customs, a whole sub-culture of transgressive rituals that provided an affront to the pious hopes of the Enlightenment: that Mankind was perfectible and could be responsive to reason.

In the above, there is little doubt that representations that are gender-specific have been set aside. Swift would appear to turn to a disrobing of polite femininity a little too often. When Gulliver is brought up close to the gigantic Brobdingnagian Maids of Honour in Chapter V of Gulliver's second voyage, their pretensions to beauty are forcibly deconstructed and, although they appear naked in his sight, the acuity of his senses renders the scene anything but aesthetic. A mole would appear 'as broad as a Trencher, and Hairs hanging from it thicker than Pack-threads' and the Maids urinate in his presence, 'to the Quantity of at least two Hogsheads'. It is only once this distasteful context has been established that Swift proceeds to offer some erotic material in the scene – only it is by now far from that: 'The handsomest . . . , a pleasant frolicksome Girl of sixteen, would sometimes set me astride upon one of her Nipples' (*PW*, 11: 119). This nipple is disproportionately so, and is unpleasantly translated into some raree-show display. The very next paragraph relates the monstrous spectacle of witnessing a Brobdingnagian beheading. Corinna, as 'A Beautiful Young Nymph Going to Bed' (1734), dismantles herself, removing hair, eyebrows, teeth and false breasts in the process, and it is decency, in 'Strephon and Chloe' (1734), that 'must fan the lover's fire', not Beauty which is merely 'supported by Opinion' (ll. 222, 224). Beauty in Brobdingnag and Covent Garden can only be skin-deep. The wonder is, to Swift, that such daily agonies of reconstruction take place. Is Beauty only a trick of the light, a matter of perception, and derived only from the deft application of cosmetic powers?

In the essays here by Penelope Wilson, Margaret Anne Doody and Carol Houlihan Flynn Swift's relations with women are discussed both in biographical and symbolic terms. For Wilson, the critical men's clubbery of Augustan criticism almost replicates the very blindspots evident in the writers themselves. Sexual difference is exploited as grounds for moralistic comment about forbidden fruit. Doody places Swift among his Irish women friends and other imitators, and uncovers a common set of themes related to dirt and disorder, as if writers such as Mary Leapor or Laetitia Pilkington, in answering Swift's overt iconoclasm of the ideal female, actually found the emphasis liberating. Flynn, in her comparative study of the body in the work of both Defoe and Swift, is insistently aware of the latter's misogyny and how it incorporates pervasive patterns of imagery to do with consumption and desire. At the same time as regretting the 'disorderly nature of women', he is acutely aware of his own 'personal fears of dissolution' – both of vital male energy and individual identity. The question remains, for Swift particularly among the Augustan satirists: wherein can the pure or rational be found? Are we merely just Yahoos under a suit of clothes?

'But Where is the Sense of a General Satire, if the Whole Species be Degenerated?'

In the third number of *The Intelligencer* (1728), Swift turned to his own status as a satirist, and wondered about his motivation and political persuasion. Was the writing of raillery merely a matter of 'Humour', an uncontrollable bias of mind that precluded his turning out to be a lyricist, or did it issue from a deliberate programme of reform with certain realizable political and cultural goals? He concluded that a satirist obeyed a dual allegiance: the 'less noble' issued from 'the private Satisfaction and Pleasure of the Writer' (but did not involve '*personal Malice*'), whereas the other instinct derived from 'a *publick spirit*, prompting Men of *Genius* and Virtue, to mend the World as far as they are able' (*PW*, 12: 34). What is so disarming about this is Swift's own quest for self-knowledge. Not for this writer the sanctimonious comfort of the gladitorial satirist, drawing only on the strong antipathy of good to bad, but rather an unsparing anatomy of the being behind the rhetoric. One of the sermons ascribed to Swift from 1744 onwards, 'The Difficulty of Knowing One's Self', displays deep scepticism about how the inner relates to the outer, 'for a Man can no more know his own Heart than he can know his own Face, any other Way than by Reflection'. If one can stand it, one can only examine one's heart 'with a steady Eye' by an effort to 'contract his

Sight, and collect all his scattered and roving Thoughts into some
Order and Compass' (*PW*, 11: 356). What if, however, one saw all?
Again, with reference also to the deeply ambiguous figure of the
woman, Swift might eventually be some Cassinus or Strephon,
unable to avert his gaze and yet unable quite to live on with the
added knowledge that there is a difference between necessary
fictions and a darker, and more amorphous, reality. Conversely,
one could read much of Swift's *œuvre* as immensely realistic, too.
Yeats sensed that Swift was 'a practical politician in everything he
wrote',[20] in that his moral sense was rarely divorced from quotidian
reality and also needed to be (somehow) demonstrable to common
understanding.

Swift's public spirit is most obviously commemorated in his Irish
writings. Lauded as the Hibernian Patriot in the title of the London
edition of *The Drapier's Letters* (1730), Swift became, whether he
always wanted it or not, a defender of Irish rights and an opponent
of English economic individualism. In 1784, Thomas Sheridan
recorded the 'Drapier's' triumphant return to Ireland in 1726 as a
'kind of triumph, where he was received and welcomed on shore by
a multitude of his grateful countrymen',[21] and yet Swift can hardly
have relished all of this fraternal attention. Not published until
1882, his two poems written while waiting for the Holyhead ferry,
Holyhead. September 25, 1727 and *Ireland*, are text-book studies in
anomie and deracination. Anxious for the health of his dearest friend,
Stella (Esther Johnson), in Dublin, Swift felt a 'rage impatient' to
make the crossing to 'the land I hate' (*Holyhead*, ll. 27–28). In Swift's
own political mythography, Ireland was a place that almost willed its
own despoliation by the English:

> Remove me from this land of slaves,
> Where all are fools, and all are knaves;
> Where every knave and fool is bought,
> Yet kindly sells himself for naught; . . .

(Ireland, ll. 1–4)

From his first Irish tract, *The Story of the Injured Lady* (1707), to
one of the last to be published, *A Modest Proposal* (1729), Swift
imaged Ireland as a victim from which he quite strenuously strove to
distance himself. As the Drapier, the bluff unintellectual tradesman,
he found not only a persona to catch the Irish popular imagination,
but he also mined a deep seam of his own materialism that pre-dated
the situation of 1724/25. In opposing William Wood's scheme to
debase the Irish coinage for short-term (English) profit, the *Letters*

promote through a shopkeeper's unlettered wisdom that same identity of sign and essence that often coloured Swift's linguistic philosophies.[22]

If Ireland were so undeserving, then it seems strange that Swift should have so frequently striven to defend its interests. Similarly, any glance at his poetry would convince us that his Irish 'exile' provoked a stream of pithy occasional verse, from Stella's Birthday Odes to bantering exchanges with Lady Acheson and Patrick Delany. In Robert Mahony's comprehensive study of Swift's Irish reception,[23] it is now clear that the Irish needed a champion in the 1720s and so helped create one out of, in Oliver Ferguson's phrase, this 'patriot-in-spite-of-himself'.[24] Drapier's letters appeared well after Swift's death and monuments were readily funded to maintain the Dean's standing in Irish culture quite apart from his standing in any purely literary canon.

Investigations of Swift's politics usually sketch a gradual move away from some formal alignment with either the Whig party (up to 1710) or the Tories (sometimes seen as more or less supplying guiding principles until death or increasingly as merely a nexus of friends). The degree to which Swift's 'publick spirit' can be identified directly with eighteenth-century political causes is much in doubt. Parties were not organized on clear manifesto lines. Certain interests seemed perennial, such as trade and the growing financial markets (predominantly Whig) versus land (mainly Tory) and, in some quarters, the Stuart cause (Jacobitism), and/or freedom of conscience (increasingly Whig from 1710) versus an adherence to the established Church (Whig, in that they brokered the Revolution Settlement in 1689, but very much the Tory position throughout the 1720s). What is significant for the work of interpretation in all this is how Swift regarded traditional authority. Allegiance and passive obedience are required by a legally instituted sovereign ruling by consent of parliament. The motives for the Glorious Revolution had, therefore, had to be taken at face value: James II had abdicated rather than that his subjects had rebelled successfully.[25] The Settlement was, however, hardly a direct act of God, even if Swift saw it as a necessary bulwark against papist tyranny. Liberty was guaranteed by consensus and a free surrender of the individual will, but it was also achieved in a secular spirit of negotiation and compromise.

Gradually, and with some force when in 'exile', Swift developed a self-image of the embattled outsider, of threat to centralizing power. The contrast with Pope was illuminating: he had a genius that could transcend faction, but, on the other hand, Swift felt on 20 September 1723 that he was sunk under the prejudices of another Education, and am every day perswading my self that a Dagger is at my Throat, a halter about my Neck, or Chains at my Feet, all prepared by those in Power, [and so] can never arrive at the Security of Mind you possess.[26]

Here there is no attempt at rational assessment, and Power is here no beneficent protection. Again, in correspondence with Pope on 1 June 1728, he is at pains to draw a distinction between his being a Patriot, a title which he did not deserve, and a satirist, who acts 'owing to perfect rage and resentment, and the mortifying sight [in Ireland] of slavery, folly, and baseness about me'.[27] Instead of stressing the labels that usually accompany the description of a writer's 'publick spirit', it may be more accurate, using Warren Montag's valuable term, to find Swift's mode of thinking 'spontaneous philosophy',[28] where the pursuit of method is an undesirable victory of the body over the soul. One is saved by common understanding and a sense of right educed from common forms. To *search* for truth is inevitably self-defeating.

On the one hand, it is quite clear that Swift was a committed writer – the pungent metaphors and precisely calculated interrogation of his readers make that plain – but on the other, there is a curiously deep and *emotional* scepticism at all programmes of reform. The disappointed romantic has nothing left to sustain her/him once a favourite Utopia fails to match reality. William Warburton may not have been the most percipient of Swift's early readers, yet his resistance to such gloom in his *Critical and Philosophic Enquiry into the Causes of Prodigies* ... (1727) has found many supporters: where is the 'Benefit of Mankind', for 'where is the sense of a general Satire, if the whole Species be degenerated?' (*CH*, p. 72). Has Swift all along been a Gulliver returned from the Houyhnhnms, with no time for Yahoo-humans and their insufferable pride? If so, where does the critique stop, if at all, and where are its foundations?

Like Pope's freedoms when he modelled his idiom on Horace's during the 1730s, Swift discovered a flexibility and a style in filtering his prose through personae – and personae which were not just a means to avoid legal redress. As Deborah Baker Wyrick observes (this volume, p. 72), Swift's pseudonyms 'are more complete divestitures than is anonymity'. For example, the Drapier laid claim to an identity in the public mind quite aside from the more historical Dean Swift, even when the pretence of anonymity was known only to be a rhetorical device. Wyrick also notes how Swift could thereby 'maintain his absence from the text, [could] defer responsibility for his words, and [could] prevent meaning from being tied to – or closed by – the speaking or writing subject'. Swift's views on the

Wood scheme were given authority and conviction by the Drapier, his freely-chosen textual identity, and not directly from the actual author, whose reception would derive from a reader's prior knowledge of Swift himself. The complex ironic gesture of disowning one's words actually leads to the assembly of non-mimetic fictions, including personae that, as Everett Zimmerman explores in his contribution to this volume, were at the same time part of his larger purpose: to dissociate his writing from aesthetics itself. To observe this fully, it is perhaps essential to work alongside, but not be confined to, 'literary' definitions of satire (or either the essay or proposal). Hence it is that, as Dustin Griffin has usefully noted,[29] the voices within the texts we now deem satirical are rarely 'monological' in Bakhtin's sense, that is, experienced in a clear hierarchy either as regards the integrity of a supposed 'speaker' or in terms of the actual satiric design. The semantic divide in irony between intended and stated meaning is often erased.

Just as the high and the low collide so often in Swift's writing, so the surface rhetoric and the intention behind it so often form a symbolic impasse, not only in a reader's attempt to master its interpretation but also as Swift's fullest expression of frustration and dislocation. The Modest Proposer is as wearied as the historical Swift by suggesting practical schemes to solve Irish poverty; when secretary to the venerable but decidedly unwitty Sir William Temple, Swift writes one of the wittiest prose works of the century (*A Tale of a Tub*) which would appear to display the horrors of too much wit, and Gulliver ends up abhorring the sin of pride in humankind much as Swift did in so much of his writing. It is as if the writing is less sternly moralistic than desperately revelatory. Swift and his readers are often implicated in the errors displayed for our disapproval, an aversion therapy that can be radically unsure of its eventual direction. In terms of the 'publick spirit' that we can trace in many of Swift's more straightforward avowals of faith, he is a particularly shrewd analyst of a reader's defence mechanisms and calculates exactly how to pierce them in the service of traditional Anglican certainties. In terms, however, of a writer's 'private satisfaction and pleasure' the picture is less clear. In the verses on his death, Swift felt he was 'born to introduce' irony, and, indeed, 'refin'd it first, and showed its use' (ll. 57–58). The 'impersonal' verdict on him in the poem locates his vein as 'ironically grave' (l. 315). I have already mentioned Leavis's verdict (above p. 9) that such irony was a trope that allowed a fiercely destructive tone. This nervousness at the heart of most readings of irony can be regarded as a legacy of the stylistically complex means to a more paraphraseable goal: the carefully contrived entrapment of the otherwise negligent reader.

This is eventually to prise meaning away from the implicit *effect* the writing actually has on a reader.

In Paul Ricœur's *The Rule of Metaphor* (1975; trans. 1978)[30] this potential contradiction at the heart of irony, between a meaning discerned once the rhetoric is discounted and a meaning discerned to be within the rhetoric, is true of all metaphor: a pull towards the specific and local set of meanings generated in the sentence-unit and a counterbalancing impulse towards a reflection of the world, which is also the motive, for example, for consulting a dictionary. The former bias is what Ricœur names an 'interaction theory' of language, where the sense of any one unit of meaning is primarily determined by its syntactical (or, in narrative terms, strategic) position within a closed system. Travelling, in *Gulliver's Travels*, loses its more general semantic power once we realize that most of the signs created out of Gulliver's loss of identity (and wisdom?) are not derived from a more general experience of anyone travelling, but are specific to how this particular text constructs a meaning for the term. In the latter 'substitution theory' of language any reference is primarily derived from how a reader brings a knowledge of the world to an understanding of any one sentence. The system is not closed; we are meant to construe a Modest Proposer out of our recognition of Restoration and early eighteenth-century econometric discourses, and a Drapier out of our knowledge of Irish drapers and similar small shopkeepers. Complex irony thus exploits the duality of metaphor.

It therefore does not do to be too positivistic about Swift's writing. He proceeded on the assumption that his readers were conversant with current events, yet his comments were rarely just about such events. At moments of especial force one was forced to comprehend the many in the one, the universal in the historical, and sense the urgency in the scatological or shocking. For E. D. Hirsch it is irony pre-eminently that disturbs any writing's claim to final meaning:

> Possible irony is not a special case, only a particularly telling one ... that exemplifies the potential plurisignificance of all word-sequences. Irony is particularly convenient because its presence or absence changes nothing in the text except its fundamental meaning.[31]

Any study of Swift that reduces his writing to 'official', probable meanings may well be in tune with his historical context, his 'publick spirit', yet at the cost of the more individual aspects of his work, and, I would argue, fatally misunderstands the full expressiveness of his irony. This eventually may also simplify the very specific circumstances in which he wrote: the clash between private and public which were only on very isolated occasions ever ignored.

For Northrop Frye, in his exhaustive mapping of literary genres, 'ironic myth' stands in a parodic relation to romance: 'the application of romantic mythical forms to a more realistic content which fits them in unexpected ways', and so, realism in the service of fantasy *and* the reverse. What is more, this amalgam is curiously flexible. The inventiveness of the creation of an alternative world can be comic satire, but, minus much of this, irony could be simply 'the non-heroic residue of tragedy, centering on a theme of puzzled defeat'.[32] Frye understands this dialectic in ways that, I suspect, the more impatient critic does not. Swift does not come right out and say what he means and we should be glad that this is so.

In collecting together these pieces on Swift I am now aware of just what I have had to leave out. As with many of the *Readers*, however, the act of selection has been an attempt to represent the state of a very complex art. When Swift is especially attractive to students, I suspect it is when they respond both to the comedy as well as the tragedy in his work. The study of satire today can often be a matter just of lengthy footnotes and learned scholarship. So much has to be assembled, it would seem, to gain even a preliminary understanding of how Swift stood in relation to his culture and his public image. There is no avoiding this, and many of the essays you will find here attempt this necessary, though rewarding, task. How one does this can illustrate much about Swift's own society, of course, but I have tried to include contributions that also engage with our own theoretical grasp of basic interpretational issues: how are we supposed to read irony? *How* does the historical Swift appear in his satiric work? To what extent can or should our own contemporary awareness of gender difference bear on that of the early eighteenth century? And finally, though not as an afterthought, are we supposed to be *entertained* by satire? The more we read Swift's work, especially during his latter years, the more we may be convinced that he anticipates so much of this critical mood – and that this intractable and complex state of mind is very much a part of what he communicates.

Notes

1. In *Swift: The Critical Heritage*, ed. KATHLEEN WILLIAMS (London, 1970), p. 317.

2. For example, 'Almost all his works are libels; generally upon individuals, sometimes upon sects and parties, sometimes upon human nature. Whatever be his end, however, personal abuse, direct – vehement, unsparing invective, is his means' (*CH*, p. 317). Scott was more forgiving, yet he regarded

Gulliver's fourth voyage with some pain: 'The source of such a diatribe against human nature could only be, that fierce indignation which he has described in his epitaph as so long gnawing his heart' (*CH*, p. 292). The epitaph was cut in a black marble tablet, set seven feet above his final resting place in St Patrick's Cathedral. Swift wrote his own final verdict on himself (in Latin) which mentions the final end to the savage indignation that had lacerated his heart in life. The full text can be found in *PW*, 13: 149–58.

3. MARTIN BATTESTIN, *The Providence of Wit: Aspects of Form in Augustan Literature and the Arts* (Oxford, 1974), p. 216.

4. The text of Pope's verse used in this Introduction is that of the Oxford Authors edition, ed. PAT ROGERS (Oxford, 1993).

5. *The Correspondence of Alexander Pope*, ed. GEORGE SHERBURN, 5 vols (Oxford, 1956), III: 401.

6. The text of Swift's verse used in this Introduction is *Jonathan Swift: The Complete Poems* (New Haven, CT, 1983).

7. Swift was anticipating his epitaph as early as *c.* 1714 when he penned his poem, 'The Author Upon Himself' (published finally in the *Works* of 1735). The comparison, however, with his later acts of self-assessment is striking. Here Swift name-drops at will and clearly hopes to create the impression of one who is beginning to have some measure of influence. In the last line, when he 'decently' retires from the public arena, 'by faction tired' (ll. 74, 71), it was only to a friend's house (Rev. John Geree) in Letcombe Bassett in Berkshire. He was not to know it, but, with the death of the Queen just a couple of months later, the retirement came eventually to be not just forced but also long-lasting.

8. *Lives of the English Poets*, ed. GEORGE BIRKBECK HILL, 3 vols (Oxford, 1905), III: 51–2.

9. The most recent (and reliable) account of this linguistic aspiration and its opponents can be found in TONY CROWLEY, *Language in History: Theories and Texts* (London, 1996), pp. 54–98.

10. Patrick Delany, in his *Observations upon Lord Orrery's Remarks on the Life and Writings of Dr. Jonathan Swift* (1754), gave the most complete account of Swift's linguistic philosophy. His style observed the 'power, and propriety of words', which still had to be annexed to a 'strength and harmony arising from their arrangement' (*CH*, p. 137).

11. JACQUES DERRIDA, *Writing and Difference*, trans. ALAN BASS (Chicago, 1978), p. 284.

12. See MARTIN PRICE, *Swift's Rhetorical Art: A Study in Structure and Meaning* (Carbondale and Edwardsville, IL, 1953), especially pp. 15–35.

13. The full title of Swift's 'Verses on the Death . . .' includes 'Occasioned by Reading a Maxim in Rochefoucauld', which is then reproduced: 'In the adversity of our friends, we find something that doth not displease us'. François, duc de La Rochefoucauld (1613–80) published his *Reflexions ou Sentences et Maximes Morales* in 1665, and was immediately regarded as part of the Jansenist zeal for confirming the doctrine of the fallibility of human nature. La Rochefoucauld suffered at the court of Louis XIII, and in 1653, at the age of forty, eventually found himself exiled from the court, his main family castle, Verteuil, burnt to the ground, and with no hope of a public career. His writings stem in the main from his time at the salon of Mme de Sablé – independent, objective and taking succour from literature and like-minded friends rather than the hopes of preferment. Swift published his own

maxims in *Thoughts on Various Subjects* (complete in 1735, but published in instalments in both 1711 and 1727), and in 1725 he confessed to Pope that he found his 'whole character' in La Rochefoucauld (*The Correspondence of Jonathan Swift*, ed. HAROLD WILLIAMS, 5 vols [Oxford, 1963–65], III: 118).

14. Most interestingly in CLAUDE RAWSON, *Gulliver and the Gentle Reader: Studies in Swift and Our Time* (London, 1973), pp. 1–59.

15. F. R. LEAVIS, 'The Irony of Swift', in *The Common Pursuit* (London, 1952), p. 75.

16. RAWSON, *Gulliver*, p. 33.

17. NORMAN O. BROWN, *Life Against Death: The Psychoanalytical Meaning of History* (rev. edn, 1970, Middletown, CT; orig. pub. 1959), pp. 179–201.

18. In his *On the Universal Tendency to Debasement in the Sphere of Love (Contributions to the Psychology of Love II)*, in *The Standard Edition of the Complete Psychological Works of Sigmund Freud*, ed. J. STRACHEY et al., 24 vols (London, 1953–74), XI: 189.

19. The Webster text used here is that of René Weis, *The Duchess of Malfi and Other Plays* (Oxford, 1996).

20. W. B. YEATS, 'Introduction' to *The Words Upon the Window-Pane* (1934), in *Yeats: Selected Criticism and Prose*, ed. A. NORMAN JEFFARES (London, 1964), p. 477.

21. THOMAS SHERIDAN, *The Life of the Reverend Jonathan Swift . . .* , 19 vols (Dublin, 1801), I: 261.

22. See my own account in NIGEL WOOD, *Swift: Harvester New Readings* (Brighton, 1986), pp. 105–18.

23. ROBERT MAHONY, *Jonathan Swift: The Irish Identity* (New Haven, CT, 1995).

24. OLIVER FERGUSON, *Jonathan Swift and Ireland* (Urbana, IL, 1962), p. 185.

25. The overall context is best summarized in J. A. DOWNIE's *To Settle the Succession of the State: Literature and Politics, 1678–1750* (London, 1994), especially pp. 31–62. The best studies of Swift's politics during this period are J. A. DOWNIE, *Jonathan Swift: Political Writer* (London, 1984), see especially pp. 73–86, 135–63; DAVID NOKES, *Jonathan Swift, A Hypocrite Reversed: A Critical Biography* (Oxford, 1985), pp. 266–91; IAN HIGGINS, *Swift's Politics: A Study in Disaffection* (Cambridge, 1994), pp. 1–37; and DANIEL EILON, *Faction's Fictions: Ideological Closure in Swift's Satire* (Newark, DE, 1991), pp. 94–122.

26. *Correspondence*, II: 465.

27. *Correspondence*, III: 289.

28. WARREN MONTAG, *The Unthinkable Swift: The Spontaneous Philosophy of a Church of England Man* (London, 1994), especially pp. 1–41.

29. DUSTIN GRIFFIN, *Satire: A Critical Reintroduction* (Lexington, KY, 1994), especially pp. 35–70.

30. PAUL RICŒUR, *The Rule of Metaphor: Multi-disciplinary Studies of the Creation of Meaning in Language*, trans. ROBERT CZERNY, with KATHLEEN MCLAUGHLIN and JOHN COSTELLO, SJ (London, 1978), especially pp. 101–33.

31. E. D. HIRSCH, *The Aims of Interpretation* (Chicago, 1976), p. 23.

32. NORTHROP FRYE, *Anatomy of Criticism: Four Essays* (Princeton, NJ, 1957), pp. 223–4.

Part One

Reading and Identity

In the four essays in this section the main topic under consideration, for both Swift as satirist and his readers, is the search for the particular degree of identity between his texts and some external referent. How can writing best incapsulate and then communicate an intention? In Swift's case, this perennial question of interpretation is more urgent as, following Roland Barthes's distinction, here repeated by Edward Said, between an *écrivant* and an *écrivain*, there is an unstable duality about the satirist's relationship with the context of both the reader ('How am I to register the precise tone and implied meaning of the writing?') and the indicated objects of his invective ('Is Swift's meaning, derived, for example, from his William Wood / Modest Proposer / Modern Writer, always a public one?'). For Barthes (see Barthes, 'To Write: an intransitive verb?', in *The Structuralist Controversy: The Languages of Criticism and the Sciences of Man*, ed. RICHARD MACKSEY and EUGENIO DONATO [Baltimore, MD, 1970], pp. 134–56, and 'Écrivains and Écrivants' – in *Essais Critiques* [Paris, 1964], pp. 147–54) there was a significant difference between an *author* and a *writer*, for the former (an *écrivain*) tends to regard the verb, 'to write', as an intransitive activity, where the aesthetic qualities outweigh the referential, and the latter (an *écrivant*) tends to write only as a means to a non-literary end, where the aesthetic or formal impact of the writing is inevitably just a part of the rhetoric. In the case of Swift, the boundaries between these two sorts of literary activity are interestingly interdependent, as he frequently finds writing an event, but an event that often gestures to intensely-felt personal as well as 'worldly' loss. This essay is taken from a collection entitled, *The World, the Text, and the Critic* (1984), a wide-ranging set of explorations around the interpretational challenges posed whenever a text is viewed in the world, that is, not so much creating its own parenthetical comment so much as joining more directly the main discourses of History. For Said, Swift is a fascinating case study: never a vocational writer, always alert to the particular constraints of context, and thereby an ironic manipulator of readerly response. In the essay immediately following this one, Said makes a persuasive claim for 'Swift as Intellectual' (pp. 72–89), and thus attempts to exclude him for critical consideration from the ranks of merely a Tory satirist. He is then a writer caught up in ideas and ethical choices, reacting to historical and cultural events in the process of attempting to mould them.

For Richard H. Rodino, the emphasis is rather more on the variety of ways readers travel with Gulliver and Swift in reading the *Travels*. Rodino, who died tragically early in his life in 1990, had just completed his *Swift Studies, 1965–1980: An Annotated Bibliography* (New York, 1984) and, with Hermann J. Real, edited *Reading Swift* (Munich, 1993), and this essay is part of an assessment of the patterns of response to Swift's work that he promised (here, p. 47) would dwell less on some teleological critical progress towards a 'correct' reading than a focus on how each generation of readers projects prior assumptions on to the text just as they apparently receive messages only from 1726. This situation is part of what has been variously termed intertextuality, the original literary text (once written into existence by Swift) actually encounters quite different patterns of understanding, 'texts' contemporaneous with the reader. It is therefore entirely probable that the most important factor in our present interest in any text lies in how it intersects with our deepest contemporary assumptions. In Hans Robert Jauss's seminal collection of essays *Toward an Aesthetic of Reception* (trans. TIMOTHY BAHTI; Minneapolis, 1982), he expounds a theory as to why interpretations differ about works as complex as *Gulliver's Travels*: it is an historical document, not a monument, and as such accrues significance through time. The hope is that history can be united with aesthetics:

> The aesthetic implication lies in the fact that the first reception of a work by the reader includes a test of its aesthetic value in comparison with works already read. The obvious historical implication of this is that the understanding of the first reader will be sustained and enriched in a chain of receptions from generation to generation; in this way the historical significance of a work will be decided and its aesthetic value made evident.
>
> (p. 20)

As we now read Swift's work, as Rodino painstakingly uncovers, we encounter a series of apparently distracting textual signals which gradually add up to a central statement about the printed book and literary fictions.

It is appropriate at this juncture to mention those critics who identify 'reader entrapment' in many of Swift's ironic works. Although Rodino is interested (though not exclusively) in the role of the implied reader in the projection of an author's meaning, there are several suggestive readings that find Swift's meaning bound up, sometimes exclusively, with the experience of the reader. In his recent collection of essays on such themes, *Reader Entrapment in Eighteenth-Century Literature* (New York, 1992), Carl R. Kropf has defined 'reader entrapment' as occurring 'when an author seems to force his reader into choosing among unacceptable readings, forces him into an unacceptable role, arouses expectations he does not fulfill, or otherwise causes the reader significant discomfort' (p. xiv). This fits Swift's tactics closely, and in the earlier work of David M. Vieth and W. B. Carnochan (see VIETH, 'Entrapment in Restoration and early Eighteenth-Century English Literature', *Papers in Language and Literature*, 18 [1982], 227–33 and CARNOCHAN, *Confinement and Flight: An Essay on English Literature of the Eighteenth Century* [Berkeley, CA, 1977]), there are demonstrations of how this claustrophobic impression actually provokes an opposite reaction from the reader: the depiction of disorder similarly calls forth such disorientation on the reader's behalf that the end result is an embracing of purity and straightforwardness. This may suggest that Rodino is interested only in the proliferation of alternative readings – for variety's sake. He concludes, though, with reflections on Paul De Man's recurrent theme throughout the essays in his *Allegories of Reading: Figural Language in Rousseau, Nietzsche, Rilke, and Proust* (New Haven, CT, 1979) that different readings cannot peacefully co-exist, but rather have to contest each other as a necessary condition of their 'proof'.

As Swift is drawn so much to pseudonymous projections of the 'author' in his writing, there is a constant temptation in any reading to search for a 'real' set of characteristics that may underlie the fallible narrator. For Deborah Baker Wyrick, this is no consistent tactic, but rather permits an array of dramatic incongruities where the reader can never for long accustom her/himself to a patterned response. Perhaps all name-calling or -assuming inevitably involves fiction. In Jacques Lacan's theory of the specular image, he traces what happens when a child first becomes aware of the self. On looking into a mirror an impression of unity is given the child that s/he cannot *feel*. Forever after, there is an inexorable quest for the 'proper' name that will heal the fractured sense of self that one senses, and yet the very nature of language means that this is doomed to failure, as stable meaning can never exist in language. What we actually join when we both register meaning in language and try to express it is a chain of signifiers with no final act of exact definition, no matter how much we may desire such a union. We travel 'in the rails of metonymy', and are actually 'eternally stretching forth towards the *desire for something else*' (*Écrits: A Selection*, trans. ALAN SHERIDAN [New York, 1971], p. 167). When Swift selects a persona, he is attempting an affirmation of an authorial self. M. B. Drapier or Gulliver, because they exist only in literature, cannot exhibit any of that startling lifelike unpredictability that the real presents every day.

1 Swift's Tory Anarchy*

EDWARD SAID

Swift's work is a persisting miracle of how much commentary an author's writing can accommodate and still remain problematic. The efforts on his behalf have been mainly restorative, since few major authors in English have presented themselves so resolutely in a long series of occasional pieces that defy easy classification. One way of checking this intransigence is to note how much more certainly we can use the adjective 'Swiftian' than we can identify, locate, and see 'Swift'. The latter seems often to be little more than an adjunct to the former, even as 'Swift' somehow energetically covers thirteen volumes of prose, three of poetry, seven of correspondence, and innumerable pages of strange jottings. Thus Swift is restored by editors to a definitive text, by biographers to a chronology of events from birth in 1667 to death in 1745, by psychological critics to a set of characteristics, by historians to an age, by literary critics to a genre, a technique, a rhetoric, a tradition, and by moralists to the norms he is said to have defended. His identity has been very much in the shadow of claims made on his work, and if this is always true with major authors it doesn't, in Swift's case, make it seem any less of what Norman O. Brown has called a housebreaking and domestication of the tiger of English literature.

Yet despite their differences each of these restorations, consciously or not, is also taking Swift as a *resistance* to the order in which he will come to be placed. In no author do the regulations of order and the challenging anarchy of dispersion cohabit with such integrity. R. P. Blackmur's remark that 'true anarchy of spirit should always show (or always *has* showed) a tory flavor' is, I think, best applied to Swift.[1] His work can be approached and characterized as the highly dramatic encounter between the anarchy of resistance to the written page and the abiding tory order of the page. This is the most literally

* Reprinted from *The World, the Text and the Critic* (Cambridge, MA: Harvard University Press; London: Faber and Faber, 1983), pp. 54–71.

basic form of encounter: it is capable of great multiplication, going from the difference between waste and conservation, absence and presence, obscenity and decorum, to the negative and positive dimensions of language, imagination, unity, and identity. The life of such an encounter is, so to speak, the active content of Swift's mind as we are able to grasp it in its essential resistance to any fixed boundaries. Nevertheless, the limits of that mind's play seem to have been set by the exclusion of everything but highly specialized and obsessive work – I am recalling Swift's own reference to his conjured spirit. So constant an experience of force and pressure warrants Yeats's granting to Swift the discovery of the intellect's madness.

The tension between an individual author, as an irreducible existence, and the tory institutions of literature to which the writing contributes is, of course, an implicit one, always to be taken into account by the critic. This tension is exploited, rather than tolerated, by critical methods whose bias stresses the anterior privileges of the writer's experience to his finished product. Whether as phenomenology, *Lebensphilosophie*, or psychoanalysis, such methods investigate dimensions of privacy, what we may call literal pretexts, whose mastery of the text is asserted either from within (see Ortega's essay *Pidiendo un Goethe desde dentro*), from all sides (Jean-Pierre Richard's *L'Univers imaginaire de Mallarmé*), or from without (Bernard Meyer's *Joseph Conrad: A Psychoanalytic Biography*). What results is an often impressive totality and the achievement of an intimate partnership between critic and writer, in which each in a sense is part of the other.

A number of important preconditions inform these critical enterprises. The texts examined are problematic in every way except *as texts*. That is, the critic is concerned with interpretations of a text, but not with asking if the text is a text or with ascertaining the discursive conditions by which a so-called text may, or may not, have become a text. Clearly, for example, a work like Swift's 'Some Considerations upon the Consequences Hoped and Feared from the Death of the Queen' (1714) does not occupy the same place in the canon as *Gulliver's Travels* (1726); yet in any integral account of Swift's oeuvre it would be very hard to say what place the *Travels* ought to stand in without considering its relation to 'Some Considerations'. Is one work more of a text than the other? The uncomplicated facts of either completion or publication cannot so easily determine whether one piece of writing is a text and another not. Furthermore, the tautology text-pretext-text is not questioned because the pretext is shown to inhabit the text on a different spiritual, temporal, or spatial level (anterior, more profound, interior); the critic's job therefore is to assemble pretext to text in a new order of simultaneity that eradicates

the differences between them – so long as one has a transcendant
principle of convertibility at hand that transforms the differences.
Without such a principle the pretext would remain extrinsic, and
hence useless. Finally, there is an assumption made about a space
common to text, pretext, and criticism, in which important hidden
things become visible, in which nothing crucial is lost, and in which
whatever merits saying can be said and connected. It is not accidental
that these methods are best suited to romantic and postromantic
authors for whom all writing is an apparently imperfect metaphor of
consciousness and writing as mirrors of each other's topographies.
The debt to criticism has become evident, since it is criticism that
lines things up in this way.

Studied in this manner, writing is also a form of temporal duration.
Literary language in particular contains its intention and, during
the reader's efforts, acquires its varied significations by virtue of
its temporality: this is a commonplace of interpretation. No matter
how severe the interruptions, the continuity of serial movement
must always be established even if the direction of that movement
is ultimately circular. Georges Poulet's *Les Métamorphoses du cercle*
demonstrates the figure with formidable insistence. At its best, then,
the restorative method is extraordinarily absorptive and catholic;
at its worst it can become reductive and exclusive. What underlies
the critic's project of restoration is an attitude that resembles
acquisitiveness, for one cannot restore what one does not possess.
And what can be possessed is only what is believed previously to
be *there*.

It is against this ideological premise of fundamental appropriation
that Swift's work militates.[2] With a few exceptions, most of his
writing was precisely occasional: it was stimulated by a specific
occasion and planned in some way to change it. This is as explicitly
true of *A Tale of a Tub* (1704) as it is of *The Conduct of the Allies*
(1711), *The Examiner* (1711), and *The Drapier's Letters* (1724). Moreover,
the publication and subsequent dissemination of most of his
individual pieces, including *Gulliver's Travels*, occupied his attention
in many ways as event, not as art in our sense of the word or as
craftsmanship for its own sake. What the manic narrator of *A Tale
of a Tub* admits, that what he says is true only for the moment, is a
comic foreshadowing of what was literally to be true of Swift's later
writing. *The Conduct of the Allies* and *The Public Spirit of the Whigs*
(1714) take place, as it were, in their actual dispersion on the streets
of London: their efficacy as instruments of urgent Tory policy during
the Harley–St. John regime is essentially in the fact that they got to as
many people as possible, as quickly as possible, and as unerringly as
possible. Distribution and skillful rhetoric are aspects of each other

and of an event they aim to promote. Once enacted, they become historical events that have taken place; if they remain at all, they do so as shadowy traces that adumbrate an occasion, monuments of a specific time whose original power has been exhausted.

Swift himself seems to have been haunted by the impermanence of events, a concern that accounts not only for his life-long interest in conversation (a speaking event) but for his solicitude for history, for correct language, for his stubborn distrust of everything that could not be verified by direct experience. Dr. Johnson's portrait of Pope, writing letters with a jealous eye cocked at their future publication, is nicely balanced by the malicious anecdote in his *Life of Swift* in which the Dean reflects with an old man's disbelief on the genius of a youth that had produced *A Tale of a Tub*, a unique event. Indeed most apocryphal stories about Swift, whether told by Mrs. Pilkington, Johnson, or Nichols, have a curious discontinuity to them. In the same narrative, one version of Swift contradicts another: so Mrs. Pilkington tells stories of Swift's gratuitous nastiness alongside those in which he is the kindest of men. Certainly these stories belong to Swift, but they waver in their fidelity to Swift, the once dynamically alive and complex man, and to another being disjunctive with him, the mythic figure who later looms so impressively in Yeats's poetry, Joyce's fiction, or Beckett's entire oeuvre. The lapse between what Swift actually said or did and what could be said about him is exactly the gap that exists between words spoken specifically for an occasion and words recorded in writing whose situation has fallen away from it. The difference is between strict, and sometimes even unpleasant, events and a permissive aftermath that beseeches interpretation and reconstruction. Not surprisingly, *A Tale of a Tub* and *Gulliver's Travels* are at once Swift's best-known 'texts' and, concomitantly, those whose intention is most general, most textually bound, and those that have welcomed the most critical attention. They are also works most amenable to generic and technical classification.

Yet, judged by most of his other works, these possessions of the library and of the critic seem like accidents intended by Swift to dramatize the fact that he was really a writer of paraliterature who used literary institutions when it suited him, or during moments of enforced idleness. Swift's purposely ingenuous letters to friends in England about Gulliver, the various guides and keys to *A Tale of a Tub* cleverly incorporated into later versions of the work, such oddities as Smedley's *Gulliveriana* – all these are comic appendages to writing that has already indicted itself for being an appendage to reality. What distinguishes the most literary of Swift's writings from his numerous political and religious tracts is that the latter are embedded as events in a complex of events in the world, whereas the former are comic or literary or textual because they are not events at all; on the contrary the *Tale* is explicitly written to forestall an event and to distract serious attention. In *The Stoic Comedians* Hugh Kenner brilliantly discusses the *Tale* as a book that parodies the sheer bookishness of books. And whatever else it is, *Gulliver's Travels* is a work that uses the historical preterite as a self-conscious literary barrier between the reader and the pseudo-present tense in which most of Gulliver's exploits are narrated. We are then forced to take seriously Swift's discovery that words and objects in the world are not simply interchangeable, since words extend away from objects into an entirely verbal world of their own. If words and objects ever coincide, it is because at certain propitious times both converge into what the prevailing polity can readily identify as an event, which does not necessarily involve exchange or communication. Yet the contrast between an event and writing as a substitute for an event is an important working opposition in Swift.

In addition, Swift seems to have been very sensitive to the differences between writing and speaking. Each activity – and this notion is entirely apt for the severity of his thought – can take two forms, which we may call correct on the one hand and debased on the other. Correct speaking is conversation, defined in 'Hints towards an Essay on Conversation' (1710–1712) as being more readily achieved than any idea, because incapable of refinement into mere ideality:

> Most Things, pursued by Men for the Happiness of publick or private Life, our Wit or Folly have so refined, that they seldom subsist but in Idea; a true Friend, a good Marriage, a perfect Form of Government, with some others, require so many Ingredients, so good in their several Kinds, and so much Niceness in mixing them, that for some thousands of Years Men have despaired of reducing their Schemes to Perfection: But in Conversation, it is, or might be otherwise; for here we are only to avoid a Multitude of Errors, which, although a Matter of some Difficulty, may be in every Man's Power, for Want of which it remaineth as meer an Idea as the other. Therefore it seemeth to me, that the truest Way to understand Conversation, is to know the Faults and Errors to which it is subject, and from thence, every Man to form Maxims to himself whereby it may be regulated.
>
> (*PW*, 4: 87)

One reason for this assertion is of course the necessary physical presence of at least two people, and all of Swift's subsequent hints are designed to preserve the presence to each other of the conversants. The rules of conversation are made subordinate to that presence, which ought to prevail and in whose interest the subject, mode, and style of exchange must serve. Even in his description of a good sermon, Swift's concern is to make the fact of speaking and listening into an event with duration, and this can only happen if the prior facts of presence are respected. There is, however, one obvious handicap to conversation. For once said in a conversation, words are lost forever, except perhaps as pleasant memory. Now 'debased' conversation, of which *The Polite Conversation* (1738) is the prime example, is speaking without respect to presence. A social occasion is only license for speaking: that turns speaking into the formalism of modish cliché, which really needs nothing specific either to set it going or to keep it going. The rationale of *The Polite Conversation*, as set forth in its introduction, is that polite talk really speaks itself. It can be learned by heart, it is always applicable, it is finite and closed, and its rules are intrinsic to it, that is, not really subordinated to the presence of speaker or listener: hence, the 'success' of Wagstaff's years of transcription. Above all, debased conversation is economical and capable of preservation since it works on the all *and* nothing principle: it never means anything and it always means the same thing – polite conversation, an absolute constant, language using people.

Swift's views on conversation remain relatively unchanged throughout his life, even if we consider such works as *The Journal to Stella*, his birthday poems to Stella, the Anglo-Latin games, the Castilian experiments, and the Scriblerus Club enterprises as variations on the theme of conversation. Or if not variations, then the closest Swift ever came to demonstrating the peripheries at which conversation shades subtly into writing. What needs to be remarked here is that Swift's writing itself was a far less integral activity than speaking; and that, I believe, is something Swift understood about his own work and more universally about writing in general. Formulas like 'the plain style', affixed by Johnson to Swift's writing, and 'proper words in proper places' (Swift's own catch-all) do little service to the fineness of his writing. Correct writing for him did not merely conform to reality. It was reality; better still, it was an event necessitated by other events, and leading to still other events. The best writing, such as *The Conduct of the Allies*, was a matter of exquisite timing and placing. Conversely, debased writing was a matter of bad timing and bad placing.

The consequences of this notion of writing, which appears to be a simple one, are of immense importance – and not only for Swift but for his reader. Consider, first of all, how relative good writing is to its time and place. Retrospectively, good writing has happened, like the past. Its force is lost to the later present of the historian or the critic; ironically again, the writer himself is no less cut off from that force. To Swift the 'simple' truth meant a great deal: it meant that (as the work he did in Letcombe shortly after the Tory demise so poignantly testifies) his time and place as a writer of worth had happened and had passed. From being a good writer he had changed into a writer of confused reminiscence, then of projections.

Roland Barthes's distinction between *écrivant* (someone who writes about subjects that exist and who is a transactor of events and ideas) and *écrivain* (someone whose subject is, if not nonexistent, then merely writing itself) applies respectively to Swift's work in 1710–1714 and the periods before and after it. Here are two passages, taken first from *A Tale of a Tub* and then from 'Memoirs, Relating to That Change which happened in the Queen's Ministry in the Year 1710' (written in 1714). Both are statements about why the work is being undertaken, although in the first passage Swift uses a mask and in the second his own voice. What is strikingly true of both passages is that the same stratagem is used – the present work is a diversion produced by an *écrivain* – with the same consequences: the style is roundabout, as if to conceal the fact that the real subject is the act of writing itself. The author, for various reasons, does not feel justified in honestly standing at the center of what he says. In the *Tale* digression is a technique; in the 'Memoirs' digression has almost become Swift's way of life away from the center of things. As we shall see, it was not until his old age that Swift could allow himself to grow confidently into the subject of his writing.

The Wits of the present Age being so very numerous and penetrating, it seems the Grandees of Church and State begin to fall under horrible Apprehensions, lest these Gentlemen, during the intervals of a long Peace, should find leisure to pick Holes in the weak sides of Religion and Government. To prevent which, there has been much Thought employ'd of late upon certain Projects for taking off the Force, and Edge of those formidable Enquirers, from canvasing and reasoning upon such delicate Points. They have at length fixed upon one, which will require some Time as well as Cost, to perfect. Meanwhile the Danger hourly increasing, by new Levies of Wits all appointed (as there is Reason to fear) with Pen, Ink, and Paper which may at an hours Warning be drawn out into Pamphlets, and other Offensive Weapons, ready for immediate Execution: It was judged of absolute necessity, that some present Expedient be thought on, till the main Design can be brought to Maturity. To this End, at a Grand Committee, some Days ago, this important Discovery was made by a certain curious and refined

Observer; That Seamen have a Custom when they meet a Whale, to fling him out an empty Tub, by way of Amusement, to divert him from laying violent Hands upon the Ship. This Parable was immediately mythologiz'd: The Whale was interpreted to be Hobbes's Leviathan, which tosses and plays with all other Schemes of Religion and Government, whereof a great many are hollow, and dry and empty, and noisy, and wooden, and given to Rotation. This is the Leviathan from whence the terrible Wits of our Age are said to borrow their Weapons. The Ship in danger, is easily understood to be its old Antitype the Commonwealth. But, how to analyze the Tub, was a matter of difficulty; when after long Enquiry and Debate, the literal Meaning was preserved: And it was decreed, that in order to prevent these Leviathans from tossing and sporting with the Commonwealth, (which of itself is too apt to fluctuate) they should be diverted from that Game by a Tale of a Tub. And my Genius being conceived to lye not unhappily that way, I had the Honor done me to be engaged in the Performance.

(*PW*, 1: 24–25)

Having continued, for near the space of four years, in a good degree of confidence with the ministry then in being, though not with so much power as was believed, or at least given out, by my friends as well as my enemies, especially the latter, in both houses of parliament: And this having happened during a very busy period of negotiations abroad, and management or intrigue at home, I thought it might probably, some years hence, when the present scene shall have given place to many new ones that will arise, be an entertainment to those who will have any personal regard for me or my memory, to set down some particularities which fell under my knowledge and observation, while I was supposed, whether truly or no, to have part in the secret of affairs.

(*PW*, 8: 107)

For Swift, and for the critic, the distinctions between the two passages are only secondarily literary ones. They are primarily linguistic and ontological – and I use the word hesitantly. The writing's status in the world has changed with the status of political and historical reality. In the *Tale*, Swift imitates diversion, whereas in the later piece his work really has become a diversion. Each work, however, is produced by an *écrivain*, albeit for different reasons. Held rigidly to a regime that, Swift thought, his efforts entered into and partnered, his writing maintained a position of supremacy over all other writing between 1710 and 1714. The Tory policy Swift supported and wrote about was policy in the world of actuality:

here he was an *écrivant*. The Whig opposition was projection,
mere scribbling. This was always the basis of his strategy. After
1714 Swift occupied no place except as outsider to the Whigs'
monolithic machine. He had become the scribbler and projector he
once impersonated (in *A Tale of a Tub*) and attacked (in *The Examiner*
and elsewhere).

Recent works of historical research (J. H. Plumb's *The Origins of
Political Stability: England, 1675–1725*, Peter Dickson's *The Financial
Revolution*, or Isaac Kramnick's *Bolingbroke and His Circle*) vindicate
Swift's sense of loss. In many ways England changed after 1714,
but chiefly in that political authority was no longer vested in
personalities but rather in the impersonal machinery of bureaucracy,
devised and perfected by Walpole. The change was England's version
of the changes in the structure of European society at the end of the
seventeenth century, changes studied by Franz Borkenau, Lucien
Goldmann, and Bernard Groethuysen. Events were no longer linked
directly to individuals. The solid values of blood and land were
transformed into the shifting values of currency, a perpetual national
debt, and city mercantilism. The Tory aristocracy of merit, which for
Swift embodied the English people at their best, was dislodged from
power by a Whig oligarchy of special interests. If previously Swift
had seen his pamphlets as events that existed in a state of homology,
or as coevals, with political reality, after 1714 he saw that both he
and his writings repeatedly demonstrated the intractable *opposition*
between language and actuality, two versions of inauthenticity cut
off from what he called nostalgically 'life in the common forms'.

This is why the role of Irish patriot suited him so eminently: it
was a role full of the infuriating contradictions between the pen and
the polity. Perfect in itself, the written language of Irish protestation
exacerbated the discontinuity between the intolerability of what was
(Ireland) and the improbability of what could be (English colonialist
plans for it). Wood's halfpence, for instance, was just the wrong Swift
could attack in *The Drapier's Letters*, mainly by taking the scheme as
a scheme and, in those brilliant fancies where squires went shopping
with carriages full of debased coin trailing after them, projecting the
project in its own element – imagination.[3] An imaginative event and,
by extension, writing that involved imaginative projections comically
displaced real events; thus Swift's mind remained faithful to the
presence of events, if only by mocking merely verbal fictions of
reality, like Wood's scheme, with alternative fictions.

What I have so rapidly summarized requires much further
exposition and demonstration. If this outline has any value, however,
it is to have situated Swift's work at the axes of the basic oppositions
and discontinuities that make the work's total accessibility to the

twentieth century so limited. We are challenged therefore by an
oeuvre that exists recalcitrantly as a negative judgment passed on
itself for not having succeeded as an event, which would have meant
its extinction and dispersion in time past. To Swift, history supported
itself adequately without need of interpretation, so long as language
(as his public letter to Harley on the maintenance of the English
language tries to prove) was synonymous with political power. Too
proud to believe that his writing merely served the Tory power,
Swift saw his pamphlets retrospectively as part of the regime, events
in its history; yet the obsessive way in which, very early and very
late in his career, he recognized the inherent dangers of language
loosed from political power and social reality suggests that he felt
himself in need of assurances that his control over language was
strong. He realized ultimately that only he could assure himself by
periodically exposing the abuses to which language far too easily
lent itself. The symmetry, for instance, between Swift's dismissal
of the muse in 'Occasioned by Sir William Temple's Late Illness
and Recovery' (1693) and his attack forty years later, on the blasts
of 'poetick Fire' (in 'On Poetry: A Rapsody', 1733) is striking. The
following passages show first the muse dismissed in anticipation of
the poet's espousal of reality, and then poetry debased by the loss of
a real subject. What intervenes between the two poems is a period
during which Swift was only a poet incidentally, 1710–1714. Those
four years, in the context of his entire life's work, are the gap over
which writing, interpretation, and memory – all verbal and all
imperfect – put down a cloud of words:

> To thee I owe that fatal bend of mind,
> Still to unhappy restless thoughts inclined;
> To thee, what oft I vainly strive to hide,
> That scorn of fools, by fools mistook for pride;
> From thee whatever virtue takes its rise,
> Grows a misfortune, or becomes a vice;
> Such were thy rules to be poetically great,
> 'Stoop not to interest, flattery, or deceit;
> 'Nor with hired thoughts be thy devotion paid;
> 'Learn to disdain their mercenary aid;
> 'Be this thy sure defence, thy brazen wall,
> 'Know no base action, at no guilt turn pale;
> 'And since unhappy distance thus denies
> 'To expose thy soul, clad in this poor disguise;
> 'Since thy few ill-presented graces seem
> 'To breed contempt where thou hast hoped esteem.' –
>   Madness like this no fancy ever seized,

Still to be cheated, never to be pleased;
Since one false beam of joy in sickly minds
Is all the poor content delusion finds. –
There thy enchantment broke, and from this hour
I here renounce thy visionary power;
And since thy essence on my breath depends
Thus with a puff the whole delusion ends.

(ll. 131–154)

How shall a new attempter learn
Of different spirits to discern,
And how distinguish, which is which,
The poet's vein, or scribling itch?
Then hear an old experienced sinner
Instructing thus a young beginner.
Consult yourself, and if you find
A powerful impulse urge your mind,
Impartial judge within your breast
What subject you can manage best;
Whether your genius most inclines
To satire, praise, or humorous lines;
To elegies in mournful tone,
Or prologue 'sent from Hand unknown'.
Then rising with Aurora's light,
The muse invoked, sit down to write;
Blot out, correct, insert, refine,
Enlarge, diminish, interline.
Be mindful, when invention fails,
To scratch your head, and bite your nails.

(ll. 71–90)

The rhyme of 'sinner' and 'beginner' is eloquent, for it ties the
habitual practitioner to the novice with inevitable firmness. Both
are writers, *écrivains*, for whom the practice of poetry is an exercise
in trying vainly to insert literary composition into the real world.
A muse dismissed and, with a sense of savage inferiority, writing
installed alongside reality: these are the beginning and the end of
a career that abides both for Swift and for his critic. The career is a
literary one whose record exists in works that ought to have become
political history but which linger on, like the Struldbruggs, as
ineffectual remnants. 'On Poetry' derives its strength not only from
the vehemences of its attack on debased poetry, but also from a
despair that this debasement after all is what poetry now really is.
Is it not an unhappy fact that Swift's instructions – here and in the

Directions to Servants (1745), *The Polite Conversation,* and so on – were always manuals of bad work elaborately described? What could be described then was what was accessible to written language, and both subject and medium were infected substitutes for the realities that remained outside their field. The productive force of Swift's energy as a writer need not be portrayed as emanating from a vision we create of him as an Anglican divine whose life can be described as a sequence of events over a period of time. On the contrary, we do him a greater service if we accept the discontinuities he experienced in the way he experienced them: as either actual or imminent losses of tradition, heritage, position, history, losses located at the center of his disjointed verbal production. And this acceptance is not so much a psychological interpretation as it is a set of conditions that makes the whole range of Swift's psychology possible, from a concern with 'fair liberty' to an excremental fixation.

To Swift, then, modern literature was the displacement of older literature; this observation, of course, is made to work throughout *A Tale of Tub.* A modern author writes *during* the loss of a tradition. He is present because of the absence of the ancient authors who were being crowded out by a fading memory of the classics. Frances Yates's book *The Art of Memory* sheds important light on the demotion of traditional mnemonic remembrance in the later seventeenth century: this change was there for Swift to witness. Thus the private inner light that the Quakers or Presbyterians claim for their guides replaces the common heritage, and it is this dislodgement that *A Tale of a Tub* enacts. Moreover, the orderly sequence of historical progress had, for Swift, been dismantled by the Puritan revolution and regicide. As the vagaries of his own history attested, continuity was largely a matter arranged between interested parties, but not a *given* in which everyone could be located securely. *The Sentiments of a Church of England Man* (1711) and the ill-fated *History of the Four Last Years of Queen Anne* (1712–13) were two of Swift's attempts to correct the unreliable opinions upon which the nation's sense of its history and meaning depended. Those works were his rather more problematic, earth-bound versions of Pope's deism and cosmic toryism.

It was in Ireland during the 1730s, however, that Swift more deliberately than before began to provide the stabler framework in which he wished the future to regard him. An incorrigible revisionist, an habitual keeper of accounts whom Taine characterized as the businessman of English letters, and a man with what Nigel Dennis has described as a schoolmaster's attitude to life, it befitted Swift to make sure that the last things to be said about him should be controlled by him. For the last memory he left behind would necessarily be the first to which the future would turn, and in the 'Verses on the Death of Dr. Swift' (1731) he constructed the continuity he wished to perpetuate. In that magnificent poem he chooses courageously, even arrogantly, to see himself in the entirely negative aspect of his own death, at once a loss to the world and a gain for history – but in either case an exemplary *subject*. This summational fiction of his own death is made to take place in the course of the poem as fragmentary responses to a loss being transformed into an event. Thus Swift could become a part of history and a master of it despite the misfortunes attributed by him to language.

The last point needs special emphasis. Whatever else he may have been, Swift realized that so far as posterity was concerned he was primarily a man committed to (that is, both involved in and imprisoned by) language. After he died he would be received by future generations as what they read: he would no longer be seen or heard. What survived of him therefore would be a verbal protrusion into the future, provided he could arrange for that in some way. Yet he would be working against himself. During most of his life he had relied confidently on his personality and on the ubiquitous personality – rather than the undoubted authorship – of his writing. No matter what he did, the supervening fact of his presence overcame the dispersion of his efforts and the variety of his disguises on behalf of the church, the state, Ireland, traditional learning, and morality. If, as I suggested above, those institutions were felt to be in imminent danger of disappearing, then he took his task to be one of assuring their continued presence. The cast of his mind, however, made him undertake these assurances in the form of written imitations of the enemy, imitations that exceeded the opposition several times further in imagination, fantasy, and ostensible disorganization. His element was language, as was the enemy's, but far more than anyone he was able to exploit the negative aspects of the medium: its airiness, its impermanence, its potential for solipsistic debasement. Coleridge, for one, saw this as Swift's tremendous gift. What, to the enemy he attacked, had been an inevitable consequence of flawed thought was for him the willed function of his orderly self-defeating logical and virtuosic analysis. This was Swift's style.

The threat to his posthumous reputation is obvious. Today, for example, we still approach him on the basis of some coherence imputed to his work, which we consider connected to him filiatively as the product of his labor. But it is precisely this connection that so much of his writing denies. 'A Modest Proposal' announces itself as the thought of everyone but Swift, yet it is indubitably by Swift. Thus, as Joyce says in *Ulysses*, absence is the highest form of presence. And this insight is above all true of language, which exists in its written

form as a substitute for the presence of its author. Any substitute
for the real thing is ruled by transience, and by a law of endless
substitution. It was fear of this fate that Swift reckoned with in the
'Verses' by allowing himself to die at cards, at Walpole's levee,
in the booksellers' shops. The event of his death, 'news [which]
thro' half the town has run', is a loss welcomed – according to La
Rochefoucauld's cynical law – as one 'no more easy to supply'.
Yet with the dissipation of all the news' energy, paralleled by the
quickness of shifting scenes in the poem exhausted by the passing of
time, Swift's death is transformed from a variety of gossipy stories
into an event on which a dispassionate, anonymous voice can pass
true judgment.

The poem is governed by a series of elaborate paradoxes that are
not merely rhetorical: hence, to my mind, the poem's special place as
a point of departure for any reading of Swift and any ascertainment
of his text. These paradoxes are all consequences of the untenable
structure that holds human existence together. This is the opposition
between the absolutes of life (birth, death, individuality, community,
in short, Nature) and particular manifestations of them that relativize
and distort them. The strength and fruitfulness of this opposition
is that the absolutes never really appear in the poem because the
particulars dominate them so fully. Yet so thorough is the competence
with which Swift illustrates this that, by the time we chafe at how
impoverished the world has become, we begin to be impressed at the
supreme art with which the impoverished has been rendered. This is
very similar to the achievement of 'On Poetry'.

The proverb by La Rochefoucauld initiates us immediately into a
world drawn from Nature, but since the maxim's import is mankind's
fault it implicates La Rochefoucauld as well.

> In all Distresses of our Friends
> We first consult our private Ends,
> While Nature kindly bent to ease us,
> Points out some Circumstance to please us.

The poem is therefore shut off from any recourse outside it, and
to this somber imprisonment the narrator quickly assents, asking,
however, 'for one Inch at most' in which to illustrate his desire,
thoroughly congruent with the world's way, to rise above his equals.
For the writer this means literally that his verbal composition will
occupy a space he denies others, and Swift proceeds without delay
to show the validity of La Rochefoucauld's observation. Yet we must
note how the examples Swift gives are what he called raillery, for
what he begrudges friends like Pope and Gay is their talent; this is a

negative way of praising them. When at lines 60 and 61, he accuses 'them' of having driven him 'out of date', a shift in tone has occurred: raillery at friends gives way to a serious indictment of the times, now the property of ministers of state who can (and did) maul him, because *his* time and good fortune – the heyday of Tory power – displeased them. La Rochefoucauld is a double-edged blade.

From this point on, the poem is dominated by the inevitable temporal order that leads every man to his death. And this order is large enough to contain not only the trivial pastimes of the idle but the transcendent judgment of history. The focal point in time is the event of Swift's death and it is set, like a fixed node, amid three movements that emanate from it and surround it. First of all, there is the movement of dispersion by which the news of Swift's death is spread through town. Second, and less apparent, is an objective chronology that carries us forward into a future considerably beyond Swift's death. Third, there is the poem's movement itself, an inch that spreads out into a powerful verbal structure. The poem's purpose is to let dispersion occur. The Dean begins to die, 'he hardly breathes', then he dies – and 'what is Trumps?' What is dispersed and lost is a negligible part of the Dean, the part of him possessed by other people. The ingenuity of dispersion is exhausted, not because, as was the case with Swift's political pamphlets, history has absorbed it but rather because the source of its energy is gossipy meanness, a form of polite conversation that has no real duration or status. Above all, this conversation belongs neither to the public nor to the private world, but to an entirely independent verbal order that obliterates every worthwhile distinction. It is a social version of the same order that overcomes the world at the end of *The Dunciad*.

Swift's death, it needs to be said, occurs in conversation, in language – nowhere else. Neither the reader nor the poet can penetrate beyond the verbal dimension, which is the imposition of a human standard upon nature ('a world drawn from nature'). Thus even so serious and natural a subject as death cannot be treated except as a function of language: hence the unashamed artificiality of the poet's stage directions and shifting of scene by which the death is literally arranged. It becomes Swift's problem then to show language as the arena in which fictions battle each other until only the most worthy remain. What remains of Swift can only be described, a long time later, by an impartial, anonymous voice that – and this is a sign of Swift's extraordinarily proleptic sense of himself as a problem for the future – understands Swift as a man who was *too much* for his own time.

The setting of the poem's final scene is one of the most carefully engineered things Swift ever did.

Suppose me dead; and then suppose
A club assembled at the Rose;
Where from discourse of this and that,
I grow the subject of their chat:
And, while they toss my name about,
With favour some, and some without;
One quite indifferent in the cause,
My character impartial draws.

(ll. 299–306)

We watch discourse of this and that exhausting itself, whereas Swift the subject, that is, the topic of history, grows: not the personality whose human situation had likewise aged and been exhausted by the common human time, but an impartial character that emerges to fuller and fuller presence. Such a character can persist in history as a supplement to the specific time he outlived because of his having been too much for it: 'Had he but spared his Tongue and Pen, / He might have rose like other men.' He does rise now, not as a man but as a subject. The terms of description are almost uniformly those of excess, of incongruence with the manners and habits of his time, so much so that sovereign and state cannot contain him.

'With princes kept a due decorum,
But never stood in awe before 'em:
And to her Majesty, God bless her,
Would speak as free as to her dresser,
She thought it his peculiar whim,
Nor took it ill as come from him.
He followed David's lesson just,
"In princes never put thy trust."
And, would you make him truly sour;
Provoke him with a slave in power:
The Irish senate, if you named,
With what Impatience he declaimed!
Fair LIBERTY was all his cry;
For her he stood prepared to die;
For her he boldly stood alone;
For her he oft exposed his own.
Two kingdoms, just as factions led,
Had set a price upon his Head;
But, not a traitor could be found,
To sell him for six hundred pound.'

(ll. 339–58)

His innocence defended by Heaven (1. 429), Swift achieves his own sovereignty by transgressing the ordinary limits, symbolized by queens and princes, with 'due decorum'. Here then Swift portrays himself in a state that is properly his own, the unity between decorum and liberty – a state that recalls Blackmur's phrase 'tory anarchy'. Paulson calls this the merging of 'Swift's satiric exploitation of his situation and his serious reflections on it'.[4] I think, however, that the explicitly satiric portion of the poem is reserved by Swift deliberately until the very end, where it becomes apparent that rather than being a technique or a genre (which is Paulson's argument), satire for Swift was the mode of his sovereignty and transgression and indeed, finally, of his intelligible existence. In fine, satire was the name of his excess and, as his legacy to Ireland proves, the objective structure of his negative duration in history.

> Perhaps I may allow the Dean
> Had too much satire in his vein;
> And seemed determined not to starve it,
> Because no age could more deserve it.
> Yet, malice never was his aim;
> He lashed the vice but spared the name.
> No individual could resent,
> Where thousands equally were meant.
> His satire points at no defect,
> But what all mortals may correct. . . .
> 'He gave the little wealth he had,
> To build a house for fools and mad:
> And showed by one satiric touch,
> No nation wanted it so much:
> That kingdom he hath left his debtor,
> I wish it soon may have a better.'
>
> (ll. 459–68; 483–88)

The 'Verses' deliver Swift to history at the poem's end. A real event is projected into the fictive element of language and submitted bravely to the chaos of gossip and transience, until what must be lost cedes to the assertion of posterity's 'impartial' gain. In the process Swift the man, of course, dies, buried in the trivia of an age that neither could nor would let him live. This must be the source of the persistent legend of his madness – his alienation from the prescriptive canons of decency that he himself yearned for but which the unendurable honesty of his last years forced him to believe were lost. So he believed himself to have lived and died in that loss. Yet the poem demonstrates how his Irish exile is reinstated as a subject of discourse, but not at all as a personality, nor as a body of works, but rather as a presence *for* those who can simultaneously accept, as he did, waste and power. It is in that condition, between the world and the archive, sharing both, that Swift lasts. His imagination was the transactor of that difficult business, and an extraordinarily difficult challenge for the twentieth-century reader.

Notes

1. R. P. BLACKMUR, *A Primer of Ignorance* (New York, 1967), p. 13.

2. For an interesting discussion of the general problem of the eighteenth-century writer in society and the consequences of this for literary history, see BERTRAND BRONSON, 'The Writer', in *Man Versus Society*, ed. JAMES L. CLIFFORD (Cambridge, 1968).

3. Some of these points are examined with great perspicacity by RONALD PAULSON, *The Fictions of Satire* (Baltimore, MD, 1968), pp. 129–222.

4. PAULSON, *Fictions of Satire*, p. 199.

2 'Splendide Mendax': Authors, Characters, and Readers in *Gulliver's Travels**

RICHARD H. RODINO

> After prolonged research on myself, I brought out the fundamental
> duplicity of the human being. Then I realized that modesty helped
> me to shine, humility to conquer, and virtue to oppress.
>
> (Camus, *The Fall*)

> Gulliver vexeth me more than any.
>
> (Swift to Charles Ford, 20 November 1733)

In the history of interpretation of *Gulliver's Travels* there has never
been an instant when readers would hesitate to debate any given
statement about the book, though the site of controversy has shifted
several times.[1] As early as 1726, the anonymous poem *The Blunder of
All Blunders* observed:

> Poor Lemuel's laid upon the Table,
> And every one, as he is able,
> In blust'ring Words and smart Orations,
> Begins to vent his Observations.
>
> (13–16)

A serious attempt to understand how and why Swift's text has
continuously generated such emphatic disputation can reveal
much, for the persistent swirl of controversy not only reflects the
predispositions of various communities of readers but also mirrors
the attitudes toward meaning expressed within the text itself.

Eighteenth-century critics generally agreed about the first level of
meaning for *Gulliver's Travels*: Swift and Gulliver intended to attack
human nature and human behavior. Nonetheless, the critics quarreled
intensely over the second level, namely, the import of the attack,
manifested in how readers would and should respond to the meaning

* Reprinted from *Publications of the Modern Language Association of America*,
106 (1991), 1054–70.

Swift and Gulliver apparently authorized. Hostile commentators
warned against readers' abasement: 'In this last part of his imaginary
travels . . . the representation which he has given us of human nature,
must terrify, and even debase the mind of the reader who views it. . . .
[W]e are disgusted, not entertained; we are shocked, not instructed,
by the fable' (Orrery 57). Defenders, however, described a therapeutic
process of response to the horrifying narrative:

> Our general answer to all those whose mistaken delicacy, or rather
> affected squeamishness, may be offended thereat, is; that if the
> brutality and filthiness of the Yahoos be painted by the powerful
> genius of Dean Swift, in Colours the most Shocking and detestable,
> as these certainly are, and, in fact, they ought to have been; the
> picture is the more striking, as well as the more terrible: and upon
> that very account the more likely to enforce the obligation of
> religion and virtue upon the human mind.
>
> (Dilworth 74)

By the end of the century, controversy had spread to the first
level of meaning, beginning with the objection Thomas Sheridan
(the younger) raised to the conventional view:

> The last charge . . . against Swift, and which has gained most
> general credit, is that of perfect misanthropy; and this is chiefly
> founded upon his supposed satyr on human nature, in the picture
> he has drawn of the Yahoos. This opinion has been so universally
> adopted by almost all who have read *Gulliver's Travels*, that to
> controvert it would be supposed to act in opposition to the
> common sense and reason of mankind. And yet I will undertake
> to overthrow it.
>
> (502)

Notwithstanding such support for Swift, the nineteenth century's
emphasis on texts as authorial self-expression generated *ad hominem*
attacks on the dean (Thackeray's 'shameful, blasphemous, unmanly'
is not the harshest [446]) and, through chagrin and alarm that a
hallowed masterpiece should express such anticanonical meanings,
concocted the theory of Swift's nervous breakdown or actual insanity.

In one of literary history's most cherishable ironies, the twentieth-
century 'defense' of *Gulliver's Travels* first took the form of denying
that Swift had ever intended the very meanings that had elevated
his magnum opus to preeminence. Operating on post-Jamesian
assumptions about the psychological consistency of characters,
distinguishing persona from author, and adopting a less doctrinal
reading of historical context, the still predominant 'soft school'

45

described by James Clifford finds *Gulliver's Travels* a satire on
frustrated idealists like Gulliver; its sentiments on human nature
more comic than satiric; the Yahoos merely an impossible image
of what human beings would be without reason; the Houyhnhnms
impracticable, even ridiculous figures; Captain Pedro de Mendez
the embodiment of the central moral values of the work; and so on.
In response, what Clifford terms the 'hard school' retrenched by
adopting 'eighteenth-century attitudes': *Gulliver's Travels* is a tough-
minded satire that extends little or no comic hopefulness; Swift
speaks his own mind through Gulliver, who is a satirical device, not
a novelistic character; the Yahoos are a reminder of the depths to
which human beings can and do sink whenever they cease pursuing
the higher ideals embodied sincerely in the Houyhnhnms; and so on
(Clifford; Rodino, *Studies* xxx–xxxvi).

At loggerheads since the 1950s, the hard and soft schools are
still going strong, despite the pose, lately fashionable, of dismissing
the controversy as no longer relevant – a conclusion that is little
more than wishful thinking. (By my count, roughly sixty percent of
the critics of *Gulliver's Travels* are still of the soft school.) Because
compromise positions almost invariably continue to approach
Gulliver's Travels from formalist-historical premises, they are limited
to arguing that the opposing set of meanings is mistaken or
fraudulent; they merely document the never-ceasing vitality of
the debate, because they cannot avoid using it as their point of
departure and the measuring stick of their success. Only a handful
of interpretations rooted in quite different assumptions offer new
and larger perspectives, not through pinning down the meaning
of *Gulliver's Travels*, but through accepting the debates about its
meaning as important symptoms of its essential linguistic nature.
As the twentieth century wanes, however, it is striking how little
influence these new directions have had on the study of Swift,
perhaps one (largely unperceived) reason that many Swiftians
consider the current enterprise of Swift studies to be in slump.

Phenomenological readings (W. B. Carnochan's is by far the best
known) rise above the hard-versus-soft controversy by positing
a state of mind for Swift more complicated and ostensibly more
contradictory than has routinely been assumed. His epistemological
anxiety glitters through his constant making and unmaking of
meanings; convinced that satire is a folly, Swift includes himself in
his satirical indictments, while continuing to press them on others as
well. The considerable insights of this approach are limited, however,
by their dismissal of disagreements as deriving from mistaken or
partial understandings of the larger, historically definable entity that
is Swift.

Outside the specialist guild, criticism of Swift has something of a reputation for reader-oriented approaches. Nearly all of them, however, are rooted in positivistic rhetorical premises, with 'The Reader' conceived of as a monolithic consciousness identifiable at every point. As a result, such criticism has almost always ended up serving some interpretation that is either hard-school (e.g., Claude J. Rawson) or soft-school (e.g., Wayne C. Booth) or else a typical attempt at rapprochement (e.g., A. E. Dyson).

Poststructuralist perspectives, though they would seem to have much to offer on the vexed question of *Gulliver's Travels*, have appeared only in dribs and drabs since 1980.[2] One needed project is a full history of the critical reception of *Gulliver's Travels*, based not on the traditional premise that the history of reading is a melioristic record of earlier errors erased and correct meanings discovered but rather on the concept that grasping the larger meaning of *Gulliver's Travels* must include acknowledging the various meanings readers have generated in response and the readers' unavoidable implication in intertextuality (see Jauss). The present chapter tackles a complementary task by analyzing structures of discourse dramatized in Swift's and Gulliver's tales and in the relations between them. The *Travels* has been a battleground where readers, both within and outside the text, resist the authorial powers of Swift and Gulliver and author their own texts in contrast to those of other readers. These battles reflect and therefore contain, rather than exclude, additional searches for meaning in *Gulliver's Travels*.

In Faulkner's 1735 edition of *Gulliver's Travels* the first words identify the protagonist as 'splendide mendax', a liar for the public good (Teerink 41). Thus the text is introduced as a nexus of fiction making and power wresting, for the allusion is not only to Horace but also to Plato's vastly influential statement of the 'noble lie', in *The Republic*. Plato's term, *gennaion pseudos*, describes a lie at once high-minded and well-bred, the instrument of a privileged social class, of those in power. His example is a fabrication about the origins of class distinctions, designed to quell the subversiveness of less privileged classes toward the existing power structure (see Bok).

Gulliver's story, too, conflates the power of language with the language of power. Acts of interpretation within *Gulliver's Travels* – acts of creating and of reading, of inventing characters and of becoming characters in the fictions of others – signal both the text's complex relations to truth and its readers' unceasing stratagems for gaining power over its meaning. The story within reflects the story without: a struggle in which readers willfully characterize Swift and rewrite Gulliver while opposing their own texts to those of others. The ambivalent returns of Gulliver's eager upward mobility in each voyage suggest not only Swift's own lifelong complaints of missed opportunities and unrewarded merits, of political and social deprivation and exile, but also his readers' double-edged gestures of self-assertion and control (see McKeon 338–56).

In *Gulliver's Travels*, interpretation, by the human characters at least, is never merely a quest for truth and virtue; it always contains a desire to control the flux of meaning. The potential for fictions and other lies is at once creative and pernicious. Language conceals even as it reveals. The text opens up a central difficulty in eighteenth-century culture, in that the will to determine the self's experiences can never free itself from a struggle for authority over others as well as over the self. Thus, instead of realizing Habermas's 'ideal speech situation' – where the self can use language freely, where speech can be action, and where truth claims can be made – the century's heavy investment in dialogue is shown to conflict with the usurpative role of language in constituting self and other.[3]

Even a preliminary exploration of this battle-ground requires an unusually complex understanding of the rhetorical relations involved. We must, for instance, go beyond Everett Zimmerman's pioneering description of the *Travels* as 'a book not about a man who undergoes certain experiences but about a man who writes a book about experience that he has undergone' – a view that regards the reader simply as a receiver of meaning (115–17) and sees the text as a movement toward truth and away from lying, away from each author, reader, and character unavoidably playing the role of *mendax* – *splendide* or otherwise. At a minimum, we need to acknowledge that Swift the author writes the story of Gulliver the author writing the story of Gulliver the character, who in turn becomes an author of various texts for various readers within the *Travels*. In addition, Gulliver is constantly the reader and interpreter of others' texts and frequently (and most often uncomfortably) also a character in them, as well as in his own and Swift's stories.[4]

A somewhat fuller description that incorporates readers outside the text would need to include a text (Swift's, signaled by the phrase 'Vol. III of the Author's Works' on Faulkner's 1735 title page) that urges readers to infer an author (Swift) who has invented an author (Gulliver) who is inventing a text that urges his own readers to assume a new relationship to him as character and through that relationship to construct his desired image of himself, that is, Gulliver as he intends to be understood. During any given reading, then, the reader is invited to play at least three roles: docile interpreter of Gulliver's authorial intentions; metacritic of Gulliver's motives and strategies; and metametacritic of Swift, who glimpses the levels and loops of textuality in which the *Travels's* other readers, authors,

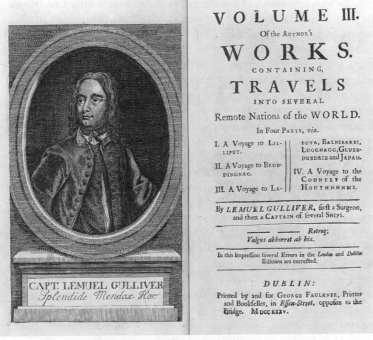

VOLUME III.

Of the AUTHOR'S

WORKS.

CONTAINING,

TRAVELS

INTO SEVERAL

Remote Nations of the WORLD.

In Four PARTS, *viz.*

I. A Voyage to LIL- | PUTA, BALNIBARBI,
LIPUT. | LUGGNAGG, GLUBB-
 | DUBDRIB and JAPAN.
II. A Voyage to BROB- |
DINGNAG. | IV. A Voyage to the
 | COUNTRY of the
III. A Voyage to LA- | HOUYHNHNMS.

By *LEMUEL GULLIVER*, firſt a Surgeon,
and then a CAPTAIN of ſeveral SHIPS.

———— *Retroq;*
Vulgus abhorret ab his.

In this Impreſſion ſeveral Errors in the *London* and *Dublin*
Editions are corrected.

DUBLIN:

Printed by and for GEORGE FAULKNER, Printer
and Bookſeller, in *Eſſex-Street*, oppoſite to the
Bridge. M DCC XXXV.

CAPT. LEMUEL GULLIVER
Splendide Mendax. Hor.

Reproduced by permission of the Houghton Library, Harvard
University.

and characters are situated. The reader's unstable roles thus also
include the parts of author and character. But this model of the
reading process is trite (though complicated) unless we bear in mind
that slippage is always occurring among the various roles, during
individual readings as well as over the readings of a lifetime (see
Prince 128–32). For, in practice, the reader as interpreter of intention
is necessarily reinvented by the friction between the reader as critic
of Gulliver and the reader as critic of Swift and in turn, sooner or
later, must reinvent these readers. Of course, through the reciprocal
processes of critical analysis, it is the reader as critic of Gulliver who
distinguishes Gulliver the character from Gulliver the author and
from Swift the author and, yes, even distinguishes between the
reader's own roles as critic of Gulliver and critic of Swift.

These tensive and slippery activities outside the text are mirror
images, always with some distortion, of the writing and reading
experiences of Gulliver: as author he aspires to pure control of a
whole meaning synonymous with his intention; as reader he desires
pure interpretive freedom from authorial constraint. (To analyze this

49

reciprocal repression in Gulliver necessitates bracketing, to a degree, the way in which readers' own senses of self are threatened in precise synchronization with Gulliver's.[5]

Swift's disguises of his own identity, his deliberate autocorruptions of his texts and his blurring of fictional levels and the borders of reality and fiction, though long recognized as narrative signatures, are usually understood as mere signs of some whole and intelligible signified that existed before and inside them, a hidden heart of discourse into which readers can burrow. However, as Michel Foucault and other post-Saussurian philosophers of language have warned, this signified is illusory, though enticing (215–37). The reader may experience Swift's disguises as pointers in a system of glassy surfaces – tempting illusions of windows but in practice only mirrors in which one sees other faces without, perhaps, recognizing one's own.[6]

The mirroring and looping of roles begin with the contrast between the 1735 title page and modern readers' expectations of the famous, though even more fictive, common title – a fiction rung upon the original fiction, which itself is of the conventional travel variety that, Gulliver later complains, 'impose[s] the grossest Falsities on the unwary Reader' (see Adams 1–18; Lawry). The familiar title is a reassuring assertion of subject-object duality: only an eponymous Gulliver has done or will be doing any traveling; readers by implication will be engaged in altogether distinct activities, that is, witnessing and perhaps assessing. The original title, in contrast, inscribes no such detachment, merely asserting that contained herein are (someone's) voyages into remote nations and identifying Gulliver by titles of sheer authority: author, captain, and surgeon. This bare hint of adversarial relations between voyagers and captain (exacerbated for all in later voyages), between readers and author, is enhanced by the quotation from *De rerum natura*, which not only claims a bitter, though medicinally pure, textual meaning but in the quoted scrap itself – 'Vulgus abhorret ab his' – insults recalcitrant readers as the vulgar who distance themselves from textual authority. Though ostensibly a negative model, Lucretius's vulgar reader turns out to be an uncanny mirror of both Gulliver and his readers over 264 years. Faulkner's title page insists on a metatext ('the Author's Works') containing these voyages, an author ('by Jonathan Swift') inventing Gulliver, and, most interestingly, errors in earlier editions that have been 'corrected'. Gulliver's attempt to make meaning will occur within the context of yet another story, this one a tale of textual transmission, corruption, and emendation that itself signifies within the story of Swift's own vexed and insufficient struggle to restore his text's original purity, as retold time and again.[7]

THE

WORKS

O F

J. S., D.D, D.S.P.D.

I N

FOUR VOLUMES.

CONTAINING,

I. The Author's MISCELLANIES in PROSE.

II. His POETICAL WRITINGS.

III. The TRAVELS of Captain *Lemuel Gulliver.*

IV. His Papers relating to *Ireland,* confifting of feveral Treatifes; among which are, The DRAPIER'S LETTERS to the People of *Ireland* againft receiving *Wood's* Half-pence: Alfo, two Original DRAPIER'S LETTERS, never before publifhed.

In this Edition are great Alterations and Additions; and likewife many Pieces in each Volume, never before publifhed

D U B L I N:

Printed by and for GEORGE FAULKNER, Printer and Bookfeller, in ESSEX-STREET, oppofite to the Bridge, M DCC XXXV.

Reproduced by permission of the Houghton Library, Harvard University.

These concentric fictional levels are reflected more obviously in the frontispiece, which, as Grant Holly has remarked, amounts to a series of regressive mirrors: an engraving of a portrait of a literary character (or, for most modern readers, a photocopy of an engraving, etc.), an image of an image of an image (149–50). The potential for slippage is mirrored, too, since the pedestal, frame, and orientation, as well as Gulliver's features and expression, are virtually identical with those in the portrait of Swift in the frontispiece of the metatext, *The Works of J.S., D.D., D.S.P.D.* (Mezciems 48–54). The title-page layouts are also reflective: both delineate a four-part division and announce the variable histories of their texts by declaring corrections, alterations, and additions.

The inscription under Gulliver's portrait is what transmutes this infernally hilarious, but seemingly analyzable, joke into a strange loop. If Gulliver is a liar, then what must Swift be when he identifies his portrait with Gulliver's? Is the identification itself therefore a lie? But that possibility, of course, would reinforce the identification of these two liars. And if Swift is not Gulliver but, rather, a man of

51

truth, then his claim that the two portraits are alike is a lie. Both distinguishing Swift from Gulliver and attempting to identify the two are locked in paradox, equally excluded, in principle, from analytical definition (see Mezciems 53). As Epimenides the Cretan might murmur, 'This complaint is made by a liar'; or, 'All fiction makers are liars, including this one.'

The 'Letter to Sympson' focuses these mirrors of textuality. At stake is an 'original Manuscript', which, in Gulliver's tortured nostalgic view, was once the site of uncorrupted authorial intention and therefore of truth and over which he had wielded absolute power. 'I do not remember that I gave you Power' to meddle with my text, complains Gulliver (*PW*, 11: 5). The lies, deletions, additions, and commentaries perpetrated by others are willful falsehoods. Yet Gulliver palpably lies even in the 'Letter to Sympson' and thus is himself a falsifier of his own texts. For instance, his claim that the truth of the first three voyages 'immediately strikes every Reader with Conviction' (*PW*, 11: 8) is a prevarication; Gulliver himself amply documents that neither in Houyhnhnmland nor in England are Yahoos susceptible to immediate conviction by truth.[8]

The Gulliver of the 'Letter to Sympson' is not only post-Houyhnhnm but also post-textual. In Europe, Gulliver cannot privilege the orality he admired in Houyhnhnmland; Europeans are 'so new fangled in their Words' that 'when any *Yahoo* comes from *London* out of Curiosity to visit me at mine own House, we neither of us are able to deliver our Conceptions in a Manner intelligible to the other' (*PW*, 11: 7).[9] Yet neither can he endorse the uncoerced publication that Swift himself pursued. Gulliver regrets not that he wrote his memoirs but that he 'suffer[ed his] Travels to be published' (*PW*, 11: 6). His wistfulness is for a text that is written but unread, or at least unpublished; in his fantasy of pure authorial control over reading circumstances and consequences, an author need never become a character in another's fiction or allow a reader to transmogrify into author.

Since only unpublished writing has power both to reveal the mind's thoughts and yet to avoid interpretive degeneracy, Gulliver recommends (for others) a reversal of the publication process, the reabsorption of the printed artifact into the being of its author, the redigestion of the external sign into the internal realm of one who signifies: all those pilers of texts upon texts, he complains, should be 'condemned to eat nothing but their own Cotten, and quench their Thirst with their own Ink' (*PW*, 11: 6). Yet the very image betrays Gulliver's intended sense of cure, of restoration of some primal whole, by suggesting a potentially endless cycle of ingestion and evacuation.[10]

Even Gulliver's fantasies fail to satisfy, and his practical efforts are self-defeating. Everywhere apparent in the 'Letter to Sympson' is his anxiety that readers' responses have made lies of his truths; he resents being implicated in a network of falsity. For the critics 'loading our Carrier every Week with Libels, and Keys, and Reflections, and Memoirs, and Second Parts' are all liars (*PW*, 11: 7), some claiming that Gulliver is not the author of the *Travels*, others that he wrote books he never saw. Nevertheless, readers operating on the critic-of-Swift level know that the libelers and key makers also manage to tell the truth in senses Gulliver can never grasp: Swift, author of books Gulliver has not seen, is at least as truly the author of the *Travels* as Gulliver is. Moreover, Gulliver can hardly claim innocence of instigating the keys and continuations of his story (see Tippett 89–90). On the contrary, he plunges even further into intertextuality by voluntarily adding his own remedial emendations, comments, and corrections to the textual 'bundles' – in this, of course, copying Swift.

Gulliver bears another complex family resemblance to his kinsman and ostensible adversary Richard Sympson, who, though by profession a meddler with texts (i.e., an editor), is every inch a 'simp's son' about language and meaning. This simp believes that read words can nevertheless remain disentangled of interpretation, can be more than what Gulliver calls 'meer Fiction' (*PW*, 11: 8), even while paradoxically leaving Sympson as reader 'Liberty to dispose of them as I should think fit' (*PW*, 11: 9). Sympson tries to defend this putative transparency of the text by comparing its ideally docile readers (those who simply interpret Gulliver's intentions) with Gulliver's Redriff neighbors, whom he imagines solemnly treasuring Gulliver's every word. Sympson will never see the neighbors' raised eyebrows or hear the delicious ambiguity of their paradoxical 'Sort of Proverb': 'it was as true as if Mr. *Gulliver* had spoke it' (*PW*, 11: 9). An audience less naive than Sympson knows a 'splendide mendax' when it hears one neighing.

In his next breath, Sympson admits that he has honored the author's 'air of truth' by tampering with (or perhaps even engineering – which is not beneath the lying simp) these organic virtues for rhetorical effect, 'to fit the Work as much as possible to the general Capacity of Readers' (*PW*, 11: 10). To demonstrate his own power over Gulliver's text, this simple and silly man offers to show curious readers the Ur-text itself, 'the whole Work at large' (*PW*, 11: 10) – a gesture repeated by most critics for 264 years after him. But this offer involves another lie, as Gulliver confirms nine years later: Sympson and other readers, however conservatorially minded, have destroyed the original textual meaning by their very perceptions of it. Now even Gulliver 'cannot stand to' the corrections and leaves it to 'my judicious and candid Readers to adjust it as they please' (*PW*, 11: 7). The remainder of the *Travels* is a history of how Gulliver reached this startling acquiescence to readers' arrogation.

Gulliver enters Lilliput with attitudes much like those of Sympson. Lilliput is, above all, a world dominated by texts, a world of ritual gestures, proclamations, ceremonies, and 'Articles', and Gulliver quickly assumes a citizen's prerogatives by becoming a docile decoder of those texts and deluding himself that he is quite at liberty. On the surface, language appears less enigmatic in Lilliput than in the other lands he visits: even on a first encounter, gestures and intonations, if not yet words, convey the meaning of both parties well enough; and Gulliver learns the idiom quickly. Underneath, bubbling away, however, is his belief in what might be called Sympson's paradox: the truth will set a reader free, but the true knowledge of any text is what its author intended. And so Gulliver's pursuit of personal liberty throughout book 1 is in essence a pursuit of freedom both to interpret and to express meanings authorized by his own intentions.

The problem with Lilliputian texts, one that the character Gulliver cannot see, is their hidden agendas – a bit like the narrator Gulliver's concealed motives toward his own readers (Castle, 'Houyhnhnms', 39–40; Swaim, 51–70). Gulliver the character does not realize the tension between his constant collaboration with Lilliputian codes of meaning and the rather blustery image of himself as a hero of freedom, the impression he wants to inculcate in his readers. His first words in Lilliputian empower him to request liberty, and he perceives his increasing participation in Lilliputian textuality as a process of liberation: 'I had sent so many Memorials and Petitions for my Liberty' (*PW*, 11: 42). Yet Gulliver is set free only to obey Lilliputian authorial intentions, to interpret and express only within the Lilliputian system of discourse, which simply denies whatever threatens its authorial power. Thus, when Gulliver painstakingly translates the emperor's proclamation 'Word for Word', he fails to catch – though he does not mask from his readers – the irony of this *splacknuck*'s dubbing himself the 'Delight and Terror of the Universe' (*PW*, 11: 43). Learning the language quickly, Gulliver has already begun to lose the double context that not long before permitted him to 'wonder at the Intrepidity of these diminutive Mortals' (*PW*, 11: 24). In fact, the 'full Liberty' Gulliver boasts of after swearing to the Articles signifies only that he has been lulled into complete readerly docility by the illusion of interpretive free play. For instance, while Reldresal's 'convenient' close reading of the key Big-Endian text, the directive to break eggs at the convenient end, appears objective and seems to avoid 'a meer Strain upon the Text' (*PW*, 11: 49), in actuality it merely reinvests meaning, as do all formalist interpretations, in the desires and practices of his particular interpretive community. But Gulliver, mistaking this sort of interpretation for a mode of personal freedom to seek truth, is so roused that he pledges his life to the emperor's defense.

Gulliver cannot wake up to the emblematic significance that all Lilliputian writing is slanted (*PW*, 11: 57). As late as chapter 6, he approvingly recites a little allegory in which breach of trust is the greatest of crimes and the roles of master, criminal, sum of money, order, and running away reflect all too uncomfortably the power relations among author, reader, signifier (text), authorial intention (signified), and interpretation in the system of discourse that holds Gulliver prisoner (*PW*, 11: 58). For Gulliver as character can neither read nor convey his intentions freely, no matter how naively he protests that his 'Heart was wholly free' (*PW*, 11: 54). For one instance, his freest and most generous expression of biddability, his prodigious urination on the roof of the Imperial Palace to extinguish a fire (*PW*, 11: 56), is inexorably read as disrespect; the Lilliputians do not interpret by searching for Gulliver's authorial intention.

The narrator Gulliver is a different story. In fact, he treats his readers very much the way the Lilliputians treat theirs, including the character Gulliver. Once 'at full Liberty', Gulliver pointedly refrains from repeating the emperor's compliments word for word (*PW*, 11: 44), ostensibly to 'avoid the Censure of Vanity', though even more effectively forestalling his reader in the critic-of-Gulliver mode from the subversive sneering that details of these compliments would certainly promote at Gulliver's expense. He trains readers in how to read him; his word-for-word rendering of the Lilliputians' inventory of his pockets (*PW*, 11: 34–36), for example, invites readers to share the misleading joke that language is merely an interpretive riddle, a screen before an intelligible, whole truth.

The story within a story in chapter 7 is pivotal, not only providing Gulliver with a crucial metaperspective from which to understand his delusive trust in authorized meanings but also warning his critic-of-Gulliver readers about their parallel trust in him. The teller, text, characters, and readers of His Lordship's story – as in Fielding's, Sterne's, and Cervantes's interpolated stories – echo and reveal much about the main story. First, both stories are locked in chains of writing, reading, and rewriting. Just as Gulliver is the audience for a pointed summary of other discourse, including both a dramatic rendition of Reldresal's slanted importuning and the 'Abstract' His Lordship has edited from the language of the Articles, so do Gulliver's readers read what Gulliver has re-created of His Lordship's story from notes taken after the visit had ended – all this contained within the text edited by Sympson, written by Swift, edited by Motte, re-edited by Faulkner et al., and so on. Second, as a character in His Lordship's story, Reldresal exhibits a cruelly ambiguous 'friendship', reminiscent of the narrator Gulliver's own double motives. Third, and perhaps most interesting, as His Lordship's reader, Gulliver reflects one version of his own readers' responses. His response forms three crests. At first, he imagines he can assert his independent consciousness against the calumnious text – 'being conscious of my own Merits and Innocence . . . I was going to interrupt' (*PW*, 11: 68). Then, as he better understands the interrelations of these textual layers, he senses his constraint, and so, in a second wave of response, he is 'under many Doubts and Perplexities of Mind' (*PW*, 11: 72).

The third wave of Gulliver's response to this uncertainty and textual dependence is an incipient understanding that reading the apparent intentions of authors can only lead to blindness. Instead of seeking to escape textuality, Gulliver realizes he must inscribe his 'Liberty' among, rather than in isolation from, Lilliputian texts. Instead of merely fleeing Lilliput, he issues a text to Reldresal, 'signifying my Resolution', and later addresses the emperor of Blefuscu so strategically that even readers outside the text are persuaded that he has not betrayed the truth, though in effect his explanation is nearly a pure lie (*PW*, 11: 73–74). Although the character Gulliver professes to be newly sensitive to rhetorical abuses of power, the narrator offers no fresh circumstantial candor but continues declining to 'trouble the Reader' with details of his reception in Blefuscu, as if to thwart the double context that would render ridiculous the 'Generosity of so great a Prince' (*PW*, 11: 74) – and, more important, would very likely subvert the story of good versus evil that the refugee Gulliver finds useful to promulgate.

The emperor of Blefuscu's devious letter to his counterpart in Lilliput only reaffirms a lesson Gulliver has already begun to absorb: that neither mastering the secret intentions of authors nor issuing counter, revisionist texts of interpretation creates freedom. The same lesson is gradually becoming available for Gulliver's reader-critics, although their adversarial authors include Swift and Gulliver himself. On the trip back to England, Gulliver the character demonstrates his new awareness of the battle between authors and readers. All pretense of circumstantiality dropped, he carefully limits his story for the crew to 'few Words', and when even these few are read as a text of lunacy, he authorizes his 'Veracity' (*PW*, 11: 79) by proffering things in place of words, first tiny cattle and sheep, then gifts of gold.

By the end of his first voyage, then, the character Gulliver has freed himself of persecution only by participating to some degree in the same rhetorical tactics by which he was persecuted, including, most important, stylistic reduction and concealment from his readers. At the same time, since Gulliver the narrator cannot escape language, he seeks power through metadiscourse, generating his own commentary on and outside the texts that oppress him. On his next voyage, the narrator Gulliver immediately talks more freely to his readers about the inadequacies of the very text they are reading. At the end of chapter 1, for instance, he validates exhaustive circumstantiality as the mode of 'Truth' but confesses in the next breath that, 'upon a strict Review, [he] blotted out several Passages of less Moment' to avert reader tedium (*PW*, 11: 94). Gulliver's self-editing of truth is both an appeal for sympathy for such service and, at the same time and for other readerly roles, a flaunting of his power and willingness to occult and reorder the text for his own purposes.

A bit later, Gulliver admits that any stylistic decision will trap him in lies: the departicularized style needed to evade censure as a liar in Europe ('I should hardly be believed') necessarily perpetrates a lie in Brobdingnag ('a false and diminutive Representation' [*PW*, 11: 115]). And so, even while airing his text's insufficiency to rise above lying, Gulliver the narrator offers an alternative, metatextual honesty as his readers' access to truth.

Gulliver the character, however, lacks metadiscourse inside Brobdingnag and therefore quickly loses control of the meanings his audience desires to make. His fate there is always to be freely interpreted, consistently to be made a character in the discrediting fictions of others: 'I was every Day furnishing the Court with some ridiculous Story'; even his beloved Glumdalclitch writes such stories (*PW*, 11: 124). Gulliver can only retell these fictions to readers outside Brobdingnag, trusting the metacontext to restructure ridicule into sympathy. But if the reader as interpreter of intention is inclined to sympathize, the reader as critic of Gulliver is just as tempted to share the giants' amusement; additionally, part of the consciousness of the reader as critic of Swift is continually stimulated to contemplate Gulliver's textual dilemma. For though Gulliver officially deplores the distorting liberties of the giants' way of reading, he nonetheless desires precisely the same freedoms for himself. He grotesquely misinterprets the king's request for 'as exact an account' as possible of England, conjuring it into a new willingness on His Majesty's part to concede Gulliver's authority: 'The King . . . began to conceive a much better Opinion of me than he had ever before'; 'he should be glad to hear of any thing that might deserve Imitation' (*PW*, 11: 127).

Gulliver becomes no more than a collection of unreliable fictions to the Brobdingnagians, as the king acknowledges by denouncing all European culture as a corrupted text: 'I observe among you some Lines of an Institution, which in its Original might have been tolerable; but these half erased, and the rest wholly blurred and blotted by Corruptions' (*PW*, 11: 132; Castle, 'Houyhnhnms' 40). Gulliver counterblasts by condemning Brobdingnagian legal texts and readers as immobilized by single meanings (i.e., he makes the same assumption that was near fatally wrong about the Lilliputians): 'They are expressed in the most plain and simple Terms, wherein those People are not Mercurial enough to discover above one Interpretation' (*PW*, 11: 136). To Gulliver, the Brobdingnagians have self-administered the same punishment the Lilliputians sought to inflict on him: reduction of insight and even of physical sight ('*short Views!*' exclaims Gulliver of the king [*PW*, 11: 135]). Although Gulliver continues to trumpet his 'extreme Love of Truth' (*PW*, 11: 133), he cannot assert the validity of his own intended meanings without paradoxically endorsing a multiplicity of interpretations and expressing hostility toward the idea that a single meaning may be synonymous with truth.

Glumdalclitch's 'little old Treatise' on human weaknesses (*PW*, 11: 137–38) mirrors the dilemma confronting Gulliver, his readers, and his authors (Quintana 298–99). For the treatise is an undeniable image of the *Travels* itself, treating a good many of Swift's long-standing themes – especially the diminutiveness of the human species in modern times when compared with the ancients and even with certain animals – and achieving, even Gulliver has to admit, 'several moral Applications useful in the Conduct of Life' (*PW*, 11: 137). Even so, Gulliver's more pressing complaint, that the book quarrels with the author of humanity, also rings true – at least until we realize that Gulliver's quarrel repeats the treatise's. Since nature did not give human beings foresight, complaints about nature are only natural. Likewise, since the treatise is an interpreter's quarrel with the authorship of nature, so it echoes Gulliver's quarrel with its own quarrelsomeness, not to mention the quarrel that the critic of Gulliver has with Gulliver's quarrelsome criticisms, the quarrel that the interpreter of intention has with the quarrelsome criticisms advanced by the critic of Gulliver, and on into the critical commentaries of the critics of Swift and *Gulliver's Travels*, and eventually so back into the text, in a circle of quarreling by readers made authors by virtue of their quarrels with other authors.

As if in extension of the Brobdingnagians' marginalization of him, Gulliver's character begins in Laputa utterly deprived of readers. His discourse is no longer even 'turned into Ridicule' (*PW*, 11: 133); indeed, he is barely noticed, despite Flapper intervention. This authorship of virtually unpublished texts may seem close to Gulliver's fantasy in the 'Letter to Sympson', but in Laputa the character Gulliver, still the enthusiast of unfettered interpretation that

Brobdingnag made of him, longs in vain for readers of his own. For their part, the Laputans claim perfect authorship; they scarcely need readers. On the one hand, their language assigns names to things, aping the epistemology of Adam in Eden or perhaps of euclidean mathematics, in which signs bear natural and unvarying relations to reality (Reiss 328–32). On the other hand, as readers the Laputans connect with the words of others only by threads (*PW*, 11: 163). No wonder Gulliver, though he can and does exercise every freedom of reader response, is soon 'heartily weary' of this world. He cannot bear to be a pure reader – however unrestrained – if he is consequently deprived of authorship; but his own words hardly reach Laputan ears.

Lagado further projects this alienation of author and reader in alternating fantasies of control and freedom. Many of the experiments are bent on rescuing some original whole from corruption: cucumber flesh is merely a container for some anterior essence; excrement may be returned to its original food; houses may be built so that the bottom can never determine the shape of the top (an idea reminiscent of the Laputans' unresponsiveness to what is below); colicky patients are reinjected with outside air until the external is realigned with the internal (*PW*, 11: 179–81; see Ehrmann). Other experiments are images of pure freedom to nose about: acorns, dates, and chestnuts are distributed for the convenience of hordes of rooting and fertilizing pigs; a spider's web, the famous symbol of private and personal art in *The Battle of the Books*, is converted into a mere vehicle to 'fit every Body's fancy'; readers of Lagadan sundials find meanings that reflect 'all accidental Turnings of the Wind' (*PW*, 11: 180–81).

The next four experiments carry the fantasies explicitly into language. The book machine is a nearly perfect image of reader gratification: a text utterly free of authorial control – literally authorless – in which 'the whole Disposition of the Words was entirely changed' by any sudden turn of the wheel (*PW*, 11: 184). (Similar, of course, are the uninhibited artists in the school of political projectors, 'dextrous in finding out the mysterious Meanings of Words, Syllables and Letters' [*PW*, 11: 191].) But the last three experiments, in the school of speculative learning, are an author's fantasy of perfect control: shorten discourse to just the names of reality; abolish words altogether and discourse transparently through real things themselves; or, more 'practically', let readers swallow one's propositions (rendered in 'natural' mathematical symbols) without mediation, so as to imprint signs directly on the brain, without need for the corrupting intervention of eyes and mind (*PW*, 11: 186). (Readers, of course, at least the critics of Gulliver and Swift, are inclined to steal aside and vomit.)

Fleeing these grotesque disjunctions of author from reader, Gulliver eventually stumbles on apparent images of wholeness in the three interpreters who figure in his last adventures on the third voyage. Since interpreters are hybrid creatures, by definition always authors and readers at the same time, so in their company Gulliver is again simultaneously author and reader; the price is that he once again is constantly a character in others' fictions. This dilemma he learns to address by lying. Sailing to Luggnag, Gulliver resorts to lies about his nationality, but they succeed only in bringing about his confinement (*PW*, 11: 203). But as soon as he hires a young interpreter (to keep, as it were, Gulliver's tongue in his mouth), Gulliver is able to control the meaning of conversations to his own advantage, without resorting to lies (or at least to any he deems worth mentioning). His Majesty is delighted with the Englishman's interpreted company; the floor Gulliver is given to lick is almost dust-free; and as he modestly observes, 'I had many Acquaintances among Persons of the best Fashion, and being always attended by my Interpreter, the Conversation we had was not disagreeable' (*PW*, 11: 207).

However, assigning away one's tongue, authorizing another to clarify one's meaning, is potentially an abdication similar to the assignment of one's awareness to Flappers, as Kathleen Swaim has shrewdly remarked (136). The second interpreter, a volunteer, gives an expurgated account of the Struldbruggs that tricks Gulliver into a ridiculous burst of enthusiasm. Chagrined, Gulliver learns, in dealing with his third interpreter in Japan, how not to be exploited by a highly unstable chain of readers and authors: he lies to his interpreter. This tactic works spectacularly well, outside as well as within the text; interpreters of intention are preponderantly receptive to Gulliver's anxiety and apparent powerlessness in Japan, while in fact Gulliver is inducing the emperor himself to conspire in, even to initiate, keeping Gulliver's secrets (*PW*, 11: 216–17). The lesson is reinforced by Gulliver's voyage home among Dutch sailors, which in the absence of a mediating translator proves 'very long and troublesome'. Although Gulliver resorts to brevity – 'I made up a Story as short and probable as I could, but concealed the greatest Part' – and evasion by 'general answers', he is constantly threatened with unmasking (*PW*, 11: 217).

Having learned to lie to others, the character Gulliver learns a penultimate strategy in Houyhnhnmland, lying to himself; and the author Gulliver teaches the art of the 'splendide mendax' to his readers, even those who do not care to learn it. Among the Houyhnhnms there seems no tension or communicative conflict of interest – at least none is permitted – no changefulness or competition of desires; authors and readers are linked by 'immediate Conviction' (*PW*, 11: 267). All this and truthfulness as well. Yet Gulliver is still limited by Sympsonian notions of the relations between language and reality. As he habitually learns languages by treating words as mere names for a reality that precedes and creates the need for language, so he analyzes the Houyhnhnms:[11] 'their Language doth not abound in Variety of Words, because their Wants and Passions are fewer than among us' (*PW*, 11: 242); for example, the Houyhnhnm tongue has no terms for 'Power, Government, War, Law, Punishment, and a Thousand other Things' (*PW*, 11: 244). Readers who buy into this sort of explanation wholeheartedly can scarcely avoid perceiving apparent contradictions in Houyhnhnmland, and indeed the majority opinion among twentieth-century critics has been that the Houyhnhnms must be hypocrites.

That the Houyhnhnm tongue has no terms for 'Power, Government, War, Law, Punishment, and a Thousand other Things' hardly denies that these exist in Gulliver's description of the horses' world. The soft school has for decades rampaged over this fact. Punishment? Why, the Houyhnhnm master has no trouble imagining that any Yahoo who dared venture on a Houyhnhnm's back would shortly be squeezed to death (*PW*, 11: 241). As for government, what else is the Grand Assembly or Representative Council that meets every four years and, despite Gulliver's insistence that disputes are unknown among the Houyhnhnms, regularly debates exterminating the Yahoos? Regarding law, what about the 'Exhortations', which do not indeed need to compel a 'rational Creature', because by definition any creature not obeying an Exhortation is not rational and so, chillingly, has no rights at all in Houyhnhnmland? And so on.[12]

These perceptions leave much unexplained. Yet bald-faced denial of the contradictions, as in some hard-school interpretations, is also inadequate. The larger question is, Just how can these utterly contrary signals come from the same text? It is easy to forget that all any reader ever can know of the Houyhnhnms comes from Gulliver's account of them. It is Gulliver's, and our own, very different language that invents our sense of the reality of Houyhnhnm 'Power, Government, War, Law, Punishment, and a Thousand other Things'. Gulliver cannot interpret the Houyhnhnms, or use the concepts of his language to conceive of them, without destroying their perfection for himself and, as narrator, for us as well. In this way, the fourth voyage brings to a climax a book massively concerned with the problems of representation, interpretation, and power.

Instead of claiming that the Houyhnhnms have few words because they have few needs, one could as plausibly contend that they have few wants because they have few words, as post-Saussurian language theory suggests. It is less their orality than their linguistic economy that creates the seeming dispensation of Houyhnhnm discourse. Before Gulliver ever spoke about and interpreted the horses, their reality may well have coincided with their language. In an otherwise brilliant study, Timothy J. Reiss has accused the Houyhnhnms of occulting their vices; but this interpretation presupposes a reality existing prior to and outside language, which the Houyhnhnms' words can only either acknowledge or obscure, that is, surreptitiously fail to acknowledge (345).[13] It also gives Gulliver's readers too much credit for metacritical astuteness and distance. The concealment is as likely Gulliver's and theirs as it is the Houyhnhnms'; the situation is parallel to the Houyhnhnm master's comment that it is 'not unwise' for Gulliver to cover and conceal his ugly body (260); but because the master exists outside Gulliver's codes of representation, it never would or could occur to him to follow suit.

On the absence of lying, Reiss similarly remarks that 'the use of a paraphrase is hardly proof that the idea is absent: on the contrary, it suggests rather that the idea is being concealed for some reason' (341). True, but who is concealing it and from whom? Here, Reiss's reading illustrates the paradox that even if Gulliver's critics do not allow Gulliver to lie to them, they may not avoid lying to themselves. The Houyhnhnms speak truth, but Gulliver's language cannot say as much without lying about them. The phrase 'the Thing which is not' reduces to paradox, simultaneously denying and asserting the same thing. Gulliver cannot celebrate the Houyhnhnms' perfection without delineating its imperfections. His readers, therefore, cannot be relied on even to envy the Houyhnhnms' bliss. Internally realized though the horses' paradise may be, it is violated by outsiders' very acts of knowing it.

And so the character Gulliver finds his linguistic utopia, where simple truth may be promulgated, but he cannot help interpreting, reauthoring, and for many readers destroying it. All that is left is lying to himself that this text, too, is perfect, luminous. Yet the claim that his truth can rise above the vicissitudes of fortune leads Gulliver to identify with yet another classical example of the confluence of truth claims, lying, and power – the importunities of Sinon, whose self-inflicted 'misery' and proclamations of truthfulness pried open Troy to conquest. This allusion, overlying Gulliver's braying about truthfulness, evokes not so much Plato's noble lie as Nietzsche's will to power:

> There is only *one* world, and that world is false, cruel, contradictory, misleading, senseless. . . . We need lies to vanquish this reality, this 'truth', we need lies in order to live. . . . That lying is a necessity of

life is itself a part of the terrifying and problematic character of existence.

(451)

As we have seen, by the time of the 'Letter to Sympson', Gulliver is complaining that his readers have corrupted his intentions, his truth. But the most profound truth about this text is that his readers did not do it alone.

Readers who pay particular attention to Gulliver's efforts at reading and at writing may see sobering reflections of their own procedures. Of course, many would prefer not to. But some do learn from Gulliver's abuses of these processes to interpret subversively against his intentions. They willy-nilly participate in chipping away the epistemological foundations that underpave the insoluble ambiguity of many Swiftian meanings. The recent attention to Swift's use of indirection, by David Nokes and others, is another reminder that, in attempting to provoke individual acts of responsibility, Swift had to invite – not simply to suffer – a multiplicity of responses. No writer has ever documented more persuasively both the relentless human ambition to totalize systems of understanding and, at the same time, the ultimate futility of those systems.

Nevertheless, the existential pleasure of anarchic or mendacious linguistic experience is not inevitably liberated from potential guilt and regret. As recent studies of Swift's linguistic views have convincingly argued, Swift never believed that linguistic redemption could be institutionalized or codified; instead, he put his stock in triggering individual acts of will (Kelly 1–5, 73–103; Wyrick). It is perhaps worth remembering the process of redemption that Augustine long ago defined for the careful reader of Scripture, for it seems an epistemological model for some readers' experiences with Swift's work (e.g., Dyson; Rodino, 'Varieties'). This is a process at once intellectual, moral, and psychological, beginning with the experience of error or abuse, then fear and guilt, next rejection of transitory things, and so on to regeneration of the individual will (Augustine 39–40; see also Fish 2–3 for a discussion of this passage).

The power struggles of authors, characters, and readers, both within and outside *Gulliver's Travels*, anticipate Paul de Man's revisionist point that differing meanings cannot simply exist side by side but, rather, 'have to engage each other in direct confrontation, since the one reading is precisely the error denounced by the other and has to be undone by it' (*Allegories* 12). At the same time, if it is true that any reader of *Gulliver's Travels* can be regenerated, the process will begin with a certain humility about the manifold errors and lies of human knowledge and the further recognition that all interpretation risks becoming a deathly struggle to defeat its other, to silence that which is different. Only when interpreters understand the nature of their understanding, its unavoidable fallacy and ineluctable ties to power, can they begin to move away from violence and arrogation toward a discourse that examines the 'larger political context in which exegesis always takes place – the context of desire and conflict' (Castle, *Ciphers* 187).

I conclude with a word on what this chapter does not do, or at least what it tries hard not to do. A reading of this sort, which attempts to understand how almost three centuries of contradictory interpretations can have been generated by the same text, does not presuppose that any documented positions in the traditional thematic controversies over the *Travels* are necessarily irrelevant or wrongheaded. For instance, Clifford's hard-school readers have given ample evidence of the narrator Gulliver's strenuous labors to gain the sympathy of his interpreters of intention and win them to his authorized meanings. Likewise, most soft-school readings have testified to the strength of critic-of-Gulliver suspicions of the narrator's motives.

Among the most notorious bones of contention has been whether to interpret Gulliver as a character with sufficient psychological consistency to be distinguished crisply from Swift or whether, as C. J. Rawson has perhaps stated most emphatically, he is less a character in a novel than 'a satirist's stance of ultimate exasperation', treated externally as a satirical device (27–29). Still, it makes as little sense to ignore the sometimes gigantic evidence of Gulliver's unstable identity as to deny his powerful efforts to create an exploitably plausible image of himself in his readers' minds. Although any reader, by conscious or unconscious critical decision, may see Gulliver as rabbit or duck, either perception is smaller than the conditions of representation – the topic of this analysis – that generate these alternative illusions. Nor does this analysis seek out the author's consciousness, not even to identify it as confused or paradoxical, at least not to imply a definable whole anterior to and outside the text of *Gulliver's Travels*. And yet such phenomenological interpretation is also highly relevant, in fact is essential, to this reading, since the text of *Gulliver's Travels* plays quite knowledgeably on expectations of author-oriented meanings.

Nor, finally, does this reading want to privilege 'the reader', except as defined by a network of unstable relations, inseparable from other elements of textual transmission, including other readers. This is not a 'strong misreading', or an allegorical reading, or a 'grid' (in Foucault's terms) imposed on the text without reference to the vocabulary used in the text or by its author. Rather, it is a reading rooted in the text's language and also in the text's implication in historical sites, as perceived nonpositivistically through the ways reading has gone on, both within and outside the text (see McGann). By contrast, traditional reader-response critics of Swift, from Booth to Rawson, have tended to hypostatize the reader into a formal rhetorical element that they sooner or later offer in support of 'hard' (Rawson) or 'soft' (Booth) thematics. And yet these approaches too are a *sine qua non* of a reading that seeks to understand a little more about how 264 years of intelligent reading has both revealed and sought to conceal such multiplicity.

This sort of attention to *Gulliver's Travels* suggests that, in his most brilliant acts of artistic creation, Swift understood very well certain inevitabilities about the paradoxical nature of texts in the world, of authorship and reading. With a nod to the perils of sea travel, the text of *Gulliver's Travels* might best be described not as 'pearls that were his eyes' – or even as the ocean floor stretching firmly, though apparently infinitely, below – but as what the ocean water itself is to the finny creatures that are buoyed up by it, ingest through it, live because of it, and die within it, all without ever recognizing that it is there.

Notes

1. See K. Williams; Berwick; Clubb; Tobin and Landa; Stathis; Clifford; Rodino, *Studies* xxx–xxxvi, 179–238.

2. See, for example, Holly; Barnett; and Castle, 'Houyhnhnms'. Poststructuralist essays written in French – e.g., Bony; Ehrmann – appeared a few years earlier.

3. See Said's 'preliminary investigation of how Swift's work can be approached and characterised as the highly dramatic encounter between the anarchy of resistance (agraphia) to the written page, and the abiding tory order of the page' (1969: 48–49): see also Eagleton, esp. 58.

4. The system of relationships in the *Travels* lends itself to vast schemes of description. Quintana, for example, distinguishes five Swifts with reference to the book: the historical personage, the writer, the satirist, the author of the *Travels*, and the commentator on the *Travels* (297–98). Aikins describes three categories of readers.

5. Bony suggests that the 'character' of Gulliver has no objective reality independent of the reader's own illusions and needs; see also Brady; and Prince 16–26, 125–32.

6. See Holly: 'What is it that the beholder sees but fails to recognize in the glass but his own beholding, i.e., the process by which the text as an empty signifying is given a face by his reading' (145). On the signified as illusory, see also Reiss: 'The assumption of objectivity and the consequent exclusion of whatever cannot be brought to fit its order are necessarily accompanied by the occultation of the enunciating subject as discursive activity' (42).

7. See, for example, H. Williams, Introduction and *Text*; Davis; Woolley; Lock; Treadwell; and Hubbard.

8. According to Dalnekoff, Gulliver illustrates Berkeley's theories that new perception creates relative senses of truth.

9. In 'Why the Houyhnhnms Don't Write', Castle relates Gulliver's infatuation with Houyhnhnm orality to Derrida's critique of the central myth in Western culture that separates speech from the written word and privileges a natural connection between speech and reality, while nurturing suspicion of writing as an unnatural imposition and corruption of meaning.

10. In contrast to Gulliver, Swift would force his words down the throats of others, as Pope perceptively noted: 'I find you would rather be employ'd as an Avenging Angel of wrath, to break your Vial of Indignation over the heads of the wretched pityful creatures of the World; nay would make them *Eat your Book*, which you have made as bitter a pill for them as possible' (*Corr.* 3: 108). Ehrmann studies reversals of interior and exterior, with particular reference to medical practices in the fourth voyage. For a penetrating discussion of betrayal by metaphor, with a discussion of the subversiveness of Locke's language against his own criticism of figurative language, see de Man, 'Epistemology'.

11. Kelly points out that this theory of language is reminiscent of John Wilkins's elaboration of Francis Bacon's theory of 'real characters' (73–82).

12. For example, although the Houyhnhnms lack a word for power, the Yahoos run away at their approach; the Yahoos are tied by the neck, continually watched, forced into servitude, and – after Gulliver's eviction – perhaps subjected to castration or extermination. The Houyhnhnms have often seen Yahoo battles, and so on. See Reiss 345.

13. In the work of linguists and ethnolinguists such as Quine, Whorf, and Saussure, language provides the conceptual scheme by which a given community of speakers will habitually interpret their world. Rorty suggests that the 'Wittgenstein–Sellars–Quine–Davidson attack on distinctions between classes of sentences is the special contribution of analytical philosophy' to this anti-Platonist insistence on the ubiquity of language (xvii–xxi). For example, following Heidegger, Gadamer argues that 'language speaks its own being'; it is 'a universal ontological structure'. The truth of objects 'comes-to-be' in the activity of language. The 'being which can be understood is language'; that is, language is the possibility condition of truth (*Truth and Method* 431–32). In a later essay Gadamer denies that linguistically articulated consciousness determines the material being of life praxis, yet points out that no social reality fails to bring itself to representation in language ('Scope'). See also Held 307–17; Mendelson 66.

Works Cited

ADAMS, PERCY G., *Travelers and Travel Liars, 1660–1800* (Berkeley, CA, 1962).

AIKINS, JANET E., 'Reading "with Conviction": Trial by Satire', in *The Genres of Gulliver's Travels*, ed. FREDERICK N. SMITH (Newark, DE, 1990), pp. 203–29.

AUGUSTINE, *On Christian Doctrine*, trans. D. W. ROBERTSON (New York, 1958).

BARNETT, LOUISE K., 'Deconstructing *Gulliver's Travels*: Modern Readers and the Problematic of Genre', in *The Genres of* Gulliver's Travels, ed. FREDERICK N. SMITH (Newark, DE, 1990), pp. 230–45.

BERWICK, DONALD M., *Reputation of Jonathan Swift, 1781–1882* (New York, 1941).

The Blunder of All Blunders: Or, The Wonder of All Wonders: Or, Gulliver Devoured by Butterflies: Or, The Fops Observation on Lilliput, &c. (Dublin, 1726).

BOK, SISSELA, *Lying: Moral Choice in Public and Private Life* (New York, 1978).

BONY, ALAIN, ' "Call Me Gulliver" ', *Poétique*, 14 (1973), 197–209.

BOOTH, WAYNE C., *The Rhetoric of Fiction* (Chicago, 1962).

BRADY, FRANK, 'Vexations and Diversions: Three Problems in *Gulliver's Travels*', *Modern Philology*, 75 (1978), 346–67.

CARNOCHAN, W. B., *Lemuel Gulliver's Mirror for Man* (Berkeley, 1968).

CASTLE, TERRY J., 'Why the Houyhnhnms Don't Write: Swift, Satire and the Fear of the Text', *Essays in Literature*, 7 (1980), 31–44.

CASTLE, TERRY J., *Clarissa's Ciphers: Meaning and Disruption in Richardson's* Clarissa (Ithaca, NY, 1982).

CLIFFORD, JAMES L., 'Gulliver's Fourth Voyage: "Hard" and "Soft" Schools of Interpretation', in *Quick Springs of Sense: Studies in the Eighteenth Century*, ed. LARRY S. CHAMPION (Athens, GA, 1974), pp. 33–49.

CLUBB, MERREL D., 'The Criticism of Gulliver's "Voyage to the Houyhnhnms", 1726–1914', in *Stanford Studies in Language and Literature*, ed. HARDIN CRAIG (Palo Alto, CA, 1941), pp. 203–32.

DALNEKOFF, DONNA ISAACS, 'A Familiar Stranger: The Outside of Eighteenth-Century Satire', *Neophilologus*, 57 (1973), 121–34.

DAVIS, HERBERT, 'Textual Notes'. Swift, *Gulliver's Travels*, 301–22.

DE MAN, PAUL, *Allegories of Reading: Figural Language in Rousseau, Nietzsche, Rilke, and Proust* (New Haven, CT, 1979).

DE MAN, PAUL, 'The Epistemology of Metaphor', in *On Metaphor*, ed. SHELDON SACKS (Chicago, 1979), pp. 11–28.

DILWORTH, W. H., *The Life of Jonathan Swift, Dean of St. Patrick's, Dublin* (London, 1758).

DYSON, A. E., 'Swift: The Metamorphosis of Irony', in *The Crazy Fabric: Essays in Irony* (London, 1965), pp. 1–13.

EAGLETON, TERRY, 'Ecriture and Eighteenth-Century Fiction', *Literature, Society, and the Sociology of Literature*. Proceedings of the Conference held at the University of Essex, July 1976, ed. FRANCIS BARKER et al. (Colchester, 1977), pp. 55–58.

EHRMANN, JACQUES, 'Le dedans et le dehors', *Poétique*, 9 (1972), 31–40.

FISH, STANLEY, 'Discovery as Form in *Paradise Lost*', in *New Essays on* Paradise Lost, ed. THOMAS KRANIDAS (Berkeley, CA, 1969), pp. 1–14.

FOUCAULT, MICHEL, 'Appendix: *The Discourse on Language*', *The Archaeology of Knowledge and the Discourse on Language*, trans. A. M. SHERIDAN SMITH (New York, 1972), pp. 215–37.

GADAMER, HANS-GEORG, 'On the Scope and Function of Hermeneutical Reflection', in *Philosophical Hermeneutics*, ed. DAVID LINGE (Berkeley, CA, 1976).

GADAMER, HANS-GEORG, *Truth and Method* (New York, 1975).

HELD, DAVID, *Introduction to Critical Theory: Horkheimer to Habermas* (Berkeley, CA, 1980).

HOLLY, GRANT, 'Travel and Translation: Textuality in *Gulliver's Travels*', *Criticism*, 21.2 (1979), 134–52.

HUBBARD, LUCIUS L., *Contributions towards a Bibliography of* Gulliver's Travels (1922) (New York, 1968).

JAUSS, HANS ROBERT, *Toward an Aesthetic of Reception*. Theory and History of Literature 2 (Minneapolis, 1982).

KELLY, ANN CLINE, *Swift and the English Language* (Philadelphia, PA, 1988).

LAWRY, JON S., 'Dr. Lemuel Gulliver and "the Thing Which Was Not"', *Journal of English and Germanic Philology*, 67 (1968), 218–22.

LOCK, F. P., 'The Text of *Gulliver's Travels*', *Modern Language Review*, 76 (1981), 513–33.

McGANN, JEROME, *The Beauty of Inflections: Literary Investigations in Historical Method and Theory* (Oxford, 1985).

McKEON, MICHAEL, *The Origins of the English Novel, 1600–1740* (Baltimore, MD, 1987).

MENDELSON, JACK, 'The Habermas–Gadamer Debate', *New German Critique*, 18 (1979), 44–73.

MEZCIEMS, JENNY, 'Utopia and "the Thing Which Is Not": More, Swift, and Other Lying Idealists', *University of Toronto Quarterly*, 52 (1982), 40–62.

NIETZSCHE, FRIEDRICH WILHELM, *Will to Power*, ed. WALTER KAUFMANN (New York, 1967).

NOKES, DAVID, *Jonathan Swift, a Hypocrite Reversed: A Critical Biography* (London, 1985).

ORRERY, JOHN, EARL OF, *Memoirs of the Life and Writings of Jonathan Swift, D. D., Dean of St. Patrick's, Dublin* (London, 1752).

PLATO, *The Republic*, trans. H. D. P. LEE (Harmondsworth, 1955).

PRINCE, GERALD, *Narratology: The Form and Function of Narrative* (New York, 1982).

QUINTANA, RICARDO, '*Gulliver's Travels*: Some Structural Properties and Certain Questions of Critical Approach and Interpretation', in *The Character of Swift's Satire: A Revised Focus*, ed. CLAUDE RAWSON (Newark, DE; London, 1983), pp. 282–304.

RAWSON, C. J., *Gulliver and the Gentle Reader: Studies in Swift and Our Time* (London, 1973).

REISS, TIMOTHY J., *The Discourse of Modernism* (Ithaca, NY, 1982).

RODINO, RICHARD H., 'Varieties of Vexatious Experience in Swift and Others', *Papers on Language and Literature*, 18 (1982), 325–47.

RODINO, RICHARD H., *Swift Studies, 1965–1980: An Annotated Bibliography* (New York, 1984).

RORTY, RICHARD, *Consequences of Pragmatism* (Minneapolis, 1982).

SAID, EDWARD, 'Swift's Tory Anarchy', *Eighteenth-Century Studies*, 3 (1969), 48–66. [See also Chapter 1 in this volume.]

SHERIDAN, THOMAS, *The Life of the Rev. Dr. Jonathan Swift, Dean of St. Patrick's, Dublin* (London, 1784).

STATHIS, JAMES J., *A Bibliography of Swift Studies, 1945–65* (Nashville, TN, 1967).

SWAIM, KATHLEEN M., *A Reading of* Gulliver's Travels (The Hague, 1972).

SWIFT, JONATHAN, *The Correspondence of Jonathan Swift*, ed. HAROLD WILLIAMS (5 vols) (Oxford, 1963–65).

SWIFT, JONATHAN, *Gulliver's Travels 1726*, ed. HERBERT DAVIS (1941; 2nd edn Oxford, 1965).

TEERINK, HERMAN, *A Bibliography of the Writings of Jonathan Swift*, ed. ARTHUR H. SCOUTEN (Philadelphia, 1963).

THACKERAY, WILLIAM MAKEPEACE, 'The English Humourists of the Eighteenth Century', in *The History of Henry Esmond, Esq., and the Lectures*. Vol. 7 of *The Works of William Makepeace Thackeray* (New York: 1899), pp. 423–617.

TIPPETT, BRIAN, Gulliver's Travels: *An Introduction to the Variety of Criticism* (Atlantic Highlands, 1989).

TOBIN, JAMES E. and LOUIS A. LANDA, *Jonathan Swift: A List of Critical Studies Published from 1895–1945* (New York, 1945).

TREADWELL, MICHAEL, 'Benjamin Motte, Andrew Tooke and *Gulliver's Travels*', in *Proceedings of the First Münster Symposium on Jonathan Swift*, ed. HERMANN J. REAL and HEINZ J. VIENKEN (Munich, 1985), pp. 287–304.

WILLIAMS, HAROLD, Introduction. Swift, *Gulliver's Travels*, xxii–xxviii.

WILLIAMS, HAROLD, *The Text of* Gulliver's Travels (Cambridge, 1952).

WILLIAMS, KATHLEEN (ed.), *Swift: The Critical Heritage* (London, 1970).

WOOLLEY, DAVID, 'Swift's Copy of *Gulliver's Travels*: The Armagh *Gulliver*, Hyde's Edition, and Swift's Earliest Corrections', in *The Art of Jonathan Swift*, ed. CLIVE T. PROBYN (New York; London, 1978), pp. 131–78.

WYRICK, DEBORAH BAKER, *Jonathan Swift and the Vested Word* (Chapel Hill, NC, 1988).

ZIMMERMAN, EVERETT, *Swift's Narrative Satires: Author and Authority* (Ithaca, NY, 1983).

3 Extract from *Jonathan Swift and the Vested Word**

Deborah Baker Wyrick

The Idea from an Empty Name

In an age given to protective pen names and anonymous authorships, Swift stands out as a particularly resolute concealer of his proper name. Swift's evasive authorial tactics shielded him from censure and, at times, prosecution while allowing him to write freely in a variety of modes on a variety of subjects. They also allowed him to wait for public reaction before deciding whether to continue dissembling or to acknowledge authorship, at least tacitly.[1] This strategy of withholding formed part of Swift's tongue-in-cheek advice to literary novices in *On Poetry: A Rapsody*; after the poem is begotten, the poet should be quiet, giving up 'fond paternal pride' to allow the work to be 'read without a name' until critical judgment has been passed (ll. 127, 129). In addition, these tactics also conformed to the custom of anonymous pamphleteering, nurtured by the real and present dangers of seventeenth-century English politics, and to the ideal image of the gentleman-author, who could indulge his avocation by withholding the patronage of his signature from his own written words. Yet these gestures of concealment also provide oblique means of revelatory identification, identification not necessarily of a received, historical self but of a conceived, textual self. In so doing, they touch on the network of problems surrounding verbal meaning, the power of a text to control the interpretation of its own words.

Sometimes anonymity produced delightful confusion and a rather transparent defense against culpability that allowed true authorship to shine through: Swift wanted readers to think that he wrote a piece without being able to prove it. False discernments of authorship that did not discomfit his targets, however, infuriated Swift. After the anonymous *A Tale of a Tub* was attributed to his cousin Thomas,

* Reprinted from *Jonathan Swift and the Vested Word* (Durham, NC: University of North Carolina Press, 1988), pp. 95–108.

for example, Swift asked his publisher to help expose 'the foolish impertinence' of 'that little Parson-cousin' (letter to Benjamin Tooke, 29 June 1710);[2] and in the postscript to the 'Apology' of the 5th edition, Swift wrote: '*The Author farther asserts that the whole Work is entirely of one Hand, which every Reader of Judgment will easily discover*' ('Postscript', *Tale*, 20–21). Such claims for authorial control indicate a more complex characteristic of many of Swift's anonymous works. They usually demand to be read as if they harbored a pseudonymic presence who has chosen to remain unnamed. Perhaps this is why commentators cannot resist giving titular or generic names to the 'creators' of these works: the Grub Street Hack, the Modern Author, even the Modest Proposer. Thus there is a double covering: anonymity disguising the fictional 'real' author disguising Swift. Investiture and divestiture work at cross tensions, allowing Swift to be in and out of the text at the same time. Swift divests himself of authority by creating an authorial character that he invests with an individual shaping voice and set of attitudes, then divests this character of an authorizing proper name so that Swift can reinvest himself in the reopened possibilities of the text.

This strategy permits various effects. For example, the righteously infuriated 'Swift' can erupt through the calm calculations of the Modest Proposer because the 'me' in a phrase such as 'let no Man talk to me of these and the like Expedients' (*PW*, 12: 117) has been left officially vacant; the bothersome anonymous voice embedded in *Verses on the Death* may or may not be impartial, ironic, or self-praising. These crossings of unnamed voices can cause artistic short circuits, in the sense that Swift loses tonal uniformity or the detachment that the very fact of anonymity is often considered to produce. But they do not seem haphazardly unintentional. In part, Swift delighted in the sheer play, in the mystifying trickery that unstable and layered anonymity makes possible. His deliberate chicanery in *A Panegyric on Reverend Dean Swift*, ostensibly written by an unnamed Irish Whig masquerading as Delany, is a case in point. Swift went as far as having it published by a Whig printer and publicly complaining about its libelous nature.[3] This poem also weaves intertextual anonymity by incorporating and reinterpreting the anonymous verse satires by Swift against Delany that preceded it; it therefore demonstrates the peculiar elasticity of Swiftian anonymity, one that stretches to encompass the competing ends of authorial exposure and concealment yet can snap back to catch and sting false interpretive certitude.[4] Like Swift's Jove in *The Day of Judgment*, whose inscrutable designs are framed to falsify and damn all interpretations of them, Swiftian anonymity turns pranks to traps. The bite not only hurts, it condemns.

Swift's pseudonyms, however, are different kinds of coverings. On the one hand, they are more complete divestitures than is anonymity. Twentieth-century criticism has shown how pen names evolved into personae, not only masks through which Swift, disguised, can speak, but also characters in their own rights who multiply the levels of satire by concurring and disputing with their creator, fictional authors who nonetheless exercise considerable authority over their works.[5] On the other hand, pseudonyms are divestitures of authority that do not leave texts naked and language exposed to random usurpations. The theory of deictics proposes that linguistic 'indicators' or 'shifters' such as personal pronouns are empty signs waiting to be seized in order to turn *langue* into *parole*; as Émile Benveniste explains, 'language is organized in such a way that it allows each speaker to appropriate the entire language by designating himself as the I'.[6] Instead of giving the pronoun the concrete, originating status of his own proper name, Swift uses pseudonymic presences to inhabit the 'I'. Therefore, he can maintain his absence from the text, can defer responsibility for his words, and can prevent meaning from being tied to – or closed by – the speaking or writing subject. In this way, Swift can circumvent some of the problems, long-term as well as immediate, inherent in the straightforward appropriation of the deictic. Seizing the deictic can actually decenter the proper name, setting it adrift in textual time, at risk of becoming a floating, empty signifier. Swift's chaotic early poem, 'Ode to the Athenian Society', outlines this troubling paradox:

> Were I to form a regular thought of fame,
> Which is perhaps as hard t' imagine right
>   As to paint Echo to the sight:
> I would not draw the idea from an empty name;
>   Because, alas, when we all die
>   Careless and ignorant posterity,
>   Although they praise the learning and the wit,
>   And though the title seems to show
>   The name and man, by whom the book was writ,
>   Yet how shall they be brought to know
> Whether that very name was he, or you, or I?

(ll. 158–68)

This ode offers no solutions, but it demonstrates the dangers of losing one's name in an effort to preserve it. The solutions come later, as Swift experiments with anonymous and named personae, and as he discovers that he can create concealed versions of the self that will 'show / The name and man, by whom the book was writ' better than can an unmediated authorial self. The critical history of one of Swift's rare signed works, *The Proposal for Correcting . . . the English Tongue,* attests to the validity of Swift's query in the 'Ode to the Athenian Society'; many readers refused and still refuse to take Swift at his word and believe that Swift did not truly advocate a closed authoritarian language system or, if he did in 1707, that he did so in a transient bout of reactionary pique and that the Swift of this *Proposal* is not the 'real' Swift of the anonymous *A Tale of a Tub* or the pseudonymic *Gulliver's Travels.*

Pseudonyms have privileged status among the varieties of nominal disguises because they specifically substitute a new name for an old. Thus, even as they de-authorize or re-authorize texts, they mark a quest for self-authorization. Finding the name entails defining – and knowing – the self. It also permits superscription of a textual family romance upon the preexisting biographical context: author, language, and text replace father, mother, and child. Such a search refashions the Adamic referential theory of language into a hunt for the proper name or, more specifically, a hunt for the specular name.

This idea is based upon Jacques Lacan's theory of the specular image.[7] A mirror shows a unified vision of self, offering a picture of wholeness in contrast to the fragmented body perceivable through unmediated self-scrutiny, imaginable through fears of castration, and translatable into the functional body of language. Recognizing one's specular image marks a child's first awareness of his [*sic*] individuality, but the mutability of the image and its puzzling otherness yet oneness with its beholder make it unstable and vulnerable. Geoffrey Hartman, commenting upon Jacques Derrida's commentary upon the self-baptized Jean Genet, has shifted the Lacanian search for the elusive specular identity into the domain of psycholinguistics. It becomes the search for the specular name – the true, 'found name behind the given name', 'a name much more genuinely one's own than a signature or proper name'. The quest involves 'the effacing or defacing of the proper name' and 'often leads to the adoption of pseudonyms and nicknames, and even to anonymity'.[8] Certainly Swift adopted false names and no-names and divorced himself from his patronym: the questions are whether the new family of names he fathered upon himself are random or carefully bred nominations, how these names refashion the meaning of the name that engendered them, and by what methods they prescribe the play of meanings in the texts attributed to them.

Above all else, Swift's pseudonyms constitute a rather joyous array of task-directing names that affirm the authorial self, and through emanative meaning, the scriptory mission. 'Isaac Bickerstaff', for instance, may be the most apt self-baptism ever devised by a satirist: *Isaac* means 'he who laughs' in Hebrew and alludes to the suspended

sacrificial offering of the father to the Father; *bicker* means to argue,
to move back and forth; *staff* signifies the crook of guidance, the rod
of chastisement, the penis, the pen, the written sign. As a name
specifically designed for a specific task, the exposure and annihilation
of the astrologer Partridge, it announces the program of substitution
that informs the Bickerstaff papers and predicts the desired response
to it. Partridge replaces the victims of his fallacious prophecies,
misread signs become modes of punishment for misreaders, and
death becomes a laughing matter because it is admonitory, not actual.
As a more general specular name, 'Isaac Bickerstaff' brilliantly reflects
the methods and goals and compulsions of Swift as satirist. It is a
name so well-tailored that, once worn, it can be handed down to
others. 'Bickerstaff' is refashioned, however, in a late pseudonym:
Simon Wagstaff, 'author' of Swift's *Polite Conversation*. The secondary
meaning of *bicker* moves to the front in *wag*, which has its own
secondary meaning of *joker*, thereby incorporating the laughing
'Isaac'. 'Simon' (Simon Magus, Simon the Zealot, Simon Peter)
confers the illusionary, fanatic authority suitable to this indefatigable
compiler of banalities. Yet the Hebrew signification, 'that which is
to be heard', accommodates satiric desire as well as Wagstaffian
material.

Swift's attacks on etymologists and mockeries of significant names
in pieces like 'A Discourse to prove the Antiquity of the English
Tongue' evidence great skill in nominal parsing along with great
skepticism of the truth such parsing may reveal. Naming oneself,
however, is a different matter. The skill to invest a name with puns
and multiple meanings can be employed to mirror a present truth,
perhaps to predict a future state, rather than to dig up meanings
hidden in the past. The brace of staffs framing Swift's pseudonymic
career forms a true name – a proper, a self name that assumes and
projects the texts it authorizes and covers the texts in between.
However, the playful differences in these two names, as well as the
series of names that separates them, indicate Swift's desire to protect
onomastic flexibility. The covert task of each specular name is to
orchestrate response not just to a particular text but to the composite
intertext that creates and preserves the meta-authorial 'Swift'.

Swift's reluctance to claim a singular specular name, *vide* the
passing of Isaac Bickerstaff to Sir Richard Steele, may account for the
fate of the name Martinus Scriblerus. This seems to be Swift's name:
Swift (Lord Orrery evidently called Swift 'Dr. Martin', both birds
being members of the swallow family)[9] the Scribbler, the writer. Yet
it becomes a corporate name for Swift, Pope, Arbuthnot, Gay, and
Parnell, and it finally fragments into individual Scriblerian projects
that cast off the Scriblerian name, the name itself lodging in footnotes

or recovered by Fielding years later. For Swift, the name may have been too general, too tautological, too undirectional. Other of Swift's pseudonyms are so specific that their use is restricted. For instance, Swift signed his *Preface to the Bishop of Sarum's Introduction* with the name 'Gregory Misosarum' (the watchman against [the Bishop of] Sarum), a meaning perfectly consonant with the aim of the tract and perfectly useless for any other undertaking. The usefulness of 'Lemuel Gulliver' was limited by the success of *Gulliver's Travels* and the relative fullness of the pseudonymic persona's characterization; Gulliver, identified by the public so closely with his journeys, could not be a credible author for other types of work. The name itself, however, does seem to have been constructed with attention to its shaping resonances. *Gulliver* resembles the word *gullible*, an appropriate description of the voyager's impressionability. *Lemuel*, Hebrew for 'belonging to God', was perhaps selected for its similarity to *Samuel*, the given name of one of the seventeenth century's most illustrious travel writers, Samuel Purchas, or perhaps because the prophecy of King Lemuel, lauding the rarity of a virtuous woman (Prov. 31), was a text Swift enjoyed. Swift also may have enjoyed the specular and spectral sedimented words *lemma* (a textual note, a gloss) and *lemures* (night-wandering spirit). In any event, the name designates a (fictional) person who is not Swift. Lemuel Gulliver is an Other, not a double.

'Isaac Bickerstaff' and 'Simon Wagstaff' are not attached to identities so resolutely separate from Swift's, though, and they can function as specular names for Swift as writer, just as can more obvious self-namings like 'pdfr' and 'Cad[enus]'. These names epitomize Swift's relationships with women. The Latin, the use of title, and perhaps the aural similarity with 'Caduceus', the authoritarian staff, make Cadenus exemplify the hierarchy of Swift's relationship with Esther Vanhomrigh; thus the name brings to the surface hidden dynamics, and Swift finally casts off the name, as we have seen, by treating it as a separate consciousness. In contrast, 'pdfr' is an unpronounceable quartet of consonants drawn from the intimate little language Swift shared with Esther Johnson, a humble and obscure tetragrammaton that answers the question 'Who am I?' with a mumbled acronym for a self-deprecating phrase.

'Who am I?' is answered in a different manner by the pseudonym 'M. B. Drapier'. The proper name transvests itself in generic identification: the Drapier, the purveyor of clothing, of woven fabrics of words that make the self visible, of the texts that make the microcoatic literary world spin from the skill of the tailor-God. It also hides in its initials. The initials may refer to Marcus Brutus,[10] one of the few historical figures whom Swift regards as a hero (see *PW*, 11:

196); certainly the *Verses on the Death* reveal that if Swift saw himself
as heroic at all, his heroism wore the guise of the Drapier. But the
initials also suggest reading this name as Swift's revisionary response
to the Cartesian cogito. 'M. B.' is pronounced as 'am, be'. The
syllables conjugate the existential verb and reveal a first-person
existential declaration: *texo ergo sum*. To think is not enough; to
write is to sew the self into the material, to sow the self in the field
of being. The specular name writes the creations and the creator
through the metaphor of meaning that Swift employs repeatedly
throughout his work. The search for the name, in itself, provides
a corollary affirmation: *nomino ergo sum*.

Thus near the end of his life, when illness curtailed his writing,
Swift's self-definition loses its context; 'I am what I am', Swift
explains, according to Thomas Sheridan's account.[11] Such an assertion
hollowly echoes Yahvist mystery, replacing the fullness of creative
power with tautological emptiness. The texts are gone, the words
contract, and the self disappears: 'I have been many months the
Shadow of the Shadow of the Shadow, of &c&c&c of Dr. Sw——'. So
Swift, with the help of Mrs. Whiteway, wrote to the Earl of Orrery
in February, 1737/38 (*Corr.* 5: 89). Shadows and abbreviations and
dashes no longer signify illusionary losses, as they did in *A Tale of a
Tub*; the losses are real and vital, typographic translations of the pain
of a decomposing body and a discomposed mind, of the dissolution
of the textual self. The '&c of Dr. Sw——' is not 'the very name'
engraved on the collective memory of 'careless . . . Posterity'. It is an
empty name, and the meaningful idea drawn from it is based instead
on inventive and self-definitional fillings and substitutions that Swift
performed throughout his career. It was through his divestitures
that he invested himself in his texts. His texts are mirrors for his
undressings and dressings of the textual self. And they are more
than mirrors, because the inscription of the specular name etches
the specular image permanently into the glass.

Indulging our Reflections

A story exists about Swift, in his declining years, facing a mirror and
muttering, 'poor mad old man'.[12] The vignette is poignant because it
indicates a divided image: the beholder judges the reflection as if it
were an image of a third person. Swift, through age and illness, had
returned to the Lacanian premirror stage, the condition of seeing the
fragmented body as unrelated to the self. Swift's biographers agree
that his last years were marked by extended periods of silence; thus
Swift had lost the tool of language that, according to Lacan, allows

one to glue together the perceived pieces of identity. If it was difficult
for Swift to speak in the 1740s, it was even more difficult for him
to write. His writings had formed a succession of mirrors, not only
for the follies of mankind but also for a series of self-investitures
that revealed and concealed the textual self. By 1743, the ability to
write new names on new mirrors was gone, and the paradoxical,
precariously held identity that grew from the erasures and rewritings
of specular names had stabilized in a permanently broken form. At
the end of his life Swift was powerless to invest the mirror's passive
illusion of truth with alternate meanings, unable to deface the glass
so that reflections would conform to desires. All he could do was
to detach himself from the image, leaving it vacant, divesting it of
personal identity.

The relationship between mirror image and textual self is the
subject of the following specular and spectral riddle poem, first
published in Swift's *Miscellaneous Poems* in 1729. As is common in
rhymed riddles, it flaunts a naked and empty 'I' that seduces the
'you' into providing fulfillment:

By something form'd, I nothing am,
Yett ev'ry Thing that you can name;
In no Place have I ever been,
Yet ev'ry where I may be seen;
In all Things false, yet always true,
I'm still the same – but ever new.
Lifeless, Life's perfect Form I wear,
Can shew a Nose, Eye, Tongue, or Ear,
Yet neither Smell, See, Taste, or Hear.
All Shapes and Features I can boast,
No Flesh, no Bones, no Blood – no Ghost:
All Colours, without Paint, put on,
And change like the *Cameleon*.
Swiftly I come, and enter there,
Where not a Chink let's in the Air;
Like Thought I'm in a Moment gone,
Nor can I ever be alone;
All Things on Earth I imitate,
Faster than Nature can create;
Sometimes imperial Robes I wear,
Anon in Beggar's Rags appear;
A Giant now, and strait an Elf,
I'm ev'ry one, but ne'er my self;
Ne'er sad I mourn, ne'er glad rejoice,
I move my Lips, but want a Voice;

I ne'er was born, nor e'er can die,
Then prythee tell me what am I.
                    (as in *Swift Poetical Works*, ed. Kathleen Williams
                    (Oxford, 1967), pp. 634–5)

The answer, 'reflections in a mirror', is both fulfillment and
nonfulfillment. The identity of the signified is just as multiform
and potential as the uninhabited 'I'; the riddle is a tautological
indeterminancy, since mirror reflections can be 'ev'ry Thing that
you can name'. One suspects another of Swift's familiar traps to
undermine a reader's interpretational certainty. The assignment
of significance becomes problematic because the text continues
to challenge the investiture of meaning it has itself invited.

Through the dialectic of soliciting meaning and denying its
adequacy, Swift superimposes another solution upon his riddle: the
'I' is the textual word, the mysterious and tempting replacement
for the human voice that, in the eighteenth century, was inalterably
bound to the presence of a living human body. More precisely, the 'I'
is verbal meaning, the significatory potential of the written sign. The
riddle conveys Swift's authorial fear of textual instability through its
succession of easy but mutually destructive paradoxes. Its images of
hollow investiture show that the body of originating significance has
decomposed underneath the textual clothes. In a sense, a published
text is dead, as it cannot be changed. It is still (up to whatever time
it is read) still (motionless), and its vitality depends upon how it is
filled with meaning: 'I'm still the same – but ever new'. Therefore,
the line 'Nor can I ever be alone' refers to readers not as unwanted
company but as postrequisites for textual existence. The text, like a
mirror, is absolutely dependent upon a separate exterior presence for
emancipation from the state of being an inert material object. Unlike
a mirror, however, a book is not a blank space of infinite imaging
capability. It is instead a glass made dark with ink, prescriptions
of meaning that may or may not hold their integrity against the
onslaughts of interpretation.

Looking in a mirror or another reflecting surface is an obvious
trope for the quest for self-knowledge, as clear in the myth of
Narcissus as in the theories of Lacan. Likewise, the mirror is an
ancient metaphor for the mimetic properties of art.[13] In Plato's
Republic, Socrates disparages artistic imitation by analogizing its
facile derivativeness to 'turning a mirror round and round – you
would soon enough make the sun and the heavens, and the earth
and yourself, and other animals and plants, as in a mirror'.[14] Swift's
riddle could be read as a gloss on Socrates' simile, but the riddle's
personal tone emphasizes Swift's essentially humanist concern with

the capabilities of textual mirrors to reflect their makers as well as the outer world. This issue is tucked away in the middle of Socrates' comments, but by the time the trope had passed through the pens of the late medieval moralists who wrote mirrors for humankind to George Puttenham or John Dryden's reading of an author's personality in his style,[15] it had moved to the forefront. Swift frequently refers to this inherited metaphor, and he integrates its emphasis on self-revelation with his own emphasis on man's ability to delude himself. For example, he writes that *'Satyr is a sort of* Glass, *wherein Beholders do generally discover every body's Face but their Own; which is the chief Reason . . . that so very few are offended with it'* ('A Preface of the Author', *Battel of the Books, PW,* 1: 140). Since the specular text must alternate revelatory clarity with covering darkness, it can tell us what we want to know but it does not always reflect the truth. When readers can hide behind prescriptions, the text loses its mirror functions. When readers erase prescriptions, the text becomes pure mirror, tautologically irrelevant, as Swift maintains when he disproves the maxim that critics' *'Writings are the Mirrors of Learning'* (*PW,* 1: 63) by literalizing it.

Ignoring textual prescriptions can be shatteringly unbearable, as Gulliver's glimpses of his reflection in Houyhnhnmland pools and streams prove to be. Gulliver's vision of himself has no context. The meaning he assigns to his image is arbitrary; since no pre-scribed Yahoo images float on the water, he writes his own fears into his blank reflection. Swift describes this process in 'Thoughts on Various Subjects':

> Imaginary Evils soon become real ones, by indulging our Reflections on them; as he who, in a melancholy Fancy, seeth something like a Face on the Wall or the Wainscot, can, by two or three touches with a leaden Pencil, make it look visible and agreeing with what he fancied.
>
> (*PW,* 4: 251)

Gulliver is victimized by his own reflections because his imagination escapes the constraints of reality. The textual reality he inhabits, however, does give the prescriptions against the blank despair of unmediated imagination; men may look and behave more like Yahoos than like Houyhnhnms, but they do not look identical to, or behave exactly the same as Yahoos. The Yahoos present a possibility, a potential terminus of human corruption.[16] Their fictional being is a prescription – waiting to be filled, or unfilled, or misfilled – against their actual becoming. A similar misinterpretation of a mirror image occurs when Gulliver stares at the double reflection of himself and the Brobdingnagian queen. He feels silly, diminished, inconsequential: '[T]here could nothing be more ridiculous than the Comparison: So that I really began to imagine my self dwindled many Degrees below my usual Size' (*PW*, 11: 107). Gulliver's retrospective choice of the word *imagine*, though, indicates that he has not isolated this particular reflection from its contexts, the reversed context of Lilliput and the framing contexts of England, where all humans are of similar size. The prescriptions of the specular text, then, are necessary mediations for self-discovery.

Gulliver's ability to contextualize his image in the Brobdingnagian mirror by recognizing the dangers of decontextualized imagination indicates a concept of personal identity based on placement within a social network, an epistemology Swift shared with both Locke and Hobbes.[17] As alien traditions and institutions repeatedly confront Gulliver, they decompose him. The *Travels* record his attempts to recompose himself according to new cultural imperatives. In one sense, Gulliver's abhorrence of his self-styled Yahoo reflection negatively ratifies the social context theory of personal identity, yet in another sense it challenges it. The episode emblematizes the face-to-face encounter of self with self.[18] Its unmediated nakedness is powerful and frightening, as if Swift feared that the self stripped of social definitions would be loathsomely demonic.

The episode also emblematizes the search for the specular name, the unifying concept of self that heals fragmentation. Throughout *Gulliver's Travels*, Gulliver never refers to himself by his proper name; instead, he dons a succession of names given by the people he encounters. *Quinbus Flestrin* (Great Man Mountain), *Grildrig* (mannikin), and *naiah Yahoo* (gentle Yahoo) serve as proper names although they are actually generic descriptions, whereas *Nardac* (honored courtier), *Splacknuk* (weasel-like animal), and *Relplum Scalcath* (freak of nature) classify Gulliver within a set of cultural norms.[19] The only self-naming occurs in book 3 when Gulliver calls himself a Hollander, even making up names for fictitious Dutch parents (which, however, he does not reveal to the reader), in order to facilitate his travels in Asian waters. Such politically expedient nomination clearly equates name with disguise; it also reflects one of the motivations for Swift's use of pseudonyms and anonymous authorships. Gulliver is identified as Captain Lemuel Gulliver only on the title page and in the letters prefatory to his *Travels*, a ploy necessary to Swift's idea of travel-book verisimilitude and to Swift's own need for nominal disguise. The prefacing proper name also acts as a prescriptive authorization against which Gulliver's textual search for his specular name can be measured, and against which his final acceptance of the specular name *Yahoo* can be judged an act of folly.

Gulliver has confused metonymy with metaphor; he has mistaken physical proximity for conceptual similarity. By clinging to a specular name at best only somewhat applicable in the limited context of Houyhnhnmland even when he changes venue to the contexts of the Portuguese ship or Redriff, he absconds with the signifier and replaces the original signified with a belated and essentially bogus one – himself. In this way, he binds himself into a single, partial, and arbitrary fiction, a textual imprisonment that Swift's succession of authorial specular names avoids. Furthermore, Gulliver's errors are sins of interpretation. He reads his own text as a Laputan would: one eye on abstract metaphor, one eye on himself.

Although Swift allows Gulliver to be lost in his own interpretive blind spots, Swift does act as a flapper for the extratextual reader. Repeated emphasis on Gulliver's clothes, cleanliness, cooperation, and communicative ability reminds us of the profound differences between man and Yahoo. We are tempted to overlook these differences on metonymic grounds; since it is a fictional human, Gulliver, rather than a fictional animal, like an intelligent baboon or orangutan, that is set down in Houyhnhnmland, we conclude that Yahoos are metaphors of degenerate humanity.[20] When we follow Gulliver further, hardening the metaphor from resemblance to identity, we are captured by our own interpretation. Thus readers who label men as Yahoos do not prove that men are really like Yahoos but that they are like Gulliver. Swift's satire is of course designed to make us ask, 'Is this my reflection in the text?' However, it is not designed to give a straightforward answer. Instead, it exposes how our self-centered delusions operate, how they lead us into misreading or erasing the multiple contexts that give meaning to our existence.

Yet in the last chapter of the book, when Gulliver makes his concluding vows 'to behold my Figure often in a Glass, and thus if possible habituate my self by Time to tolerate the Sight of a human Creature' (*PW*, 11: 295), it seems that his search for the lost name may continue, that he may try to rewrite his humanity over the fearful Yahoo image that his indulgent fancy has inscribed upon his own reflection. Perhaps his final answer to the question of 'Who am I' is not final at all, and Swift has designed Gulliver's search for the specular name that will unify his identity as a guide to interpretation. Gulliver's stubborn habitation of a stolen signifier shows the consequences of self-authorized textual trespass. The hint that he may ultimately abandon it is a reminder that metonymy is not necessarily metaphor, even though the pressures of the text tend to squeeze one figure into another, and that metaphor is but a partial and potential reflection of truth.

Notes

1. The social backgrounds of authorial disavowal are discussed in 'A Social History of Fact and Fiction: Authorial Disavowal in the Early English Novel', in *Literature and Society: Selected Papers from the English Institute, 1978*, ed. EDWARD W. SAID (Baltimore, MD, 1980), pp. 120–48.

2. As quoted in *A Tale of a Tub*, ed. A. C. GUTHKELCH and D. NICHOL SMITH, 2nd edn (Oxford, 1958), p. 349. Hereafter, noted in the text as *Tale*.

3. See JOHN MIDDLETON MURRY, *Jonathan Swift: A Critical Biography* (London, 1954), p. 449.

4. And the traps continue to snap. Two recent articles conclude that *A Panegyric* was written not by Swift but by James Arbuckle (AUBREY L. WILLIAMS, '"A Vile Encomium": That "Panegyric on the Reverend D – n S – t"', in *Contemporary Studies of Swift's Poetry*, ed. JOHN I. FISCHER and DONALD C. MELL, JR. (Newark, DE, 1980), pp. 178–90; JAMES WOOLLEY, 'Arbuckle's "Panegyric" and Swift's Scrub Libel: The Documentary Evidence', in FISCHER and MELL, pp. 191–209. If so, Swift, as well as subsequent readers, was caught by his own devices. The intricate mechanisms and surprising results of Swiftian anonymity are demonstrated just as well by Swift not having written the poem as by Swift having been the true author.

5. The seminal study is by WILLIAM B. EWALD, *The Masks of Jonathan Swift* (Cambridge, MA, 1954).

6. See ÉMILE BENVENISTE, *Problems in General Linguistics*, trans. MARY E. MEEK (Miami Linguistic Series, no. 8) (Coral Gables, FL, 1971), p. 226.

7. JACQUES LACAN, *Ecrits: A Selection*, trans. ALAN SHERIDAN (New York, 1971), pp. 1–7.

8. GEOFFREY HARTMAN, *Saving the Text: Literature, Derrida, Philosophy* (Baltimore, MD, 1981), pp. 101, 125. Hartman extends his theory to include primal 'scenes of nomination', personal annunciations that generate literature in a way similar to but more personal than Saussure's concept of the controlling name hidden in Latin poetry.

9. See notes on p. 87 of John Arbuthnot, Alexander Pope, Jonathan Swift, John Gay, Thomas Parnell, and Robert Harley, *Memoirs of the Extraordinary Life, Works, and Discoveries of Martinus Scriblerus*, ed. CHARLES KERBY-MILLER (New Haven, CT, 1950).

10. This is a reading first suggested by JACK GILBERT, 'The Drapier's Initials', *Notes and Queries*, 208 (June, 1963), 217–18. See also IRVIN EHRENPREIS, *Swift: The Man, His Works, and the Age*, 3 vols (Cambridge, MA, 1962–83), 3: 208.

11. See THOMAS SHERIDAN, *The Life of the Reverend Dr. Jonathan Swift, Dean of St. Patrick's, Dublin* (London, 1787), p. 472.

12. See MARIO ROSSI and JOSEPH HONE, *Swift, or the Egoist* (London, 1934), p. 311.

13. An excellent overview of this topos can be found in M. H. ABRAMS, *The Mirror and the Lamp: Romantic Theory and the Critical Tradition* (Oxford, 1953), pp. 8–14, 30–5. RICHARD RORTY subjects the mirror analogy to extended questioning in his *Philosophy and the Mirror of Nature* (Oxford, 1980); he asserts that Western philosophy is grounded on mistaken or at least misleading sublimation of the swerve of epistemology into metaphor.

14. PLATO, *The Republic* (Chicago, 1952), 10.596.

15. GEORGE PUTTENHAM, *The Arte of English Poesie* [1589]. in *Elizabethan Critical Essays*, 2 vols., ed. G. GREGORY SMITH (Oxford, 1904), 2: 153–4; JOHN DRYDEN, *Essays of John Dryden*, ed. W. P. KER, 2 vols (New York, 1961), 2: 251–3. See also LOCKE's view of the mind of man as mirror in *An Essay concerning Human Understanding* (Chicago, 1952), 2.1.25. Milton's depiction of Eve's awakening into self-recognition by looking in a mirroring pond and learning that the reflection *indicates* selfhood but *is* neither self nor other accurately forecasts Lacan's analysis (*Paradise Lost*, ed. SCOTT ELLEDGE (New York, 1975), 4.449–71).

16. In various private letters, Swift did refer to men as animals and, specifically, as Yahoos. But these comments are always qualified in some way, often by raillery or self-satire. The famous letter to Pope in which Swift asserts that he 'hate[s] and detest[s] that animal called man' is softened not only by the possibility of loving individuals but by the satiric close that tries to bully and bribe Pope into immediate acceptance of misanthropy (29 Sept. 1725; *Corr.* 3: 103). The letter calling Stella and Bolingbroke's wife Yahoos is a railing reproach to Ford for having injudiciously talked about Swift's work-in-progress (19 Jan. 1723/24; *Corr.* 3: 4). Swift's advice to Sheridan, 'expect no more from man than such an animal is capable of, and you will every day find my description of Yahoos more resembling' (11 Sept. 1725; *Corr.* 3: 94) comes from a letter consoling Sheridan for the loss of preferment and reminding him of the need for caution when dealing with men like the despised Sir Richard Tighe. Even in this letter, Swift emphasizes resemblance, not identity.

17. See LEO BRAUDY, 'Penetration and Impenetrability in *Clarissa*', in *New Approaches to Eighteenth-Century Literature: Selected Papers from the English Institute*, ed. PHILIP HARTH (New York, 1974), p. 181; FREDERIK M. KEENER, *The Chain of Becoming/the Philosophical Tale, the Novel, and a Neglected Realism of the Enlightenment: Swift, Montesquieu, Voltaire, Johnson, and Austen* (New York, 1983), pp. 89–126.

18. In this sense, it participates in the satirist-satirized topos; see, for example, ROBERT C. ELLIOTT, *The Power of Satire: Magic, Ritual, Art* (Princeton, NJ, 1960), pp. 188–9.

19. Swift evidently performed similar categorical namings in real life. He bestowed mock-pastoral names upon female beggars in Dublin; the epithets were determined by their diseases and deformities (e.g., 'Cancerina' and 'Stumpa-Nympha'). See EHRENPREIS, *Swift*, 3: 812–13.

20. For the possible influence of travelers' accounts about great apes and primitive men, see R. W. FRANTZ, 'Swift's Yahoos and the Voyagers', *Modern Philology*, 29 (1931), 49–57; M. F. ASHLEY MONTAGU, 'Tyson's *Orang-Outang, Sive Homo Sylvestris*, and Swift's *Gulliver's Travels*', *PMLA*, 59 (1944), 84–9; and the travel-books owned by Swift as listed in HAROLD WILLIAMS, *Dean Swift's Library* (Cambridge, 1932).

Part Two

Text and Context

I have tried to assemble in this section a variety of criticism and literary history that concentrates our attention on how we might place Swift in his immediate literary and cultural context. This is not simply a matter of identifying his politics or how he had his writing disseminated, but also an examination of the ways his texts, both material books and more abstract conceptual propositions, mirror contemporary history and culture. A link with the previous section is provided by Brean S. Hammond whose contribution examines the way that not only Swift but also his fellow-members of the Scriblerus Club, Alexander Pope and John Gay, tried to combat both the reductive effects of committing thoughts to paper – and paper that was increasingly a contribution to a market economy – and also the deleterious scientistic thinking power-less to withstand the steady creep of Dulness Pope illustrates in his *Dunciad* (1728; 1742–44), and Swift enacts whenever Gulliver sinks into the redundant details of empirical cataloguing or the Teller of *The Tale of a Tub* loses his thread – presuming that 'he' had one in the first place. For a fuller account of Hammond's thesis, see his *Professional Imaginative Writing in England, 1670–1740: 'Hackney for Bread'* (Oxford, 1997).

Marcus Walsh observes a crucial distinction between two current meanings for 'text' in current critical writing: the first needs no scare-quotes and indicates the material book that is the direct result of a writer's labour and conscious intention, whereas the second can be found in Roland Barthes's famous critical essay, 'From Work to Text' (in his *Image–Music–Text*, trans. and ed. STEPHEN HEATH [London, 1977], pp. 155–64), where he indicates it only as an object of interpretation, '*experienced only in an activity of production*' (p. 158, original emphasis). This deconstruction of the authority of the original moment of intention and thus of an original context Walsh withstands by placing modern debates within a frame that Swift would have found far more accessible and amenable. For the Anglican commentators quoted here, the written word is not inferior to the spoken, but is rather an adequate substitute for it, 'neither an accident nor a substitute, but original, apostolic, fully equal to speech' (p. 113), whereas oral tradition outranks the written for Roman apologists who grant the power of performance and thus of supplementary witness in the constitution of meaning. Hence it is that Swift, always a son of the Church of Ireland, steadfastly distrusts the labours of critics and commentators, and also graphically portrays the entropy of sense in *The Tale of a Tub* whenever the Teller becomes acutely aware of the printed destination of his thoughts. Walsh argues against a common recent tendency to regard *all* texts as an erosion of stable and ascertainable meaning. Corrupt texts are corrupt, but it is not inevitable that all printed matter is mistransmitted.

Everett Zimmerman treads similar ground in the first chapter of his *Swift's Narrative Satires: Author and Authority* (Ithaca, NY, 1983), where he analyses some of the tropes of the satiric mode, especially in relation to allegory. If allegory constantly relates all its narrative twists and turns to some unchanging, prior *schema*, then it is pervasively suggesting that the physical may always be shot through with the metaphysical. Satire can, on the other hand, use allegory to drive a wedge between the 'earthly process' and the 'moral imperative' that *should* underpin it, but rarely does. The Teller's failure at allegory implies that his insistent attempt to supply some significance to his Tale is not only a sign of the bad writer, but also of a wider malaise involving a breakdown of resemblance, between the microcosm and macrocosm and between the human and the divine. Gulliver's reportage, the keynote predominantly (though not exclusively) in the first three voyages, is representative of a certain literal ignorance, a materialistic vision that seems to suggest a failure to find significance in the travels. As does Walsh, Zimmerman is acutely aware of debates about the apparent fixity of scriptural truths. In invoking the ghost of Thomas Hobbes and his distrust of the abstract, Zimmerman uncovers certain departures in Swift's case from Hooker's more moderate sense of a mediating sense of nature. In his realism, even an occasional materialism, Swift actually proves that opposites can meet in his kinship to Hobbes.

For Carole Fabricant, Swift's landscape has both figural and topographical contours, an 'all-encompassing ideological landscape, a country for the mind as well as a concrete habitation for the body' (*Swift's Landscape*, p. 1). Fabricant perceptively isolates the many occasions when Swift associates this angle and condition with specifically political premisses. Chapters on his antipastoral gestures, his subversion of the Country House ideal and the Irish context surround a section on 'The Spectator in the Landscape' from which this extract is taken. What emerges is a two-way reflection: there is empathy both with the object of perception as well as the disinterested spectator. In his poetry and prominently in *Gulliver's Travels*, Swift feels as well as depicts the first-person voice as *within* a landscape. This has a disorientating effect, as the clear lines of perspective we might expect tend to dissolve, and often there develops an uncomfortable sense, shared with the reader, of constant inspection. Immediately following a section where Fabricant investigates the figural possibilities of a 'long view' of landscape, this section portrays those less comfortable passages where the perceiving eye ('I') is brought up oppressively against obdurate realities, most commonly Irish conditions. Compared to the 'philosophical spectacles' of his friend in exile (from 1714 on), Henry St John, first Viscount Bolingbroke, Swift's relentless physicality of seeing appears to be a refusal to synthesize into abstract thought anything actually experienced at first hand.

In its most extreme manifestations – the grotesque or scatological, for example – this reflex can be transgressive and radical. In Peter Stallybrass and Allon White's examination of the carnivalesque in the literature of the Renaissance to the early twentieth century, *The Politics and Poetics of Transgression* (London, 1986), the cultural and sociological divide between high and low and between thought and the body is regarded as a tenuous demarcation. Here, in an extract from the chapter on 'Authorship in the Eighteenth Century', they trace the attempts made within bourgeois ideologies (as represented within such ideals) to re-draw the lines that cordon off the hybrids and miscegenation they found in the fairs or popular festivals from courtly decorum. Unexpectedly, though, in the hands of satirists such as Pope and Swift, such a neat world tended to get turned upside down. An absence of cultural leader-ship at court (they forgot about Handel, though their fellow Scriblerian, John Gay never did) provoked in works such as *The Dunciad* and espe-cially Swift's later poetry a graphic displacement of anxieties about the dissolution of older certainties on to grotesque depictions of the fair and the body that actually tapped into (and perversely celebrated) that same unofficial energy they elsewhere denounced. A fuller account of this folkloric underworld can be found in E. P. Thompson's *Customs in Common* (London, 1991), where an apparently disorderly array of rituals has its own rationale. Here, the sense of transgression issues less from the visceral details themselves than the renewed vigilance to avoid the body and so the need to deem such details prohibited material. (See also Dennis Todd's 'The Hairy Maid at the Harpsichord: Some Specu-lations on the Meaning of *Gulliver's Travels*' (*Texas Studies in Literature and Language*, 34 [1992], 239–83) for more relevant research into Swift's knowledge of fairground culture.) Stallybrass and White's use of the term 'carnival' is in direct reference to its use by Mikhail Bakhtin in his study of *Rabelais and His World* (trans. Helen Iswolsky, Cambridge, MA, 1968), where it appears as a transgressive realm, full of images that are 'opposed to all that is finished and polished, to all pomposity, to every ready-made solution in the sphere of thought and world out-look' (p. 3). This mercurial quality gains its energy from its knowing departures from official good form, marking the 'suspension of all hierarchical rank, privileges, norms and prohibitions', and therefore 'hostile to all that was immortalized and complete' (p. 109). This radical element is one that the Augustan satirists are proverbially taken to have just simply either excoriated or ignored; Stallybrass and White, however, emphasize how much of their satire needed carnival and its vital challenge to empty regulations.

4 Scriblerian Self-Fashioning*

BREAN S. HAMMOND

Will any Man say that if the words *Whoring, Drinking, Cheating, Lying, Stealing,* were by act of parliament ejected out of the *English* Tongue and Dictionaries; we should all awake next Morning chaste and temperate, honest and just, and Lovers of Truth?

(*PW*, 2: 32)

I

An enduring preoccupation of Jonathan Swift's writing is the attempt to find an acceptable relationship between words and their objects. Throughout his life Swift was tormented by the dangerous plasticity of language. Its bewildering evolutions were capable of reducing language to a set of arbitrary signifiers that severed the connexion between utterance and meaning. It was not that he shared the age's aspiration towards a linguistic purity that would ensure the complete transparency of language: as Thomas Sprat, the historian of the Royal Society, expressed it so memorably, a desire to 'return back to primitive purity, and shortness, when men deliver'd so many *things*, almost in an equal number of *words*'.[1] Swift was contemptuous of the various attempts to re-create a lost linguistic Eden where words were identical with the realities they signified, free of the inevitable distortion that occurs when, as Locke argued, they become concepts in the human mind. In *Gulliver's Travels* the proposal for abolishing words and replacing them by things is a *reductio* of such schemes as that of Bishop Wilkins to introduce a philosophical language. When Denis Donoghue says that 'Swift was uneasy with anything that did not occupy space; so he treated words as if they were things' he emphasizes only one side of the equation.[2] It is truer to say that Swift struggled to find a language that was truly human, a language in which the words that we produce are meaningful sounds that secure

---

* Reprinted from *Yearbook of English Studies*, 18 (1988), 108–22.

the relationship between the material world and the spiritual being of man. Any kind of systematic thought, including any product of artificial intelligence such as a systematic language, is associated in Swift's work with belligerence and intimidation.[3]

Allegory is the battlefield on which the struggle between *res* and *verba* is most bloodily contested in Swift's prose. In allegory words say less than they mean and they communicate ambiguously, referring to one set of 'things' but cryptically encoding a further set of 'things' to be understood by initiates and deciphered by jacks in office. In an important study of allegory Maureen Quilligan has argued that allegory proper is characterized by a kind of word-magic that turns words into concrete entities through the structural use of the pun.[4] But Swift lived at the fag-end of this essentially Catholic form of sacramentalism, and he lost no opportunity of ridiculing it. In *A Tale of a Tub*, that most sacred of all allegories, the Catholic doctrine of transubstantiation is exposed as a mere case of 'saying the thing that is not' when Lord Peter obsessively insists that what is manifestly a 'Slice from a Twelve-peny Loaf' is a shoulder of mutton. In secular contexts, too, Swift employs allegory in a way that destroys its own mode of functioning. It has been established that the Tribnia passage in *Gulliver's Travels* (III. 6) refers to the Atterbury trial and the ludicrous decoding of allegorical letters that led to his prosecution.[5] The passage is a satire on allegorical reading, but in order to know this the reader has to read allegorically. Punishing the unsavoury desire to 'apply', this passage also indulges that desire to the full. Allegory becomes yet another Swiftian technique of reader 'entrapment'. David Nokes has written well on the characteristic strain of Swiftian irony that works by materializing the abstract or by literalizing the figurative, and in particular on the part played by pun in the process:

> Swift was a lifelong punster, a man whose love of riddles, verbal games, 'pun-ic wars', crambo, and Anglo-Latin doggerel demonstrated his adherence to the motto *'vive la bagatelle'*. Yet he shared with his fellow Dubliner Joyce an interest in pun at a deeper level, as a form of ironic revelation. Epiphanies, Joyce called them; acts of verbal magic that could transform old words into new ideas. Swift's puns are not so much epiphanies as incarnations, a constant process of words becoming flesh and spirit becoming substance.[6]

This perhaps underestimates the extent of Scriblerian equivocation over allegory and pun. Although in *God's Revenge against Punning* (1716) Pope could mock the enthusiasm of those who regard punning

as the end of civilization as we know it ('the woful Practice of
PUNNING . . . does occasion the Corruption of our Language, and
therein of the Word of God translated into our Language; which
certainly every sober Christian must Tremble at') the puns devised
by Swift's friend Thomas Sheridan to illustrate his *The Art of Punning;
or, the Flower of Languages* (1719) do not suggest that great claims can
be made for it:

Q. Where did the first Hermaphrodites come from?
A. Middlesex.
Q. What part of England has the most Dogs?
A. Barkshire.

Puns are allegories in little, and allegories themselves involve a
kind of linguistic materialism that Swift and his fellow Scriblerians
took to be a defining characteristic of modern intellectual life.
Transubstantiation of words into objects is typical of such sects as the
Aeolists, who 'maintain the Original Cause of all things to be *Wind*',
and of those who 'held the Universe to be a large *Suit of cloaths*'.
Separation of subject and object, and hence of word and referent, was
one consequence of the Cartesian dualism. R. S. Westfall, biographer
of Newton, introduces the world that the great scientist inherited as
one divided from itself by Cartesian philosophy:

The Cartesian dualism . . . attempted rigorously to separate mind
or spirit from the operations of physical nature . . . most of the
functions of the human body, from digestion and growth on the
one hand to reflex actions on the other, proceed independently
of the human will. And the overwhelming majority of nature's
phenomena, from the panorama of the heavenly vortices above
us, through the realm of animal and vegetable life about us, to
the motions of the particles of bodies below the threshold of
perception, are never affected by an act of a human will.[7]

It was also the world the Scriblerians inherited, and they never felt
at home in it. From the outset the Scriblerus project was aimed at
arresting the development of natural science and philosophy by
satirizing its more extravagant absurdities. To Gay, writing in 1711,
Steele's *Tatler* had broken important ground in educating public
sensibilities:

'Tis incredible to conceive the effect his Writings have had on the
Town; How many Thousand follies they have either quite banish'd,
or given a very great check to; how much Countenance they have

added to Vertue and Religion . . . how intirely they have convinc'd
our Fops, and Young Fellows, of the value and advantages of
Learning. He has indeed rescued it out of the hands of Pedants
and Fools, and discover'd the true method of making it amiable
and lovely to all mankind.[8]

Scriblerian satire was a harder-hitting and more muscular attempt
to distinguish the chaff from the bran of contemporary learning.
It was aimed at the new scientific methodology that was being
injudiciously applied (as the Scriblerians thought) to the entire world
of learning; at the new 'professional' scholars and scientists who were
engaged in this falsely rigorous research; and at the debasement
and prostitution of literary standards that the expression of their
conclusions seemed to entail. The rising tide of materialism could
be stemmed only by renewing a commitment to polite writing as the
expression of humane values. 'Great writers' were the apparatus that
could alone stave off disaster.

But what, in the early eighteenth century, was the writer? In this
period the professional identity of the author was in a transitional
phase. Authors marketing their talents for a public readership were a
late seventeenth-century development, but it took some considerable
time to replace patronage as the dominant means of literary
production. Respectability for writing as a means of earning a living
was hard won. Although opportunities for making a living by the
pen increased as the century progressed, lump-sum payments to
authors meant that only by writing a great deal could one hope to
prosper. Before the establishment of limited copyright and royalty
payment writers existed in a limbo somewhere between marketing
their labour and being sponsored by patrons. For the Scriblerians,
however, purely professional writing could not produce great
literature, which had to be the result of independent endeavour,
born after a long gestation-period of leisured study. If the writer, as
custodian of the verbal culture, was to be entrusted with the task of
restoring an organic harmony between body and soul, the material
and the immaterial, he had to be worthy of it. Few writers were,
as far as the Scriblerians could see, because, for most, writing was
simply another way of making a living, just another way of keeping
body and soul together any old how. Scriblerian satire foregrounds
instances of writing where sub-literary effusions are directly
exchanged for bread. Such writings call attention to their own
materiality because they can be reduced, without residue, to the
paper they are printed on. In Swift's 'On Poetry: A Rapsody', for
example, hack poetry is presented as a set of brittle physiological
and typographical tricks:

The muse invoked, sit down to write;
Blot out, correct, insert, refine,
Enlarge, diminish, interline.
Be mindful, when invention fails,
To scratch your head, and bite your nails.

Your poem finished, next your care
Is needful, to transcribe it fair.
In modern wit all printed trash, is
Set off with numerous breaks — and dashes —

To statesmen would you give a wipe,
You print it in *italic type*.
When letters are in vulgar shapes,
'Tis ten to one the wit escapes;
But when in CAPITALS expressed,
The dullest reader smokes a jest

(ll. 86–100)

Later, again harping on the mechanical performance that bad poetry becomes, the kind of figurative padding with which the hack poet stuffs his work is likened to various other material compensations for deficiency:

Or oft when epithets you link,
In gaping lines to fill a chink;
Like stepping stones to save a stride,
In streets where kennels are too wide:
Or like a heel-piece to support
A cripple with one foot too short:
Or like a bridge that joins a marish
To moorlands of a different parish.

(ll. 169–76)

Swift's early prose repeatedly features writing that short-circuits its own inspiration, becoming a mechanical set of operations that makes the pen a conduit for bodily nourishment. From the outset the teller of *A Tale of a Tub* situates himself with respect to that pervasive eighteenth-century icon, the hack in his garret:

The shrewdest Pieces of this Treatise, were conceived in Bed, in a Garret: At other times (for a Reason best known to my self) I thought fit to sharpen my Invention with Hunger; and in general, the whole Work was begun, continued, and ended, under a long

Course of Physick, and a great want of Money. . . . And this I lay down as my principal *Postulatum*.

(*PW*, 1: 27)

Thereafter the narrator adopts this postulatum at will, writing at varying degrees of distance from the 'Grub Street brotherhood'. Throughout the text he sustains an attack on ephemeral and on professional writing, singling out for special attention such authors as Dryden and L'Estrange, whose careerist complaints are parodied; speaking of Dryden's use of panegyrical prefaces aimed at boosting sales, he comments: 'Our Great *Dryden* . . . has often said to me in Confidence, the World would never have suspected him to be so great a Poet, if he had not assured them so frequently in his Prefaces, that it was impossible they could either doubt or forget it' (*PW*, 1: 81–82). In 'On Poetry: A Rapsody', he revisits Dryden with another sideswipe at that author's money-making tactics:

Read all the prefaces of Dryden,
For these our critics much confide in,
(Though merely writ at first for filling
To raise the volume's price, a shilling.)

(ll. 267–70)

Swift's later quarrel with the almanac-maker Partridge, hilariously documented in *The Bickerstaff Papers*, gains its edge, as David Woolley points out, from the tremendous value of almanacs as literary products: 'These publications were the most valuable literary properties of the day; monopoly in the several titles of the half a million or so almanacs printed each autumn was held, under royal charter, by members of the Stationers' Company . . . [Partridge's] was the leading almanac title, *Merlinus Liberatus*, with an annual circulation of over 20,000 copies.'[9] Almanacs were precisely the kind of profit-making sub-literary product that the Scriblerians felt were most damaging to the interests of polite letters. Bickerstaff's persona is that of the serious practitioner of the astrological art, to be distinguished from 'a few mean illiterate Traders between us and the Stars': 'My Fortune hath placed me above the little Regard of writing for a few Pence, which I neither value nor want: Therefore, let not wise Men too hastily condemn this Essay, intended for a good Design, to cultivate and improve an antient Art, long in Disgrace by having fallen into mean unskilful Hands' (*PW*, 2: 149). When Bickerstaff announces Partridge's 'death' in a later paper, he produces a magnificent 'dying hack' genre-piece, in which the penitent astrologer, terrified at the judgement to come, confesses all

95

his petty frauds and their mercenary motivation: 'The rest was my own Invention to make my Almanack sell; having a Wife to maintain, and no other Way to get my Bread; for mending old Shoes is a poor Livelihood' (*PW*, 2: 155). Later, in a *Tatler* essay, Swift expressed anxiety about the proliferation of Grub Street lucubrations, relating linguistic corruption directly to the spread of popular prints:

> I cannot but observe to you, that until of late Years, a *Grub-street* Book was always bound in Sheep-skin, with suitable Print and Paper; the Price never above a Shilling; and taken off wholly by common Tradesmen, or Country Pedlars. But now they appear in all Sizes and Shapes, and in all Places: They are handed about from Lapfulls in every Coffee-house to Persons of Quality; are shewn in *Westminster-Hall*, and the Court of Requests. You may see them gilt, and in Royal Paper of five or six Hundred Pages, and rated accordingly. I would engage to furnish you with a Catalogue of *English* Books published within the Compass of seven Years past, which at the first Hand would cost you an Hundred Pounds; wherein you shall not be able to find ten Lines together of common Grammar, or common Sense.
>
> (*PW*, 2: 174)

These early writings survey the ground for the distinction between 'classic' and 'popular' literature that the later poems of Swift and Pope did so much to establish. According to the Scriblerians, 'classic' literature has 'value' in the moral or spiritual sense, whereas 'popular' literature only has, and is intended by its worthless authors only to have, value in the sense of material exchange. Scriblerian writing reinscribes the Cartesian dualism by giving to some writers a monopoly over spirituality, taste, moral worth, politeness, and refinement, whereas the productions of others are condemned to the realm of the material. The serious side of the Scriblerian project was to replace in the world the spirituality that mechanistic natural philosophy and the professionalization of writing had taken away.

Forming the link here is the world of 'professional learning' that, pre-eminently, is the Scriblerian target. Elsewhere I have commented on the gradually emerging split between gentleman-amateurs and methodical scholars in this period, to which the Ancients/Moderns quarrel imparted militancy.[10] Penelope Wilson's thorough study of this process as manifested in classical scholarship and translation deserves quotation:

> To a humanist like Pope, the kind of scholarship represented by Bentley and his Dutch colleagues . . . involved not just a petty

obsession with the incidental details of classical literature but also an abandonment of responsibility for the upholding of established literary standards. . . . A strong moral resistance to the autonomy of words in isolation from 'things' permeates every level of eighteenth-century thinking about the study of the classics.[11]

The result of a rigorous scientific method as applied to the humanities, to history, and to archaeology was the appearance of a critical tribe who, in Pope's view, confined their 'whole debate' to mere words, mere verbiage, words as the empty husks of departed meanings. Behind the attack on recent trends in education in *Dunciad* IV is Pope's fear of reification, of an unnatural perversion of relationship between language and the objects to which words refer. Those, like Annius and Mummius in *Dunciad* IV, or in real life the perennial Scriblerian target John Woodward, who fetishize objects are most likely to press their hypotheses into extravagance and absurdity because of a quality of literal-mindedness. Such scholars are bound to produce only reductive explanations, because they are materialists who strip nature of her mystery. Another identifying feature, therefore, of the writing designated Scriblerian is its ironic parody of reductive explanatory models.

A fine comic example of this is a little treatise, probably a Pope/ Arbuthnot collaboration written around 1714 but not published until 1732, *An Essay of the Learned Martinus Scriblerus, concerning the Origine of Sciences. Written to the most Learned Dr. —— F.R.S., from the Deserts of Nubia.*[12] Pope said to Spence that the design was 'to ridicule such as build general assertions upon two or three loose quotations from the ancients'.[13] Like most Scriblerian pieces it promotes to polite attention a sub-literary type, the learned essay, in this case on the subject of historical anthropology. Scriblerus claims to write 'from the Deserts of Aethiopia, from those plains of sand which have buried the pride of invading armies' (*Prose Works*, 11, 286). What follows is truly Scriblerian fieldwork. In 1699 Dr. Edward Tyson had published his pioneering work of comparative anatomy, *Orang-Outang, sive Homo Sylvestris*, showing that the orang-utan closely resembles man and conjecturing that this animal may have given foundation to ancient stories of races of undersized men, previously dismissed as mere fictions. The extraordinary thing about Tyson's science is that it is actually employed to serve the ends of polite letters. His investigation is philological as much as it is anatomical, as the appended *Philological Essay concerning the Satyrs of the Ancients* makes plain. Satyrs were '*Monkeys* or *Baboons*, that in *Africa* were worshipped as the *Gods* of the Country; and being so, might give the *Poets* the Subject of the Stories which they have forged about them' (p. 46).

It is the combination of scientific enquiry and humane scholarship that particularly invites Scriblerian parody. In a farrago of part-mythical, part-historical, part-literary erudition, Scriblerus shows that modern monkeys in Ethiopia and India are descendents of an early race of satyrs (originally led by Pan/Bacchus) who are themselves survivors of ancient pygmies. Among other mythological stories that this fantastic genealogy is held to explain is the Orphic myth, the ancient stories of Orpheus charming the beasts and 'the fabulous story of the Gods compressing women in woods under bestial appearances' (notice the mock-learned 'compressing' and the scholarly periphrasis of 'under bestial appearances'). To the objection that no stories actually exist of women being compressed under the appearances of monkeys, Scriblerus gives a reply that anticipates the Yahoo couplings in *Gulliver's Travels* and the monkey couplings in *Candide*: 'I am sensible it may be objected, that they are said to have been compress'd in the shape of different animals; but to this we answer, that women under such apprehensions hardly know what shape they have to deal with' (*Prose Works*, 2: 289).[14] Here is the true voice of Scriblerus.

The treatise is grounded in a received eighteenth-century belief that Egyptian and Oriental learning was in an advanced stage of development when Greece was still barbaric. Pope himself believed that Homer had learned from the religion of the Egyptians, and the Hebrew patriarchs were thought to have learned the rudiments of their faith there.[15] Again, however, the view of the Middle East as the matrix of Western culture was one that could be pushed by the collectors and scholars into hyperbole, and could be falsely systematized on the basis of a few loose hints. Here the result is a genealogy based on unnatural miscegenation. Gay's collaborative play *Three Hours After Marriage* takes a similar dim view of the Egyptologist. Its protagonist, Dr. Fossile, is cuckolded by one of his own museum-pieces. Arbuthnot's later *Brief Account of Mr. John Ginglicutt's Treatise concerning the Altercation or Scolding of the Ancients* has smaller fish to fry, doing little more than pressing copious learning into the service of a ludicrous argument: to show that contemporary parliamentary mud-slinging has an ancient pedigree. Mock-heroically it collects examples of 'objurgation' (name-calling) in Homer and elsewhere to sanction modern political Billingsgate. As Pope put it, 'when I die, be sure you let me know, / Great *Homer* dy'd three thousand years ago'.

Ponderous drudgery in establishing an argument not worth making is, of course, the hallmark of all activity satirized in Scriblerian writing. Literal-mindedness, a lack of imagination so chronic that it amounts to inhumanity, is the culpable folly of the Scriblerian butt. Arbuthnot's *An Account of the Sickness and Death of DR. W——DW——RD by DR. TECHNICUM* (1719) cribs Swift's Bickerstaff joke, announcing the death of Woodward and, by means of an autopsy, exposing the murderous theories to which he subscribed and which this pamphlet claims to have been the death of him. Just as in *The Bickerstaff Papers*, where astrology, Partridge's own trade, is turned against him in predicting his death, so here Woodward's own technology is employed to undermine him. Again the Scriblerian touches come through the laborious documentation of Woodward's misguided remedies, the mathematics of dulness: 'I heard him say not long ago (and no man was more punctual in his arithmetic) that in the course of his practice he had administered 20473 vomits, 756 hogsheads, four gallons, and a pint of sack-whey, and above 50 ton of oil.'[16] Swift was fascinated by this kind of imaginative limitation. His personae are often men who cannot understand metaphors other than literally, though in some cases this is not a limitation but a rhetorical advantage. He makes use of it in works not essentially Scriblerian, as in *The Drapier's Letters*. The Drapier can pose as such an individual when it suits him. In the fourth *Letter* the Drapier replies to William Wood's threat that Walpole will force the Irish to '*Swallow his Coin in Fire-Balls*':

> To execute this *Operation*, the whole Stock of Mr. *Wood*'s Coin and Metal must be melted down, and molded into hollow *Balls* with *Wild-fire*, no bigger than a *reasonable* Throat can be able to swallow. Now, the Metal he hath prepared, and already coined, will amount to at least Fifty Millions of Half-pence to be *Swallowed* by a Million and a Half of People; so that allowing Two Half-pence to each *Ball*, there will be about Seventeen *Balls* of *Wild-fire* a-piece, to be swallowed by every Person in the Kingdom.
>
> (*PW*, 10: 68)

Though not actually a Scriblerian passage, this extract, with its imagery of melted metal, *aurum potabile*, is very suggestive of Scriblerian metaphor. An impressionistic response to such Scriblerian works as *Peri Bathous* and the early *Dunciad* might issue in an associative train (rising–sinking–weight–gravity–heavy metal–brass–lead–Age of Gold–Age of Lead), and indeed such an image-repertoire is a hallmark of Scriblerian writing. *Peri Bathous* is an inverse manual of rhetoric in which the Longinian sublime is converted into Popean profound. It deals with the alchemy by means of which dunces convert the sublime into the low, conflating lofty and natural styles. Scriblerian butts are of course alchemists in reverse. They are looking to convert gold into base metal, and as scientists, therefore, they are in touch with an older tradition that pre-dates mechanical philosophy, even if they have its quest arsy-versy. Alchemy is wedded to an entirely organic model of nature, in which matter, far from being inert, is inspirited with vital principles. Dunces, however, fail in the alchemist's desire to purify nature of its dross, and are frequently left with only the faeces. As Pope puts it in the *Bathous*, 'the Physician, by the study and inspection of urine and ordure, approves himself in the sciences; and in the like sort should our author accustom and exercise his imagination upon the dregs of nature' (*Prose Works*, 2: 198).

It is in the Scriblerian centrepiece, the *Memoirs of Martinus Scriblerus* itself, that the scientific method is most obviously a limitation, resulting in unnatural and inhumane behaviour. Our hero, on first introduction, is a Cervantic prototype of Frankenstein. Cut off from ordinary human intercourse by the weight of unshareable knowledge (the *Arcanum Magnum*) he is confined to his lonely attic as much by poverty as by the pursuit of science:

> His Cloak so completely covered his whole person, that whether or no he had any other cloaths (much less any linen) under it I shall not say. . . . His lodging was in a small chamber up four pair of stairs, where he regularly payed for what he had when he eat or drank, and he was often observed wholly to abstain from both.[17]

Martin is a peculiarly Scriblerian Quixote, a divided self whose financial means are not adequate to his aristocratic pride and altruistic ambition to extend the frontiers of knowledge. From the outset, therefore, farce dogs the footsteps of the Scriblerii. As usual in Scriblerian satire, applied science is on a collision course with the dictates of natural behaviour or common sense. Martin's father Cornelius is a parent whose practice is always defined against a norm of natural parentage. He uses Galen's diet 'for the generation of Children of Wit' and is soon outraging natural feeling by 'treasuring up' his wife's aborted embryo 'in a Vial'. In the bibliographically-mysterious 1723 version of the *Memoirs* our hero (therein called Tim) is announced as unnatural through his first intelligible sound, which articulates his desire to scribble, not his desire for parental comfort: 'One Day the Nurse, with great Joy, came running to the Father to tell him Master *Tim* call'd Papa, but the Father soon found the Mistake, and that the first Word *Tim* utter'd was, Paper' (p. 380). On the introduction in Chapter 7 of Martin's servant Crambo, who is addicted to punning, another Scriblerian chord is sounded. Language is reduced by him to mere sound-value, 'Dennis and Dissonance':

'*Words*, which as they are said to be the counters of wise Men, and ready-money of Fools, Crambo had a great store of cash of the latter sort' (p. 118). To fall in love with one of a pair of Siamese twins, as Martin does, a man surely needs more scientific curiosity than imagination.

II

The above textual discussion suggests that there is a satiric mode that we can confidently designate 'Scriblerian'. The period 1713–14, during which the Scriblerus Club convened, is only an approximate date of birth, because, as I have described, the early works of Swift (and one might add of Garth and William King) disseminate some of its characteristic attitudes. Its conception is the result of the widening gap between polite letters and more scientific 'professional' research conducted by members of the Royal Society and others in the late seventeenth century. It is born out of a period of transition in the economics of authorship, and at a particular historical moment when the status of writing itself was under active renegotiation. Questions about whether writing was an activity of the spirit (issuing, to be sure, in a set of marks on paper, but not reducible to these marks), or whether writing was a mechanical and material act which produced goods exchangeable for the wherewithal to buy necessities of life, are focused through this mode. The Scriblerian target is *homo mechanicus*, a species both produced by and producing the new scientific learning, but at a cost to fundamental humanity, to naturalness, and to good writing. 'Scriblerian' satire inhabits many different kinds of writing, but in its early phase it employs as its 'host' sub-literary kinds such as the biography or learned essay or critical treatise, because initially it works by parodying the kinds that seem to endanger 'valuable' writing. Mature eighteenth-century works such as the *Dunciad* or *Gulliver's Travels* are far too diverse to be described satisfactorily as Scriblerian satires, but parts of them are certainly informed by this mode. Scriblerian satire is capable, in my view, of relative autonomy from the historical moment that produced it, so that it might make sense to say of Beckett or of Borges that their satire is in some respects Scriblerian.[18] Perhaps the term 'Scriblerian' should be assimilated into the vocabulary of criticism in the same way as the term 'Menippean' has been.

In prose the Scriblerians circulated a set of narratives whose purported authors, or whose principal personae, exemplify undesirable authorial practices. Despite the paradox and complexity of the *Tale* and the frequently sympathetic treatment of the Scriblerus family in the *Memoirs*, these texts do finally attack 'modern' conceptions of authorship which express 'modern' modes of knowledge. This side of the Scriblerian enterprise is identified by its epidemic pseudonymity. The names of the Scriblerians are legion, although all are to an extent controlled by the master disguise of Martinus Scriblerus: to the names already mentioned we might add Sir Humphry Polesworth; E. Parker, Philomath; Esdras Barnivelt; William Cleland; P. P., Clerk of this Parish; and others.

If the central thrust of the Scriblerian project was to write the spoof-biography of a pseudonym, charting the ideally typical career of the contemporary virtuoso, it also had ramifications beyond that. In poems written for the most part after Scriblerian energy had burned itself out, Pope, Swift, and Gay all try to justify their lives and writing careers. (Conspicuously absent from this list is Arbuthnot, who seems not to have felt the self-justificatory urge. We can speculate that his relatively normal family life (he was the only Scriblerian to marry and have a family) offered him many more conventional routes to self-definition.)[19] For Pope, and more indirectly for Gay, the Scriblerian endeavour helped to hew the rough shape that normative autobiography would take. It partially defined the nature of the space into which Pope and Gay inserted their self-images. If Scriblerian texts had sharpened up an image of what authorship was not, they had also prescribed some respects in which the poet's life could be held up as exemplary. When Pope, in the *Epistle to Dr. Arbuthnot*, presents himself as an independent poet without visible means of support we have to recognize this levitation-trick as a response to the Scriblerian view of the hack's client status. Study of Scriblerian texts helps us to understand the gradually-forming ideology of authorship that made poetic autobiography an imperative by the 1730s.

Pope's career shows how oblique the process was. Terry Bélanger points out that, as far as the economics of authorship go, Pope was 'the watershed figure ... who by careful management of his literary productions was able to earn a good deal of money from them'.[20] 'Careful management', in Pope's case, meant the marketing of patronage, an ingenious way of profiting by his writing without incurring the opprobrium of being a 'hack', a professional writer: that is, without ending up on the wrong side of the great divide that he and his fellow Scriblerians were opening up. Earlier in his career, before the Homer translation established his talent and his independence, Pope was not so certain that there was a firm dividing line between genius and duncehood. Pope's preface to the 1717 edition of his *Works* treads a cautious line on this. Well it might, since this publication was the poet's first bid for the status of genius:

I think a good deal may be said to extenuate the fault of bad
Poets. What we call a Genius, is hard to be distinguish'd by a man
himself, from a strong inclination: and if it be never so great, he
can not at first discover it any other way, than by that prevalent
propensity which renders him the more liable to be mistaken.
The only method he has, is to make the experiment by writing,
and appealing to the judgment of others. . . . We have no cause
to quarrel with [the worst authors] but for their obstinacy in
persisting, and this too may admit of alleviating circumstances.
Their particular friends may be either ignorant, or insincere; and
the rest of the world too well bred to shock them with a truth,
which generally their Booksellers are the first that inform them
of. This happens not till they have spent too much of their time,
to apply to any profession which might better fit their talents; and
till such talents as they have are so far discredited, as to be but of
small service to them.[21]

At this stage in Pope's thinking, Mother Nature herself is not
credited with making dunces. Dunces are created by the thumbs-
down of the reading public: 'What's aught but as 'tis valued?' Some
immigration into Parnassus from Grub Street is possible on this view.
In Arbuthnot's third John Bull pamphlet, *John Bull Still in his Senses*,
'the Publisher', pleading with Sir Humphrey Polesworth for more
copy, implies just such a flexible view of literary merit: 'I represented
to him the good Reception the two first Parts had met, that tho' they
had been calculated by him, only for the Meridian of *Grub-street*, yet
they were taken notice of by the better sort; that the World was now
sufficiently acquainted with *John Bull*, and interested it self in his
little Concerns' (*History of John Bull*, p. 47). But if the chrysalis of
literary genius sometimes gives birth to moths, quite inevitably and
through no fault of the author, Pope is also careful to insist that the
crime lies in continuing to write. Writing then becomes a profession
and displaces other serious callings. Later in the preface, in terms
that will recur in the *Epistle to Dr. Arbuthnot*, Pope himself disclaims
any professional motive for writing: 'I writ because it amused me;
I corrected because it was as pleasant to me to correct as to write;
and I publish'd because I was told I might please such as it was a
credit to please' (*Prose Works*, 1: 292). Thus Pope frees himself from
the taint of professionalism.

As early as 1717, then, Pope was tentatively formulating an
ideology that was able to establish him as a genius while putting
distance between himself and those who, not possessing genius, were
condemned to a life of writing for bread. When in the *Miscellanies*
Pope and Swift collected some of their occasional writings into two

spirited and humorous volumes they were careful to let the public know that this was the product of genius on holiday. Only published at all through the muck-raking activities of those who 'have fished the very Jakes, for Papers left there by Men of Wit', the *Miscellanies* are winsomely presented as the follies of youth or as the results of less guarded moments: 'We are obliged to confess, that this whole Collection, in a manner, consists of what we not only thought unlikely to reach the future, but unworthy even of the *present* Age; not our Studies, but our Follies; not our Works, but our Idlenesses' (*Prose Works*, 2: 92). Hot on its heels, the *Dunciad* further widened the gap between 'classic' and 'popular' writing, between writing worthy of serious critical notice and writing worthy of neglect. Subsequently Pope embarked on a career of image-making which David Piper has aptly described in terms of a 'need to rectify the tragic twisted reality of his crippled body with an image worthy of the lucid, beautifully articulated construction and spirit of his poetry – the need, very literally, to put the image straight'.[22]

Swift's poetic autobiography owes less to Scriblerian writing for its precise lineaments. If, as Timothy Keegan says, Swift's aim is always self-justification when he writes explicitly about himself as a public figure, the self he justifies is different from Pope's in a fundamental respect.[23] Pope's sense of self is almost completely expressed in terms of his sense of himself as a writer. Swift's is not. For him the perlocutionary effect of his writing was more important than its literary merit and so his poetic autobiography seeks to justify his writing as securing the objectives of the public man.[24] Although he was as wedded to the concept of independence as was Pope, his was a rugged and militant version. When, in *A Libel on Dr. Delany*, he tried to clothe Pope in these borrowed robes, Pope repudiated the image that his friend was trying to fashion for him:

> Hail! happy Pope, whose generous mind,
> Detesting all the statesmen kind!
> Contemning courts, at courts unseen,
> Refused the visits of a queen;
> A soul with every virtue fraught
> By sages, priests, or poets taught:
> Whose filial piety excels
> Whatever Grecian story tells:
> A genius for all stations fit,
> Whose meanest talent is his wit:
> His heart too great, though fortune little,
> To lick a rascal statesman's spittle.

(ll. 71–82)

Pope rejected this aggressively-politicized version of his conduct, not only because he was still maintaining diplomatic relations with Walpole but because it misconceived the way he wanted to inhabit his poems. As a piece of image-making it was inept, failing to capture the effortlessness of Pope's own brand of independence. It does, however, draw attention to a fascinating aspect of Scriblerian self-fashioning. After 1728, when Swift left England for the last time and the Scriblerian dream of a satiric 'think tank' was finally over, Pope and Swift began to project images of each other in a way that neither found satisfactory. Only by going through a procedure as circumspect as a courtship ritual could Pope persuade Swift to part with his letters, allowing Pope to put the finishing touches to the improved version of himself that his correspondence promoted.[25] More significantly, Pope was largely behind the attempt to doctor Swift's self-image as expressed in the *Verses on the Death of Dr. Swift*. When the poem was printed by Bathurst in 1739 it was without 165 of Swift's lines and contained sixty-two extra lines from another poem, the *Life and Genuine Character of Dr. Swift*. The result, as Hume and Scouten say in their important article on the *Verses*, replaces the Rose Tavern spokesman's panegyric by Horatian 'rapid-fire dialogue', thus giving a much more controversial sense of Swift's place in history.[26] Like many later readers Pope was embarrassed by the monologic way in which Swift presents himself as noble and incorruptible, requiring at the very least that this come through the distance of dialogue and alternative presentations of self.[27] Pope is remaking Swift in the image of his own rhetorical strategies of the *Epistle to Dr. Arbuthnot*. Swift, however, liked this compromise no more than Pope had liked his picture in the Delany poem.

III

Though the public-relations work they did for each other was so gauche and unwelcome, Pope and Swift found common ground in John Gay's writing career. As advertising agents for Gay, the other Scriblerians found a more productive site for their endeavours. Here, in their promotion of an image for Gay, the implied contrast with authors stigmatized in Scriblerian writing is most obvious. Elsewhere I have talked about the means Pope and Swift employed to put John Gay's image straight, to fashion a life-history for Gay as a neglected genius never considered worthy of his hire by a philistine Court and Government.[28] In an early number of the *Intelligencer*, for instance, Swift defends *The Beggar's Opera* in the following terms: 'It is true, indeed, that Mr. GAY, the author of this Piece, hath been somewhat singular in the Course of his Fortunes; for it hath happened, that after Fourteen Years attending the *Court,* with a large Stock of real Merit, a modest and agreeable Conversation, a *Hundred Promises,* and *five Hundred Friends,* he hath failed of Preferment' (*PW,* 12: 34). This 'authorized version' of Gay's life is at least in part the creation of the other Scriblerians, who had a vested interest in presenting him as exactly the kind of writer who was losing ground to the hacks and professionals. Early poems such as *Rural Sports* and *The Shepherd's Week* show Gay's consciousness that he had a way to make in the world, and they make quiet bids for Tory and royal patronage. The first of these poems opens with Gay's confession that he is far less well qualified than Pope or Virgil to write a peace-poem celebrating the virtues of rural life:

> You, who the sweets of rural life have known,
> Despise th' ungrateful hurry of the town;
> In *Windsor* groves your easie hours employ,
> And, undisturb'd, your self and Muse enjoy.
> *Thames* listens to thy strains, and silent flows,
> And no rude wind through rustling osiers blows,
> While all his wond'ring Nymphs around thee throng,
> To hear the *Syrens* warble in thy song.
> But I, who ne'er was bless'd by Fortune's hand,
> Nor brighten'd plough-shares in paternal land,

will nevertheless 'the same road ambitiously pursue, / Frequented by the *Mantuan* swain, and you'. But it proved for Gay a hard road to follow, and after the failure of his early bid for political patronage his poetry is beset by the need to come to an accommodation between genius and its hire. In 'A Letter to a Lady' he makes poetry out of regarding frankly this very problem. It was written to solicit the Princess Caroline's entrée into Hanoverian favour, and comments in meta-poetic mode on its own processes of composition. Gay's failures with ode, complimentary epistle, and epigram are ruefully recorded. All raise the same problem; that the muse remains sullen when she suspects that she is being coerced by the necessity to write. Without employment the Muse has not the ease to flow, so how is the poet to compose the kind of panegyric that can alone secure patronage?

> Another ask'd me, why I had not writ:
> A Poet owes his Fortune to his Wit.
> Strait I reply'd, With what a courtly Grace
> Flows easy Verse from him that has a Place!
> Had *Virgil* ne'er at Court improv'd his Strains,
> He still had sung of Flocks and homely Swains;

And had not *Horace* sweet Preferment found,
The *Roman* lyre had never learnt to sound . . .
Still ev'ry one I met in this agreed,
That Writing was my Method to succeed;
But now Preferments so possess'd my Brain,
That scarce I could produce a single Strain.

(ll. 99–106, 125–128)

Even in Gay's single attempt to combine panegyric with elegy, his 'An Epistle to Her Grace Henrietta, Dutchess of Marlborough', he is unable to praise without self-consciousness. The poem develops a mannerism of commenting on the fact that elegy, in praising the deceased and recalling his virtues, is liable to aggravate the grief of the mourners. If elegy has that ambivalent effect, the poem muses, then *commenting* on the effect can only magnify it further, and the poem worries its way to a contradictory close. In truth, the problem with this elegy on the Duke of Marlborough is precisely that it is a hack job, written to gain favour. If we compare its unctuous sentiments with Swift's 'A Satirical Elegy', or his *Examiner* piece on the Duke, it is hard to believe that Gay meant what he said.

Objectively considered, Gay made a very comfortable living out of being, in effect, a professional author. He could never reconcile himself to that image, however, because Pope and Swift were demanding that he be given the financial independence that alone guarantees the functioning of genius. Gay was actually an author in the mode of those attacked by Scriblerian satire, a thorough professional well able to market his pen. Yet the conservative tectonics of Scriblerian texts created inevitable rifts, so that he could not settle comfortably into this coming model of authorship. Swift and Arbuthnot had other professions. Pope, in many ways the first great professional writer, had artfully covered his tracks. In Gay, Scriblerus made a victim of himself.

Notes

1. THOMAS SPRAT, *History of the Royal Society* (London, 1667), p. 113.

2. Wilkins's and other 'Adamic' linguistic schemes are discussed in ANN CLINE KELLY, 'After Eden: Gulliver's (Linguistic) Travels', *ELH*, 45 (1978), 33–52, and A. C. HOWELL, '*Res et Verba*: Words and Things', *ELH*, 13 (1946), 131–42; DENIS DONOGHUE, *Jonathan Swift: A Critical Introduction* (Cambridge, 1969), p. 131.

3. ROBERT C. GORDON makes this point well in 'Jonathan Swift and the Modern Art of War', *Bulletin of Research in the Humanities* (Summer, 1980), 187–202.

4. MAUREEN QUILLIGAN, *The Language of Allegory* (Ithaca, NY and London, 1979).

5. EDWARD ROSENHEIM, JR, 'Swift and the Atterbury Case', in *The Augustan Milieu: Essays presented to Louis A. Landa*, ed. HENRY KNIGHT MILLER, ERIC ROTHSTEIN, and G. S. ROUSSEAU (Oxford, 1970), pp. 174–204.

6. DAVID NOKES, *Jonathan Swift: A Hypocrite Reversed* (Oxford, London and New York, 1985), p. 49. See also his ' "Hack at Tom Poley's" ': Swift's Use of Puns', in *The Art of Jonathan Swift*, ed. CLIVE T. PROBYN (London and New York, 1978), pp. 43–56.

7. R. S. WESTFALL, *Never At Rest: A Biography of Isaac Newton* (Cambridge and London, 1980), pp. 14–15.

8. From *The Present State of Wit*, in *John Gay: Poetry and Prose*, ed. VINTON A. DEARING, with assistance from CHARLES E. BECKWITH, 2 vols (Oxford, 1974), 2: 452. Subsequent references are to this edition.

9. *Jonathan Swift*, ed. ANGUS ROSS and DAVID WOOLLEY, Oxford Authors (Oxford, London and New York, 1984), p. 639.

10. BREAN S. HAMMOND, *Pope*, Harvester New Readings (Brighton, 1986), Chapter 4.

11. PENELOPE WILSON, 'Classical Poetry and the Eighteenth-Century Reader', in *Books and their Readers in Eighteenth-Century England*, ed. ISABEL RIVERS (Leicester, 1982), pp. 69–96 (p. 86).

12. ROSEMARY COWLER, printing this in her recent edition of Pope's later prose works, argues the case for Pope's authorship in *The Prose Works of Alexander Pope*, 2 vols, Vol. II (Oxford, 1986), p. 279.

13. JOSEPH SPENCE, *Observations, Anecdotes and Characters of Books and Men: Collected from Conversation by Joseph Spence*, ed. JAMES M. OSBORN, 2 vols, Vol. I (Oxford, 1966), p. 57.

14. Some of the ancient descriptions of satyri that Tyson quotes are quite close to Swift's Yahoos. Pliny's *Natural History*, in Tyson's paraphrase (p. 50), characterizes them as having 'something of the shape of Men, but can't speak, they are hairy, they go sometimes upon all four, sometimes erect, they have Dog's Teeth, they are wild mischievous Animals'.

15. See JAMES SAMBROOK, *The Eighteenth Century: The Intellectual and Cultural Context of English Literature, 1700–1789*, Longman History of Literature in English (London and New York, 1986), p. 187.

16. *The Life and Works of John Arbuthnot*, ed. GEORGE A. AITKEN (Oxford, 1892), pp. 467–68.

17. *The Memoirs of Martinus Scriblerus*, ed. CHARLES KERBY-MILLER (New Haven, CT, 1950; reprinted London and New York, 1966), p. 91.

18. In referring to Scriblerian satire as a 'mode' I am employing a terminology argued for by ALASTAIR FOWLER in *Kinds of Literature: An Introduction to the Theory of Genres and Modes* (Oxford, 1982), *passim*, but see pp. 110–11, 188–90. CLAUDE RAWSON makes the suggestive comparison between Scriblerian satire and Borges in his editorial introduction to *English Satire and the Satiric Tradition* (Oxford, 1984), p. xii.

19. This is suggested, as an explanation for Arbuthnot's relatively careless attitude to his literary works, by ALAN W. BOWER and ROBERT A. ERICKSON, editors of Arbuthnot's *The History of John Bull* (Oxford, 1976), p. xxxi.

20. TERRY BÉLANGER, 'Publishers and Writers in Eighteenth-Century England', in *Books and their Readers*, pp. 5–25 (p. 21).

21. *The Prose Works of Alexander Pope*, 2 vols, Vol. I, *The Earlier Works, 1711–1720* (Oxford, 1936), p. 290.

22. DAVID PIPER, *The Image of the Poet: British Poets and their Portraits* (Oxford, 1982), p. 58.

23. TIMOTHY KEEGAN, 'Swift's Self-Portraits in Verse', in *Augustan Studies: Essays in Honor of Irvin Ehrenpreis*, ed. DOUGLAS LANE PATEY and TIMOTHY KEEGAN (Cranbury, NJ and London, Ontario, 1985), pp. 127–43 (p. 127).

24. A point clearly made by PETER J. SCHAKEL in *The Poetry of Jonathan Swift: Allusion and the Development of a Poetic Style* (Madison, WI, 1978), pp. 129–30.

25. See MAYNARD MACK's illuminating account of this in *Alexander Pope: A Life* (New Haven, CT and London, 1985), pp. 664–71.

26. ARTHUR H. SCOUTEN and ROBERT D. HUME, 'Pope and Swift: Text and Interpretation of Swift's Verses on His Death', *Philological Quarterly*, 52 (1973), 205–31; reprinted in *Essential Articles for the Study of Jonathan Swift's Poetry*, ed. DAVID M. VIETH (Hamden, CT, 1984), pp. 315–45.

27. JAMES WOOLLEY has all but captured the ground for the view that the problematic encomium is not ironic; see his 'Friends and Enemies in *Verses on the Death of Dr. Swift*', *Studies in Eighteenth-Century Culture*, 8 (1979), 205–32, and 'Autobiography in Swift's Verses on His Death', in *Contemporary Studies of Swift's Poetry*, ed. J. I. FISCHER, DONALD MELL, JR, and DAVID M. VIETH (Newark, DE, 1981), pp. 112–22. Most readings depend on a set of assumptions not only about Swift's self-estimation but also about what is biographically true or accurate. Biographers do not always agree, however: see IRVIN EHRENPREIS, *Swift: The Man, his Works and the Age*, 3 vols (London, 1962–83); J. A. DOWNIE, *Jonathan Swift: Political Writer* (London, 1984); DAVID NOKES, *A Hypocrite Reversed*. For a stylistic analysis that brings us very close to understanding why Pope was embarrassed by the poem, and that does not depend on biography, see C. J. RAWSON, ' "I the Lofty Stile Decline": Self-apology and the "Heroick Strain" in Some of Swift's Poems', in *The English Hero, 1660–1800*, ed. ROBERT FOLKENFLIK (Newark, DE, 1982), pp. 79–115.

28. ' "A Poet, and a Patron, and Ten Pound": John Gay and Patronage', in *John Gay and the Scriblerians*, ed. PETER LEWIS and NIGEL WOOD (London and New York, 1988), pp. 23–43.

5 Text, 'Text', and Swift's *A Tale of a Tub**

MARCUS WALSH

Few printed texts make so apparent, or are so ingenious about, their textual nature and status as Swift's *A Tale of a Tub*, and few have given rise to so much interpretative controversy. The *Tale* has been a focus of some of the key disagreements in modern critical theory.

It has been possible to think of the *Tale* as embodying, as the Apology of 1710 so repeatedly suggests, 'the Author's Intentions', its satiric purpose being 'to expose the Abuses and Corruptions in Learning and Religion' (*PW*, 1: 26). Readings of the *Tale* which explain that Swift uses the *persona* of a mad modern writer to exemplify and satirize scholastic and modern incoherence in learning and belief, and readings of the *Tale* (notably Ehrenpreis's) which deny the use of a persona and invite us to seek 'the direct sense implied by the irony',[1] have this in common: that they insist the *Tale* has an originating author, that this author's meaning intention is there to be found, and that, despite all of the *Tale*'s evident complexity, a valid interpretation of its essential message can be offered. In particular such readings tend to argue that Swift sets up standards of plain, comprehensible expression, against which the vacancy and chaos of the Modern's own writing, and interpretative principles, are found wanting.

More recently, however, the discussion of *A Tale of a Tub* has been dominated by a very different argument: that, far from satirizing expressive and interpretative incoherence, the *Tale* is a narrative without an authoritative voice, which sets out to exemplify the inevitable polysemy of writing, and, more especially, of print. In this view, it would be deluded to see *A Tale of a Tub* as even potentially stable, authoritative, bounded. The *Tale* is, in Barthesian terms, not a 'work' but a 'text', which 'goes to the limit of the rules of enunciation (rationality, readability, etc.)'.[2] Textualizing studies have explored a number of the implications of this. In a recent essay Clive Probyn argues that, far from implicitly confirming by its satiric negatives a

---

* Reprinted from *The Modern Language Review*, 85 (1990), 290–303.

confident humanist belief in the comprehensibility and permanence of good writing and good printing, the *Tale*, as well as *Gulliver's Travels*, reveals and explores Swift's most fundamental fears about the transience of all printed texts: 'a fear of supersession, the prospect of literary obsolescence, the anxiety of loss, the horror of obscurity, and the cancellation of history'.[3] Nigel Wood has claimed that a key problem for the 'Modern' narrator of the *Tale* is 'how to maintain one's authority over the *printed* word. . . . The mediation of the printing-press did not necessarily ensure clarity or even a desirable measure of survival for one's thoughts'.[4] Other textualist critics suggest that Swift himself experienced and viewed this dilemma much as his modern persona did. Thomas Docherty takes the hack's invitation to 'every Prince in Christendom' to appoint commentators on his *Tale* as evidence that Swift believed 'a multiplicity of readings are sanctioned by the words of the text, independently of a supposedly pre-linguistic authorial intention or psychology'.[5] In an essay which argues, or assumes, that Swift thought of writing as dangerous supplement, Terry Castle describes the *Tale* as part of a 'Swiftian critique of Text', which takes in all writing, including the Bible:

> Every writing is a source of corruption, no matter what authority – natural, divine, or archetypal – we may wishfully invest in it. Because they constitute an earthly text, the Scriptures themselves pathetically and paradoxically make up part of the fallen world of writing. . . . Swift does not state . . . baldly that God's text itself is corrupt, but . . . the possibility is implicit everywhere in his satire.[6]

Such recent readings of the *Tale* arise not only from the presumed difficulty or impossibility of identifying a securely present voice but also from the difficulties of establishing a context which might validate any voice. As Wood puts it, 'as interpretation of the basic satiric context is problematic (such as, what is being attacked and on what authority), most textual critics have concluded that the main point of the *Tale* is to demonstrate the extreme difficulty of interpreting anything without a divine yardstick' (p. 47). I would like to offer some qualifications of the textualist position by beginning to set *A Tale of a Tub* in a context which has been surprisingly little discussed, and which seems to me to have an immediate intellectual bearing on Swift's discussion of Scripture, text, and meaning: that is, the argument between the Roman Church and the Anglican Church through much of the seventeenth century concerning Scripture as a rule of faith.

This polemic in very large part concerned itself, inevitably, with fundamental problems about the nature, determinacy, stability,

and comprehensibility of the printed book. Questions of text
and hermeneutics were obsessively debated, notably in William
Chillingworth's *Religion of Protestants* (1638), in the *Dialogues* (1640)
of the exiled Romanist William Rushworth (and Chillingworth's
Answer),[7] in John Sergeant's *Sure-Footing in Christianity* (1665) and in
Tillotson's reply *The Rule of Faith* (1666),[8] in Bossuet's *Exposition de la
doctrine de l'Église Catholique* (Paris, 1671) and its numerous English
defenders and opponents, in Père Richard Simon's magisterial *Critical
Histories* of the Old and New Testaments (1678, 1689),[9] and, most
voluminously and passionately, in the debate of the 1680s between
Anglican Churchmen (Tillotson, Sherlock, Stillingfleet, and others)
and their Romanist adversaries led by John Gother. This was in no
sense a set of peripheral pamphlet skirmishes, but a major war in the
history of ideas, in which big guns on both sides were employed.
The chief polemicists of the reign of James II engaged as officially-
sanctioned public representatives rather than private individuals,
the works of Gother and many of the other Roman Catholic writers
being regularly published by Henry Hills, 'Printer to the King's Most
Excellent Majesty', and those of their opponents commonly appearing
under the imprimatur of the English Church. The arguments
employed in these debates have significant resonances for modern
textual and hermeneutic theory, and for the assessment of Swift's
textual and hermeneutic position in the *Tale*. In this chapter I shall
address myself chiefly to issues of textual theory.

'Of Wills', as the Peter of the *Tale* remarks, '*duo sunt genera*,
Nuncupatory and scriptory' (*PW*, 1: 51). Peter's preference for oral
over written tradition is of course distinctly Roman, and as certainly
not Swift's. The written Testament consists of 'certain plain, easy
Directions' (*PW*, 1: 121) and says nothing about gold lace; but oral
tradition will allow, for Peter, a desirable extension of its licence: 'For
Brothers, if you remember, we heard a Fellow say when we were
Boys, that he heard my Father's Man say, that he heard my Father
say, that he would advise his Sons to get *Gold Lace* on their Coats,
as soon as ever they could procure Money to buy it' (*PW*, 1: 52).
The official Roman position, from the Counter-Reformation onwards,
was that truth was to be found equally in the written Scriptures
and in unwritten tradition.[10] In their continuing polemic against
Protestants, and against the inevitable Protestant dependence on
Scripture as a rule of faith, however, Romanist writers repeatedly
stressed what they thought to be the stability and continuity of oral
tradition as preserved in the Church, the uncertainty of textual
transmission and intrinsic textual interpretation, and the necessity of
tradition to any safe understanding of Holy Scripture. Bossuet, in his
Exposition, regarded by many as an official account of belief, insists

that the Church is founded on an original spoken word: 'JÉSUS-CHRIST ayant fondé son Église sur la prédication, la parole non écrite a esté la première regle du Christianisme; et lors que les Écritures du Nouveau Testament y ont esté jointes, cette parole n'a pas perdu pour cela son autorité' (pp. 158–9). Similarly, John Gother, the leading, most 'official', and certainly the wittiest polemicist on the Catholic side of this debate in the reign of James II, insisted that Christ's teaching was by word of mouth, and that the Apostles' '*Writing* was only *Accidental*, occasion'd by reason of their Absence from those they would teach'.[11] So the oral discourse takes precedence over the written text. The word of truth has been passed down from Christ to his Apostles, and thence through the agency of the Church to the modern believer. It is precisely the long, unbroken series of transmission, so much a joke to the Anglican Swift ('we heard a Fellow say . . . , that he heard my Father's Man say, that he heard my Father say . . .') which for an orthodox Roman Catholic validated oral tradition: 'n'étant pas possible de croire qu'une doctrine receûë dès le commencement de l'Église vienne d'une autre source que des Apôtres' (Bossuet, *Exposition*, p. 160). By contrast with the institutionalized certainty of the chain of oral tradition, Scripture was characterized by Roman polemicists as inadequate, on its own, as a rule of faith: uncertain in its transmission, dubious in its translation, and dangerously ambiguous in its sense. 'If we join not Tradition with the Scripture we can hardly affirm any thing for certain in Religion.'[12]

Anglicans resisted this privileging of the spoken word. Writing is neither an accident nor a substitute, but original, apostolic, fully equal to speech. If speech may be plain and comprehensible, so, argues Chillingworth, may writing. If the preaching of Christ and the Apostles could be understood by those who heard it, 'why may we not be as well assured, that we understand sufficiently what we conceive plaine in their writings?' (*Religion of Protestants* (1638), p. 111). Similarly, John Tillotson insisted that the Scriptures, not the oral tradition preserved in Peter's Church, 'are the means whereby the Christian Doctrine hath been brought down to us'. Like many of his Anglican contemporaries Tillotson understood that the defence of the Scriptures as a rule of faith inevitably depended on a defence of all writing and of all printed text as a determinate and reliable vehicle for the communication of meaning, fully equivalent to speech: 'Whatever can be spoken in plain and intelligible words, and such as have a certain sense, may be written in the same words . . . words are as intelligible when they are written as when they are spoken.'[13] In principle books may be written 'in plain and intelligible words', just as the Father's Will in *A Tale of a Tub* consists of 'certain plain, easy

Directions', and just as the unambiguously comprehensible laws of Brobdingnag 'are expressed in the most plain and simple Terms' (*PW*, 11: 136).

Clearly, a crucial difference between oral and written (or printed) tradition is the presence or absence of the speaking subject. Nigel Wood, in his discussion of the Modern's problem of control and authority over his published words in *A Tale of a Tub*, sums up a modern 'textualist' view of the uncertainties of writing and print consequent upon the disappearance of voice: 'The printed word may bear the same marks [as "living" speech] of the author's possession, but these are nominal compared with the speaker's power to retract, qualify and employ physical indicators (facial expression, posture of the body or gestures)' (pp. 38–9). The same argument was well known to Roman apologists. To have set down in writing even *exactly* the words Christ used in his spoken preaching could not have been enough, argues William Rushworth for example, to communicate Christ's meaning:

> Let him have written in the same language, and let him have set downe everie word and sillable, yet men conversant in noting the changes of meanings in words, will tell you, that divers accents in the pronunciation of them, the turning of the speakers head or bodie this way or that way, . . . may so change the sense of the words that they will seeme quite different in writing from what they were in speaking.
>
> (*Dialogues* (1640), pp. 275–6)

For Tillotson, however, the Scriptures are a fully adequate replacement for the presence of the speaking subject. In *The Rule of Faith* he quotes Eusebius to the effect that Matthew 'by the diligence and pains of Writing, did abundantly supply the want of his presence to those whom he left' (*Works*, p. 751). Tillotson quotes Rushworth's words on 'divers accents' and 'the turning of the speaker's head', and comments with a fine ironic anxiety for the necessary preservation of the gestural machinery:

> I hope that Oral and Practical Tradition hath been careful to preserve all these circumstances, and hath deliver'd down Christ's Doctrine with all the right *Traditionary Accents, Nods* and *Gestures*, necessary to the understanding of it; otherwise the omission of these may have so altered the sense of it, that it may be now quite different from what it was at first.
>
> (*Works*, p. 696)

Oral tradition is reduced by Tillotson to an actor's inherited repertoire of poses. It is perhaps a disappointment not to find such a traditionary pantomime portrayed in *A Tale of a Tub*.

Modern accounts of the status and independence of text cover the spectrum, from the view that texts not only have an objective existence but contain meaning, to the view that texts are mere constructs, without physical existence. In *Objective Knowledge* Karl Popper argues that printed texts belong to the 'third world' of *'objective contents of thought*, especially of scientific and poetic thoughts and works of art'. A book, and its inherent meaning, have an objective existence, whether or not they are perceived by a knowing subject.[14] Perhaps the closest to Popper's view among modern literary theorists is E. D. Hirsch, who, though he accepts that 'meaning is an affair of consciousness' and that 'the text does not exist even as a sequence of words until it is construed', none the less insists that an author's text embodies a determinate, self-identical, bounded meaning.[15] On the whole, however, recent theorists of text have not been willing to accept Popper's invitation to consider 'the objects of our understanding' in the humanities as 'third-world' objects, rather than as objects belonging to the 'second world' of mental states (pp. 106, 160–2). In particular, Derrida offers a 'graphocentric' model in which the text, shorn of the delusory presence of the speaking voice, becomes marks on paper, 'noir sur blanc', signifying only through difference. 'Text' has become open, destabilized, indeterminate, subject to interpretation, and indeed already multiply-interpreted.

Forms of the argument that truth and life inhere in spoken language, whereas writing is necessarily dead and incapable of explaining itself, go back to Plato's *Phaedrus*. Here Socrates denies that 'one can transmit or acquire clear and certain knowledge of an art through the medium of writing'. Written discourses, consisting merely of ink marks, are no more than the 'shadow' of 'the living and animate speech of a man with knowledge'.[16] St Paul platonizes, influentially, in II Corinthians 3.6: 'The letter killeth, but the spirit [*pneuma*] giveth life.' A similar emphasis is offered by the cabalistic tradition that 'the written Torah can take on corporeal form only through the power of the oral Torah'. The 'ink on parchment' of the written Torah cannot be understood, *does not exist*, except through the oral Torah, the interpretation which realizes it, which gives it sense. (My reference here, traditionally, is to Harold Bloom, quoting Scholem, quoting Rabbi Isaac the Blind.)[17]

As far as questions of the relative status of speech and writing were concerned, Romanist apologists in the century before Swift were the heirs of Plato and of the cabalists, insisting on the certainty

115

and life of speech, against what they considered the dangerous indeterminacy, the deadness, of the written or printed text. The theme appears explicitly and repeatedly in the writings of French and English Romanists. John Sergeant's *Sure-Footing* insists, typically, on the difference between the living truth of Christ's words, and the 'dead Letters' or 'dead Characters' of the Scripture (pp. 127, 194).[18] Sense is not inherent in the 'Scripture', by which word Protestants can mean only 'that Book not yet senc't or interpreted, but as *yet to be senc't*' (p. 13). Worse, the black marks of Scripture are 'waxen-natur'd' characters, dangerously polysemous, 'fit to be plaid upon diversly by quirks of wit' (p. 68). Sergeant is one of those who take what Popper calls the 'mistaken subjective approach to knowledge', believing that 'a book is nothing without a reader: . . . otherwise it is just paper with black spots on it' (*Objective Knowledge*, p. 115). For Sergeant, as for other Romanist apologists, it is Tradition which provides the text with a reader, giving determinate and living sense to the inert and mouldable words of the Holy Book: 'Tradition is to sence Scripture's Letter; and so that Letter no Rule but by virtue of Tradition. . . . Tradition gives us *Christ's Sence*, that is, the *Life* of the Letter ascertain'd to our hands' (pp. 130, 149).[19] Similarly, Richard Simon argues that 'the Church . . . alone is possess'd of the Scripture, because she possesses the true sence thereof'. Even if 'there were no Copies of the Bible in the World, Religion would be preserv'd, because the Church would always subsist' (III. 160). Religion and civilization are preserved not in the physical Bible (or in a complete set of Everyman's Library floating on the waters) but in the continuing mind of the living Church. The contrast between such a textual scepticism and the objectivism of Popper could scarcely be clearer: one of Popper's most dramatic knock-down arguments is the proposal of a 'thought experiment' in which all 'our subjective learning' (tradition, in fact) is destroyed, but '*libraries and our capacity to learn from them* survive' (*Objective Knowledge*, pp. 107–8), enabling the continuation of our world.

Seventeenth-century Anglican apologists were conscious of the need to argue that the sense of Scripture, in essential points, is inherent in the words of Scripture, and may be understood without tradition's explication. William Chillingworth cast his *Answer to some Passages in Rushworth's Dialogues* in the form of a dialogue between 'Uncle' and 'Nephew'. The Roman Catholic Uncle is made to assert that the sense of Scripture is 'a distinct thing from the naked Letter', belonging 'to Tradition rather than Express Text of Scripture'. The Protestant Nephew replies that, in all those parts of Scripture which belong 'to faith and good manners' the sense is inherent and clear; such passages 'carry their meaning in their foreheads' (*Works*, p. 58).

Later in the century Tillotson similarly rejected Sergeant's premise 'that [Protestants] cannot by the Scriptures mean the Sense of them but the book'. Just as books of statute law can sufficiently convey knowledge to men, so Scripture can sufficiently convey Christ's doctrine; sense is inherent in both. Protestants 'mean by the Scriptures, Books written in such words as do sufficiently express the sense and meaning of Christ's Doctrine' (*Rule of Faith*, pp. 672, 673).

Ultimately the Protestant belief, that the Scriptures have an inherent and determinate sense, validly interpretable, required justification by a developed hermeneutic theory, including especially questions of authorial intention and historical context. John Wilson argued that the Scriptures 'have a true Sense *Originally* and *Essentially* in themselves, given them by their Author when they were first indited'; that 'the Sense of Scripture is fixt and immutable, not varying with the times, . . . no other than what it always had, and ever will have to the Worlds end'; that 'the Rule of Interpretation is that which gives us the objective Evidence by which the true Sense of Scripture is discern'd' (*The Scripture's Genuine Interpreter Asserted* (1678), pp. 5–6). Such a hermeneutic was essential to a sophisticated defence of the Anglican view of the status of the Holy Scripture in particular, and of the book in general. It is also strikingly, and unsurprisingly, close to the position of such a modern objectivist as Hirsch.

The Roman argument for oral tradition shifts meaning, and authority, away from the text itself, and places both in the hands of Rome, the divinely-authorized interpreter. The argument is, explicitly, not confined to the Bible, but applicable, in principle, to any book. John Sergeant argues that if we read Aristotle (an author who was to become the standard example for this area of the debate), we cannot be sure of his 'Certain Sence' unless

> the Point he writes on be first clear'd to us through a Scientifical discourse by word of mouth, made by some Interpreter vers'd in his Doctrin and perfectly acquainted with his meaning. . . . Now what a well-skill'd and insighted Interpreter or scientifical Explicator . . . is to such an Author, the same is *Tradition* to Scripture.
>
> (*Sure-Footing*, pp. 146–7)

In his reply to Sergeant, Tillotson concentrated on questions of the relative status of text and traditional commentary:

> Suppose there were a controversie now on foot, how Men might come to know what was the true *Art* of *Logick* which *Aristotle* taught his Scholars; and some should be of opinion, that the only

way to know this would be by Oral Tradition from his Scholars;
which he might easily understand by consulting those of the
present Age, who learned it from those who received it from them,
who at last had it from *Aristotle* himself: But others should think it
the surest way to study his *Organon*, a Book acknowledged by all
his Scholars, to have been written by himself, and to obtain that
Doctrine which he taught them.

(*Works*, p. 668)

Tillotson does not attempt to prohibit commentary, or to deny the
possible value of tradition: 'These have been of good helps.' To argue
for the possibility of valid interpretation does not logically presage
an end to all commentary, the mere reproduction of a supposedly
pristine text, untainted by explication. But Tillotson does insist on
the central status of the text as the 'measure and standard' of the
author's doctrine, communicated in 'the obvious sense of his words'.
There is a clear parallel with the Father's Will in the *Tale*: known to
have been written by its author, consisting of 'certain plain easy
directions', the repository of truth to which Martin and Jack have
eventually to appeal if they are to challenge Peter's forced and
forcing commentary. Peter is 'the Scholastick Brother' (*PW*, 1: 54),
not merely because he applies perverse ingenuity to particular
interpretative *cruces* but because he is characteristically a scholastic
commentator, heir to a tradition which decentralizes and destabilizes
Scripture. For Peter, his *scholia* replace the text itself; he allows no
appeal beyond his subjective interpretations to any objective, publicly
accessible truth.

Swift's examination of the relation of text and commentary is
not confined to Peter's interpretation of the Father's Will. At one
point the hack is confident that the '*Learned* among Posterity' 'will
appoint . . . Commentators upon this elaborate Treatise' (*PW*, 1: 70);
at another, that 'sublime Spirits . . . shall be appointed to labor in a
universal Comment upon this wonderful Discourse' (*PW*, 1: 118). He
proposes that each Prince of Christendom might 'take seven of the
deepest Scholars in his Dominions, and shut them up close for *seven*
Years, in *seven* Chambers, with a Command to write *seven* ample
Commentaries on this comprehensive Discourse' (*PW*, 1: 117). The
text indeed already presents itself as overwhelmed by commentary.
The kernel tale is introduced by a hack whose digressions, from the
start lengthy, become less and less discrete, and at last force the 'text'
out of sight altogether. The hack's account is reached only through a
maze of prefatory materials attributed to a variety of voices. Wotton's
notes are hoisted in, only to become themselves the subject of further
commentary: for example, to call the coats given to each of the three

sons 'the Garments of the *Israelites*' is 'an Error (with Submission) of
the learned Commentator; for by the Coats are meant the Doctrine
and Faith of *Christianity*' (*PW*, 1: 44). Clearly, the 'text' is becoming
replaced by, is *becoming*, its commentaries. The principle that *A Tale of
a Tub* exemplifies is stated clearly by the hack. Arguing as a Modern,
he insists that, 'tho' Authors need be little consulted, yet *C021icks*, and
Commentators, and *Lexicons* carefully must' (*PW*, 1: 93).

Formal parody of the gloss-making excesses of dull scholastic
pedantry was of course to become a familiar method of Augustan
humanist satire, reaching its apogee no doubt in the *Dunciad
Variorum*. There are, however, some theoretical and historical
implications of Swift's use of the form in *A Tale of a Tub* which need
further exploration. An article by Louis Hay discusses the history
of 'text' as term and concept. Hay points out that for a long time
an important sense of 'text' was 'les propres paroles d'un auteur,
considérées par rapport aux notes, aux commentaires, aux gloses'.[20]
These are the words of the French Academy Dictionary of 1786. Hay's
further citations make it clear that this sense of 'text' as something
specifically distinct from gloss or commentary was pervasive. The
examples in the *Oxford English Dictionary* ('text' sense 2) show that
this sense operated in England at least as early as the fourteenth
century. *OED*'s definition reads thus: '**text**: The very words and
sentences as originally written, . . . in the original form and order,
as distinguished from a commentary . . . or from annotations. Hence,
in later use, the body of any treatise, the authoritative or formal part
as distinguished from notes, appendices, introduction, and other
explanatory or supplementary matter.' The last sentence of *OED*'s
definition is obviously pertinent to the *Tale*, where distinction
between text and 'notes, appendices, introduction, and other
explanatory or supplementary matter' collapses.

Such a definition of 'text' is of course tendentious. The text
may be thought of as pure, formal, original, authorial, canonical.
Its commentary may be thought of as unauthorized, derivative,
distorted, corrupt, apocryphal. As Hay points out, 'what is implied
in such an arrangement is a distinction between the sacred and the
profane' (p. 65). To make the distinction so as to privilege the text,
to give it canonic status and accept it as the determinate statement
of an identifiable voice, is the Anglican position, the position of
Martin and, I think, of Swift. Anglicans regarded the text of the
Bible as, to use Barthes's changed terminology, a 'work'; 'the author
is reputed the father and the owner of his work: literary science
therefore teaches *respect* for the manuscript and the author's declared
intentions' ('From Work to Text', p. 160). Martin attempts to reform
his religion by 'serving the true Intent and Meaning of his Father's

Will' (*PW*, 1: 85). To collapse the distinction between text and gloss, to allow the original text to become subordinate to and lost in a controlling critical apparatus, is the position of Peter and the Modern writer. Both are scholiasts, writers of *scholia*. Both operate with a 'modern', scholastic view of textuality. In Barthes's words, 'no vital "respect" is due to the Text: it can be *broken* (which is just what the Middle Ages did with two nevertheless authoritative texts – Holy Scripture and Aristotle); it can be read without the guarantee of its father' ('From Work to Text', p. 161). The difference is that Peter and the Modern know that a text need not be 'broken' if it can be submerged or displaced by commentary.

The discussion of 'text' and Swift's *Tale* needs also to include another specific sense of the word: the material form of what we read, and its transmission. For most of this century, academic editing has worked on the assumption that it is the editor's task to recover the text intended by an author. The genealogy of this assumption may be traced back to the Renaissance humanists, who attempted to establish reliable texts of classical authors and, more especially, to go beyond the corrupted Vulgate and recover God's pristine Word. For the last two decades, however, debates about scholarly editing have increasingly had to address problems of textual ontology as well as technical problems of transmission. Is there an 'author'? What can 'intended' mean? What sense does it make to speak of 'the text', to entertain the belief that there is an original text to recover, or that confident reconstruction is possible? The posing of such questions acquired a special impetus from Roland Barthes's essay 'From Work to Text', and has grown stronger in the post-structuralist years. As early as 1971 Morse Peckham insisted, in an article entitled 'Reflections on the Foundations of Modern Textual Editing', that the textual editor works not with 'printed artifacts as physical objects' but with 'human behaviour in the past, human behaviour that no longer exists and cannot now be examined'. Inevitably, the editor's text is not a recovered original but a 'construct'. For Peckham, analytical bibliography, like historiography, cannot be 'scientific'; 'It is not talking about anything which is empirically, phenomenally, observable *now*, about anything which lies outside discourse.'[21] The Popperian answer is that discourse itself belongs to 'the world of intelligibles, or of *ideas in the objective sense*' (*Objective Knowledge*, p. 154), and is as much a real object for 'scientific' enquiry as nuclear physics. Popper makes the point explicitly in reference to textual editing. The 'method of problem solving, the method of conjecture and refutation', is common to science and the humanities; 'it is practised in reconstructing a damaged text as well as in constructing a theory of radioactivity' (p. 185). Deconstruction, however, has continued to mount a theoretical challenge to the notion that there is an 'ideal' text to reconstruct. Lee Patterson's words, in an essay on the iconoclastic Kane/Donaldson *Piers Plowman*, may be taken as a representative application of Derridean concepts to the theoretical field of editing: 'For the postmodern critic, the text is a *bricolage* . . . insofar as the subject is constituted by its enunciation rather than vice versa, the very concept of a holograph as a text inscribed by its author becomes problematic.'[22]

There is no disputing that *A Tale of a Tub* 'as a text inscribed by its author' is 'problematic'. The work does not bear Swift's name, and the Apology intimates, with what credibility it is hard to establish, that 'in the Authors Original Copy there were not so many Chasms as appear in the Book' (*PW*, 1: 9). The words of the 'modern' author come to us, sometimes for the modern's own tactical reasons, with the signal losses of faulty transmission: here there is a '*Hiatus in MS.*' (*PW*, 1: 37–38), there '*multa desiderantur*' (*PW*, 1: 107), in another place '*desunt nonnulla*' (*PW*, 1: 128). The modern's whispered explanation concerning one of the students of Bedlam evaporates into the safety of blanks (*PW*, 1: 113), and the note emphasizes that such chasms invite 'conjecture', and 'more than one interpretation'.

Such textual absences and polysemy seem certainly attributable to the Modern, but may not be so safely attributable to Swift. Whatever accidents the 'Original Copy' referred to in the Apology may have met with, it is at least clear that a concept of original copy exists. There is a stable text in the *Tale*, though the Modern author (understanding that to offer quotation as evidence is a deluded humanist empiricism) naturally does not attempt substantially to reproduce it. Swift himself, however, might be thought to have been so convinced of the effectiveness and value of humanist textual scholarship that he could think the project of textual reconstruction credible, if not unproblematic. Martin and Jack are able, once they have found the Father's Will, to make a '*Copia vera*' without apparent difficulty (*PW*, 1: 75). For Swift a true humanist textual criticism, whose business is to recover the lost original, is possible: 'By the Word *Critick*, have been meant, the Restorers of Antient Learning from the Worms, and Graves, and Dust of Manuscripts' (*PW*, 1: 57). This is the Modern's second kind of 'false' critic, by clear implication for the intelligent reader therefore not a Grubean pedant but a humanist scholar. Guthkelch and Nichol Smith's note here makes the appropriate comparison with Temple's praise of those editors who have 'restored' old copies, and 'recovered' the jewels of ancient learning from the dust and rubbish. Also possible, however, to those of less pure motive and more duncely skills, has been the perversion and distortion of the text. The 'main Precept' of the Father's Will is that the sons must not add to, or diminish, their religion without a 'positive Command in the Will' (*PW*, 1: 49). Where a command does not exist, commentary may supply it. Here, as elsewhere, the Modern does not quote from the Will, but the note of 1734 makes the obviously germane reference to the anathema in Revelations 22. 18, 19, against *textual* omissions and additions: 'If any man shall add unto these things, God shall add unto him the plagues that are written in this book: And if any man shall take away the words of the book of this prophecy, God shall take away his part out of the book of life.' Both Peter and Jack invite the curse. Peter justifies the addition to their coats of '*flame Coloured Sattin* for Linings' (the addition to religion of the doctrine of purgatory) by arguing the desirability of appending to the Will a new-fangled (in fact an Apocryphal) 'Codicil' (*PW*, 1: 52–53). Jack uses pieces and scrapings and inches of the Will on every occasion of his life. Taken short, he remains filthy because of his application of a 'Passage' (Revelations 22. 11) which may have been 'foisted in by the transcriber' (*PW*, 1: 122).

The *Tale* arguably presents a contrast, then, between a stated humanist belief in the possibility of recovery and transmission of a true copy, and that modern scepticism which displays the incoherence of textual transmission and allows subjective application of the text. In this the *Tale* echoes, once more, a characterizing disagreement between Roman and Anglican polemicists in the later seventeenth century. Romanists argued that all textual transmission is inescapably subject to error and corruption, whether accidental or malicious, and that the *Copia vera* is an impossible dream. Anglicans had to defend the Scripture as a rule of faith by arguing that true texts could indeed, given scholarly effort, good will, and God's help, be recovered from the dust and worms.

Rushworth sets out the normal Roman arguments particularly fully and clearly. Salvation or damnation are at issue; if Scripture is to be a judge of controversies, 'everie word, everie letter, and everie tit[t]le must be admitted of absolute and uncontrolable certaintie' (*Dialogues*, pp. 244–5). Scripture, however, is inevitably faulty, because of 'the multitudes of nations and languages' and the 'mutabilitie of the world, ever subject to a thousand accidents' (pp. 247, 248). Familiarly, to a modern editor of secular texts, the process of transcription introduces errors 'by the negligence of Servants, which copied the Bible', who may have been mercenary, or 'witlesse', or 'weary' (pp. 250–2, 253). For John Sergeant, similarly, the 'material characters' of Scripture are as liable to destruction, to be 'burnt, torn, blotted, worn out', as any other object in this fallen world. Its transmission has inevitably been subject to the weakness of mortal behaviour, and the many diverse readings of the numerous surviving copies show that 'Scripture's Letter may be uncertain in every tittle'.[23] For Romans, so long as textual transmission is a human activity, the certainty essential to faith is impossible. Just as meaning can be guaranteed only by the divine presence (immediately in God's own spoken words, mediately in the Church), so textual accuracy can be guaranteed only by divine providence. Just as Scripture's 'sense' is located not in the Scripture itself but in the Church, so the accuracy of a text of Scripture cannot be established by textual criticism, and may be validated only by the conformity of its readings with Church doctrine.[24]

In this debate the Romans had some inevitable laws of information transmission on their side. Human transcription must produce error. The attempt to bypass the series of transmission and return to a now-lost original is bound to involve some degree of editorial construction. In their replies Protestant apologists argued that reliable transmission of the Holy Scripture, as of other books, was in principle possible. Tillotson's words in *The Rule of Faith* are typical: 'The Books of Scripture are conveyed down to us, without any material corruption or alteration. And he that denies this, must . . . reject the authority of all Books, because we cannot be certain whether they be the same now as they were at first' (*Works*, pp. 660–1). Absolute textual accuracy, the 'tittles' on which Rushworth and Sergeant had insisted, was not essential, provided that those passages which communicate truths necessary to faith were not substantially faulty. Arthur Bury, Rector of Exeter College, insisted that:

> *The Scriptures cannot be denied to be sufficient*, though they may have suffered the common Fate of all long-lived Books, by Carelessness of Copiers, Fraud of Hereticks, or Dust of Time . . . if all the rest of the Scripture were lost, but only those Texts which proclaim those Truths, to the Belief whereof eternal Life is promised; those few texts would be sufficient.
>
> (*The Naked Gospel* (1690), p. 43)[25]

However much of a concession this may seem, there lies behind it a confident assumption that the Scripture, like other texts, like 'all long-lived Books', contains an essential message, and continues adequately to communicate even where noise intrudes. The evident contingency of transmission is not allowed to lead to a despairing scepticism. For Swift and his Anglican contemporaries, that scepticism was familiar both as a Romanist and as a deist position. John Sergeant had warned his Protestant opponents that to make Scripture, with its 'almost innumerable *Variae Lectiones*', a sole rule of faith was to leave

themselves without an answer to a deist's challenge, which Sergeant
imagined posed in these terms: 'All depends on the Truth of the
Copies immediately taken from the Original, or the very next to
them; which, what they were, by whom taken, where and how
preserved from time to time, how narrowly examined when they
were first transcribed . . . is buried in obscurity and oblivion' (*Sure-
Footing*, pp. 31–2). Sergeant was prophetic: precisely such a charge
would be made by the deist Anthony Collins in his *Discourse of
Free-Thinking* (1713). Understanding his position in the history
of this idea, Collins pointed out that 'the *Priests* of all Christian
Churches differ among themselves' about the copies, readings, and
senses of Scripture, and reminded his readers that 'the Popish Priests
contend that the Text of Scripture is so corrupted, precarious, and
unintelligible, that we are to depend on the Authority of the Church'
(pp. 54, 55). Worse, the chaos of text undercuts all books. Collins
quotes (translating from the original Latin) Whitby's apocalyptic
response to John Mills's listing of some thirty thousand textual
variants in the Greek New Testament: 'Nothing certain can be
expected from Books, where there are various Readings in every
Verse' (p. 89). Swift's parodic 'abstract' of Collins's, and Whitby's,
words on the textual unreliability of the Bible clearly implies Swift's
understanding that to attack scriptural authority is inevitably (and
in Swift's view absurdly) to question the book itself, to deny the
possibility of the transmission of doctrine and information in any
book at all:

> All *Christian* Priests differ so much about the Copies of [their
> Scriptures], and about the various Readings of the several
> Manuscripts, which quite destroys the Authority of the Bible: For
> what Authority can a Book pretend to, where there are various
> Readings? And for this reason, it is manifest that no Man can know
> the Opinions of *Aristotle* or *Plato*, or believe the Facts related by
> *Thucydides* or *Livy*, or be pleased with the Poetry of *Homer* and
> *Virgil*, all which Books are utterly useless, upon account of their
> various Readings.
>
> (*PW*, 4: 33)

Richard Bentley's devastating demolition of Collins (*Remarks upon
a Late Discourse of Freethinking* (1719)) insists, just as Swift does here,
that the textual case of Scripture is the same as that of other books.
Mills's listing of the Greek Testament's numerous variants did not,
as Whitby had feared and Collins had claimed, 'prove the Text of
Scripture precarious'; such variants, Bentley insists, 'must necessarily

have happened from *the Nature of Things*, and what are common and in equal proportion in all Classicks whatever'. The Scriptures are no less, and no more, subject to textual variation than other books. Like Swift, Bentley can afford to be relaxed about textual variance in Scripture, not because (with Père Simon, or modern textualists) he believes all text vulnerable and corrupt but because he is convinced the message an author intends can be adequately transmitted in a written text despite the inevitable accumulation of (generally minor) error. The ocean of meaning cannot be swallowed by one, or thirty thousand, soiled fish of the textual sea. Of ancient writers, such as Cicero and Plutarch, the 'Remains are sufficiently pure and genuine, to make us sure of the Writer's design'; the presence of 'a corrupt line or dubious reading' need not be thought 'to darken the whole Context'. Just as secular texts sufficiently communicate the author's intended meaning, so, despite all its textual changes, Scripture 'is perfect and sufficient to all the great ends and purposes of its first Writing'.[26]

This contextual evidence leads me to venture qualifications of some common assumptions in recent textualizing criticism of *A Tale of a Tub*. I am not convinced that the *Tale* is 'the most devastating onslaught on the authenticity of The Book in literary history to date' (Probyn, p. 189). Attacking the Book was a Roman Catholic activity: Anglicans tended to avoid sawing off the branch they sat on. It is reading particularly sharply against the grain to impute to Swift a radical textual scepticism which was evidently associated in his mind with the scholiasts, medieval and contemporary (and both 'modern') that he mocks, and with controvertists whose concern, for many decades before the *Tale*, had been to attack the Anglican Church and the assumptions about the nature and status of text upon which the Anglican Church indispensably and explicitly founded itself. The 'Apology' claims that the *Tale* 'celebrates the Church of *England* as the most perfect of all others in Discipline and Doctrine, it advances no Opinion they reject, nor condemns any they receive' (*PW*, 1: 2). Unless we are prepared to think this claim wholly disingenuous, or by reason of lapse of time or otherwise a wholly inaccurate account of Swift's intentions, we might do well to be cautious about reading into *A Tale of a Tub* attitudes to text radically opposite to fundamental Anglican positions.

Clive Probyn argues, in the context of the later debate with Collins, that for Swift the Bible was a special case; precisely because 'all language and therefore all texts are prone to deconstruct themselves', the anarchy of individualist reading must be corrected, must, 'in the single case of the Bible', be controlled by expert interpretation (p. 193). For Swift the Scriptures, for political as well as for religious reasons, needed to be vested with a distinguishing authority and respect. He knew that in a mortal world language and text are prone to be corrupted and forced (not, however, 'to deconstruct themselves'), and he had no naive misconception that the text of Scripture was angel-guarded. None the less, he did not consider Scripture a 'single case', and did not give up all the rest of written discourse as inevitably indeterminate, unstable, or opaque. Earlier Anglican writers, as I have said, in defending the text of Scripture as a rule of faith, explicitly and repeatedly defended the Bible on the grounds that, *like any other printed book*, it is determinable and comprehensible, an adequate means of conveying meaning. Any writing, in principle, may be good writing; though it may very well also be possible to write on nothing, to write darkly, deliberately to solicit misleading commentary.

We have learnt to collapse distinctions between primary and secondary texts, between author and critic. 'A strong reading is the only text', as Bloom puts it. Recent comment on *A Tale of a Tub* has therefore been less concerned with the possible difference between text and commentary. Probyn, for example, writes that '*self*-assertion as author *or* textual commentator is the sure Swiftian sign of amor sui' (p. 190). Authorship as the 'modern' conceives it, no doubt, for Swift is mere self-love. *A Tale of a Tub*, however, exemplifies throughout the essential Anglican (and humanist) distinction between a present real author and a parasitic commentator, between sacred original text and corrupt gloss. In *Gulliver's Travels* Swift uses Aristotle, as earlier Anglican apologists had done, as his exemplary case in the argument against self-serving commentary and its distortions of authorial meaning; Gulliver summons Aristotle, and Homer, to Glubbdubdrib, and learns that their commentators keep their distance in the lower world, shamed 'because they had so horribly misrepresented the Meaning of those Authors to Posterity' (*PW*, 11: 197).

Is it safe to assume Swift finds text problematic and speech divine and safe? Terry Castle argues that Swift's model of speech and writing is Platonic: 'The written object is a material rendering of something ideal, the pure world of speech' (p. 34). This does not in fact seem very convincingly supported by Castle's references to Swift's text itself, either to the fourth Voyage of *Gulliver's Travels* (in which the Houyhnhnms' purely oral traditions lead them to debate repeatedly the single proposition, 'whether the *Yahoos* should be exterminated from the Face of the Earth') (*PW*, 11: 271), or to the *Tale*, which includes a lengthy satire on aeolist oral preaching. (The aeolists should perhaps put us in mind of the Platonic view of good, 'pneumatological', 'natural writing', 'immediately united to the voice and to breath'.)[27] According to Castle, the account in the 'Apology' of the imperfect transmission of the text of the *Tale* 'hints' that all texts are 'impure in regard to the world of spoken discourse, which maintains here an assumed priority' (p. 34). This assumption of the priority of the voice seems to me nowhere stated or implied in the 'Apology' or in the *Tale* itself. Such an accommodation of Swift's writing as Castle makes to an originally Platonic, and wholly alien, textual value-system, seems to me possible only as a consequence of seeking what meanings the *Tale* may have through its absences, and, more especially, by operating without reference to contexts of textual theory in the years immediately before Swift wrote the *Tale*, contexts which at least define the terms of debate and at most delimit the lines of textual argument open to Swift.

Criticism of *A Tale of a Tub* used to assume that Swift made a distinction between competent and incompetent writing. The Hack writes badly, and invites indulgent interpretation, but there is a plain and meaningful text, the Will, whose interpretation is possible and necessary. Castle, however, denies that it is possible to 'separate good texts from bad texts'; 'No text is privileged in regard to truth; no text is scriptural' (Castle, p. 37). The Will is not only corrupted and distorted but also, in itself, 'a deathly, parasitic, artefact' (p. 35), feeding off the speech that gave it birth. These conclusions do not follow logically from the *Tale*. The aim of the *Tale* is 'to expose the Abuses and Corruptions in Learning and Religion' ('Apology', *PW*, 1: 6). To attack abuses and corruptions is not, as the 'Apology' insists, necessarily to attack learning or religion themselves, nor does such an attack logically deny the possibility of a genuine learning or a true religion. Many of the abuses and corruptions are, certainly, textual. The existence of corrupt texts is not, however, proof that all texts are, because of the nature of textuality itself, corrupt. More especially, the practice of abusive methods of interpretation of the Will is not proof either of the Will's inherent corruption or of the impossibility of believing in good interpretation. There is no disputing that Swift's satire reflects 'upon the problematic status of the written word' (Castle, p. 33), its vulnerability to mistransmission and misinterpretation. It is natural that a modern textual scepticism would wish to appropriate this central concern and energy in the *Tale* in support of the much more radical proposition that *all* text is fundamentally and inevitably 'compromised, de-natured, separated from truth at its moment of origin' (Castle, p. 35). Nothing in the *Tale*, however, gives clear indication that Swift held this much more extreme position, and the powerful and immediately relevant intellectual context I have outlined makes it very unlikely that he could possibly have done so.

I do not wish to simplify. Clearly the meaning or meanings of *A Tale of a Tub* are not straightforwardly given by, or in any simple way controlled by, the context of intellectual debate I have outlined. Recent textualizing critics have indispensably focused attention on Swift's obsessive concern with the nature, status, and stability of writing itself. I do, however, wish to argue that we now too readily impute to Swift a notion of text to which he simply cannot have subscribed. Of course, Swift is not Chillingworth, or Tillotson, or Ehrenpreis. But he is not Rabbi Isaac, or Bossuet, or Derrida, either.

Notes

1. IRVIN EHRENPREIS, *Literary Meaning and Augustan Values* (Charlottesville, VA, 1974), pp. 49–60 (p. 54).

2. ROLAND BARTHES, 'From Work to Text', in *Roland Barthes: Image, Music, Text*, selected and trans. STEPHEN HEATH (London, 1977), p. 157.

3. CLIVE PROBYN, 'Haranguing upon Texts: Swift and the Idea of the Book', in *Proceedings of the First Münster Symposium on Jonathan Swift*, ed. HERMANN J. REAL and HEINZ J. VIENKEN (Munich, 1985). pp. 187–97 (p. 188).

4. NIGEL WOOD, *Swift* (Brighton, 1986), p. 38.

5. THOMAS DOCHERTY, *On Modern Authority* (Brighton, 1987), pp. 246, 247.

6. TERRY CASTLE, 'Why the Houyhnhnms Don't Write: Swift, Satire and the Fear of the Text', *Essays in Literature*, 7 (1980), 31–44 (p. 37).

7. *The Dialogues of William Richworth or the Judgment of Common Sense in the Choise of Religion* (Paris, 1640); *An Answer to Some Passages in Rushworth's Dialogues*, printed in Chillingworth's *Works*, ninth edition (1719).

8. *The Rule of Faith; Or, An Answer to the Treatise of Mr. J. S. Entituled, Sure-Footing, &c* (1666). All quotations from Tillotson in this chapter are from the *Works*, third edition (1701).

9. Quotations in this chapter from PÈRE SIMON are from *A Critical History of the Old Testament. Written Originally in French by Father Simon . . . Translated into English by a Person of Quality* (London, 1682).

10. See, for example, PAOLO SARPI, *Histoire du Concile de Trent*, 2 vols (London, 1736), I: 242, 254.

11. *The Catholick Representer*, Second Part (1687), p. 45.

12. SIMON, *Critical History of the Old Testament*, Author's Preface b1ʳ.

13. TILLOTSON, *Rule of Faith, Works*, pp. 658, 659, 674.

14. See KARL POPPER, *Objective Knowledge* (Oxford, 1979), pp. 106, 115.

15. E. D. HIRSCH, *Validity in Interpretation* (New Haven, CT, 1967), pp. 4, 13.

16. PLATO, *Phaedrus*, trans. WALTER HAMILTON (Harmondsworth, 1973), pp. 97–9.

17. 'The Breaking of Form', in HAROLD BLOOM et al., *Deconstruction and Criticism* (New York, 1979), pp. 7–8.

18. See RUSHWORTH, *Dialogues*, pp. 276–7.

19. See Bossuet, *Exposition*, p. 162.

20. Louis Hay, 'Does "Text" Exist?', *Studies in Bibliography*, 41 (1988), 64–75 (p. 64).

21. *Proof*, 1 (1971), 122–55 (pp. 127–8, 131, 132–3).

22. Lee Patterson, 'The Logic of Textual Criticism and the Way of Genius: The Kane–Donaldson *Piers Plowman* in Historical Perspective', in *Textual Criticism and Literary Interpretation*, ed. Jerome J. McGann (Chicago, 1985), pp. 55–91 (p. 89).

23. See *Sure-Footing*, pp. 37–8.

24. See Simon, *Critical History of the Old Testament*, III, 166.

25. See Tillotson, *Works*, p. 678.

26. *Remarks upon a Late Discourse of Freethinking*, in *Enchiridion Theologicum*, ed. John Randolph, 5 vols (1792), V: 156, 160, 163, 173–4.

27. See Jacques Derrida, *Of Grammatology*, trans. Gayatri Spivak (Baltimore, MD, 1976), p. 17.

6 The Authority of Satire*

Everett Zimmerman

Narrative tends to represent itself as a version of the flux of life,
always including too much to be intelligible without some systematic
reduction. Even the parables of the New Testament are often not
convincingly circumscribed by their apparent point: 'A narrative of
some length, like the Good Samaritan, works hard to make the answer
obvious and in so doing provides a lot of information which seems
too important to be discarded, once the easy act of completion is
performed.'[1] Historians too find that narrative, itself an interpretation
of prior events, is not easily subdued to its intended analytical
meaning: 'The historian must "interpret" his data by excluding
certain facts as irrelevant to his narrative purpose. On the other hand,
in his efforts to reconstruct "what happened" in any given period
of history, the historian inevitably must include in his narrative
an account of some event for which the facts that would permit
a plausible explanation of its occurrence are lacking.'[2] Literature,
Northrop Frye suggests, exhibits a tension between linear movement
and 'the integrity . . . of completed form'.[3] Linear movement is
narrative, and formal integrity is meaning. Formal integrity is,
however, sometimes defined only in relation to an extrinsic
interpretive theory, which is granted authority by a privileged
institution. Furthermore, like history, some works of literature
claim a relationship to an external reality or system that does not
adequately subsume their narrative aspects.

In allegory, for example, an opposition of narrative to meaning
is sometimes apparent. The narrative is, on occasion, presented as
yielding to a meaning rather than being identical to it, needing a
figure like Interpreter in *The Pilgrim's Progress* or a book like the Bible
to control the narrative. Satire has an obvious affinity to allegory,
although only some satires are accepted as allegorical. Both presume

---

* Reprinted from *Swift's Narrative Satires* (Ithaca, NY: Cornell University Press,
1983), pp. 17–35.

that reader and author share a context that remains incompletely represented in the narrative. Consequently, the interpretive model provided by allegory – the narrative read as if it were an oblique version of a prior book, scheme of thought, or historical situation – is widely accepted as appropriate to satire.[4] Satire thus shares allegory's difficult relationships to narrative. Satire aims to confine the apparent fluctuations of narrative within an evaluative framework. The genre invites us to share the godlike vision of the satirist, in which our usual imperceptiveness is regarded as symptomatic of our debased condition. Satire is static and conceptual; narrative is a process and evades conceptualization.

Satire often uses allegory to reveal the gap between earthly process and moral imperative. The allegorical as a creative, or interpretive, strategy is conveniently adaptable to the metaphysical view that the secular and the sacred, body and spirit, are intimately connected. But allegory alternatively implies that the physical is only an appearance beyond which lies a spiritual reality. These differing uses of allegory can be seen if we compare *The Divine Comedy* to *The Pilgrim's Progress*: Dante emphasizes the connections of the sacred to the secular, Bunyan their opposition. Narrative is allied to the secular and the literal – the world treated as independent – while allegory implies the incompleteness and disorder of narrative and of the world that narrative reflects. It is exaggerated but not entirely wrong to regard our assumption of an affinity between the terms 'literal', 'realism', 'narrative', and 'novel' as a reflection of the triumph of secularism. As the novel becomes the dominant narrative form, its claim of literalism is thought to give it a validity that allegory lacks.

Swift's major satires, *A Tale of a Tub* and *Travels into Several Remote Nations of the World*, make the oppositions of the literal and the allegoric, and of narrative and satire, into both formal and thematic concerns. The tale-teller divides his work into narrative segments and digressive commentary, losing both narrative continuity and satiric focus. Eventually he questions even the premises of satire, having eroded the moral framework by which he distinguishes what we praise from what we abominate. Gulliver imposes a travel narrative on his satire, implying that satire is embedded in the very movement of existence. But his generic distinctions become risible as his narrative encapsulates materials that are not assimilable to travel literature.

Swift satirizes the interpretive procedures of both of his narrators. In the *Tale*, he puts in narrative form a satirical account of the history of biblical interpretation in which the dominating issue is the relationship of the literal to the allegorical. He replicates the distinction between the two in formal aspects of the *Tale* and the

131

Travels, in one of which the narrator embraces the allegorical, in the other the literal. *A Tale of a Tub* is heavily metaphoric and allusive, the *Travels into Several Remote Nations of the World* resolutely literal and spare. Both the dogged secularization in the *Travels* and the frenetic attempts at spiritualization in the *Tale* represent the self-serving choices of their putative authors, who illustrate the unstable elements in the Protestantism of Swift's time. Swift creates a vision that reveals the limits of these styles. While providing a critique of the metaphysical underpinnings of the secular literalism that Ian Watt and others have regarded as exemplified in the new fiction of the eighteenth century, Swift's satires also expose the allegorizers as obscurantists who act from self-interest.

Swift's *Tale of a Tub* reflects both the changing biblical interpretation of the Reformation[5] and the implications of biblical criticism for the interpretation of secular works. In the brothers' manipulations of the will, Swift parodies both the allegorization characteristic of Roman Catholic biblical interpretation and the literalism characteristic of Protestant, especially Puritan, interpretation. Furthermore, he extends the specifically religious issues of the *Tale* to more general questions about writers and readers, about allegory and allegoresis. As Maureen Quilligan remarks, Swift is concerned with 'the dangerous tendencies of readers, particularly "modern" readers, to become more powerful than their texts'.[6] In addition, Swift explores the authority of writer over reader, in which lies the possibility of a demagoguery that exceeds the restraints of a text and of the world external to the text but putatively reflected in it. The *Tale's* narrator adapts the methods of biblical exegesis to the production of meanings that exalt the writer: his description of 'Oratorial Receptacles or Machines, contains a great Mystery, being a Type, a Sign, an Emblem, a Shadow, a Symbol, bearing Analogy to the spacious Commonwealth of Writers, and to those Methods by which they must exalt themselves to a certain Eminency above the inferiour World' (*PW*, 1: 37). When Swift erupts into the controversies of biblical interpretation in the crucial period of the late seventeenth and early eighteenth centuries, he focuses on the demand for private authority that characterizes authors and interpreters alike. The three brothers' operations upon the Will are governed by their own wills, and the narrator demands that his text too be interpreted in accord with his desires for acclaim.

In adopting an allegorical form for his *Tale* in a time when allegory was vanishing, Swift emphasizes the questions of interpretation and authorial authority that result from the shift in the religious and epistemological situations of his time. Maureen Quilligan argues that 'allegory always presupposes at least a potential sacralizing power in language, and it is possible to write and read allegory intelligently only in those cultural contexts which grant to language a significance beyond that belonging to a merely arbitrary system of signs'.[7] Writing in a context in which language is increasingly granted only the power to represent the private vision of its user, Swift measures the implicit claims of allegory against the explicit desires of his putative author. The narrator of the *Tale* claims a sacralizing power for his language but exposes his entirely secular aims as he does so. In Protestant literalism, the incarnate Word, God in history, was used to retain both letter and spirit within the language of Scripture. But in a world in which writing reveals a private vision and interpretation another, perhaps incongruent, one, the Word becomes words. Appropriately enough, after the failure of the Puritan revolution and ·during the rise of empiricism, Swift uses an allegorical form to scrutinize inspiration and interpretation in relation to both sacred and secular texts.

The narrator of the *Tale* accords his work scriptural status, hoping to be translated by 'the most Reverend Fathers the *Eastern* Missionaries' (*PW*, 1: 65). The reader is encouraged both to interpret the *Tale* and to see it, like Scripture, as a compendium of interpretations of all thought and history. The narrator connects his work to biblical exegesis and to the interpretive tradition in which classical texts are allegorized to expose the true meaning hidden in an ostensibly different story. The work contains '*Innuendo's*' for the benefit of the commentators who must illuminate its dark points (*PW*, 1: 118), and it attempts to draw other works into its own compass: for example, the *Tale* completes Homer, having 'exhausted all that Human Imagination can *Rise* or *Fall* to' (*PW*, 1: 80). The various systems from which the tale-teller derives his authority, however, are blatantly arbitrary. Although he claims to absorb all history into his text, he obliterates history: 'But I here think fit to lay hold on that great and honourable Privilege of being the *Last Writer*; I claim an absolute Authority in Right, as the *freshest Modern*, which gives me a Despotick Power over all Authors before me' (*PW*, 1: 81). His modernist claim substitutes the author for history.

The *Travels into Several Remote Nations of the World* appears to be a very different kind of book. Gulliver resolutely avoids both the allegorization and the figural claims that are characteristic of the tale-teller. The narration of the *Travels* is determinedly flat, avoiding historical and literary analogies even when they seem obvious. The tale-teller takes every opportunity, even a pun, to imply that his work has some deeper, or higher, or broader, or just 'other', meaning than is apparent. But when, in one of his very few acknowledged allusions to other writers, Gulliver quotes Virgil to defend his own veracity, he writes with no suggestion that he knows the context that gives Sinon's speech a meaning differing from the literal (*PW*, 11: 292).

A Tale of a Tub parodies the text that accretes authority from a prior text, the *Travels* the text that acquires authority from its literal rendering of nature. The *Tale* mimes an attempt to subsume all other claims to authority, the *Travels* an attempt to supplant all other claims to authority. These sharply dissimilar procedures have a similar aim – authority and autonomy for the narrator. The tale-teller makes his book so indiscriminately suggestive that he seems to be attempting to imply in figure and allegory all other thought. Gulliver makes his book so singular that he seems to be claiming all its implications as his own. He suppresses the suggestiveness of his story, making it his unique experience. In one case, the inclusiveness of the story gives its author final literary authority. In the other case, exclusivity achieves the same end. Both Gulliver and the tale-teller exert a 'Despotick Power over all Authors before' (*PW*, 1: 81). Gulliver, like the tale-teller, attributes a scriptural authority to his book. Not only does he insist on the absoluteness of the truth of his book, but he believes that his vision of the goodness embodied in the Houyhnhnms would have put a stop 'to all Abuses and Corruptions' if the English Yahoos had not been incorrigible (*PW*, 11: 6).

Allegory relies on some prior condition, conceptualization or, often, book for its authority. But instead of giving the source outside the text, the pre-text, a privileged position (for example, as *The Pilgrim's Progress* is related to the Bible), satire demeans it.[8] When related to a privileged pre-text, allegory acquires an authority external to its author, but when the pretext is suppressed or demeaned, this authority is weakened, making us rely on the author. Instead of suppressing this sense of diminished authority in a satirical allegory, Swift emphasizes it. One method of acquiring authority for the author of a narrative is to consolidate the forces of author and narrator, having the narrator display a wisdom within the narrative that reflects his creator's wisdom. Another method is to set author and narrator against each other, the obvious failures of the narrator pointing to the author's superiority. In the first of these methods the narrator becomes part of a personal allegory as the author's representative; in the second, the narrator represents some evil within an historical allegory. But Swift's narrators are only with difficulty relegated to either function. Instead, they resist identification with the author by usurping his role. Both the tale-teller and Gulliver are satirists who are aware of the evils that are represented in their narratives. And both explicitly display themselves as authors and discuss questions of their craft. Their self-display is bumptious and aggressive, however, not a sober display of authorial responsibility. Instead of being a conduit for Swift, these narrators make it difficult to apprehend him.

The distinction may be made more apparent by means of a comparison to *The Drapier's Letters*. The drapier is biographically distinguished from Swift, but he controls the ironies of the letters, and he shows his awareness of the evils that he describes rather than his implication in, or obfuscation of, them. Although he represents only one version of Swift's view, he is used as a particularly apt explicator of the dangers of Wood's halfpence and not as an oblique example of a complex evil that he does not acknowledge. This interpretive model will work only imperfectly for the *Travels*. Gulliver is indeed an apt viewpoint from which to observe the satiric scene. As a character, he undergoes experiences that convince him that humans are justly an object of satire. He also interacts with that scene, sometimes becoming an exemplar of evils that he describes. Still, we need posit no great separation between Gulliver and Swift as long as the failures of the character are marked, even implicitly, by the narrator: noting the failures of a life, especially our own, is a way of showing our perspicuity as well as our continuity with the flawed life. But the attempt to reduce the dissonance between Gulliver and Swift is sabotaged by Gulliver's explicit manipulation of generic conventions. Gulliver aggressively and unbelievably defines his book's origin as bare truth unaccommodated to the conventions of fiction. He suppresses his book's obvious similarities to a multitude of other familiar works, insisting that it embodies only the eyewitness veracity characteristic of the best travel literature. Gulliver's ruminations on the appropriate genre for the *Travels*, and his invidious comparisons of lying books to his truthful one, are not just the conventional claims of satire to truth. While attempting to establish his literal perspective, Gulliver calls attention to his literary ambitions and his shaping imagination rather than to his veracity. He attempts to place his reader at the appropriate vantage not only for understanding the experiences recorded in the book but also for understanding the achievements of Gulliver as author.

Questions of genre inevitably raise questions of authorial stance, putative or real. Genre suggests both a certain kind of event and a shaping of the event to fit a conventional literary pattern. In satire the event is often pitted against its literary shaping, as when in mock epic an inappropriately small event is shaped according to the patterns conventionally used for epic events. But whether the result is a satire or an incompetent imitation depends on the reader's hypothesis about authorial stance: 'As Virgil is said to have read *Ennius*, out of his Dunghill to Draw Gold; so may our Author read Shakespear, Milton, and Dryden, for the contrary End, to bury their Gold in his own Dunghill.'[9] When the author implied by the work is aware of the demeaning effects of an incongruous juxtaposition of

135

form and content, we have a satire either of the content or of the form – satiric parody. If the parody is unmarked by an external perspective, however, we have a difficult problem of interpretation. Hugh Kenner makes the interesting observation that 'To Augustus' is just the kind of poem an inept poet (Ambrose Philips, for example) might have written. It becomes a satire when Pope signs it, identifying himself as the obviously knowing creator of an inept work.[10]

Swift complicates rather than simplifies this interpretive problem by dramatizing his narrators themselves as ambitious authors who are also perceptive satirists. The narrator-author of the *Tale*, for example, is both aware of human weakness and perversely willful. Like Gulliver, he organizes a satiric commentary, and also, by means of his generic choices and manipulations, exhibits his own shaping imagination. His expressed intent is to narrate a story of three brothers, obviously a historical allegory, but eventually the allegory is absorbed by his mock encomium of the moderns, and the mock encomium itself becomes a praise of the fool who narrates it. The form that makes the greatest claim to objectivity – the historical allegory – is absorbed by the self who narrates. The tale-teller's exhibition of the craft of his work – his division of it into instruction and delight – finally leads to an attempted display of tale-telling without a tale. Generic choices here, and in the *Travels*, are dramatized not as inevitable results of the historical or putatively historical content of the narration but as the narrator's way of making use of his story.

The explicit introduction of authorial choices and rationalizations into the texts implies that the satirical allegory is to some degree the creation of the narrator and, consequently, is symptomatic of him. The narrator as author is not, then, simply one among other satiric targets, for example, a figure who sometimes conducts Swift's attack against dissenters and at other times exemplifies the modern authors whom Swift despises. While the satire may be grasped as a series of local effects independent of any comprehensive form, such a reading is unsatisfactory, given the presence of an author-narrator whose literary shapings are made so apparent. The narrator's depiction as author gives him a priority over other objects of the satire.

Swift's image of the modern author as a combination of blindness and insight depicts the possibilities for understanding at a moment in history when absolute truths are asserted but the basis for man's appreciation of them has been undermined. Nature and Scripture remain values for Swift, but he is intensely aware that man's understanding of both is the product of a private mind with solipsistic proclivities. Consequently any conception of nature figuring its own meanings is compromised. The authorial dilemma that Swift dramatizes became conventional in later fiction: no perspective is total, all is interpreted, and the shape of literature is not congruent with that of life. Swift shows his narrative coming into being because of a particular perspective, not because it has an objective, uninterpreted existence.

But placed against this dramatized subjectivity is the implication of satiric allegory that its norms are impersonal. In satire the narrative is itself presumed to imply a normative shape. These satires, with their emphasis on their creators, call into question the very possibility of satire. Without at least the pretense that it represents a pre-existent situation, the work loses any polemical import.[11] Satire ought, in a loose sense, to be emblematic or figural: it assumes a meaning in things themselves or in history itself. Its fictions imply that its words are connected to things that figure their own meanings.

The reader's position in relation to an authorial position as ambiguous as that represented in Swift's works is difficult. Swift appears in the interstices between the putative author's meaning and the meaning that is assumed to be inherent in the narrative events. The incongruities within the work imply that an author controls the limited narrator, but the incongruities are not thereby resolved. In a sense, the reader's control of the work partakes of the same arbitrary nature as the narrator's. The reader's vantage is his or her own interpretation of the narrator's tale. Readers may choose to subordinate the narrator to the historical allegory or the historical allegory to the narrator, because Swift rules out neither approach. Swift is there as the figure we may use to lend authority to either interpretive mode.[12] Indeed, a history of the exegesis of Swift's satires might divide his commentators into those who emphasize the narrative aspects of his works and those who emphasize the satiric allegory. Commentators on narrative are concerned with narrators, process, continuity; their opponents accuse them of turning satires into novels. People concerned with satiric allegory tend to focus on image and referentiality; their interest lies in the confining of history within a conceptualized moral scheme that fixes process in the summary judgment. Their opponents accuse them of reducing narrative to polemic, of discarding the richness of means that is inapplicable to their neat summations of end.

Swift exposes the literariness of satire, just as Lucian exposes Homeric epic. For Swift, satire is not a privileged form, and its author is not exempted from explicit scrutiny. Satire conventionally winks at those of its implications that do not facilitate its polemical intents. And readers blink at those aspects of satire that do not fit the polemical intent preordained by the author's biography and expository writing. Still, Swift's satires demand of us the difficult process of searching for an authoritative perspective rather than just assuming Swift's perspective.

Swift articulates a crux that occurs in the interpretation of art and nature when the relationship between words and things is perceived to be unstable. St Thomas Aquinas's view of the relationship between words and things implies that words designate things and that the things designated by the words have their own meanings. Meaning is increased without becoming contradictory. But the new science suppresses the emblematization of nature, substituting a science of primary qualities. Dealing with the gap between the differing meanings of word and thing, the Royal Society attempts to bridge it, to make the word signify a true conceptualization of a thing. This use of language is an attempt to evade the apparent truth that the words represent only the private understanding of their user. An experiment described properly ought to have its benefits conveyed with universal success. Both Aquinas and the Royal Society attempt to give to language an authority beyond the intention of its author: it represents more, or perhaps less in the case of the Royal Society, than an author's meanings. Because the gap between thing and word, or conception and word, does not quite vanish, however, there remains unacknowledged personal allegory – a private meaning always intervenes between word and thing. In tracing the consequences of the new scientific view in the later eighteenth century, Earl Wasserman remarks that the older relationship of physical, moral, and spiritual is reduced to a relationship between the material world and qualities of mind: 'Correspondences had become a phase of psychology, not ontology.'[13] Swift's narrative satires articulate this process of verbal and ontological change.

Satire's customary attack on other literature is its way of obliterating the gap between word and thing. Satire defines itself as nonliterature, making its words represent the filthy things themselves and its judgments those of nature. But as Alvin Kernan has argued, the dynamics of satire tend to draw satirists into their scene, making them at one with the things they satirize.[14] Swift's narrative satires are extreme versions of this centripetal force. In Swift, in fact, the satirist threatens to absorb the scene. Revealing their fictive manipulations, Swift's narrators expose satire as literature, as an author's product, not the world's.

There is finally no conflict between the polemical purposes and the literary forms of Swift's narrative satires. Swift's most inclusive polemical purpose is to allow no privileged human perspective. This purpose is consonant with his politics. His objection to Hobbes's politics is that Hobbes lodged in a single ruler the power that should be given to an elected legislature.[15] And Swift recognized that such a legislature too might make laws that contradict the very nature of things. With all his Hobbesian assumptions about human propensities for civil disorder, Swift was, nevertheless, not about to accept the Hobbesian solution for the conflicts engendered by human subjectivity – endowing with absolute authority another equally fallible human.

The key theorist who attempts to reconcile human and divine authority is in Swift's time still Richard Hooker, whose argument (one closely related to that of St Thomas Aquinas) is that reason and revelation are both authoritative. People are governed by Scripture and also by natural law, which is derived from God and is manifested in his creation. Consequently a human society may make laws that, in reflecting natural law, are also in accord with God's laws. Hooker views the seeming oppositions of the secular and the sacred as complementary, capable finally of being reconciled in a society with a united church and state, neither having to be subordinated to the other. This vision of society is based on a belief in the universality of reason. Conferred by God, reason allows people to organize a secular society that is in harmony with God's order.

Still, changes in the seventeenth-century conception of reason undermined Hooker's views. According to Peter Munz's analysis, Hooker's reason is 'the same [as] it had been to the Middle Ages and to Antiquity; it implied an intuitive as well as a discursive element'.[16] But the term narrowed during the seventeenth century, becoming especially relevant to the inductive and deductive processes. According to Hooker, natural laws are 'investigable by reason, without the help of Revelation supernatural and divine', but Hooker's investigation of natural laws is not advanced by Baconian empiricism or by Cartesian rationalism: 'The world hath always been acquainted with them.'[17] Considered after the débâcle of the Puritan revolution and the increased influence of the new science, Hooker's faith in reason must have seemed old-fashioned, although a version of it survived in the Cambridge Platonists. When man is studied empirically, he may appear more or less rational, but Hooker's concept of reason is philosophically and theologically derived, not empirically discovered.

Swift's writings in defense of the relationship of church and state in England generally accord with the position of Hooker. Swift's view is that the dissolution of the connections between the sacred and the secular, church and state, spirit and body, leads to unrestrained and arbitrary individualism. Even if these connections engender constant tensions, Swift regards the abandoning of either of their terms as willful. But despite this general consonance with Hooker's view, Swift also perceives the difficulties of accepting

Hooker's faith in the practical efficacy of reason in human society. Against the theoretical claims of Hooker's reason, Swift's empirical vision too makes its demands. As John Traugott observes, 'Swift's radical undermining of reason and will brings into question the fundamental assumption of Hooker's church, which is that the *societas perfectus* is founded on reason and through reason, laws, both effects of God's grace'.[18]

In the 'Argument Against Abolishing Christianity', Swift measures the distance between Hooker's formulations and a fictional version of the condition of Christian society in England. Hooker writes: 'The general and perpetual voice of men is as the sentence of God himself. For that which all men have at all times learned, Nature herself must needs have taught, and God being the author of Nature, her voice is but his instrument' (I: vii, 3). Swift's speaker reduces Hooker's 'general and perpetual voice' to 'this Majority of Opinion': 'a Design to oppose the Current of the People; which besides the Folly of it, is a manifest Breach of the Fundamental Law, that makes this Majority of Opinion the Voice of God' (*PW*, 2: 26). The speaker of the *Argument* appears to resist the majority who wish to repeal Christianity, but his argument is an analysis of their actual practical interests, not of their mistakenly assumed ones: as Christianity has no moral effects on this majority, its few practical benefits need not be forgone. Rather than opposing the majority, he is clarifying their true interests by revealing their mistaken assumptions.

Swift's speaker directly attacks freethinkers, dissenters and, less prominently, Catholics. He himself appears to be the voice of Anglicanism, defending Christianity and, in addition, the sacramental test. But he defines a world from which Hooker's reason has vanished (although his church remains established). There is no possible appeal to a discernible natural law that connects human institutions to divine law. The speaker's defense of Christianity makes no claims that are not secular and dependent purely on human self-interest. Religion itself has become a matter not of reason that compels but of arbitrary choice: 'As long as we leave in Being a God, and his Providence, with all the necessary Consequences . . . , we do not strike at the Root of the Evil' (*PW*, 2: 37).

Between Hooker and Swift's speaker, an unorthodox response to the Puritan theocracy intervenes – Hobbes's *Leviathan*, 'that *Mortall God*, to which wee owe under the *Immortall God*, our peace and defence'.[19] The Leviathan is the sovereign who includes all, even those who oppose him: 'Because the major part hath by consenting voices declared a Soveraigne; he that dissented must now consent with the rest' (II, 17, p. 231). In a Christian commonwealth, this sovereign is God's viceregent, and people should 'observe for a Rule, that Doctrine, which in the name of God, hee commanded to bee taught' (III, 36, p. 468). Hobbes's law of nature merely induces people to arrange a peace, nothing other than self-preservation having a claim before enforceable positive laws are created. Hobbes and the Puritans are, in a sense, the opposites that meet. As a consequence of the radical egocentrism of their versions of humanity, religion becomes a secular power in both. Seeing people as totally depraved, the Puritans accept a theocracy that claims biblical authority; seeing people as totally self-interested (a secular version of total depravity), Hobbes accepts only an absolute monarch. In both cases, the end result is arbitrary power.

Hobbists, Puritans, and the physico-theologians (who aimed to reach theological truth through the scientific study of nature) – each attempted to find an authority that would fix the meanings of nature and Scripture. Faced with nature, the Puritans subordinated it to Scripture, in order to provide a common standard for nature's interpretation. But then the interpretation of Scripture too needed an authoritative basis. The vilified Hobbes solved the problem without the appropriate sanctions of nature or Scripture. Faced with nature, Hobbesian man invents religion as an explanation for the causes of things – depending sometimes on 'fancy', sometimes on the authority of various other people (*Leviathan*, I, 12, p. 169). To halt this subjectivity, he then creates the commonwealth, a Leviathan to subsume him. Hobbes's solution, like the Puritan one, merely substitutes one subjectivity for another, but it does so openly. The physico-theologians seemed to have a solution that would escape both Hobbism and Puritanism. They directly harmonized Scripture and nature, seemingly reaching a confirmation of Scripture by empirical studies of nature. The results, as we now know, were not what the physico-theologians intended. Instead of confirming Scripture, they drove a wedge between it and a scientific version of nature.

To view these issues in a specifically literary context, we may turn to John Milton, who, by Swift's time, was the salient exemplar of the literary merging of the private and the sacred. Edward Said goes as far as to argue that while *The Divine Comedy* is an 'implantation of the Biblical text in the here and now', *Paradise Lost* is 'characterized by the intention to exceed all previous texts': 'To Dante the original texts require confirmation and incarnation in what Auerbach calls the earthly world, whereas Milton sees his text aspiring to the place of inauguration, as if to protest the usurpation of the beginning place by an antecedent text.'[20]

In *The Prophetic Milton*, William Kerrigan traces the tradition of the inspired poet, the *vates*, especially as the tradition undergoes the impact of the political and social upheavals of England in the seventeenth century.[21] The classical notion of the inspired poet came to be of considerable concern when Christian literature was written in the vernacular. Is poetic inspiration on Christian topics comparable to the inspiration of the prophets? Is it not heretical to regard Dante in the same context as the Psalmist? The poets of the English Renaissance were reluctant to link their inspiration directly to the divine. According to Kerrigan's analysis, Sidney, for example, regarded man as 'fallen only in will' and still able to create 'art with the "erected" faculties of his intellect' (p. 56). The artist, then, does not depend on a special inspiration for the glories of his work. And Spenser's epic, Kerrigan suggests, is more appropriately regarded as claiming inspiration from Elizabeth than from God (p. 62). But after the Puritan revolution, even the linking of inspiration with patriotism was tainted: 'The old vocabulary of *furor poeticus* was not different from the new vocabulary of religious revolution' (p. 72).

Some opponents of the Puritans reserved inspiration exclusively for the writers of Scripture. In his 'Preface' to *Gondibert*, Davenant attacked inspiration, whether poetical or political, and equated it with 'enthusiasm' (in the seventeenth- and eighteenth-century sense of mental aberration). Davenant's attack on inspiration was followed by two works that treated religious inspiration, or enthusiasm, in a way that anticipated Swift's *Tale of a Tub* volume, Meric Casaubon's *A Treatise of Enthusiasme*, and Henry More's *Enthusiasmus triumphatus*.[22] Both argued the irrationality of a belief in private inspiration. But the best-known response to inspiration was that of Hobbes, whose views are reflected in Swift's depiction of the dissenters as Aeolists: '*Inspiration* . . . is nothing but the blowing into man some thin and subtile aire, or wind' (III, 17, p. 440). Even in Scripture, Hobbes asserts, the word 'inspiration' is used 'metaphorically only'. Regarding all claims to private revelation as unverifiable, Hobbes chose to prevent anarchy by the expedient of relegating all authority to the sovereign, substituting power for inspiration.

Swift's great satires explore these issues of authority both directly and through his central fiction of the 'author', with its implicit claim to the authority of inspiration, or at least insight, The contexts alter from *A Tale of a Tub* to the *Travels into Several Remote Nations of the World*, but the hermeneutical and epistemological problems remain the same. Swift shows his authors claiming the external authority of books or nature for a vision that is gradually exposed not only as private but also as solipsistic.

Notes

1. FRANK KERMODE, *The Genesis of Secrecy: On the Interpretation of Narrative* (Cambridge, MA, 1979), pp. 24–5.

2. HAYDEN WHITE, 'Interpretation in History', in *Tropics of Discourse: Essays in Cultural Criticism* (Baltimore, MD, 1978), p. 51.

3. NORTHROP FRYE, 'The Archetypes of Literature', in *Fables of Identity: Studies in Poetic Mythology* (New York, 1963), p. 14.

4. ELLEN DOUGLAS LEYBURN, *Satiric Allegory: Mirror of Man* (New Haven, CT, 1956), discusses the close relationship between satire and allegory: 'Critics write as if there were something incongruous in the two. How foreign this impression of incongruity was to ancient rhetoricians is indicated by Quintilian's including irony and mockery, which we link with satire, under the kinds of allegory' (p. 8). GAY CLIFFORD, *The Transformations of Allegory* (London, 1974), finds Swift to be 'a crucial transitional figure in the development of allegory' (p. 111) and argues that 'works of an allegorical nature from the late seventeenth century onwards . . . are conceived in a spirit hostile (sometimes violently so) to any attempted systematization of life' (p. 110).

5. JAY ARNOLD LEVINE, 'The Design of *A Tale of a Tub* (With a Digression on a Mad Modern Critic)', *ELH: A Journal of English Literary History*, 33 (1966), 198–227, discusses the relationship of Swift's *Tale* to issues of biblical interpretation in the seventeenth century. He argues that the putative author of the *Tale* is primarily a critic of Scripture: 'The abuses in learning and the abuses in religion, then, are not only merged in Swift's basic design, but in fact emanate from one source, the egomania of the modern sacred critic, for whom the Bible is one more text to be trod upon in his assertion of self' (p. 206). PAUL J. KORSHIN, 'Swift and Typological Narrative in *A Tale of a Tub*', *Harvard English Studies*, 1 (1970), 67–91, discusses 'Swift's use of Biblical typology for satiric purposes in *A Tale of a Tub*, principally in Section VII, "A Digression in Praise of Digression"' (p. 67). Korshin finds that the narrator's 'devious misapplications of typological method . . . associate him closely with the undercurrents of Puritan dissent' (p. 91).

6. MAUREEN QUILLIGAN, *The Language of Allegory: Defining the Genre* (Ithaca, NY, 1979), p. 141.

7. Ibid., p. 156.

8. Ibid., p. 192, separates the satires of Swift and Pope from proper allegories on the basis of this changed relationship to a pretext.

9. ALEXANDER POPE, *The Art of Sinking in Poetry*, ed. EDNA LEAKE STEEVES (New York, 1952), p. 39.

10. HUGH KENNER, *The Counterfeiters: An Historical Comedy* (Bloomington, IN, 1968), pp. 92–3.

11. EDWARD W. ROSENHEIM, *Swift and the Satirist's Art* (Chicago, 1963), p. 31, defines satire as 'an attack by means of a manifest fiction upon discernible historic particulars'. He notes that satire is distinct from art 'which is purely rhetorical' (p. 23), because satire has a fiction that is a recognized departure from literal truth (pp. 17–18). Some version of the definition formulated by Rosenheim is assumed in most discussions of satire, although the arguments of ALVIN KERNAN, *The Cankered Muse: Satire of the English Renaissance* (New Haven, CT, 1959), chapter 1, against the emphasis on satire's affinities with

143

polemical writing have also exerted much influence. JOHN R. CLARK, in *Form and Frenzy in Swift's 'Tale of a Tub'* (Ithaca, NY, 1970), has argued vigorously in his introduction and in chapter 1 that the *Tale* is a work of 'mimetic art', not only a polemical work (p. 3).

12. ROBERT W. UPHAUS, *The Impossible Observer: Reason and the Reader in Eighteenth-Century Prose* (Lexington, KY, 1979), suggests that 'many eighteenth-century texts do not reinforce the expectations of "objective" criticism so much as they challenge the reader into a new or renewed awareness of just how problematical the nature and formation of all beliefs, assumptions, expectations, and value judgments are' (p. 2).

13. EARL WASSERMAN, 'Nature Moralized: The Divine Analogy in the Eighteenth Century', *ELH: A Journal of English Literary History*, 20 (1953), 68.

14. KERNAN, *The Cankered Muse*, chapter 1.

15. In this work, *The Sentiments of a Church of England Man*, Swift defines a position similar to Hooker's on the relations of church and state. Swift rejects the dissenters' attempts to separate the two, and he also rejects Hobbes's attempt to make the church subservient to the state. IRVIN EHRENPREIS, *Swift: The Man, His Works, and the Age* (Cambridge, MA, 1967), vol. 2, discusses Swift's positions on the church, the state, and their relationship. His discussion includes an analysis of *The Sentiments of a Church of England Man* (pp. 124–31).

16. PETER MUNZ, *The Place of Hooker in the History of Thought* (London, 1952), p. 64.

17. RICHARD HOOKER, *Of the Laws of Ecclesiastical Polity* (London, 1907), 1: viii, 9. Subsequent references are to this edition.

18. JOHN TRAUGOTT, 'A Tale of a Tub', in *Focus: Swift*, ed. C. J. RAWSON (London, 1971), p. 116.

19. HOBBES, *Leviathan*, ed. C. B. MACPHERSON (Baltimore, MD, 1968), II, 17, p. 227. All subsequent references will be to this edition, which is a reprint of the 'Head' edition. Part and chapter citations are given to facilitate reference to other editions.

20. EDWARD SAID, *Beginnings: Intention and Method* (New York, 1975), p. 213. Said links questions of authority in literary texts with the paternal role of the author: 'a begetter, beginner, father, or ancestor' (p. 83). MICHAEL SEIDEL, *Satiric Inheritance: Rabelais to Sterne* (Princeton, NJ, 1979), explores the lineage of satire, finding Swift's *Tale* to be about 'satirically weakened lines of descent: fathers to sons, ancients to moderns' (p. 169).

21. WILLIAM KERRIGAN, *The Prophetic Milton* (Charlottesville, VA, 1974), especially the chapters 'Prophets and Poets', 'Prophets and Protestants'.

22. CLARENCE M. WEBSTER, 'Swift and Some Earlier Satirists of Puritan Enthusiasm', *PMLA*, 48 (1933), 1141–53.

7 Extract from *Swift's Landscape*[*]

CAROLE FABRICANT

IV

In contrast to these prospects or 'long views', Swift's characteristic mode of observation is a close-up view, which, although it can produce grotesque distortions (as in his minute descriptions of the female body), can also result in a visual clarity that makes possible a more truthful, because more detailed and intense, perception of landscape. Throughout his writings we find evidence of his awareness that distance has a profound effect on one's perception. In advising Celia, 'Delude at once, and bless our sight, / When you are seen, be seen from far' (*The Progress of Beauty*, ll. 70–71), he is (however facetiously) making a point akin to the one reiterated in descriptions of landscape, where a distant vantage point is recommended to ensure an attractive view. Observing anything too closely is likely to result in visual discomfort or revulsion, as when Gulliver is filled with 'Horror and Disgust' upon seeing the Brobdingnagian maids' naked bodies at close range (*PW*, 11: 119) and when, the situation reversed, a Lilliputian friend informs Gulliver '. . . that my Face appeared much fairer and smoother when he looked on me from the Ground, than it did upon a nearer View when I took him up in my Hand, and brought him close; which he confessed was at first a very shocking Sight' (*PW*, 11: 92). Similarly 'shocking Sight[s]' are revealed when Swift examines his physical surroundings close at hand. For example, he counters a correspondent's apparently idealized conception of the Irish countryside with his own detailed account of what he saw during his trip through county Tipperary: '. . . filthy cabins, miserable, tattered, half-starved creatures, scarce in human shape; one insolent ignorant oppressive squire to be found in twenty miles riding; a parish church

[*] Reprinted from 'The Spectator in the Landscape', in *Swift's Landscape* (Baltimore, MD: Johns Hopkins University Press, 1982), pp. 186–96.

145

to be found only in a summer-day's journey, in comparison of which, an English farmer's barn is a cathedral; a bog of fifteen miles round; every meadow a slough, and every hill a mixture of rock, heath, and marsh' (*Corr.* 4: 34).

The very title of Swift's tract, *A Short View of the State of Ireland*, suggests his mode of observation, the word 'short' not only literally characterizing a brief polemic only a few pages in length but also denoting a close-up, eye-level view. The body of the tract deals directly with the differences between accurate and distorted ways of seeing; Swift instructs 'the worthy *Commissioners* who come from *England*' how to view the Irish landscape clearly and thus rid themselves of prior misconceptions as well as potential misperceptions. His advice to '. . . ride round the Kingdom, and observe the Face of Nature, or the Faces of the Natives' (*PW*, 12: 10) calls for a close scrutiny inconsistent with the sweeping, lofty gaze of the prospect viewer. The 'faces' Swift recommends for observation have little in common with 'Earth's universal face' mentioned in *The Seasons* ('Winter', 238) or '. . . the face / Of universal nature' depicted by Cowper (*The Task*, Book IV, 324–25), for in the former case the concern is with particularity, not universality – with unique characteristics that aid in making distinctions, not with general qualities that presumably create a harmonious whole. Swift's 'rider' will inevitably see sights that are shielded from the eyes of the typical English spectator: 'The miserable Dress, and Dyet, and Dwelling of the People. The general Desolation in most Parts of the Kingdom. The old Seats of the Nobility and Gentry all in Ruins, and no new ones in their Stead. The Families of Farmers, who pay great Rents, living in Filth and Nastiness upon Butter-milk and Potatoes, without a Shoe or Stocking to their Feet; or a House so convenient as an *English* Hog-sty, to receive them' (*PW*, 12: 10).

Swift's scornful reference to the '*English* Spectator', who can afford if he wishes to transform these horrors into 'comfortable Sights', and who 'comes for a short Time, only *to learn the Language*, and returns back to his own Country, whither he finds all our Wealth transmitted' (*PW*, 12: 10–11), indicates that he perceived the close connection between visual and economic exploitation. The portrayal of the activities of the typical English spectator in the *Short View* suggests how the well-bred English gentleman can plunder with his eyes and his hands alike as he feasts his gaze on desirable scenery while fattening his pocketbook on profits obtained from Ireland's natural resources. The tract makes clear Swift's abiding sense of Ireland's total vulnerability, to perceptual distortion as well as to economic abuse and political oppression. This distortion results in grossly inaccurate reports about the state of the country: '. . . because there may be a Dozen Families in this Town, able to entertain their *English* Friends in a generous Manner at their Tables [,] their Guests, upon their Return to *England*, shall report, that we wallow in Riches and Luxury' (*PW*, 12: 12). These 'Guests', who carefully limit their social activities to the 'safe' realm occupied by the well-to-do Protestant gentry in Dublin and thereby banish all signs of urban poverty from their purview, have something in common with those 'strangers from other Countries' who completely refrain from visiting Ireland, '. . . where they can expect to see nothing, but Scenes of Misery and Desolation' (*PW*, 12: 9). Swift's comment that another pamphleteer, responsible for erroneous accounts of Ireland's state of affairs, 'appear[s] to write as a Stranger' (*PW*, 12: 23), points to the kind of vision that Swift often condemned, deeming it instrumental in reinforcing the country's wretched conditions. To write about or view Ireland 'as a Stranger' is to survey the country with a remote and alien vision. A stranger's act of perception presupposes a distance similar to the one separating the Irish, as ailing 'Patients', and the English, as 'Doctors at a Distance, Strangers to their Constitution, and the Nature of their Disease' (*PW*, 12: 8), whose prescribed 'Physick' is aggravating rather than helping to cure the illness.

Another 'short view' of Ireland, similar to Swift's, appears in an account written for the periodical the *Reformer* by the eighteen-year-old Trinity College student, Edmund Burke. His essay, like Swift's, demonstrates the inextricable links between perceptual and ideological stance, between one's position as either close or remote observer of the landscape and one's insight into the nature of society. Burke too shows that an accurate view of prevailing conditions depends on which parts of the landscape one chooses to look *at*, as opposed to which parts one can afford to look *over*:

In this City [Dublin] Things have the best Face; but still, as you leave the Town, the Scene grows worse, and presents you with the utmost Penury in the Midst of a rich Soil. . . . [The people's] Cloaths [are] so ragged, that they rather publish than conceal the Wretchedness it was meant to hide; nay, it is no uncommon Sight to see half a dozen Children run quite naked out of a Cabin, scarcely distinguishable from a Dunghill. . . . Let any one take a Survey of their Cabins, and then say, whether such a Residence be worthy any thing that challenges the Title of a human Creature.[1]

Burke goes on to note that the cabins' furnishings are 'much fitter to be lamented than described', thus in effect agreeing with Dunton's point, made a half-century earlier, that the habitations of the Irish peasants 'are so very wretched things that perhaps the pen . . . would be very defective in describing them'.[2] Such descriptions of Ireland represent an ironic reversal of the literary convention, particularly evident in eighteenth-century poetry, according to which words are deemed inadequate for conveying the ineffable beauties of the landscape. Thomson, for example, reflects upon '. . . hues on hues [that] expression cannot paint' ('Spring', 554) and, acknowledging art's inferiority to nature ('. . . But who can paint / Like Nature? . . .' [468–69]), he laments, '. . . If fancy then / Unequal fails beneath the pleasing task, / Ah, what shall language do? ah, where find words / Tinged with so many colours . . .' (473–76). In eighteenth-century Ireland, it was more often than not the *wretchedness* that defied description. The best a writer could do was to focus his attention wholly upon the concrete details unfolding before his view, to marry word and thing as closely as possible, for 'things' – that is, the harsh, empirically verifiable realities of the Irish countryside – spoke for themselves, with their own form of nonrhetorical eloquence.

We see this meticulous allegiance to observed detail throughout Burke's portrayal of the Irish countryside: 'You enter [a cabin], or rather creep in, at a Door of Hurdles plaistered with Dirt, of which the Inhabitant is generally the Fabricator; within-side you see (if the Smoke will permit you) the Men, Women, Children, Dogs, and Swine lying promiscuously; for their Opulence is such that they cannot have a separate House for their Cattle, as it would take too much from the Garden, whose produce is their only Support. . . . I Appeal to any one, who knows the Country, for the Justness of the Picture.'[3] This passage reflects a mode of vision predicated on impassioned immediacy rather than Olympian detachment. The writer, far from being the typical aloof spectator like Thomson atop Hagley's hill, is an involved actor in the scene, who has emphatically rejected the visual refuge offered by geographical distance. That Burke invokes the testimony specifically of one 'who knows the Country' suggests that he, like Swift, recognized the distortions likely to result from viewing the landscape as a 'stranger'.

The 'Picture' Burke presents in the *Reformer* essay is not the kind that would ever have adorned the walls of a Houghton or a Twickenham villa. For Burke's 'Picture' derives its meaning precisely from what lies *beyond*, because inherently alien to, the Augustan frame of reference and framework of values. Its subversive implications with regard to them may be gleaned from the extent to which it approximates a class analysis of society. Following his minutely detailed account of the country's rural poverty, for example, Burke declares:

Who, after having seen this, comes to Town and beholds [the gentry's] sumptuous and expensive Equipages, their Treats and Diversions, can contain the highest indignation? . . . I fancy, many of our fine Gentlemen's Pageantry would be greatly tarnished, were their gilt coaches to be preceded and followed by the miserable Wretches, whose Labour supports them . . . that among Creatures of the same Kind there should be such a Disproportion in their manner of living; it is a kind of Blasphemy on Providence.[4]

The linguistic placing of the 'gilt coaches' next to 'the miserable Wretches, whose labour supports them' grows out of a manner of perception that has inescapable ideological implications, for through it the contemplation of visual contrasts in the landscape becomes the simultaneous perception of economic disparities in society, accompanied by the dismaying revelation of massive inequities in all aspects of contemporary life.

Similarly in Swift's writings, a careful scrutiny of existing conditions exposes the inequities of a class society. In the *Short View* we see Irish tenants 'who live worse than *English* Beggars' juxtaposed against 'those worthy Gentlemen the BANKERS; who . . . [with a few exceptions] are the only thriving People among us . . .' (*PW*, 12: 11). Elsewhere Swift deals with this matter in a less direct but no less forceful manner by dramatizing the fallacies inherent in any mode of vision based upon generalization and abstraction, which is therefore incapable of distinguishing among different landscapes, living conditions, and classes within society. His tract entitled *Maxims Controlled in Ireland*, for example, was written to challenge the supposedly universal validity of '. . . certain Maxims of State, founded upon long observation and experience, drawn from the constant practice of the wisest nations, and from the very principles of government, nor ever controlled [refuted] by any writer upon politics' (*PW*, 12: 131). The 'long observation and experience' mentioned here, like the Augustan 'long view' with regard to landscape, proves to be in direct conflict with the kind of close observation and day-to-day experience necessary for an accurate understanding of a particular set of circumstances. (Tellingly, those whose reasoning is 'founded upon long observation and experience' become identified with 'short thinkers' later in the tract.) The tract shows that the words 'observation' and 'experience' are paradoxically often put to the most unempirical of ends, made to serve the cause of general precepts or theories rather than actual circumstances. The reliance upon 'long observation', whether by prospect viewers or political analysts, is likely to result in short-sightedness, in a vision as restricted from one point of view as it is comprehensive from another.

The insistence upon clear, accurate perception is a continuing note throughout Swift's Irish tracts, which repeatedly exhort readers to take off their blinders and open their eyes to both the environmental and the political conditions confronting them: 'If I tell you there is a Precipice under you, and that if you go forwards you will certainly break your Necks: If I point to it before your Eyes, must I be at the Trouble of repeating it every Morning? Are our People's *Hearts waxed gross*? Are *their Ears dull of hearing*, and have *they closed their Eyes?*' (*PW*, 10: 22). Swift's role as combined pamphleteer and political activist is to *un*close the people's senses by *dis*closing the facts and precise details of the prevailing situation: 'Give me Leave to do what the *Drapier* hath done more than once before me; which is, to relate the naked Fact, as it stands in the View of the World' (*PW*, 10: 105). The blindness of the average Irishman, unlike the carefully cultivated 'blindness' of the Augustan spectator, is created by others, imposed from without (though reinforced from within, by his own gullibility), for purposes of political deception rather than aesthetic delectation. As Swift explains it (with the scheme for coining Wood's halfpence in mind), even 'the most ruinous project' can be rendered acceptable to the Irish natives:

> For the poor ignorant people, allured by the appearing convenience in their small dealings, did not discover the serpent in the brass, but were ready, like the Israelites, to offer incense to it; neither could the wisdom of the nation convince them, until some, of good intentions, made the cheat so plain to their sight, that those who run may read. And thus the design was to treat us, in every point, as the Philistines treated Samson, (I mean when he was betrayed by Dalilah) first to put out our eyes, and then bind us with fetters of brass.
>
> (*PW*, 9: 238)

The association made here between blindness and captivity is of particular significance for Swift's writings, which are intended to clarify as well as to focus his countrymen's perception – to direct their gaze to the most important objects and issues confronting them, as a means not only of heightening their consciousness, but also of freeing them in a very literal sense.

The perceptual distortion that appears throughout Swift's early odes, with their imagistic emphasis upon optical illusions, blindness, and visual as well as moral and physical errancy, tends to become translated into more specifically political terms in his later writings.

Instead of 'the *deluding* muse' who '. . . blinds [the poet] to her ways'
(*Ode to the Athenian Society*, l. 234), we have a deluding colonialist
power that tries to blind an entire nation to its practices. The people's
'prostituted sight', produced by their 'deflowered eye', which cannot
'face the naked light' (*Ode to Dr. William Sancroft*, ll. 221–22), is later
understood as a visual affliction perpetrated on them by the ruling
class (though unwittingly intensified by their own folly). Swift's
subsequent role as political pamphleteer, opener of his compatriots'
eyes, is foreshadowed in the *Ode to the Honorable Sir William Temple*,
where he 'expose[s] the scene' behind the curtains of 'The wily shafts
of state, those juggler's tricks' (97, 92) and 'Down the ill-organed
engines fall; / Off fly the vizards and discover all, / How plain I
see through the deceit! / How shallow! and how gross the cheat!'
(ll. 98–101). Temple's young amanuensis, who could pierce the
façade in order to expose the 'Cheat' within, later becomes the
Drapier-Dean, capable of 'ma[king] the cheat so plain to [his
countrymen's] sight'. Again and again, Swift's writings urge the
pursuit of clear-sightedness, a form of vision that in virtually every
case calls for close scrutiny and thus rejects the 'long views'
prescribed by conventional Augustan wisdom.

V

The extent to which Swift's stance as spectator differed from the
typical stance of his contemporaries is apparent in an exchange of
letters between himself and Bolingbroke in the summer of 1729. In
part responding to an epistle addressed jointly to himself and to
Pope several months earlier, in which Swift complained that 'I never
wake without finding life a more insignificant thing than it was the
day before' (*Corr.* 3: 329), Bolingbroke writes in a spirit of philosophic
detachment, assuring Swift that 'if you will come to a certain farm in
Middlesex, you shall find that I can live frugally without growling att
the world' (*Corr.* 3: 348) and advising him to adopt a more stoical
attitude toward life, which requires that Swift change his mode of
viewing the world:

> you say you are no Philosopher, and I think you are in the right
> to dislike a word which is so often abused, but I am sure you like
> to follow Reason, not custom, which is sometimes the Reason &
> oftner the Caprice of others, of the Mob of the world. Now to be
> sure of doing this, you must wear your philosophical Spectacles
> as constantly as the Spaniards used to wear theirs. You must make
> them part of your dress, and sooner part with your broad brimmed
> Beaver, your Gown, your Scarf, or even that emblematical vestment

your Surplice, thro' this medium you will see few things to be
vexed att, few persons to be angry att.

(*Corr.* 3: 349)

Bolingbroke is here proposing a presumably superior mode of
perception that is actually a call for selective blindness to 'the Mob
of the world' as well as to the existential conditions connected with
it – to the very world of poverty, disease, and starvation that Swift
was agitatedly describing in ever greater detail in his correspondence
and pamphlets. Indeed, in a letter written only two weeks before
Bolingbroke counseled use of the 'philosophical Spectacles', Swift
was telling Pope about the 'three terrible years dearth of corn' in
Ireland and concluding somberly, 'These evils operate more every
day, and the kingdom is absolutely undone, as I have been telling
it often in print these ten years past' (*Corr.* 3: 341).

Given Swift's preoccupations during this period and his sense of
urgency about the contemporary situation, it is not surprising that
he found Bolingbroke's advice inappropriate as well as uncongenial
to his own way of looking at the world. He makes this clear in his
response to the viscount two months later: 'I renounce your whole
Philosophy, because it is not your practice by the figure of Living.
. . . I wish you could learn Arithmetick, that 3 and 2 make 5, and will
never make more. My Philosophical Spectacles which you advise me
to, will tell me that I can live on 50^{ll} a Year (Wine excepted which my
bad health forces me to) . . .' (*Corr.* 3: 354–55). Swift characteristically
gets down to brass tacks and everyday realities. While Bolingbroke
waxes eloquent upon the lofty detachment enjoyed by the wise man,
affirming that he himself finds 'little Regret when I look backwards,
little apprehension when I look forwards' (*Corr.* 3: 348), Swift is
insisting in a letter to Pope that '. . . we wise men must think of
nothing but getting a little ready money' (*Corr.* 3: 355), thereby
typically shifting the basis of wisdom from an otherworldly
transcendence to a clear, unobstructed look at the concerns of *this*
world. In a situation where 'there are not two hundred thousand
pounds of species in the whole island . . . and so are all inevitably
undone' (*Corr.* 3: 355), the act of contemplating one's surroundings
through 'philosophical Spectacles' makes no more sense than the act
of admiring beautiful prospects through the barred windows of a
dungeon. The uselessness of Bolingbroke's 'philosophical Spectacles'
is indirectly underscored in Swift's poem *Upon the South Sea Project*,
which makes the point that concrete realities will not conveniently
disappear or change into something more palatable simply because
one uses an artificial, presumably superior medium through which
to observe them:

  But as a guinea will not pass
At market for a farthing more
Shewn through a multiplying glass,
Than what it all ways did before:

  So cast it in the Southern Seas,
And view it through a jobber's bill;
Put on what spectacles you please,
Your guinea's but a guinea still.

(ll. 125–32)

Undoubtedly one can, through a variety of visual manipulations, 'see few things to be vexed att, few persons to be angry att', but for Swift there is a heavy price to pay for this 'luxury': condemning oneself to a world of fantasy and self-deception. As he explains the matter in a letter countering Dean Brandreth's 'philosophical' perception of the country in Tipperary, 'I have not said all this [concerning the poverty and desolation of the Tipperary landscape] out of any malicious intention, to put you out of conceit with the scene where you are, but merely for your credit; because it is better to know you are miserable, than to betray an ill taste . . .' (*Corr.* 4: 34). Swift is in effect telling Brandreth to *remove* his 'philosophical Spectacles' so that he can view his surroundings accurately, without comforting illusion.[5] It is characteristic of Swift that he associates Brandreth's unrealistically rosy picture with the stance of 'an excellent philosopher', for throughout his writings he uses the term 'philosopher' in alternately ambiguous, mocking, or ironic ways, to denote attitudes fundamentally inimical to his own temperament and mode of perception. The pejorative associations of the word are epitomized in Swift's versified comment addressed to Lady Acheson:

You, like some acute philosopher,
Every fault have drawn a gloss over;
Placing in the strongest light
All your virtues to my sight.

(*To a Lady*, ll. 97–100)

The philosopher's mode of perception, far from being disinterested and objective, is here defined as manipulative, hence deliberately deceptive and self-serving. Systematically 'Gloss[ing] over' an entire body of earthly realities in the process of magnifying another, it results in a 'cosmetic' vision, designed to beautify through selective concealment and appealing distortion. The philosopher's mode of perception is ironically akin to the warped perspective expressed by the Tale-teller in the 'Digression on Madness': 'How fade and insipid do all Objects accost us that are not conveyed in the Vehicle of *Delusion*? How shrunk is every Thing, as it appears in the Glass of Nature? So, that if it were not for the Assistance of Artificial *Mediums*, false Lights, refracted Angles, Varnish, and Tinsel; there would be a mighty Level in the Felicity and Enjoyments of Mortal Men' (*PW*, 1: 109).

The insistence upon intractable realities, stubbornly resistant to all forms of visual rearrangement, optical illusion, and wishful thinking, is central to Swift's outlook and writings. It is an aspect that can be too easily overlooked in our understandable preoccupation with Swift's multiple ironies and with the complex ambiguities that make us feel as though we are walking on shifting sands when we read much of his work. There was an important side of Swift, however, that enabled him to cut through layers of confusion, delusion, and illusion as did no other eighteenth-century writer, in order to reveal the unalterable, often visible and tactile reality beneath. For all of Swift's acute awareness of shifting perspectives and how they affect the way in which external reality is interpreted, he remained throughout his life a firm believer in the latter's unequivocal existence and its susceptibility to being clearly defined and objectively verified. By the same token, although there was a side of Swift that could very well understand the appeal of that 'sublime and refined Point of Felicity, called, *the Possession of being well deceived* . . .' (*PW*, 1: 110) – a side that indulged the yearning for pleasing appearances since, as the Tale-teller puts it, '. . . in most Corporeal Beings, which have fallen under my Cognizance, the *Outside* hath been infinitely preferable to the *In* . . .' (*PW*, 1: 109)[6] – we should keep in mind that the major thrust of Swift's writings was directed *against* the state of being 'well deceived', and reflected his commitment to seeing things clearly, as they really are.

Thus, in a verse written on the occasion of Stella's birthday, Swift exults in the deterioration of his eyesight, which allows him to indulge in both mental and optical illusion, even as he simultaneously acknowledges the irrevocable fact of advancing age and indirectly confirms the very realities that his faulty vision negates:

> But, Stella say, what evil tongue
> Reports you are no longer young?
> That Time sits with his scythe to mow
> Where erst sat Cupid with his bow;
> That half your locks are turned to grey;
> I'll ne'er believe a word they say.

'Tis true, but let it not be known,
My eyes are somewhat dimmish grown;
For nature, always in the right,
To your decays adapts my sight,
And wrinkles undistinguished pass,
For I'm ashamed to use a glass;
And till I see them with these eyes,
Whoever says you have them, lies.

(*Stella's Birthday* [1725], ll. 35–48)

The poem, with its opening simile reminding us of the inevitable
passage of time ('As when a beauteous nymph decays, / We say,
she's past her dancing days' (ll. 1–2)) and its frank recognition of
the toll this passage has taken on praiser and praised alike, is finally
less a tribute to the 'sublime and refined Point of Felicity, called, *the
Possession of being well deceived*' than it is an affirmation of man's
ability to see things as they really are despite the ever-present
temptation of, and periodic flirtations with, comforting illusion.
Swift, as one 'ashamed to use a Glass', refuses to look at the world,
or his beloved friend, through any kind of spectacles, philosophical
or otherwise, and consequently he sees things in their natural state
even though he can playfully pretend to see them otherwise.[7]

Significantly, Swift, in playfully commenting upon Bolingbroke's
spectacles, implies a link between his friend's mode of perception
and his class affiliation, his 'station' in life. It is not coincidental
that in the same letter in which he rejects Bolingbroke's use of
'philosophical Spectacles', Swift alludes to the vast discrepancy in
social and economic status between the two men: 'My Lord I write
to Mr Pope, and not to you. My Birth although from a Family not
undistinguished in its time is many degrees inferior to Yours, all
my pretensions from Persons and parts infinitely so; I a Younger
Son of younger Sons, You born to a great Fortune' (*Corr.* 3: 354). The
characterization of himself as 'a Younger Son', although factually
inaccurate, serves to dramatize his sense of identification with a class
of estateless, disinherited beings who must struggle for their survival
in a world controlled by others. Swift's comment immediately
following ('Yet I see you with all your advantages Sunk to a degree
that could never have been so without them. But yet I see you as
much esteemed, as much beloved, as much dreaded, & perhaps
more . . . than e'er you were in your highest exaltation . . .') develops
further the imagistic contrast between height and lowness. Although
Bolingbroke's fortune has 'Sunk', he remains to all intents and
purposes in a position of 'highest exaltation', while Swift, 'many
degrees inferior', occupies a place much lower down in the social

order. This difference in elevation corresponds to a difference in angle of vision.

Despite Bolingbroke's protestations that he must resign himself to lean times and increasing economic hardships (*Corr.* 3: 348), Swift indicates that he is very well aware of the wide gap between Bolingbroke's romanticized notions about accepting 'forced Retrenchments' in order to live a simpler, more frugal existence and the realities of his situation as a lord 'born to a great Fortune': '. . . can you, could you, come over and live with Mr Pope and Me at the Deanery when you are undone. I could almost wish the Experiment were tryed. – No – God forbid, that ever such a Scoundrel as *want* should date [*sic*] to approach you. But in the meantime do not brag; Retrenchments are not your Talent . . .' (*Corr.* 3: 354). In a letter written to Pope some fifteen months earlier, Swift underscored even more emphatically the unbreachable gulf between the viscount and himself:

> By the way, I must observe, that my Lord Bolingbroke (from the effects of his kindness to me) argues most sophistically: The fall from a million to an hundred-thousand pounds is not so great, as from eight hundred pounds a year to one: Besides, he is a controller of Fortune, and Poverty dares not look a great Minister in the face, under his lowest declension. I never knew him live so great and expensively as he hath done since his return from Exile; such mortals have resources that others are not able to comprehend.
>
> (*Corr.* 3: 294)

Here Bolingbroke is perceived not merely as a man 'born to a great Fortune' but as the master of his fate and ruler over his environs. He can enjoy his philosophic flights atop a lofty peak remote from the 'Mob of the world' precisely because he has sufficient wealth and 'resources' – because he can *afford* to do so in every sense. Swift, on the contrary, condemned to remain a 'slave' in Ireland, cannot afford to become a philosopher or to view his surroundings through 'philosophical Spectacles', struggling as he must with the mundane issues of human survival.

Notes

1. ARTHUR P. I. SAMUELS, *The Early Life, Correspondence, and Writings of the Rt. Hon. Edmund Burke* (Cambridge, 1923), p. 315.

2. EDWARD MACLYSAGHT, *Irish Life in the Seventeenth Century* (New York, 1969; 1st edn 1939), p. 356.

3. Samuels, *Edmund Burke*, p. 315.

4. Ibid., pp. 315–16.

5. The significance of spectacles for Swift – specifically in connection with Gulliver's dependency upon them because of his 'weak eyes' – is discussed in W. B. CARNOCHAN, *Lemuel Gulliver's Mirror for Man* (Berkeley, CA, 1968), pp. 135–7; and in PAT ROGERS, 'Gulliver's Glasses', in *The Art of Jonathan Swift*, ed. CLIVE T. PROBYN (London, 1978), pp. 179–88. Carnochan sees Gulliver as a 'myopic hero', to whom spectacles are symbols of man's blindness after the Fall, as well as of man's 'pride in his ability to overcome it' (p. 135). Rogers, on the other hand, believes that the spectacles 'represent visual over-development, hypertrophy of the sight' (p. 183), as well as 'the intrusive intellect; the over-intent scrutiny of what is better left unexamined because it causes pain and revulsion when pried into by the modern empiricist' (p. 187). As my discussion suggests, I strongly disagree with Rogers's identification of Swift with this latter point of view and with his argument that 'on another level Swift shares Gulliver's instincts, to hide and to peer out, to avoid bodily contact which squeezes and pains us. He wants to do this while at the same time negotiating a safe distance with the physical world, through his sight' (p. 187). On the contrary, Swift tended to be contemptuous of those who sought this kind of visual refuge. Although the example of Gulliver is a somewhat complicated and paradoxical one, for Swift in general spectacles were instruments not for probing deeply into, but precisely for glossing over, empirical realities.

6. This view is put forth by ROBERT M. ADAMS in *Strains of Discord: Studies in Literary Openness* (Ithaca, NY, 1958), pp. 158–60).

7. Interestingly, Swift in actual life eschewed the use of glasses despite his failing eyesight. As Harold Williams observes in a footnote to a letter in which Swift's correspondent expresses fears that her writing 'should inconvenience [his] Eyes': 'Swift's eyesight had begun to trouble him but he consistently refused the aid of spectacles' (*Corr.* 4: 17, n. 1). Swift's refusal apparently persisted into old age.

8 The Grotesque Satiric Body*

Peter Stallybrass and Allon White

The decaying, vestigial terms of Renaissance iconography which had associated the Court with classical models and the populace with rural buffoonery were visibly disintegrating after the Civil War, yet they could be neither fully abandoned nor accurately translated to cover new conditions of writing. Neither courtiers nor clowns, yet wishing to be associated with the one and to be dissociated from the other, the writers and artists of that period are to be found furiously manipulating the inherited terms of the old feudal symbolic system in the attempt to make them fit the new conditions of literary production. How frequently in the poetry of the period we find kingship and the low-grotesque boiling together in a mixed satiric brew which is *supposed* to describe poetic life. Vestiges of the inherited court – folly provoking opposition – are everywhere to be found in the eighteenth century, satirically mismatched and therefore somehow forced into service to approximate to the felt 'neither up nor down' existence of the writer.

The matter was made more complex by the popular image of Restoration court-society itself. In a sense the traditional terms of high-classical and low-grotesque were not simply rendered anachronistic by the growth of professional middling classes to whom the language of hierarchical extremes was inapplicable: the court of Charles II itself made a farce of the chivalric and classical icons of aristocratic and regal identity. The defiant, transgressive devilry of the Restoration court seemed to betoken a crisis of nobility after the civil wars despite the control and political influence which it had maintained. That delirious immersion in violence, promiscuity, invective, duelling and theatrical excess which characterizes the Court Wits had such an element of desperate effrontery about it that it had of itself given the lie to the complacent tableaux of the masque.

---

* Reprinted from *The Politics and Poetics of Transgression* (London: Methuen, 1986), pp. 100–12.

The robbery and assassination of a tanner in 1662 near Waltham Cross by Lord Buckhurst, his brother Edward Sackville, Sir Henry Belasye and others was matched by another 'frolic' the following year when Sir Charles Sedley and Lord Buckhurst, both of them stark naked, preached drunkenly to the crowd below from the balcony of Oxford Kate's tavern in Covent Garden.

The Restoration court projected a collective image of living in ironic and even defiant incompatibility with its inherited forms of public representation. It was carelessly demonic, nonchalantly outrageous, cynical in the way that only a class which despises its compromises can be cynical. The mixture of 'frolic' and violent outrage on the part of the Wits seemed to both defy and seek some limit to transgression. In the atheistical amusements of the Restoration court we can detect an intense phase of that aristocratic hell-raking which was to carry 'all the tricks of Aretine' through the eighteenth century and which was to command a mixture of revulsion and admiration from the bourgeois writers of the period.

Thus the inadequacy of pre-Civil War repertoires of iconography for the representation of the emerging republic of letters in the late seventeenth century was compounded by the fact that all its terms were slowly altering. As the world of the Court was brought closer to the town and to the realm of the professional publishers, booksellers, pamphleteers, playwrights and poets, its 'grotesque' incompatibility with its inherited pre-eminence became both more visible and more risible. As early as 1669 Pepys talks of how 'cheap' the King made himself by condoning the behaviour of Rochester, Mulgrave, Killigrew and other members of the 'Merry Gang'. Pinkethman recorded how 'King Charles II, being in company with the Lord Rochester and others of the nobility, who had been drinking the best part of the night, Killigrew came in, – Now, says the King, we shall hear of our faults. – No, faith, says Killigrew, I don't care to trouble my head with that which all the town talks of.'

The notoriety of the Court, its patent iconographic failure to match up to its high office and the decorum, serious refinement and responsibility which that office required, led inevitably to a satirical relationship between Court and town. The Court was *both* classical and grotesque, both regal and foolish, high and low. At the fall of Clarendon Evelyn referred to 'the baffoons and the ladies of pleasure' at Court. With only occasional periods of respite (such as the reign of Queen Anne) the perceived indignities and decadence of the monarchy were to be an obsessive source of graphic and verse satire up to the coronation of Victoria.

This was only partly due to actual behaviour and to the occurrence of specific scandals at Court. Although we can trace periods, such

as the decade after the accession of George III, when graphic and
verse satire were particularly intense and vitriolic, the extraordinary
saturation of eighteenth-century culture with satire cannot be
explained by referring to particular personalities or political events,
royal or otherwise. The ambiguous iconographic representation of the
Court was only one element in a cultural set of high/low dichotomies
which through satire, were gradually to restructure the territories and
discourses of representation in themselves during the Enlightenment.
Swift is characteristically savage in his denunciation of kingship and
uses the carnivalesque inversion of high/low, king and footman, king
and beast, most maliciously:

> But now go search all Europe round,
> Among the savage monsters crowned,
> With vice polluting every throne
> (I mean all kings except our own)
> In vain you make the strictest view
> To find a king in all the crew
> With whom a footman out of place
> Would not conceive a high disgrace,
> A burning shame, a crying sin,
> To take his morning cup of gin.
> . . .
> Thus think on kings, the name denotes
> Hogs, asses, wolves, baboons and goats,
> To represent in figure just
> Sloth, folly, rapine, mischief, lust.
>
> (Swift, *On Poetry: A Rapsody*, ll. 435–44; 457–60)

But just as the Court was a source of troubled and troubling
representations after the Restoration, so too was the other pole of
the dichotomy, the realm of the rustic buffoon, the realm of Folly.

We can analyse a contradictory process taking place. On the
one hand the period appears to mark an intensification of certain
carnivalesque and popular festivities after the Civil War and this
increase and intensification precipitated a conservative desire on the
part of the upper classes to separate themselves more clearly and
distinctly from these popular activities. In 1738 the Society for the
Reformation of Manners was formed and although it only lasted a
short while a second society was set up in 1757 in an attempt, mainly
under the auspices of the clergy, to regulate popular morality and
custom.[1]

Perhaps on account of the renewed vitality of the fairs and
festivities (Bartholomew Fair undoubtedly enjoyed a period of

expansion at the turn of the eighteenth century) there was a commensurate increase in the desire to remove or at least disperse the sites and times of popular carnivalesque pleasures – the fairs, the farces, the games and entertainments.[2] Many attempts were made to curtail or shorten the duration of the big fairs: in 1750, for example, after years of struggle by the authorities, Bartholomew Fair was cut down from fourteen days to three and its importance drastically reduced.

But as the realm of Folly was being restructured within bourgeois consciousness as precisely that *other realm* inhabited by a grotesque body which it repudiated as a part of its own identity and disdained as a set of real life *practices and rituals*, so it seemed to become more and more important as a set of *representations*. The symbolic energy of carnival festivity spills out uncontrollably from over-stuffed couplets of Augustan satire and the crowded, bustling prints of Hogarth and his contemporaries. The Smithfield Muse was on the move. We find a not dissimilar movement in Paris when, even as the Commedia dell'Arte is being dismissed and exiled in 1697 and its theatre is being closed, there is a veritable explosion of artistic *representations* of the pierrots, players, tumblers and rope-dancers by painters of the time – by Gillot and Watteau in particular. A sort of refined mimicry sets into the salons and ballrooms of Europe in which the imagery, masks and costumes of the popular carnival are being (literally) put on by the aristocracy and the bourgeoisie in order to simultaneously express and conceal their sexual desire and the pleasures of the body.

Thus in a brilliant essay Terry Castle has shown the symbolic centrality of the masquerade in eighteenth-century fiction,[3] its focusing of sexual and class transgression in a purely vicarious way such that, for the novelists of the period, 'invoking the world of masquerade is typically a way of indulging in the scenery of transgression while seeming to maintain didactic probity' (p. 912).

It is wrong, therefore, to assume that the attack on popular culture is simply the story of oppression from above. The grotesque body of carnival was being re-territorialized, it was being appropriated, sublimated and individualized to code refined identity, to give the eighteenth-century nobility and the bourgeoisie masks and symbols to think with at the very moment when they were repudiating the social realm from which those masks and symbols came. These masks and symbols, the motley paraphernalia of the Smithfield Muse and the Venetian carnival, were being systematically *severed* from their anchorage in the annual calendar of contemporary festive life, from the fixed places and times of the year which sustained them as communal events, and they were being discursively reformed and redistributed to supply most powerful symbolic repertoires for the

expression of individual body/subjects – the body/subjects of the
coffee-house and the cleaned-up theatre, the spa, the pleasure garden,
the country house, the ballroom and the assembly room: *not* those
body/subjects of the street, market square, fairground, common and
village green.

Swift and Pope perpetually identify the scene of writing with the
fairground and the carnival and in both writers the festive repertoire
is satirically deformed by the vicious competitive circumstances
of the literary market. The 'marketplace' has become 'the market'
and the individual aspiring poets denigrate each other by trying to
associate *everyone else* with the vulgarity of the fair while repudiating
any connection which they themselves might have with such a
world. Spite, repulsion and envy, the very marks of *ressentiment*,
recode the figures of carnival in the satiric poetry of the eighteenth
century to capture the 'grotesque' new competitive scene:

> As a thorn-bush, or oaken bough,
> Stuck in an Irish cabin's brow,
> Above the door, at country fair,
> Betokens entertainment there,
> So, bays on poet's brows have been
> Set, for a sign of wit within.
> And as ill neighbours in the night,
> Pull down an alehouse bush, for spite,
> The laurel so, by poets worn,
> Is by the teeth of envy torn,
> Envy, a canker-worm which tears
> Those sacred leaves that lightening spares.
>> (Swift, *On Paddy's Character of the 'Intelligencer'*, ll. 1–12)

The use of the fairground as a slur in Augustan satire is so common
that the poetry and pamphlet literature becomes a riot of *tu quoque*,
little different in tone from the Punch and Judy shows with which
Augustan poets habitually tried to identify each other:

> Two bordering wits contend for glory;
> And one is Whig and one is Tory.
> And this, for epics claims the bays,
> And that, for elegiac lays.
> Some famed for numbers soft and smooth,
> By lovers spoke in Punch's booth.
> And some as justly fame extols
> For lofty lines in Smithfield drolls.
>> (Swift, *On Poetry: A Rapsody*, ll. 309–16)

Precisely because the suppression and distancing of the physical body became the very sign of rationality, wit and judgement, the grotesque physical body existed as what Macherey calls a 'determining absent presence' in the classical body of Enlightenment poetic and critical discourse, a raging set of phantoms and concrete conditions to be forcefully rejected, projected or unacknowledged. Hence the apparent paradox that writers who were the great champions of a classical discursive body including Dryden, Swift and Pope spent so much time writing the grotesque, exorcising it, charging it to others, using and adopting its very terms while attempting to purify the language of the tribe. The production and reproduction of a body of classical writing required a labour of suppression, a perpetual work of exclusion upon the grotesque body and it was that supplementary yet unavoidable labour which troubled the identity of the classical. It brought the grotesque back into the classical, not so much as a return of the repressed as a vast labour of exclusion requiring and generating its own equivocal energies. *Quae negata, grata* – what is denied is desired: Augustan satire was the generic form which enabled writers to express and negate the grotesque simultaneously. It was the natural site for this labour of projection and repulsion upon which the construction of the public sphere depended.

The excremental obsession and carnivalesque imagery of a language resolutely classical may now seem less strange. What Pope refers to as the 'Smithfield Muse' was a popular deity governing traditional feast days, carnival, Saints' Days, the Lord Mayor's Procession (an enormously popular holiday which Pope makes the basis for *The Dunciad* and to which we return below), fairs, wakes, shroving, wassailing and parish feasts. These regular cycles of festivity embodied a diacritical symbolic logic (see Introduction to Stallybrass and White, p. 15): the rhythmic ritual oscillation enabled groups to play out a set of body categories particularly to do with expenditure, consumption and pleasure. What this meant in practice was a *diachronic* separation of the normative and its obverse, of structure and anti-structure into an historical series of alternating binary terms. The *disjunctive* relation of classical and grotesque was thus mediated by temporal switching from one to the other. At set times the 'dirty', the 'excessive', the transgressive and the body as pleasurable subject of consuming and discharging were celebrated in corporate ritual.

Augustan England witnesses a particular phase of the change of mediating form, an act of inner self-regulation and internal distancing on the part of the middling sort. The festive calendar was altogether too dirty, too disruptive, and rooted in a network of sites and places which the urban bourgeoisie was rejecting in favour of new sites of assembly, like the coffee-house and the spa. Rational enjoyment and classical pleasures developed in a network of locations which not only displaced the carnivalesque topography with alternative constructions of 'rational pleasures' but which grew rapidly alongside the older network and defined itself over against that topography.

To a certain extent this was a move from outdoors to indoors, a farewell to the street, fondly ironic such as we find in Gay's *Trivia*, or full of repellent phobias such as in Swift's *A Description of a City Shower*, or full of malicious disdain, such as we find in *The Dunciad*. Street culture, in the eighteenth century, is a source of fascination and fear on the part of a bourgeois culture which must risk contamination by the low-Other, dirt, and danger whenever it steps down into the street ('Ah where must needy poet seek for aid / When dust and rain at once his coat invade?', Swift, *A Description of a City Shower*, ll. 27–28). Indeed in the first stanza of Swift's *City Shower* the coffee-house is imaged as the haven where the saunterer can escape the stink and inconvenience of the street and complain in comparative comfort. As Pat Rogers has convincingly shown in *Grub Street: Studies in a Subculture*, the urban topography of London was a fundamental symbolic resource in Pope's time and 'Grub Street' is related to an actual place and cannot be treated as a purely abstract image. The reviling of Grub Street took much of its force from the specific and local conditions of the real Grub Street as Rogers shows, but it also gained from a general cultural movement out of the streets and into other more protected middleclass enclaves as the popular urban culture of the street and market square was repudiated. One network of sites, times and bodies was being supplanted by another: the consequences were enormous.

The Enlightenment strengthened and extended the Reformation desire to destroy the popular festive tradition. Yet in the present context it is not so important to establish whether in historical fact the festive calendar was temporarily strengthening itself or in decline. There is evidence that the early eighteenth century saw something of an increase, both in fairground culture and in attacks upon it. What is in question for our present purposes is rather the *self-exclusion* of certain middling and professional classes from that popular ritual culture, irrespective of whether that culture was waxing or waning. The *symbolism* of that tradition remained extraordinarily important in 'high' culture: even as writers were attacking the events and rituals of this festive calendar they were appropriating its symbols, imagery and imaginative repertoires for their own distinct purposes. It was

the *form of mediation* which was changing, gradually giving way to
other kinds of mediation less inimical to the rules of purity, propriety
and continuous production which govern bourgeois reason. As sites
of assembly were decathected and cleaned up to provide the material
productive network for public discourse and as the carnivalesque
rituals of the open air were ironized and sentimentalized in the
'soft culture' of the masquerade, pleasure garden, opera and theatre
pantomime, so the ritual oscillation was displaced by 'transduction',
a form of mediation between classical and grotesque adhering more
closely to the demands of the classical.

The Augustans laboured to translate what they were designating
as grotesque (in Bakhtin's special sense) into discourse more in
line with the classical: discourse which is elevated, serious, refined,
tending to relate to genres of epic and tragedy, pure, homogeneous,
closed, finished, proportioned, symmetrical, dignified and decorous.
At the same time and just as important, they appropriated symbolic
elements of the grotesque and deployed them as the focal imaginative
and revivifying elements of their own discourse. This two-way
transaction thus begins by creating a discursive hierarchy with itself
at the top and a number of inferior realms beneath it where language
is deemed to be 'grotesque': impure, vulgar, of lesser epistemological
clarity, masked and muddied, irresponsibly protean, indecent and
exorbitant. In the act of reforming or rejecting these 'inferior' content-
discourses, holding them subject to new kinds of abstract restraining
device (such as the rhyming couplet), Dryden, Swift and Pope tried
to incorporate them within classical norms.

Thus while Augustan poetry witnesses an unprecedented labour
of transduction in which it battled against the Smithfield Muse to
cleanse the cultural sphere of impure and messy semiotic matter,
it also fed voraciously and incessantly from that very material. It
nourished and replenished its refined formalisms from the symbolic
repertoire of the grotesque body *in the very name of exclusion*. It took
the grotesque within itself so as to reject it, but this meant only that
the grotesque was now an unpalatable and interiorized *phobic* set of
representations associated with avoidance and with others. It could
never be owned. It was always someone else who was possessed by
the grotesque, never the self. In this way the bourgeois public sphere,
that 'idealist' realm of judgement, refinement, wit and rationalism
was dependent upon disavowal, denial, projection.

By disowning the grotesque body the Enlightenment rendered
itself peculiarly vulnerable to the shock of its continued presence or
to its unexpected rediscovery. Swift is never to be taken as normative
in anything, but his description of the critic in *A Tale of a Tub* cannot

be entirely dismissed as a matter of an insane individual excremental obsession – the fascinated disavowal in the name of cleanliness is too prevalent in the whole culture. The critics, he writes,

> In their common perusal of Books, singling out the Errors and Defects, the Nauseous, the Fulsome, the Dull, and the Impertinent, with the Caution of a Man that walks thro' *Edenborough* Streets in a Morning, who is indeed as careful as he can, to watch diligently, and spy out the Filth in his Way, not that he is curious to observe the Colour and Complexion of the Ordure, or take its Dimensions, much less to be padling in, or tasting it: but only with a Design to come out as cleanly as he may.
>
> (*PW*, 1: 56)

The excremental interest then is dissociative: the sole avowed reason for such close observation, in all bad faith, is avoidance, 'to come out as cleanly as he may'. And Edinburgh, like Ireland and Virginia, is made the suitable site for such exercises of avoidance, once more illustrating the way that the grotesque body may be topographically coded. Why Edinburgh? Not simply because it was a town renowned for mean critics, nor because, as A. L. Rowse once remarked, it was a second-rate Presbyterian city, but because a clean ideal sphere of judgement was being constructed and defined in terms of a low and dirty periphery, a notional and literal 'outside' which guaranteed a coherence and privilege to the 'inside'. Similarly in Pope's *Dunciad*, the use of 'low and base' matter in Book II is legitimated in the footnote with the remark that 'the politest men are sometimes obliged to *swear*, when they happen to have to do with porters and oyster-wenches'. The co-ordinates of geography and class intersect as a network of exclusions which underpin and guarantee the status of the refined sphere, enabling it *both* to speak about that which was rapidly becoming unspeakable *and* to define its class identity by projecting the grotesque body onto the low, foreign courts, the provinces and frequently, as in Swift, onto women.

This refined public sphere occupied the centre. That is to say, it carved out a domain between the realm of kings and the world of the alley-ways and taverns, and it did so by forcing together the high and the low as contaminated equivalents, somehow in league with each other and part of a conspiracy of exchange and promiscuity in which the low was ebbing higher to flood the court and the court was sinking into the filthy ways and pastimes of the low. In Book IV of *The Dunciad* Pope satirizes the Grand Tour, upon which the young son of Dulness:

Saw every court, heard every king declare
His royal sense of operas or the fair;
The stews and palace equally explored,
Intrigued with glory, and with spirit whored;

> (Pope, *The Dunciad* IV: 313–16, in Alexander Pope
> (Oxford Authors) ed. PAT ROGERS (Oxford, 1993))

Indeed the whole conception of *The Dunciad*, which makes Dulness at once a Monarch *and* the embodiment of the fairground spirit, guided by her own muse from Smithfield, this conception of the regal and the lumpen promiscuously compounded is the foundational structure of the poem. At the very outset Pope establishes the circuit of corruption which connects the extremes of Court and marketplace in a single figure. Even the very phrase 'The Smithfield Muse' is a dislocating and ironic compound of high classical and low grotesque which perfectly symbolizes the poetics of transgression at the heart of Pope's project:

> The Mighty Mother, and her son who brings
> The Smithfield muses to the ear of kings,
> I sing.
>
> (Pope, *The Dunciad* I: 1–3)

The Poet Laureate is a contaminating mediator who brings the carnivalesque to the Court, perversely muddling and enmiring the polar terms of the classical system. In Book III Pope envisages Dulness irrevocably rising from the fairground stalls and passing through the theatres to finally take her place at Court:

> Till raised from booths, to theatre, to court,
> Her seat imperial Dulness shall transport.
> Already opera prepares the way,
> The sure forerunner of her gentle sway.
>
> (Pope, *The Dunciad* III: 299–302)

Here 'Dulness' seems to be a synonym for carnivalesque or popular culture and nothing else. It illustrates that pervasive organizational antimony between 'Folly' and 'Wit' which, at least since Dryden, had served as the trigger words in the struggle to carve out the intermediate domain of 'judgement and sense' (Wit) from the popular culture of the period (Folly). It is also important to realize, as Robert M. Krapp has indicated, that the terms 'Wit' and 'Sense' were also polarized against each other towards the end of the seventeenth century in the attack by predominantly middle-class writers ('Sense')

upon the aristocratically inclined writers ('Wit').[4] But for Pope in
The Dunciad Dulness is Folly and he attacks those writers who are its
bearers, those vanishing mediators in the conspiracy of history who
(Theobald or Cibber, does it really matter which?) carry the plague
of Bartholomew Fair to reach, with infectious consequence, the very
ears of Royalty:

> 2. *Smithfield* is the place where Bartholomew Fair was kept,
> whose shows, machines, and dramatical entertainments, formerly
> agreeable only to the taste of the rabble, were, by the hero of this
> poem and others of equal genius, brought to the theatres of Covent
> Garden, Lincoln's Innfields, and the Haymarket, to be the reigning
> pleasures of the court and town. This happened in the reigns of
> King George I and II.
>
> (Pope, *The Dunciad* I: n. 2)

After Charles II's return, Bartholomew Fair was extended from
a market officially lasting three days to a fair of two weeks and at
one time possibly six weeks' duration. And as the fair grew and
flourished it drew the theatres into its orbit. The traffic in ideas, plays,
personnel, actors and managers between the fair-booths and the
theatres was considerable in the eighteenth century, not least because
the fairs offered theatre people the chance of employment during the
summer period when the theatres were closed. Actors could often
hope to make more money in the fortnight of Bartholomew Fair
than they could hope to make in a much longer period in the town
theatres.[5] Actors came from the fashionable theatres to perform at
the fair's booths. Henry Woodward for example, a well-known actor
of the period who appeared in Rich's Lilliputian troupe and played
Harlequin Macheath in 1737 in *The Beggars' Pantomime*, made a great
part of his reputation in playing Harlequin at the fair. In the opening
lines of Churchill's *Rosciad* which satirized contemporary actors,
Shuter (*c.* 1728–76) and Yates (1706–96), two reasonably renowned
actors, are both remarked for playing booths at the fairs:

> Shuter keeps open house at Southwark fair,
> And hopes the friends of humour will be there;
> In Smithfield, Yates prepares the rival treat
> For those who laughter love, instead of meat.[6]

William Pinkethman, a member of the Drury Lane Company, ran a
booth at Smithfield with two or three other actors, thereby earning
himself the contempt of a pamphleteer who wrote 'A Comparison
between the Two Stages':

SULLEN: But Pinkethman, the flower of –
CRITIC: – Bartholmew Fair, and the idol of the rabble.[7]

As the fair and the theatre became interfused the fear of a general contamination grew and to be associated with Bartholomew Fair was recognized by critics as a mark of inferiority. It indicated that the writer concerned was a *hybrid* creature trying to straddle the world of popular fairground culture and the 'higher' world of humanistic ethics and ideals. Since, as we have seen, it was precisely self-exclusion from the sites of popular festivity which was a major symbolic project for the emergent professional classes, such hybridization appeared as especially grotesque. The *separation* of the two cultural spheres was a specific and quite self-conscious labour for the Augustan élite, particularly since the two realms appeared to be getting closer together.

Notes

1. See T. C. CURTIS and W. A. SPECK, 'The societies for the reformation of manners: a case study in the theory and practice of moral reform', *Literature and History*, 3 (1976), 45–64, and J. M. COLBY and A. W. PURDUE, *The Civilisation of the Crowd: Popular Culture in England, 1750–1900* (London, 1984), p. 50.

2. See B. BUSHAWAY, *By Rite: Custom, Ceremony and Community in England, 1700–1880* (London, 1982); R. W. MALCOLMSON, *Popular Recreations in English Society, 1700–1850* (Cambridge, 1973); and COLBY and PURDUE, *Civilisation of the Crowd*.

3. See TERRY CASTLE, 'The carnivalization of eighteenth-century English narrative', *Publications of the Modern Language Association of America*, 99 (1984), 903–16.

4. See R. M. KRAPP, 'Class analysis of a literary controversy: wit and sense in seventeenth-century literature', *Science and Society*, 10 (1946), 80–92.

5. See S. ROSENFELD, *The Theatre of the London Fairs in the Eighteenth Century* (Cambridge, 1960).

6. CHARLES CHURCHILL, *The Rosciad* (1761), ll. 29–32.

7. See H. MORLEY, *Memoirs of Bartholomew Fair* (London, 1859), p. 364.

Part Three

The Female Monster

In placing the extract by Carol Houlihan Flynn just after that by Stallybrass and White I have tried to indicate several areas of similarity in that both note the semantic variety produced by references to the body. To some extent, the 'body' can be regarded as an integral ingredient in a whole political economy of repression. As Michel Foucault claims in his case study of the institutionalized punishment of the body, *Discipline and Punish: The Birth of the Prison* (trans. ALAN SHERIDAN, Harmondsworth, 1977; original edn, 1975), a 'history of the body' may be possible when it emphasizes the strategies power carries out on individuals, how bodies are segregated and possessed, and put to productive use (see pp. 24–31). This is not just a matter of political expediency but rather it emerges from deep impulses within society, a method of 'making sense' and thus of naturalization. For Flynn, in her provocative study of *The Body in Swift and Defoe* (Cambridge, 1990), these ideological forces are taken to establish parameters for all considerations of 'sexual connection' and competitive acquisition (p. 5). This extract occurs at the start of the fourth chapter, 'Flesh and Blood: Swift's Sexual Strategies', where Flynn isolates the often submerged fears and abhorrence of the voracious female (the 'famished womb'). Desire is not just a hunger for the 'other' but, in Swift's case, a compulsion to be fought and overcome.

In Ellen Pollak's *The Poetics of Sexual Myth: Gender and Ideology in the Verse of Swift and Pope* (Chicago, 1985) there is an analysis of the patriarchal influences within not just overt cultural practices but also language itself. As Margaret Anne Doody makes clear, part of the indecorum explored above by Stallybrass and White in relation to society in general and summarized in my Introduction was intense where the female figure was concerned. This is a central issue for feminist critics of most of early-century male-authored writing: the pigeonhole of either angel or whore seemed so convenient, the accolade of angel so apparently glorious, that there did not seem to be a problem at all. For Penelope Wilson the problem is one that is seen with particular intensity in a study of Augustan satire, which comprises texts that are 'uniquely adept at constructing the terms of [their] own criticism and at pre-emptive disablement of the opposition' (this volume, pp. 184–5). When resisting the lure of the already constructed sense of what may be relevant or true, feminists have to break rather strenuous frameworks of thought as well as aesthetics. The value of Wilson's essay and that by Doody is that they hold at bay the vicious binary oppositions offered by patriarchal simplifications. Doody, especially, is aware of how an estimate of Swift provided by female witness differs significantly from more accepted perspectives. Support for Swift from Laetitia Pilkington and Mary Barber uncovers a rather more domestic spirit than is usually the case, yet they both in their own ways adopted some of their mentor's colloquial vigour. Mary Leapor and Hester Thrale (Piozzi) also show how Swift's example could provide a model of 'ironic self-presentation', and thus he could be an 'exciting poet of limitation' eschewing both the lyrical and the heroic. In serving as this sort of example, he could therefore help the woman poet escape undue categorization.

Although I have included several essays that have made use of psychoanalytic concepts and vocabulary, the only one that exclusively addresses matters of the unconscious and how it can project deep psychic structures into imaginative form is that by Thomas B. Gilmore, Jr, who discovers a surprising integrity in 'Strephon and Chloe' by referring to Freud's understanding of narcissism. Freud's 1914 essay, 'On Narcissism: An Introduction' (*The Standard Edition of the Complete Psychological Works*, 24 vols, ed. J. STRACHEY et al., 14: 163–90) plays with the myth of Narcissus, punished by Aphrodite for his harsh rejection of Echo by the curse of gazing perpetually into his own reflection in a pool. Unable to capture his own image and possess it, Narcissus wasted away and died. As Gilmore notes, the narcissistic compulsion is always for completion of the self – not on account of some lust for another. There is a link here between this syndrome and the 'mirror stage' isolated by Jacques Lacan (*Ecrits: A Selection*, ed. ALAN SHERIDAN [New York, 1971], pp. 1–7). The ideal wholeness suggested by the mirror-image is something upon which the protean self strives to model itself or reach for. An unbroken union between outer and inner is the comforting goal, yet it functions only as myth, effacing the radical instability of the self. In 'Strephon and Chloe', Swift deploys scatological details to deconstruct the glamorous images both have of each other: both on their wedding night see the other urinating, and Strephon, 'as he filled the reeking vase / Let[s] fly a rouser [either loud fart or strong jet] in [Chloe's] face' (ll. 191–92). Their mutual (necessary?) self-delusion is destroyed, its civilized detachment exposed merely as a veneer, but an 'uncivilized' yet sensible substitute takes its place: 'On sense and wit your passion found, / By decency cemented round; . . .' (ll. 307–8). As Gilmore illustrates, the female monster can be located in the male brain. For those wanting to know more about how Gilmore's approach might help inform other readings, see *Narcissism and the Text: Literature and the Psychology of Self*, ed. LYNNE LAYTON and BARBARA ANN SCHAPIRO (New York, 1986; especially the Introduction, pp. 1–35).

9 Flesh and Blood: Swift's Sexual Strategies*

CAROL HOULIHAN FLYNN

For fine ideas vanish fast,
While all the gross and filthy last.
('Strephon and Chloe', ll. 233–34)

Unlike Defoe dreaming Moll's escape from Roxana's nightmare, Swift cannot even begin to imagine women from the inside. Keeping his ironic distance, he flails and strips 'the sex' to get at the truth of its loathsome condition. The knowledge he produces is always external and judgmental. For reasons cultural as well as psychological, Swift defines women according to a physicality that is gross, filthy, and lasting. Women threaten to scatter reason, waste energy, and destroy the possibility of civilization. The disorderly energies that Swift so actively invokes in his fictional explorations of women must be repressed or denied to be endured. In the end, he can only run from the engrossing feminine temptations of unreason that he has both exposed and invented.

Swift's consciousness of the absurdity of his position produces an ironic detachment that serves to protect him from the hysterical implications of his misogyny. Strephon, silly Strephon, is the cracked one, he blandly reassures his gentle reader, not me. *I* stuff rue up my nose. Indirectly, he displaces the burden of sexual detection upon the reader, so often blamed for all the filthy imaginings Swift both invents and attacks. His retreat from women is complicated even further by his need for them. He demonstrates repeatedly a fearful attraction for the nurse figure, that maternal surrogate who nourishes and punishes. Jealous of his own independence, yet hungry for the attentions of a governing yet servile feminine figure, Swift represents in his fictions a system of sexual strategies that allow repressed juvenile fantasies to be both explored and contained.

---

* Reprinted from *The Body in Swift and Defoe* (Cambridge: Cambridge University Press, 1990), pp. 88–94.

The explorer is always at risk. A central fictional situation
Swift offers his reader is the paralyzing discovery of the body.
Characteristically, Swiftian explorers both ferret out and run away
from their knowledge. Gulliver discloses the yahoo nature he is bent
on repressing when he taunts his 'fellow' yahoos with his physicality.
'I have reason to believe', he primly reports, 'they had some
Imagination that I was of their own Species, which I often assisted
myself, by stripping up my Sleeves, and shewing my naked Arms
and Breast in their Sight, when my Protector was with me.' On
occasion, Gulliver will even strip himself stark naked beneath the
lustful gaze of a young female yahoo who embraces him 'after a most
fulsome Manner' and quits her grasp 'with the utmost Reluctancy'.
Mortified by her 'natural Propensity to me as one of their own
Species', Gulliver spends the rest of his time on the island of the
Houyhnhnms trying to deny the fact that he has forced into
consciousness, that he possesses the body of a species he loathes
even to look at. But even his loathing seems suspect. After catching
a young male of three years, he coyly supplies a 'Circumstance' to
vex his reader: 'that while I held the odious Vermin in my Hands,
it voided its filthy Excrements of a yellow liquid Substance, all over
my Cloaths' (*PW*, 11: 265–67). Gulliver's shock of recognition is at
best a stock response to a physical drama scripted to confirm his
predictable worst suspicions.

Swift's fascinated revulsion towards the physical becomes even
more axiomatic when he confronts 'the Sex'. It takes a female yahoo,
'not ... above Eleven Years old' (*PW*, 11: 267), to make it impossible
for Gulliver to deny his yahoo nature. The horror of the physically
known 'Species', that category of creatures so like, but necessarily
unlike the self, becomes the horror of the physically known woman
caught inevitably in the act of being vile. Thus Strephon and
Cassinus lose their wits and pride with their discovery that Celia,
Celia, Celia shits, compelled as they are to seek assiduously after
well-hidden secrets of the hoary deep. Spying on nature, most
particularly feminine nature, they become debilitated by their own
discoveries of natural acts.

Corporeal knowledge becomes particularly vexing in marriage, that
dreaded state of 'Repentance, Discord, Poverty, Jealousy, Sickness,
Spleen, Loathing, &c.' (*PW*, 4: 252). A 'known' Chloe who farts and
stinks with abandon is no more acceptable than the inaccessible
Goddess exuding ambrosia. Anality might replace sublimity, but the
body still gets in the way. 'Love such niceties requires', Strephon and
Chloe learn: 'One blast will put out all his fires' (ll. 135–36). Swift's
solution to the problem: don't eat beans.

The advice is both serious and ludicrous, typical of Swift's
radically simplified sexual discourse.

> Keep them to wholesome food confined,
> Nor let them taste what causes wind;
> ('Tis this the Sage of Samos means,
> Forbidding his disciples beans)
>
> (ll. 123–26)

The sage, Swift reminds his readers in a note, is Pythagoras, infamous
for his own personal and philosophical attempts to purify the body.
Such notorious asceticism would appear to sit well with Swift, and
finds its way into the clean, bracing regimen of the Houyhnhnms,
whose nature is so very easily satisfied. But simple solutions verge
on farce in the real world, where once she 'has got the art', Miss
Moll, archetypal 'Jade', will not be able to restrain her natural self
from letting loose. 'She cannot help it for her heart; / But, out it flies'
(ll. 128–31). Swift presents here a physical nature irrepressible and
gross. Inverting conduct-manual formula, he suggests that maidens
will need to 'learn' the art of letting 'it' fly, or rather unlearn the false
modesty pasted over their base nature, but he is not implying that
the natural maid is any less disgusting. Had Strephon only been wise
enough to spy on Chloe before 'that fatal day' on her 'house of ease',
he would have detected the true woman:

> In all the postures of her face,
> Which nature gives in such a case;
> Distortions, groanings, strainings, heavings;
> 'Twere better you had licked her leavings.
>
> (ll. 239–42)

No matter how many beans incipient goddesses forebear ingesting,
they will always reveal themselves to be at bottom filthy. While
blandly advising Chloe 'from the spouse each blemish hide / More
than from all the world beside' (ll. 253–54), Swift grimly sends out
his platoons of sexual spies in search of her nature. Inverting Platonic
idealism, Swift argues that the truly 'real', the matter that is Chloe,
will overcome the ideal, 'For fine ideas vanish fast / While all the
gross and filthy last.' To reconcile the demands of flesh and spirit,
Strephon should shun the body altogether and found his passion on
sense and wit. Love will become friendship, nature will be refined
into 'good nature', while sexuality itself will turn into discourse.

The ironies implicit in Swift's discourse provide a necessary
distance, for the female body threatens not only to offend, but to
scatter reason and swallow up certainty. The women themselves tend
to fall apart, revealing a dissolution that inspires terror and sometimes
– in passing – pity. Swift graphically mangles his 'Beautiful Young
Nymph Going to Bed', before making a judgment that both approaches
and denies his satirical victim's need:

> But how shall I describe her arts
> To recollect the scatter'd parts?
> Or shew the anguish, toil, and pain,
> Of gathering up herself again?

> (ll. 67–70)

In spite of incipient sympathy, the narrator of the poem finally
withdraws to leave Corinna 'in the Morning dizened', warning that
'Who sees, will spew; who smells, be poisoned' (ll. 73–74). Similarly,
the Celia of 'The Progress of Beauty' mechanically rots away each
night to awaken to a dissolution of materials most alarming in their
mutability.[1] The dissolution becomes moral as well as physical. If
matter offends, scattered matter compounds the offense. The disorder
which results blurs distinction and makes it difficult for Swift to find
fault as precisely as he would wish. For how can he catalog chaos?[2]
Chattering over their cards, roaring and railing louder than the
rabble, grosser than a pack of fishwives over their gin, 'Modern
Ladies', each one a filthy mate, dissolve into 'The jumbling particles
of matter' that 'In chaos made not such a clatter' ('The Journal of a
Modern Lady', ll. 184–85). The scattered matter the women represent,
'Mopsa, who stinks her spouse to death', 'Hircina rank with sweat'
(ll. 156–58), threaten with a physicality that violates even the
possibility of order.

When Swift rails at the disorderly nature of women, he is not only
revealing personal fears of dissolution, but articulating the same
uneasiness we have seen in the work of Defoe and Montesquieu.
Unless they are somehow contained or occupied, women threaten to
scatter vital energy that Freud would later recuperate as materials
necessary to build civilization and its discontents. The sexual act,
scattering material most personal, and its 'necessary passion' requires,
as Mandeville complained, a medium most difficult to hit.[3] While a
'healthy' use of the body was encouraged, much discourse dwells on
the possibility of failure, waste, or excess.[4]

By nature excessive, Swift most dramatically calls up visions
of disorder that threaten to overwhelm his own plans to chastise
sense. In his sermon on 'The Difficulty of Knowing One's Self', Swift

alludes to the problems of 'collect[ing] all his scattered and roving Thoughts into some Order and Compass, that he may be able to take a clear and distinct View of them'. The only answer is retirement from the world of sense and sensuality, 'and how hard and painful a thing must it needs be to a Man of Passion and Infirmity, amidst such a Crowd of Objects that are continually striking upon the Sense, and solliciting the Affections, not to be moved and interrupted by one or other of them' (*PW*, 9: 356).[5] His solution, characteristically radical, suggests a struggle he counters with irony, for to protect his vulnerability, he insists upon the most threatening of visions made deliberately bland through a world weariness verging on parody.

Typically, he presents the terror experienced by naïve subjects enclosed within his own ironic frame. In 'The Lady's Dressing-Room', Strephon goes mad with the realization that *Celia, Celia, Celia* shits, but his narrator deflates this hysteria to reassure the reader that as long as he stuffs rue up his nose, Strephon should come to appreciate the sex he flees. By mocking Strephon's hysteria, Swift projects a more urbane acceptance of the gaudy tulips he purports to admire. But in one chilling couplet, Swift reveals the reason for the terror he barely contains by disowning Strephon's madness. 'Should I the queen of love refuse', the narrator asks, 'Because she rose from stinking ooze?' (ll. 131–32). Swift alludes here to a myth of dismemberment, of scattering, and of physical devouring that calls up everything that keeps him out of conjugal beds. For in these lines, the narrator grounds Celia's being in a stinking ooze which is not just offensive, but generative at the expense of masculine sexuality. One of the variations of the myth of Venus's birth depends upon the emasculation of Uranus. In punishment for his rebellion against the gods, Uranus's testicles were ripped from his body and tossed into the sea. Venus rose out of the ooze and froth generated from his mutilation. (It is worth remembering that the Yahoos also were believed to have originated from the ooze and froth of the sea.) The way Swift negligently tosses off such volatile material complicates the terror of the emasculation, but the image remains: Venus symbolically devouring Uranus in her ascension.[6]

Swift employs images of devouring equally troubling in much of *Gulliver's Travels*. Capable of taking up twenty or thirty smaller fowl at the end of his knife, Gulliver on Lilliput can tease his captors with his voracious ways, pretending on one occasion, penknife in hand, a readiness to eat the more impudent members of the rabble alive (*PW*, 11: 31). Gulliver on Brobdingnag, more obviously vulnerable, barely escapes being eaten alive by a large infant who is only pacified by 'the last Remedy', a 'monstrous Breast' that perfectly disgusts Gulliver (*PW*, 11: 91). Later an even more 'horrible Spectacle', a cancerous breast 'swelled to a monstrous Size, full of Holes, in two or three of which I could have easily crept, and covered my whole Body', threatens in its swollen magnitude to engulf him (*PW*, 11: 112–113). But then Brobdingnag offers room for many 'nauseous sights'. The Queen herself, although boasting a weak stomach, 'would craunch the Wing of a Lark, Bones and all, between her Teeth', while the malicious dwarf almost drowns Gulliver in a bowl of cream and manages to stuff him into a marrow bone ready to be eaten (*PW*, 11: 106–108). When the dwarf plays his naughty tricks, he is turning his enemy into material for consumption, food fit for a queen. Even on Laputa, appetite interferes with the pursuit of the ideal. While their husbands keep one eye on heaven, their notorious wives keep one eye on Lagado, threatening to break out and slide down to feed on less idealistically inclined males. Even the queen appears suspicious enough to be kept confined to the island until she is past childbearing. The fate of the prime minister's lady serves as a warning. 'On the Pretence of Health', she managed to slip down to Lagado to hide away in an 'obscure Eating-House' where she consumed the pleasures of 'an old deformed Footman, who beat her every day' (*PW*, 11: 166).

Overwhelmed by so many predators, Gulliver would have understood too well John Maubray's description in his *Female Physician* of the '*attractive Faculty*' of the famished womb. As Nicholas Venette warned, 'The Womb of a Woman is in the Number of the insatiable things mentioned in the Scriptures . . . and I cannot tell whether there is anything in the World, its greediness may be compared unto; neither Hell fire nor the Earth being so devouring, as the Privy Parts of a Lascivious Woman.'[7] For a man as (ironically) desperate for order as Swift (for 'Order governs the world. The Devil is the author of confusion'[8]), the sexual act itself threatens to subsume rationality always perilous just as surely as Venus threatens to devour Uranus's manhood. Throughout his work Swift employs powerful metaphors to contain that which threatens, but at the same time, he appears compelled to explore the stinking ooze in spite of himself. For as Defoe reflects in his fiction, and as Swift demonstrates not only in his literary productions but in his self-consciously acted out life, desire, even when desire leads into death, is most difficult to quell. Swift may advise us not to eat beans, but in spite of dieting, the appetite itself gets in the way.

Notes

1. As Felicity Nussbaum notes, 'without substantial form, woman soon fades' (*The Brink of All We Hate: English Satires on Women* [Lexington, KY, 1984]), p. 101.

2. In her study of Swift's 'Disordered World of the Gentlewoman', LOUISE K. BARNETT discusses Swift's catalogs implicating women as the source of earthly disorder (in *Swift's Poetic Worlds* (Newark, NJ, 1981), p. 159).

3. BERNARD MANDEVILLE, *A Modest Defence of Public Stews* [London, 1724], ed. RICHARD I. COOK, Augustan Reprints, No. 162 (Los Angeles, 1973), p. 28.

4. The edgy fear of emission is difficult to date. As LAWRENCE STONE suggests, when Tissot announces that the loss of one ounce of semen equals the loss of forty ounces of blood, he was offering a 'new version of Avicenna's medieval claim that one ejaculation is more debilitating than forty bloodlettings', an old belief particularly attractive to a sexual economy dedicated to exercising their complicated iatrophydraulic sexual systems (*The Family, Sex and Marriage in England, 1500–1800* [London, 1977], pp. 495–8). CHRISTOPHER FOX discusses the 'early eighteenth-century anti-masturbatory craze sparked, at least in part, by a pamphlet titled *ONANIA*' (London, 1709–10), in 'The Myth of Narcissus in Swift's *Travels*', *Eighteenth-Century Studies*, 20 (1986), 17–33. CHARLES E. ROSENBURG considers a later nineteenth-century concern with 'control' in his discussion of repression and masturbation in 'Sexuality, Class and Role', in *No Other Gods: On Science and American Social Thought* (Baltimore, MD, 1976), pp. 71–88.

5. 'As soon as the Appetite is alarmed, and seizeth upon the Heart, a little Cloud gathereth about the Head, and spreadeth a kind of Darkness over the Face of the soul, whereby it is hindered from taking a clear and distinct View of Things' (*PW*, 9: 358).

6. HESIOD, *Theogony*, trans. DOROTHEA WENDER (Harmondsworth, 1973), ll. 188–200. See ROBERT GRAVES, *The Greek Myths*, 2 vols (rev. edn, Harmondsworth, 1960), 1: 37–9, 49–50. DONALD GREENE argues that 'if one wanted to be "archetypal", one could praise Swift's awareness – in the parallel illustration of Venus, symbol of human love and warmth and the continuity of the human species, rising from the Mediterranean slime – of the great eternal facts of the human condition', and goes on to find Swift sounding 'Joycean' here, 'a robust Irish Molly Bloom in clerical garb' ('On Swift's "Scatological" Poems', *Sewanee Review*, 75 [1967], 672–89, repr. in *Essential Articles for the Study of Jonathan Swift's Poetry*, ed. DAVID M. VIETH [Hamden, CT, 1984], p. 227).

7. See ROBERT A. ERICKSON, 'The Books of Generation', and PAUL-GABRIEL BOUCÉ, 'Some Sexual Beliefs and Myths', in *Sexuality in Eighteenth-Century Britain*, ed. PAUL-GABRIEL BOUCÉ (Manchester, 1982), pp. 84, 42.

8. *Journal to Stella*, 2 vols, ed. HAROLD WILLIAMS (Oxford, 1948), 1: 72. See also 'Doing Good: A Sermon' (*PW*, 9: 238), for a less ironic discussion of the Devil, author of confusion, struggling against a 'God of Order'.

10 Feminism and the Augustans: Some Readings and Problems*

PENELOPE WILSON

Early in 1715 Pope wrote, for decency's sake in the guise of their 'brother', to Martha and Theresa Blount, describing a visit with a doctor and a divine to inspect 'the most reigning Curiosity in the town', currently a hermaphrodite. The account is in Pope's rakish mode, a set-piece of the *risqué* rather than a personal reaction: the priest has to imitate the method of the Apostle Thomas, seeing and feeling, and the Doctor opines that 'upon the whole it was a woman; whatever might give a handle to think otherwise, was a trifle, nothing being more common than for a child to be mark'd with that thing which the mother long'd for'.[1] Since the letter was included in the 1735 editions of Pope's works, it was actually published in the same year as the *Epistle to a Lady*, the poem which ends with a tribute to the same Martha Blount as an androgynous ideal, a 'softer Man', a blend of elements picked from each sex. In the letter the 'brother' concludes – 'As for this Party's temper of mind, it appears to be a most even disposition, partaking of the good qualities of both sexes. ... Of how obliging and complaisant a turn appears by this, that he tells the Ladies he has the Inclinations of a Gentleman, and that she tells the Gentleman she has the *Tendre* of a Lady.' We can hardly help noticing the natural slippage in this bawdily-tinged account from the best kind of fusion or tempering (like Martha Blount, 'Woman's at best a Contradiction still') to the nastiness of the Sporus portrait in the *Epistle to Dr Arbuthnot*, published one month earlier than *To a Lady*: 'His Wit all see-saw between *that* and *this*, / Now high, now low, now Master up, now Miss, / And he himself one vile Antithesis'. Thin partitions divide the good contradiction from the vile antithesis. The tribute to Martha Blount if set alongside that letter can be seen to hover on the borders of monstrosity: it is not only Calypso who is 'ne'er so sure our passion to create / As when she touch'd the brink of all we hate' (*To a Lady*, ll. 51–2).

---

* Reprinted from COLIN MACCABE (ed.), *Futures for English* (Manchester: Manchester University Press, 1988) pp. 80–92.

One of the earliest of the still relatively few pieces of feminist work on the period bears the telling title 'The female monster in Augustan satire'.[2] If feminism has – until very recently – left Augustan satire alone, it is partly no doubt because it can expect few rewards from an area which offers more obvious scope for recrimination than for critical insight. To set alongside Pope's hermaphrodite, based this time on the 'curiosity' of the year 1708, there is the 'double mistress' episode of the *Memoirs of Martin Scriblerus*, where the object of desire is literally monstrous, one of a pair of Siamese twins joined at the waist and with genitalia in common. The isolated figures of Vanessa and 'Stella' and Martha Blount, idealized largely by virtue of their transcendence of the differentially feminine, provide at best a frail counterweight to set against a well-documented gamut of misogyny which runs from attacks on particular women, and in particular on women writing, through satire on the *mores* and pastimes of the contemporary female world, to a representation of woman as species – whether as a physical being as in Swift's 'scatological' poems, or with the more ambivalent recoil of Pope's psychological characterization in *To a Lady* – which is aptly enough summed up in that phrase, 'the brink of all we hate'.[3] Female sexuality is a focus for fear or derision, or both: Gulliver's climactic trauma in the land of the Houyhnhnms is after all the embrace of a young female Yahoo. Motherhood has no better a press. Breast-feeding in Brobdingnag provides Gulliver with one of the nastiest sights of his voyages, and in *The Dunciad*, where the 'Mother' is figured as a force of anti-creation, a black hole drawing everything back into her vortex, images of giving birth tend constantly towards transmogrification – as 'Sooterkin', for example (I. 126), or embryo: 'How hints, like spawn, scarce quick in embryo lie, / How new-born nonsense first is taught to cry, / Maggots half-form'd in rhyme exactly meet, / And learn to crawl upon poetic feet' (I. 59–62).

There is a striking, though not unpredictable, lack of awareness in most standard commentaries that there is an issue here at all. One doesn't have to be a very humourless feminist to identify the masculine clubbery which can see the 'broad humour and farcical action' of the Double Mistress episode in the Scriblerus *Memoirs* as a 'refreshing change', nor to query the latent sexism of several now classic readings of *The Rape of the Lock* – less overt, but perhaps no less objectionable than Dr Johnson's frank commendation of its moral as exposing 'the freaks, and humours, and spleen, and vanity of women, as they embroil families in discord, and fill houses with disquiet'. The notes to the Twickenham edition of *To a Lady* offer an unreconstructed litany of prejudice, randomly exemplified by the gloss on the line 'from loveless youth to unrespected age', where

the parallel weighting given to two items of 'information' about the
Duchess of Buckingham – that she obtained a separation from her
first husband because of his brutality to her, and that 'in her old age
she became one of the town's [i.e. Horace Walpole's?] jokes' – brings
out all the potential insensitivity of Pope's zeugma. Pope *is* allowed
to have been unfair, for 'political' reasons, to Queen Caroline ('the
worst that can be said of such a sensible and tolerant woman is
that she maintained an implacable hatred of her eldest son'): sexual
politics, however, count for nothing. Because of its date, perhaps
the most startling example of the general myopia comes from a
work published as late as 1971, where we are told of Swift's *The
Lady's Dressing-Room* and other similar pieces that the scatological
elements, the relentless recitations of the details of female grossness,
'dramatize the failure of people, *as represented by the young heroes, to
reconcile the physical imperfections and animal nature of man with his
decent and spiritual side*' (my italics).[4]

Clearly there is plenty of scope for a revisionary questioning of the
ideological assumptions which tend to be brought into play as one
reads these works: and teaching early eighteenth-century literature
to today's undergraduates one is made perpetually aware of the
dimensions of the challenge. But despite that real need to free
readings from the pall of misogyny, there are acute problems for
feminism in these uncongenial waters. The political importance of
a more consciously resistant reading in this case seems to remain,
disappointingly, out of all proportion to its usefulness as a critical
tool. The potential creativity of entry into the text from the margins
too easily loses itself either in a righteous cul-de-sac of recrimination
or in a self-generating process of elaboration on the 'positions'
of feminist theory. On the one hand there is a real danger of
unproductive anachronism, the feminist reader of Augustan satire
courting comparison with the hack author of Swift's *Tale of a Tub*,
reading Homer, in current parlance, against the grain: 'What can
be more defective and unsatisfactory than his long dissertation
upon tea?' On the other hand, whereas in its own defence, to avert
the charges, or more importantly the consciousness, of naiveté or
marginality to which it is so prone, feminism must meet academic
criticism on its own terms, in doing so it can itself become at least
stylistically complicit in forms of scholastic oppression to which it
should be particularly sensitive. The justice of the cause, one wants
to remind oneself, is not necessarily a measure of its availability for
theoretical sophistication.

These problems – general problems, of course, for feminist
criticism – are, I would argue, in a special way integral to this topic.
Augustan satire is perhaps uniquely adept at constructing the terms

of its own criticism and at pre-emptive disablement of the opposition. 'Augustanism', if more than a conventional denomination, is more usefully seen as a strategy, a range of rhetorics and tactics, than as a set of absolute beliefs. It is strongly anti-theoretical in stance. Like Barthes's 'mythology' representing History as Nature, it represents itself and its values as beyond the merely partisan, timeless rather than accidental, paradoxically 'universal' in that by these values most of the world will fall. Opposition is inevitably defined as partial. From the early *Essay on Criticism* to the final *Dunciad* the good critic is for Pope the one who looks to 'the whole' rather than to parts; and as the word 'Author' suggests in the following passage from *The Dunciad*, the bad critic connects closely with the scientific investigators approved by Dulness, who 'See Nature in some partial narrow shape, / And let the Author of the whole escape' (IV: 455–56). Two tenets of characteristic circularity are hinted at here: that the proper concern of literature and criticism is with human nature in general rather than with the particular and the partisan, and that works are to be read not 'against the grain' but in the same spirit that the author writ. Feminism thus fits neatly if anachronistically into Pope's account of critical malpractice in the *Essay on Criticism*. It is particularly threatened by distinctions like those set up in the language of the following passages:

> Most Criticks, fond of some subservient Art,
> Still make the *Whole* depend upon a *Part*,
> They talk of *Principles*, but *Notions* prize,
> And All to one lov'd Folly sacrifice . . .
>
> Thus Criticks, of less *Judgment* than *Caprice*,
> *Curious*, not *knowing*, not *exact*, but *nice*,
> Form *short Ideas*; and offend in *Arts*
> (As most in *Manners*) by a *Love to Parts*.
>
> (ll. 263–66, 285–88)

In the face of such high-precision intimidation, there are few options but to hold out exactly for 'caprice' and 'curiosity' as, if not ends in themselves, at least the tools of exploration, necessary inroads into the apparent certainties embedded in 'judgement', 'knowing', and the confident representation of 'the whole'. One of the first premises of feminism is, of course, that the structures it has to confront are not those of a universal, all-embracing humanism, but are coloured by an unspoken androcentrism; that these part/ whole statements can be, and need to be, turned on their heads, so that the shape of Pope's own construction of 'Nature' is recognized as 'partial' and 'narrow'. It is hardly accidental that Augustanism, coloured as it is by the ethos of a like-minded coterie, has remained something of a masculine preserve. The parallel drawn by Pope in the lines above between criticism and 'manners' is still a resonant one in academic circles, and highlights the fear endemic to women's studies of being *mal à propos*, of being ridiculous, humourless, or banal. In doing so it may help to focus our attention on the more particular problems of the voice of feminist resistance when confronted with the refractions and complexities of specific examples of Augustan wit.

In Pope's letter to the Blount sisters the hermaphroditic penis may be a 'trifle', but sexual difference is not: the joke places the phallus as the object of the woman's longing at the centre of sexual existence. The representation of sexual difference is at the heart of this topic, and on it must depend any further judgements about what seem to me the less interesting questions of whether or not the texts or their authors are sexist, misogynist, or partly or wholly 'recuperable'. In this chapter I want to look at the question of sexual difference in two of the best-known of the Augustan poems on 'women', Swift's *The Lady's Dressing-Room* and Pope's *To a Lady*, noting in passing that for these purposes there is an imbalance in the material available to us: there is, in this sense, no *Essay on Man*. It goes more or less without saying that here and elsewhere both Pope and Swift represent positions which are properly inimical to a modern feminist consciousness. Pope's poem calls constantly for such qualification: in its validation in advance in the first lines of a sexist discourse of dumb blondes and brunettes (' "Most Women have no Characters at all" . . . And best distinguished by black, brown, or fair'); in the relegation of women to a purely private, domestic realm; in the Miltonic subordination effected through the image of the moon and its reflected light; in the collapsing of female obedience and desire – the one who 'by submitting sways'; in the notion of woman as charming in her weaknesses, 'fine by defect, and delicately weak', this last formulation being one directly challenged by Mary Wollstonecraft.[5] *The Lady's Dressing-Room* is understandably regarded as one of the most notorious sites of anti-feminist animus, no less so for being, as Felicity Nussbaum and others have shown, in a long literary tradition of obscene and scatological satire against women.

Swift's dressing-room is a far cry from the narcissistic ritual presented to public view in *The Rape of the Lock* ('And now, unveil'd, the Toilet stands display'd'): instead we are drawn in to the stealthy inspection of the closed quarters of woman and maid which had been used since Lucretius, Juvenal, Ovid, as the paradoxical site of potential redemption for the love-pangs of the suffering suitor.[6]

The accusatory *reportage* of Swift's dressing-room poem presents a room from which the lady herself has issued forth in the third line leaving the room 'void' for Strephon's inspection, 'void' only in a sense which one might most appropriately gloss as 'vacant', since in other respects it is all too full – of litter, debris, matter. In Pope's ceremonial set-piece the looking-glass is the site of beauty made manifest: here the absent image is transmogrified into the world of the magnifying glass and tweezers, of 'worms in the nose', bristles on the chin, ear-wax, snot, grease, sweat, the scrapings of teeth and gums. The catalogue of nouns, scarcely relieved by the sparse adjectival qualifiers of equal maculacy – 'begummed, bemattered, and beslimed' (l. 45) – produces a verbal texture clogged like that of Celia's own combs, 'filled up with dirt so closely fixed, / No brush could force a way betwixt; / A paste of composition rare, / Sweat, dandriff, powder, lead and hair' (ll. 21–24).

Strephon's investigations, and the narrator's rhetorical excitement – though not perhaps the reader's arc of revulsion – culminate with the discovery of the commode and its contents. The trauma of his 'peeping' turns Strephon – now fittingly 'blind' to female charms – into an out-and-out misogynist:

> His foul imagination links
> Each dame he sees with all her stinks . . .
> All women his description fits,
> And both ideas jump like wits,
> By vicious fancy coupled fast,
> And still appearing in contrast.

> (ll. 121–22; 125–28)

In the well-known coda, the narrator dissociates himself from the extremity of his hero's reaction: 'Should I the queen of love refuse, / Because she rose from stinking ooze?' (ll. 131–32) If Strephon would but stop his nose – like Gulliver on his return from his final voyage? –

> He soon would learn to think like me,
> And bless his ravished eyes to see
> Such order from confusion sprung,
> Such gaudy *tulips* raised from *dung*.

> (ll. 141–44)

Language and structure enable various utterly 'respectable' readings of the poem – Christian, proto-Freudian, straightforwardly didactic. The poem follows a characteristic Swiftian pattern: the hero, like Gulliver, is disillusioned in proportion as he had before been

gulled into accepting a false and clichéd romantic construct. Indeed,
since Strephon's case is presented to us not in his own voice but
by a commenting narrator, the coda usefully makes explicit a way
of diagnosing Gulliver's final hippophiliac disorder in terms of
associative psychology – horses and rationality, man and bestiality
bound into a dichotomy no less rigid for being inverted. As one
considers that coda more closely, however, the apparent moderation
of the narrator's pose is re-read as a hopeless and violent yoking
together of its own constituent obsessions and refusals, compromised
rather than a compromise, a symptom of that ambiguously 'ravished'
sight which constitutes a common ground between him and Strephon.
The locus of insanity shifts backwards through the poem, with the
narrator's attempts to impose a distancing literary order on Strephon's
findings, and his perfunctory authorial gestures towards reticence
or euphemism ('the stockings, why should I expose . . . ?' (l. 51),
'Why, Strephon, will you tell the rest?' (l. 69)), coming to seem an
increasingly mad and irrelevant refrain to the catalogue of disgust:
we could be again in the company of the hack of *A Tale of a Tub*. In
the mythologising and metaphoric moves of the presentation of the
excremental 'chest' – the comparison with Pandora's box, and the
lingering mutton chops simile – the narrator quite overtakes the now
'cautious' Strephon in his unmediated involvement in the survey.

> But Strephon cautious never meant
> The bottom of the pan to grope,
> And fowl his hands in search of hope . . .
>
> As mutton cutlets, prime of meat . . .
> So things which must not be expressed,
> When *plumped* into the reeking chest,
> Send up an excremental smell
> To taint the parts from whence they fell.
>
> (ll. 92–94; 99; 109–12)[7]

All this undermining – of Strephon, of the narrator, and obliquely
of the reader who lends a complicit ear – may seem to deflect much
of the attack from 'Celia' and her body on to the minds of men.
A tactful, if incongruously bland, reading is made available for
the critical consensus in the way, directly analogous with Swift's
best-known prose writings, in which the poem both suggests and
explodes a schema of compromise. We are free to conclude that,
like others in the same *remedium amoris* mode – 'A beautiful young
nymph going to bed', 'Strephon and Chloe' – 'woman' functions here
simply as the clearest image of the discrepancy between the human

– and especially the literary – capacity for idealization and the gross materiality of things as they are. The poem is not really, then, 'about' women: on the contrary, as we have seen, it is (although few critics have felt entirely comfortable with it) about man's 'decent and spiritual side'.

A feminist reading would want to resist the hermeneutic move to write out the issue of gender from the poem. Granting that Swift's scatological satire is not solely directed against women, it would not accept as merely accidental or opportunist the association in this and in other poems of the feminine with dirtiness and decay. It is hardly a twentieth-century possibility that the poem should be taken – as it largely was by contemporaries, with a brave literality – as primarily practical in its aim, to reform women's boudoir habits. That even then some sort of accommodation seemed necessary is suggested by the unlikely shift of emphasis found in one of the earliest critiques of the poem: 'whenever he offends against delicacy, he teaches it. . . . And though it may reasonably be supposed that few English ladies have such a dressing-room as Celia's, yet many may have given sufficient cause for reminding them, that very soon after desire has been gratified, the utmost delicacy becomes necessary, to prevent disgust'.[8]

It takes a rare reader to uncover here the lineaments of gratified desire; but even without them, the operation of the poem is a complex one, at once moralistic and cathartic. The generalizing, homiletic impulse of a de-gendered reading operates on a sophisticated level of interpretation, demanding to be decoded; but the poem also enacts a much more primitive ritual of control of the unspeakable, cleansing through naming. Jean Hagstrum finds the author here less like a wit or an outraged priest than 'a Freudian patient repeating compulsively the particulars that produced his trauma'.[9] The poem certainly has something pathological about it, a dimension which retrospectively, and sometimes anachronistically, taints even its more innocent locutions, as 'issues' and 'tissues' in lines 3 and 4. The purpose of this inventory, we are told in lines 9 and 10, is 'to make the matter clear'; and in the context of this extravagant be-mattering (l. 45) there seems a fleeting possibility that itemisation itself could somehow restore a kind of purity or transparence to the impurity of the congealed effluvia of the dressing-room debris.

In that context, and with sexual difference in mind, it is interesting to note the absence of disgust at any specifically feminine failures in hygiene; and one might compare a similar silence in *Strephon and Chloe*, where honeymoon disillusion is precipitated by the revelation of Chloe's bodily nature not through the menstrual anxiety which is the common currency of wedding-night jokes (hinted at no doubt in the narrator's use of the phrase 'no proper season' (l. 160)) but through a unisex Swiftian variation: 'Carminative and diuretic, / Will damp all passions sympathetic' (ll. 133–34). In anthropological terms matter issuing from the body is dangerous because of its marginal nature, and Mary Douglas suggests that the particular bodily margins to which the beliefs of each culture attribute power will depend on 'what situation the body is mirroring'.[10] What Celia represents in *The Lady's Dressing-Room* is not the otherness of the menstrual body, with its attendant disgusts and fears: Swift's 'nymphs' do produce on their respective Strephons and Cassinuses effects nearly as dramatic as those feared by some cultures to result from contact with menstrual blood, but disillusion operates through a recognition of sameness, of shared excrementality, rather than through fear of otherness. The lines 'Should I the queen of love refuse / Because she rose from stinking ooze?' very possibly contain an echo of some lines by Etherege where the reference is quite explicitly vaginal:[11] even allusion here seems to act rather as suppression, the insistence on the excremental nature of the 'smell' indicating the consistency of the urge to write sexuality out of the picture.

There is of course another side to Swift's views on women, even without an invocation of the *Journal to Stella* – the tough, unsentimental challenge of his arguments for female education, a concern introduced into the Utopian visions of Books I and IV of *Gulliver's Travels*, and expounded in his 'Letter to a very young lady on her marriage' without a vestige of the 'lullaby strains of condescending endearments' to which Mary Wollstonecraft was to take such strong exception in later male purveyors of 'advice' to young women. The 'Letter' is an important document in a version of feminism as integration, the whole direction of Swift's exhortations being that women should make themselves, and be allowed to make themselves, intellectually fit companions for men. Clearly of limited acceptability from the viewpoint of modern feminism, the letter is uncompromisingly hostile to the forms of female bonding ('A Knot of Ladies got together by themselves, is a very School of Impertinence and Detraction'); like some of the poems (e.g., 'The furniture of a woman's mind'), its most positive tribute to women is anger at what Swift sees as the almost universal misdirection of their energies. The fact that Swift has found a place in studies both of misogyny and of feminism in the eighteenth century is only apparently a paradox, as is perhaps most economically illustrated by one characteristically unconvivial statement from that letter, a statement to which I should like to give emphasis as a focal point for this chapter: 'there is no Quality whereby Women endeavour to distinguish themselves from Men, for which they are not just so much the worse' (*PW*, 9: 93).

The androgynous emphasis of Swift's construction of the acceptable woman is clear in several works addressed to his female friends – the poems to Stella, or *Cadenus and Vanessa*. His commitment is to the need for women to overcome sexual distinctions, and however enlightened a position that may be in educational terms, in physical terms the rejection – or the suppression – of femininity must be an irredeemably misogynist position. Turning from Swift to Pope we move, despite all their similarities (and it is interesting to note the incidence of Swiftian touches in *To a Lady*), into a very different mode. The difference is usefully signalled by a revealing variation of emphasis in Johnson's strikingly parallel formulation of the mechanism of disgust in Swift and in Pope. On Swift, he finds that 'the greatest difficulty that occurs, in analysing his character, is to discover by what depravity of intellect he took delight in revolving ideas, from which almost every other mind shrinks in disgust'. With Pope there is a new sense of the reader's complicity in the process of 'revolving': 'we feel all the appetite of curiosity for that from which we have a thousand times turned fastidiously away'. As a comment on *The Rape of the Lock* this is itself something of a *faux pas*, but it will serve to point to the intrusion of a new concept, essentially that of 'charm'. In Pope's words, "Tis to their Changes that their charms we owe': the concept is now bereft of its magic and its danger, denoting an ambiguous fascination with the potentially evil or disruptive disabled of its power, a weakened and more manageable version of the passion created on the brink of hatred.

It has been suggested that the peculiarly bald negativity of Swift's views on women may be accounted for as a failure to accept, or more positively a dissociation from, the essentially middle-class sexual ideology which was crystallizing during his lifetime, a myth of feminine idleness and domestication which would offer a new register to which Pope – twenty years Swift's junior – was to find no difficulty in acceding.[12] At any rate, if in Swift the otherness of women, and of a woman's world, is something to be as far as possible eliminated, Pope in the *Epistle to a Lady* is from the outset accepting and building on an acceptance of 'contra-distinction' between the sexes and their worlds. The addressee, the listener, is a woman who transcends femininity not by quelling 'the feminine' in herself, the difference of her sex, but rather by an apotheosis of it – 'Woman's at best a Contradiction still'.

Martha Blount's androgyny bears a closer relation to the angels than to the hermaphrodite, her desire not so much ambiguous as collapsed into submission. Female sexuality is a strongly negative presence in the poem, a recurrent synecdochic representation of selfishness, social disruption, or a disturbing power of detachment

191

which begins to call into question the simplification of woman's sexuality as unbridled lust – as with Chloe who, 'while her Lover pants upon her breast, / Can mark the figures on an Indian chest' (ll. 167–68). Nevertheless, sexual difference is overtly presented by Pope as a matter of degree rather than of absolute distinctions. Woman is 'a softer Man'; women are more inconsistent within themselves than men but more uniform in general character. It is notable, however, that the subject of 'women' induces a significant qualitative modification to Pope's psychological schema of the Ruling Passion, the providential *laissez-faire* expounded in the *Essay on Man* and the *Epistle to Cobham* which ensures with an easy optimism that 'the two extremes of a vice serve like two opposite biasses to keep up the balance of things', that 'one man's weakness grows the strength of all'. The difference with women is not just one of degree:

In Men, we various Ruling Passions find,
In Women, two almost divide the kind;
Those, only fix'd, they first or last obey,
The Love of Pleasure, and the Love of Sway . . .

(ll. 207–10)

Men, some to Bus'ness, some to Pleasure take;
But ev'ry Woman is at heart a Rake:
Men, some to Quiet, some to public Strife;
But ev'ry Lady would be Queen for life.

(ll. 215–18)

The uncertainty signalled by that slippage from a divided kind to blanket inclusiveness lies near the surface here, but can be seen more subtly to inform the whole poem. The 'ruling passions' in women are no longer self-cancelling in the larger scheme of things, but dialectically interactive in one individual: 'They seek the second not to lose the first'. The collapsing of those separate and divergent principles into this more challenging pleasure/power dialectic carries with it, as numerous readers have recognized, a new charge of poetic engagement. The struggle to characterize 'woman' seems to take Pope to a new level of general truth. It would be hard to argue that the portraits of some of these 'difficult women' do not in some way dramatize the poet's own awareness of a divided consciousness – that of Atossa, for example, her life, like that of a wit in Pope's 1717 preface to his own poems, 'a warfare upon earth', her schizophrenia surely the nightmare of the satirist ('Shines, in exposing Knaves and painting Fools, / Yet is, whate'er she hates and ridicules'), or even of the chameleon poet ('Scare once herself, by turns all Womankind').

As in the curiously masculine orientation of the line, 'But ev'ry Woman is at heart a *Rake*' we can here observe another version of androgyny, one which involves the poet in much the same way as the female impersonation of the early epistles, the translation of Ovid's 'Sapho to Phaon' as well as the better-known *Eloisa to Abelard*.

Ellen Pollak, in an exposition of what she sees as 'the conventional ideological imperatives regarding gender' inscribed by *To a Lady*, rightly points out that the ambiguities and complexities of a well-wrought poem do not in themselves guarantee its ideological innocence; and she goes on to argue, more problematically, that the illusion of complexity generated by Pope's paradoxes is actually a sophisticated rhetorical strategy for obscuring an ideological simplicity.[13] One is reminded of Dr Johnson's report that Pope 'hardly drank tea without a stratagem'; and if *To a Lady* is in general more resistant than Pollak allows to the dropping down of an ideological barrier against the play of meaning, it is at any rate possible to identify in its central device of address to a friend just such a muddying of the waters. Pope's satire on women takes the form of a tribute to one woman, and for many readers the tribute so radically qualifies the satire as to free the poem from any taint of misogyny.[14] The use of the exemplary woman can, obviously, however, be an anti-feminist device in itself. The technique is a commonplace of rhetorical strategy – used in an anti-feminist context as early as Simonides, who sets nine types of women reincarnated from nasty animals against the one useful type derived from the bee.[15]

In *To a Lady* the woman could be said to be constituted from the outset in the role of traitor to her sex, and her mostly silent participation in the quizzing of the figures in the portrait gallery raises a more general question about the nature of this kind of collusive adversarial relationship. The power play in wit of this sort very obviously depends on the existence, or the construction, of a suitable third party to receive and validate it. The representation of sexual difference here is not simply a product of an ideology, or of individual or communal neurosis, but is substantially informed by the interplay of poet and listener in the satiric game. We can take this further: it may be that one of the most suggestive models for feminist criticism in relation to Augustan literature is that of the triangulating technique of the 'tendentious' joke.[16] In *The Lady's Dressing-Room* we have at one level what is perhaps the classic structure of the anti-feminist joke, the aggression of the male narrator directed past the woman (and at least overtly past Strephon as well) to a third person, the colluding listener, inevitably inscribed as male. In Pope's *Epistle* (and in the letter describing the visit to the hermaphrodite) the fact of address to a woman interferes with that triangulation, apparently defusing its hostility, as the brother–sister fiction of the letter 'apparently' renders its very bawdiness innocent. In each case a social interplay is set up in which the voice of feminist resistance can hardly seem other than unmannerly, shrill, or gauche.

The first recorded voice of feminist resistance to *The Lady's Dressing-Room* is that of Lady Mary Wortley Montagu, refreshingly untroubled by any such qualms in her own octosyllabic Augustan wit, diagnosing the poem as simple revenge for sexual misadventure in a critical approximation to the knee in the groin:

> Perhaps you have no better Luck in
> The Knack of Rhyming than of —[17]

Laetitia Pilkington, whose mother deserves a place in the Critical Heritage as having simply thrown up her dinner on reading *The Lady's Dressing-Room*, has an anecdote which may serve as one last example of the repertory of techniques brought by Augustan satire to the anti-feminist animus of its wit. Interesting partly for the way in which Swift, as so often, executes a move which leaves Pope's stratagems looking transparent, it also captures the voicelessness to which one may be reduced by such 'civility', and perhaps in capturing it enacts its own more indirect revenge. She is relating 'a compliment of [Swift's] to some ladies, who supped with him, of whom [she] had the honour to be one': 'The Dean was giving us an account of some woman, who, he told us, was the nastiest, filthiest, most stinking old B—ch that ever was yet seen, except the Company, Ladies! except the Company! for that you know is but civil. We all bowed: could we do less?'[18]

Notes

1. ALEXANDER POPE, *Correspondence*, ed. GEORGE SHERBURN (Oxford, 1956), I: 277–9. Quotations from Pope's poetry are from the one volume Twickenham edition of the *Poems*, ed. JOHN BUTT (London, 1963).

2. SUSAN GUBAR, *Signs*, 3 (1977), 380–94; see also comment by Ellen Pollak, and Gubar's reply, ibid., 728–33.

3. Recently adopted as the title of a study of the tradition of post-Restoration satire on women: see FELICITY A. NUSSBAUM, *The Brink of All We Hate* (Lexington, KY, 1984).

4. See *Memoirs of the Extraordinary Life, Works, and Discoveries of Martinus Scriblerus*, ed. C. KERBY-MILLER (New Haven, CT, 1950), p. 294; JOHNSON, *Lives of the English Poets*, ed. G. BIRKBECK HILL (Oxford, 1905), 3: 234. POPE, *Epistles to Several Persons*, ed. F. W. BATESON (London, 1951); JAE NUM LEE, *Swift and Scatological Satire* (Albuquerque, NM, 1971), pp. 82–3.

5. MARY WOLLSTONECRAFT, *The Rights of Woman*, chapter 4, 'Observations on the state of degradation to which woman is reduced by various causes' (London, 1970), p. 68.

6. For a wide variety of commentaries, see the works listed in PAT ROGERS's Penguin edition of *Swift's Complete Poems* (Harmondsworth, 1983), p. 827; and on the English 'dressing-room' tradition, see especially HARRY M. SOLOMON, ' "Difficult Beauty": Tom D'Urfey and the Context of Swift's "The Lady's Dressing-room" ', *Studies in English Literature*, 19 (1979), 431–44.

7. This is a rather different reading of what HERBERT DAVIS sees as the bubbling up of Swift's 'irrepressible spirit of parody' throughout the poem: 'A Modest Defence of "The Lady's Dressing-Room" ', in *Restoration and Eighteenth-Century Literature*, ed. C. CAMDEN (Chicago, 1963), pp. 39–48. The essay would serve as a good illustration of the 'sanitizing' critical effect of devices like parody and allusion.

8. JOHN HAWKESWORTH (1755), CH, p. 154.

9. JEAN HAGSTRUM, *Sex and Sensibility: Ideal and Erotic Love from Milton to Mozart* (Chicago and London, 1980), p. 148.

10. MARY DOUGLAS, *Purity and Danger: An Analysis of Concepts of Pollution and Taboo* (London, 1966), p. 121: see also p. 147. See in general JANICE DELANEY, MARY JANE LUPTON and EMILY TOTH, *The Curse: A Cultural History of Menstruation* (New York, 1976).

11. *Poems*, ed. JAMES THORPE (Princeton, NJ, 1963), p. 38.

12. See ELLEN POLLAK in *Signs*, 3 (1978), 728–32. One might compare the myth written out by Addison in the story of the sexually segregated commonwealths in *The Spectator*, nos 433–4.

13. ELLEN POLLAK, 'Pope and Sexual Difference: Woman as Part and Counterpart in the "Epistle to a Lady" ', *Studies in English Literature*, 24 (1984), 461–81. See now ELLEN POLLAK's *The Poetics of Sexual Myth: Gender and Ideology in the verse of Swift and Pope* (Chicago and London, 1985), which appeared while this chapter was in the press.

14. See, e.g., HOWARD WEINBROT, *Alexander Pope and the Traditions of Formal Verse Satire* (Princeton, NJ, 1982), pp. 189–98.

15. Paraphrased by Addison in *Spectator*, 209: ed. D. F. BOND (Oxford, 1965), 2: 320.

16. See FREUD, *Jokes and Their Relation to the Unconscious*, trans. JAMES STRACHEY, published in Pelican Freud Library, 1976, esp. pp. 140ff. on jokes about women.

17. See ROBERT HALSBAND, ' "The Lady's Dressing-Room" explicated by a contemporary', *The Augustan Milieu*, ed. H. K. MILLER, E. ROTHSTEIN and G. S. ROUSSEAU (Oxford, 1970), pp. 225–31.

18. *Memoirs* (Dublin, 1748) 2: 144–5.

11　Swift among the Women*

MARGARET ANNE DOODY

A certain view of Swift has been powerfully represented in Middleton Murry's shocked denunciation:

> Nevertheless, it is not his direct obsession with ordure which is the chief cause of the nausea he arouses. It is the strange and disquieting combination of his horror at the fact of human evacuation with a peculiar physical loathing of women. It is an unpleasant subject; but it cannot be burked by any honest critic of Swift. The conventional excuses made for him are ridiculous. . . . Lust is natural and wholesome compared to the feeling Swift arouses.

According to this view, Swift is not only obsessed and perverted but professedly inimical to womankind. His 'animus against women became more and more disproportioned, vituperative, and shrill'.[1] The mad Irishman's wandering dirty thoughts betray the chiefest of misogynists. Swift detests the female and the feminine.

Murry's Freud-tinged view is only an elaboration of what has been said by some others before him. Lord Orrery, for instance, in his *Remarks on the Life and Writings of Swift* judged Swift lacking in appropriate sexual feelings:

> If we consider SWIFT's behaviour, so far only as it relates to women, we shall find, that he looked upon them rather as busts, than as whole figures. In his panegyrical descriptions, he has seldom descended lower than the center of their hearts: or if ever he has designed a compleat statue, it has been generally cast in a dirty, or in a disagreeable mould: as if the statuary had not conceived, or had not experienced, that justness of proportion, that delicacy of limb, and those pleasing, and graceful attitudes which have constituted the sex to be the most beautiful part of the creation.

* Reprinted from *Yearbook of English Studies*, 18 (1988), 68–92.

Swift's 'The Lady's Dressing-Room' merely discovers his inexcusable 'want of delicacy and decorum'; the author 'too frequently forgets . . . politeness and tenderness of manners'.[2]

If Swift is guilty of inexcusable misogyny, of shrill animus against women, then surely women readers in particular ought to have taken notice – and umbrage. Surely, then, women writers of the eighteenth century must have mocked Swift, or expressed horror of him, or shunned him. Indeed, we can find some examples of female censure of Swift. Sarah Green, in her conduct-book *Mental Improvement for a Young Lady; on her Entrance into the World; Addressed to a Favourite Niece* (London, 1793), quite simply advises that 'Favourite Niece' to shun all of Swift's writings save his Sermons; the other works are 'vulgar, indelicate, and satiric'. Nobody could say this is not true. But the improving aunt also disapproves of Pope: 'He was, as you will find, for I recommend his works to your perusal, no friend to our sex; as such I cannot esteem the man, though I admire the poet' (pp. 95–6). Swift's 'vulgar' works may be dismissed from the presence of refined young ladies, but it is Pope who is specifically the misogynist.

Lady Mary Wortley Montagu (1689–1762) had waxed caustic against Swift, and Pope, upon reading Lord Orrery's *Remarks*: 'D[ean] S[wift] (by his Lordship's own account) was so intoxicated with the love of Flattery, he sought it amongst the lowest class of people, and the silliest of Women, and was never so well pleas'd with any Companions as those that worship'd him while he insulted them.' Swift's letters show him 'vain, triffling [*sic*], ungratefull'. Lady Mary dismisses Pope and Swift together: 'These two superior Beings were entitl'd by their Birth and hereditary Fortune to be only a couple of Link Boys.'[3] This is the Lady Mary of 1754, still recalling the resentments of her old estrangement from Pope, and from Swift. She turns for defensive consolation, in a rather pitiful snobbery, to the rights of 'Birth'; these genius-enemies were 'low'. Her more general charges against Swift are the not uncommon ones of ingratitude and religious infidelity. But Lady Mary does not rank Swift as a misogynist; on the contrary, her Swift is meanly fond (like Richardson in certain hostile representations) of the company of women, who ought to be beneath the notice of a man of genius. This notion Lady Mary has taken from Orrery, who elaborates with fascinated hostility on Swift's friendships with women:

> You see the command which SWIFT had over all his females; and you would have smiled to have found his house a constant seraglio of very virtuous women, who attended him from morning till night, with an obedience, an awe, and an assiduity, that are seldom

paid to the richest, or the most powerful lovers; no, not even to the Grand Seignior himself.

There is something very like envy in Orrery's tone, even as he sharpens his ridicule; he blames the publication of 'many pieces, which ought never to have been delivered to the press' upon these foolishly-trusted women: 'He communicated every composition as soon as finished, to his female senate' (*Remarks*, p. 83).

In her commonplace book Lady Mary picked up and elaborated Orrery's metaphor, noting 'Dr. S[wift] in the midst of his Women, like a master E[unuch] in a seraglio'.[4] Swift in his 'constant seraglio' becomes a master Eunuch, or a tamed caponized Macheath with his doxies about him. Lady Mary raises an interesting problem. Was Swift too fond of women, of women's manners and women's company? The question is first raised by Orrery, who seems blissfully unaware of certain contradictions in his portrait of a Swift unable to appreciate the female as real men do, and yet able to attract the devoted service and admiration of all those women. Lady Mary's language plays with the feminine. If Swift was 'vain' and 'triffling' and fond of flattery, why, these are well-known feminine vices. Was Swift (again like a certain picture of Richardson) too womanly a man?

Indeed, for every female voice raised against Swift there are several to speak for him. Laetitia Pilkington (1712–50), once one of Swift's 'virtuous seraglio' (she was still 'virtuous' at that point) addressed a poetic epistle to Swift, praising him as the equal of the 'God-like Men of Old'. This 'Patriot, Bard and Sage' is a subject for Irish pride; Ireland 'in that Name / Shall rival *Greece* and *Rome* in Fame'.[5] According to her own account, Laetitia Pilkington was serving an immediate interest in writing this set of verses, for she hoped through them to gain admission to the presence of the famous Dean. Flattery operated successfully. But Pilkington also had national as well as personal interests to serve. Praise of Swift was praise of the national literary identity. Mary Davys (1674–1732), in her autobiographical novel *The Merry Wanderer* (1725), self-consciously defends both herself and Ireland through an allusion to Swift:

> To tell the Reader I was born in *Ireland*, is to bespeak a general Dislike to all I write, and he will, likely, be surprised, if every Paragraph does not end with a Bull; but a Potato's a fine light Root, and makes the Eater brisk and alert. . . . And I am going to say a bold word in defence of my own Country; the very brightest Genius in the King's Dominion drew his first Breath in that Nation: and so much for the Honour of *Ireland*.[6]

The Irish have been supposed the butts of wit, not wits, but Swift
has changed all that. The 'very brightest Genius' raises downtrodden
Ireland, as Pilkington also asserts: 'As the *Irish* are the eternal
Ridicule of the *English* for their Ignorance, I am pround *Hibernia* had
the Happiness of producing this brilliant Wit, to redeem the Credit
of the Country; and to convince the World, a Man may draw his
first Breath there, and yet be learned, wise, generous, religious, witty,
social and polite' (*Memoirs*, 1: 67). Swift redeems a group at apparent
disadvantage; he proves the potential excellence of those traditionally
judged by (imposed and alien) authority to be dull and inferior. Such
a liberation has an interesting suggestiveness for women, another
group whose writings may 'bespeak Dislike' upon identification of
the author, another group eternally ridiculed 'for their Ignorance' by
those who constitute themselves as superior. It is not surprising that
a number of Irish women writers were attracted into Swift's orbit.

The women who achieved acquaintance with Swift discovered not
only the celebrated author but also an oddly domestic individual.
Laetitia Pilkington recollects Swift entertaining her in performing a
hospitable household task:

> The bottle and glasses being taken away, the Dean set about
> making the Coffee; but the Fire scorching his Hand, he called to
> me to reach him his Glove, and changing the Coffee-pot to his
> Left-hand, held out the Right one, ordered me to put the Glove
> on it, which accordingly I did; when taking up part of his Gown
> to fan himself with, and acting the character of a prudish Lady, he
> said, 'Well, I do not know what to think; Women may be honest
> that do such Things, but, for my Part, I never could bear to touch
> any Man's Flesh – except my Husband's, whom, perhaps, says he,
> she wished at the Devil'.
>
> (*Memoirs*, 1: 58–9)

In a little riff of sudden mimicry, Swift satirically adopts the role of
the absurdly prudish woman, at the same time reminding everyone
present of 'Man's Flesh', and delivering this impromptu travesty-role
in the midst of performing a rite which might be considered feminine.
Teasingly conscious of the interplay of gender roles, the Swift of
this anecdote can remind us of the female persona in some of his
poems, in, for instance, 'The Humble Petition of Frances Harris'
(1700), or 'Mary the Cook-Maid's Letter to Dr. Sheridan' (1718), or
'A Panegyrick on the Dean in the Person of a Lady in the North'
(1730). In this last Swift imagines himself celebrated by a pleased
hostess not only as a master of conversation and a fount of
knowledge but also as a help around the place: 'You merit new

employments daily: / Our thatcher, ditcher, gardener, bailie' (l. 155–56). This Swift successfully takes a hand at churning the butter for breakfast by shaking a bottle of cream:

> Now, enter as the dairy handmaid
> Such charming butter never man made.
> Let others with fanatic face,
> Talk of their milk for babes of grace;
> From tubs their snuffling nonsense utter:
> Thy milk shall make us tubs of butter.
> The bishop with his foot may burn it;
> But, with his hand, the Dean can churn it.
> How are the servants overjoyed
> To see thy Deanship thus employed!
> Instead of poring on a book,
> Providing butter for the cook.
>
> (ll. 167–78)

The masculine calling of preaching, orating (from 'tubs'), has been displaced by the feminine calling, as 'the dairy handmaid' hopes to make 'tubs of butter', although in humble reality the three hours' tossing yields only 'an ounce at least' (l. 186). Yet the Dean thinks himself well paid for long 'jumblings round the skull' if he squeezes out 'four lines in Rhyme' (ll. 191, 195). Butter-making and verse-making are equated. This employable worthy in his round of humble tasks completes his contribution by designing two structures which might vie with the proudest architecture; these models of the 'art of building' (l. 200) are two outhouses, with separate offices for male and female. From food (breakfast butter) Swift moves to the privy, but not without reminding us that the various needs of a household's routine have their place in a not unpleasing round of daily activities. This poet of domestic life, however ostentatiously and carefully he may separate the sexes' privies, is seldom content to remain on his side of the gender line. He prefers mercurial ease (and easement) to the pomposity of generic masculine grandeur. It is this Swift that Laetitia Pilkington encountered making coffee.

Swift's kind of teasing evoked a recognition of physical realities ('Man's Flesh'), including his own reality and idiosyncrasies. Pilkington makes her own private teasing observation: 'I could not help smiling at his odd Gait, for I thought to myself, he had written so much in Praise of Horses, that he was resolved to imitate them as nearly as he could.' Swift, guessing her mental lampoon, comments that Mr. Pilkington was 'a Fool . . . to marry you, for he could have afforded to keep a Horse for less Money than you cost him, and that, you must confess, would have given him better Exercise and more Pleasure than a Wife' (*Memoirs*, 1: 79–80). This ridicule of wives and marriage is a reminder of the Swift of the satiric poems. But the open teasing is explorative, a challenge to women in the sex war to which they were allowed to respond. The effect of Swift's humour is not to silence the woman but to force her into utterance. According to Pilkington, she composed her satiric poem 'The Statues' specifically in order to answer Swift's ridicule: 'As the Dean, and after his Example, Mr. P[ilkingto]n, were eternally satyrizing and ridiculing the *Female* Sex; I had a very great inclination to be even with them, and expose the Inconstancy of Men' (1: 91–92). In her poetic tale the fair Queen Lucida must try the constancy of her enraptured bridegroom by visiting her father's under-sea realm for one day. 'Twice twenty noble Youths' have already failed the test. The youth swears undying constancy, but of course proves incapable of spending a day on his own without falling for the charms of a nymph. Led to a spacious grotto 'Where forty Youths, in Marble, seem'd to mourn, / Each Youth reclining on a fun'ral Urn', the Prince imagines he is about to consummate his new love. But the angry nymph suddenly dashes the fountain's magic water upon him, accusing him of the general male weakness: 'Thy changeful Sex in Perfidy delight, / Despise Perfection, and fair Virtue slight.' The enticing nymph proves to be the injured Queen, disguised, and the magic water turns the Prince to stone; he joins the marble group as the forty-first monument to male lightness: 'A STATUE now, and if reviv'd once more, / Would prove, no doubt, as perjur'd as before.'[7]

'The Statues' is an interesting reversal of a constant masculine trope. Women are often presented as Lord Orrery thinks of them, as statues with delicately-shaped limbs and 'pleasing and graceful attitudes'. Here a woman, both within and without the poem, turns a multitude of men into such cool shapes (elegant, marmoreal, and inanimate) but only as a punishment. The male fault for which the Prince suffers is not specifically Swift's; in fact Pilkington in her *Memoirs* takes care to defend him from the charge of unsuitable gallantries. (Her husband's infidelities were the spur to resentment.) Her satiric poem is a literary riposte to such satires as Swift's 'The Progress of Love' (1727), and, as she reconstructs the history and conditions of her writing the poem, Swift's satiric ridicule of 'The *Female* Sex' prompted this written reply. One of the first anti-masculinist satires by a woman in an age over-rich in anti-feminist satires by men, this poem is produced in a sense under Swift's aegis. The presence of Swift the satirist encourages the release of female energies in utterance.

Swift's 'female senate' was composed largely of writers or would-be writers, a matter which Orrery seems determined to ignore. Swift in fact did encourage a number of his women friends to write. He not only encouraged Mary Barber (1690–1757) but introduced her to the public, as he wrote the 'Dedication' to her *Poems on Several Occasions* (London, 1734). When she was in financial difficulties Swift not only gave her aid but ultimately offered her the manuscript of *Polite Conversation* with full rights of publication for her own benefit. Swift is a visible influence upon Barber's literary work, an influence not to be summed up as a mere source of imitation. Mary Barber endeavours to create her own kind of satire. She seizes upon the one kind of authority she certainly has that the world might acknowledge: her maternal authority. This strangely allows her access to the male world and the masculine voice, or at least to the voice of her young son, imagined ventriloquizing her words in a greater theatre of action.

An Apology written for my Son to his Master, who had commanded him to write verses on the Death of the Late Lord –

> I beg you Scholar you'll excuse,
> Who dares no more debase the Muse.
> My Mother says, if e'er she hears
> I write again on worthless Peers,
> Whether they're living Lords, or dead,
> She'll box the Muse from out my head.
>
> (*Poems on Several Occasions*, p. 50)

Just as Swift takes his clerical position as an opportunity for speaking with prophetic roughness and biting wit rather than for suave moralizing, so Mary Barber takes her position as mother as an opportunity to exercise satiric criticism rather than sweetly maternal sentiments. The poems grow out of the assertiveness of Barber's position as mother, and an almost pugnacious insistence on her real social status as the wife of a Cit. From this apparently low position she can take a high comic line against 'worthless Peers'. Those who write panegyrics on them deserve to get their ears boxed in a good bourgeois parental manner, and the Muse gives way to the assertive Mother, as schoolmasters and lords are vicariously slapped. Barber presents herself in the guise of the oft-criticized scribbling woman, careless of dress, while at the same time so careful of her children's lives and morals as to give rise to alarm in governing powers. The presentation of the self as a comic and sometimes awkward figure, not simply or smoothly in the right: this is a self-presentation common in the Swift of the *Poems*, and was perhaps learned from him.

With her son as a pretext Barber could write upon Irish topics, noting the unhappy position of young Irishmen who, even if educated, are 'Doom'd in Obscurity to dwell' while 'Strangers [the English] make the happier Claim'.[8] Taking on the man's point of view (or rather, the view of the innocent boy) she is able to promulgate female rational opinion against the abuses and constrictions of the masculine world. One of her poems takes up a subject not elsewhere treated in Augustan verse as a topic of satire: the absurdity of *masculine* wear for male grown-ups. Ridicule of women's dress is a standard satiric topic, but Barber, through voicing her son's distress, makes a criticism ultimately levelled at the whole great male world:

What is it our Mammas bewitches,
To plague us little Boys with Breeches?
To Tyrant *Custom* we must yield,
While vanquish'd *Reason* flies the Field.
Our Legs must suffer by Ligation,
To keep the Blood from Circulation, . . .
Our wiser Ancestors wore Brogues,
Before the Surgeons brib'd these Rogues
With narrow Toes, and Heels like Pegs,
To help to make us break our Legs.

Then, ere we know to use our Fists,
Our Mothers closely bind our Wrists;
And never thinks our Cloaths are neat,
Till they're so tight we cannot eat.
And, to increase our other Pains,
The Hat-band helps to cramp our Brains.
The Cravat finishes the Work,
Like Bow-string sent from the Grand Turk.[9]

Male costume is absurd, tyrannous, damaging to the physical being. Men, as well as women, undergo socialization by dress, which in their case too is oppressive: here 'Tyrant *Custom*' is associated with English invasion and the suppression of Irish tradition ('Our wiser Ancestors wore Brogues'). One can see how Barber's witty contempt for authority and custom, for public English authority and custom, would appeal to Swift, who wrote of Mary Barber's poems:

They generally contain something new and useful, tending to the Reproof of some Vice or Folly. . . . She never writes on a Subject with general unconnected Topicks, but always with a Scheme and

Method driving to some particular End; wherein many Writers in Verse, and of some Distinction, are so often known to fail. In short, she seemeth to have a true poetical Genius, better cultivated than could well be expected, either from her Sex, or the Scene she hath acted in, as the Wife of a Citizen.[10]

The influence of Swift's own verse style on Mary Barber's poems is evident. His kind of quick colloquial rhymed tetrameter offered her, as it was to offer other women writers, more control with less pretension than would be involved in the pentameter heroic measures. The rhymed pentameter assumes a grand ideal, a public language, and the hope that private and public self may become one. The women could not adapt the private to the public self with anything like equal ease, because women had no public function, no available public persona. They had to start with the private self, and invent a public voice. This manoeuvre is one that many of Swift's poems are engaged in, and his manner of quick, colloquial, impudent rhyme provides a usable model for effective criticism of life. In Mary Barber, an Irishwoman who saw the state of Ireland much as he did, Swift apparently recognized a kindred tough impishness.
He acknowledged her right to utter 'Reproof of some Vice or Folly'.

The private Swift was sometimes hectoring, often teasing, about female behaviour and roles. But he did not demand constant pastel femininity. His disgusted remark on Addison, 'let him fair-sex it to the world's end' is peculiarly satisfying.[11] Many Western writers (not satirists only) instinctively (if often unconsciously) reach for images of woman when they wish to symbolize the inadequacies of human intelligence, the uncomfortable demands of the physical, and the eternal obstruction that lies between the heart and the heart's desire. Swift is not one of them. He never attributes to womankind the earthy conspiracy against the (male) grand spiritual aspiration, nor is woman presented as the deranged and fearful underside of consciousness. To a woman reader the fact that 'Celia shits' is probably less upsetting or annoying than the Magna Mater business in the *Dunciad*. In Pope's poem femaleness and motherhood are in effect condemned as obscene images of frightening power. But in Swift's satiric world, when things go wrong it is not because women are in control.

In *Cadenus and Vanessa* (1726), that verse compliment at once convoluted and straightforward, cryptic and open, Swift could at least imagine a woman endowed with qualities that womankind is customarily supposed to lack, qualities 'For manly bosoms chiefly fit', such as 'knowledge, judgment, wit . . . justice, truth and fortitude' (ll. 204–5, 207). Pallas and Venus combine to produce a lady who

outdoes the men so much that they cannot even comprehend her.
Men's complaints about women's ignorant shallowness prove
empty clichés; shallowness is what they want. Swift's poem implies
a sympathy for the intelligent woman who does not fit into the
socially-prescribed role, and could not fit into that mould without
self-injury and diminution.

The poem itself can be read by women as sympathetic to the
hardships of their position, unlike Pope's *The Rape of the Lock* or
Epistle to a Lady. So Ellen Pollak has recently read it in a full and
lengthy analysis.[12] Certainly, while the 'Lady' in Pope's *Epistle* must
learn to accept, submit, and obey, Vanessa in Swift's poem is praised
for accepting nothing that she does not like. Disdainful of feminine
behaviour, she is 'silent out of spight' (l. 406), but she is silent only
when she chooses to be. She has no notion of charming by submitting.
She 'condescend[s] to admit' (l. 447) those who please her. She acts
according to her own judgement and power, which includes the
power of speech. 'All humble worth she strove to raise; / Would not
be praised, yet loved to praise' (l. 456–57). When Vanessa realizes
she loves Cadenus she openly debates with him, speaks her feelings;
she reasons, urges, and argues. The lady is not only a seducer but a
seducer with powers of argument, all without censure from the poet.

That Swift is at the same time paying himself as Decanus the most
terrific compliment need not be disputed; masculine critics tend to
find the affair unsavoury and the poem indelicate. But Swift presents
his unhandsome hero in an oddly 'feminine' position, as observed
and desired object rather than subject; Cadenus's awkward reactions
show a masculinity that does not rely on cultural phallic certainty. In
any case Swift could compliment himself only by presenting himself
as loved by a woman of intelligence, learning, force of character, and
full command of language. His Vanessa, like the Mary Barber he
praises, speaks forcefully, 'with a Scheme and Method driving to
some particular End'. We do not know the end: 'But what success
Vanessa met, / Is to the world a secret yet' (ll. 827–28). Ellen Pollak
suggests in effect that Swift could find no ending to his poem
because his culture, as he knew, allowed for no women save for the
well-known types of docile (or shrewish) wives, longing old-maids,
and light-minded whores, none of which suited the 'Vanessa' of life
or fiction. 'How', Ellen Pollak asks, 'could he pay tribute to a woman
within the confines of a language and a logic by whose terms she
was either fallen or unloved?' (p. 151). That Swift's portrait of an able
and lively woman was distressing in itself is evidenced in Orrery's
comments. All Orrery wants us to see in Vanessa is a lightminded
foolish female: 'Vanity makes terrible devastation in a female breast.
It batters down all restraints of modesty . . . VANESSA was excessively

vain' (*Remarks*, p. 70). Orrery wants to say that no such woman as Swift describes could exist.

Lord Orrery in effect tries to shut Vanessa up. In his relations with women Swift (inside and outside his own poems) never shuts them up. Women writers were likely to find in him an encouragement to speak. It is not surprising that a little group of Irish women writers forms part of Swift's personal circle, particularly if we remember that the condition of Ireland encouraged men and women who felt alike about political issues to band together. All the members of Swift's 'seraglio' of writing women (Mary Davys, Laetitia Pilkington, Constantia Grierson, Mary Barber) might be described as 'self-made women'. They were middle class, perhaps, but close to the working class, and most of them worked at something aside from writing (and housework) at some point in their lives in order to earn a living or to eke out that of a spouse.[13] Swift's Irish women friends were 'low', appropriately 'low' if we take Lady Mary's view of 'Birth'; the offspring of a man-midwife and the spouse of a haberdasher are fit associates for a being entitled by Birth and Fortune to no higher status than that of a Link Boy. Uppity women surrounded an uppity man. They are an unusual group, these Irish writing women of Swift's circle: energetic, self-reliant, self-conscious, and witty. They might perhaps be seen as a group of Vanessas, new women freshly compounded 'of Wit and Sense', illustrating Vanessa's maxim (learned from Cadenus himself) 'That common forms were not design'd / Directors to a noble mind' (l. 620–1).

The case for Swift's influence on women writers cannot, however, be made properly by considering only those women he himself knew. Swift was an influence on women writers who had never met him. Much of the poetry written by Englishwomen during the middle and later eighteenth century exhibits an awareness of Swift and a sense of his importance as a model. This is evident as soon as one turns to the poetry columns of the *Gentleman's Magazine*, which in its early years was an important medium for women writers, as Phyllis J. Guskin has shown.[14] The poetry pages, in which Swift and Barber appeared, might in some respects be seen as an extension of Swift's 'seraglio'. The verse of 'Fidelia' of Lincoln, for instance, acknowledges Swift in brisk tetrameters as the author humorously complains about the inadequacy of a fifty-pound prize for a poetical essay on 'Life, Death, Judgment, Heaven and Hell':

> But 50 pounds! – A sorry sum!
> You'd more need offer half a *plumb*;
> Five weighty subjects well to handle?
> Sir, you forget the price of candle;

And leather too, when late and soon,
I shall be pacing o'er my room; . . .
'Tis known old *Swift, Dan Pope,* and *Young,*
Those leaders of the rhiming throng;
Are better paid for meditations,
On the most trifling Occasions;
The *Broomstick, Benefit of Fa*——*ing,*
Or any whim they shew their art in.[15]

Though Swift may be better paid, 'Fidelia' proclaims in a later
poem 'I love the Dean with the utmost affection; / I'm charm'd with
his writings, I admire his brave spirit', and she bids Sylvanus Urban
tell the Dean that 'Fidelia' is quite willing to marry him, and 'That
Vanessa, that favourite of *Vulcan*'s fair dame / For her dear *Decanus*
ne'er felt such a flame'. If 'good Mr. Urban' will only speak to Swift
in her favour, 'Fidelia' can forego the fifty pounds: 'And then for
your prizes your poets may shift. / I shall have all I wish, when I
get Doctor *Sw*——*t*'.[16] After this mock-proposal of November 1734
various masculine correspondents express in comic verse their
objections to her offer for Swift: 'Strange is Fidelia's passion! – for I
swear, / I thought to match him with my sorrel mare' says one prize
epigram on the subject.[17] The topic became a running joke in the
poetry section of the *Gentleman's Magazine* in 1735. While pretending
to be hurt that the 'dear dean . . . continues mum', 'Fidelia' repeats
her admiration; though correspondents 'call the doctor ugly names',
she loves him so unswervingly 'That whoe'er hopes to gain my
favour, / Must not speak ill of him however'. Even Swift's satiric
verses on women, such as 'The Furniture of a Woman's Mind' (in the
Gentleman's Magazine for February 1735), show 'That while he chides
he pleases too; / A secret, known to very few'.[18] The marriage
proposal is a joke, expressing that attraction towards Swift that many
women feel and that men evidently find hard to comprehend in
them. 'Fidelia', too, wants to be a Vanessa, and the successfulness of
the true Vanessa of wit and sense and independence is ultimately
equated with success in writing and publishing. 'To get Doctor
Sw——*t*' is not to marry the aged deaf dean, but to become like the
poet, to take advantage of his voice.

Swift had distinguished himself in finding an immediate and
quite unheroic voice, a critical grumbling impish voice that emerges
not from the centre of authoritative power but from somewhere on
the sidelines. The tetrameter verse form Swift inherited from Butler,
but the bullying public narrative manner of the Hudibrastic style is
modulated into something suited to the private meditative personality
in touch with gritty fact. This personality does not cease to be satiric

while relating thoughts to homely experience and undramatic events, or non-events. Swift's is a good mode for pointing our uncomfortable truths in a bearable way. In his tetrameter verse, and in parodic mimicry of other breathless voices (as in 'Mrs. Frances Harris's Petition'), the manner seems to make up its own rules as it goes along. This effect is often emphasized by the touch-and-go rhymes and sprightly running of the four-beat verse. It is not Swift's verse form alone but the voice and manner in general that could attract female writers. Women poets were to pick up Swift's kind of energy, pungency, and pointedness. They appreciated the absence of ponderous *gravitas*, the celebration of the unignorable not dressed up as the noble. They could share his kind of interest in that which is homely, unofficial, and truthful.

Above all, perhaps, the women poets of the mid-century are affected by the gender-related topics of Swift's verses (we can see how 'Fidelia' has picked up the sexual teasing in Swift). The conflict between masculine and feminine as Swift presented it might disgust men such as Orrery, who wished their females presented by the poet-statuary as figures of 'delicacy of limb' and 'pleasing and graceful attitudes'. The women writers who respond to Swift are hardier than Orrery, and less interested in the pleasing and graceful. They, like Swift, are moved to question the romanticizing of conventional behaviour. In their works the conflicts between men and women are picked up and developed from a female point of view.

Mary Leapor (1722–46) is another of the women writers both energetic and low born who dared to speak out. Leapor (commonly known as 'Molly') gives herself the romantic name of 'Mira', but defies the conventions of feminine propriety and beauty, and the pastoral ideal, in her comic pastoral 'Mira's Picture' in which she is discussed by two 'swains' in the most unflattering terms. Her self-presentation, which picks up the conventions of men looking at a woman and the conventional repudiation of the woman writer as physically ugly, mockingly makes Leapor unbelievably repulsive (dirty, hump-backed, with teeth falling out). Leapor plays with the fascination of female ugliness in such a manner as to free herself from conventional claims of feminine proprieties. Unheroic (or, rather, unheroinic) 'Mira' is able to assume a parodic masculine voice, as Swift had adopted and ventriloquized a feminine one.

Freeing herself of conventional expectations, Leapor casts a cool amused eye at the half-truths of a socially-trained sexual sensibility. She picks up Swift's characters, or anti-characters, of Strephon and Chloe and introduces us to her own version of these anti-pastoral persons in two poems. In 'The Mistaken Lover' the husband Strephon has fallen out of love with his wife Chloe, and finds fault with her appearance:

'Your Lips I own are red and thin,
But there's a Pimple on your Chin:
Besides your Eyes are gray, – Alack!
Till now I always thought 'em black.'

The reader expects that poor Chloe will be offended and unhappy, and is surprised when she cordially agrees that the marriage is a vexatious mistake. The pair will, she says, channel their energies into the techniques of polite separation:

'But now, my Dearest, as you see
In mutual Hatred we agree,
Methinks 'tis better we retreat,
Each Party to a distant Seat;
And tho' we value each the other,
Just as one Rush regards another:
Yet let us often send to hear
If Health attend the absent Dear'.

Another of Leapor's mock-pastoral couples appears in '*Strephon* to *Celia*. A modern *Love-Letter*':

Now, Madam, as the Chat goes round,
I hear you have ten thousand Pound:
But that I as a Trifle hold,
Give me your Person, dem your Gold;
Yet for your own Sake 'tis secur'd,
I hope – your Houses too ensur'd,
I'd have you take a special Care,
And of false Mortgages beware.[19]

What such women as Molly Leapor evidently heard most clearly in poems like Swift's 'The Lady's Dressing-Room' was a refreshing challenge to the ideology of courtship, the conventional romanticizing of the female, and other absurdities of male–female relations. Taking up the Swiftian style of verse (though the 'modern *Love-Letter*' has echoes of Hudibras to the Widow, as well) Leapor can offer parodic ventriloquizing of the masculine voice and masculine pretensions and pretences. A feminine word can be put in against marriage as so often constituted. Such a word is put in by Ann Yearsley, for

instance, at the end of the century, in her iambic tetrameter narrative
'Lucy. A Tale for the Ladies'. Lucy suffers from an unhappy middle-
class marriage to the dull Cymon. She eventually finds a friend in her
husband's friend, a man she can talk to, and she is then accused of
adultery. The wretched marriage, however, drags miserably on until
Lucy finds release in death:

> She dies! and Cymon's poignant grief
> Is finely wrought in bas-relief.
> To prove he does his wife lament,
> How grand, superb, her monument:
> There weeping angels cut in stone,
> The rose snapt off ere fully blown,
> The empty urn – must surely prove,
> Cymon's deep sorrow, and his love.[20]

Women poets of the period seem inclined to record a suspicion that
men want their women static and monumental. The conventional
images evoked by Yearsley, the stone angels, rose, and urn are all,
like the urn, empty; real living women are despised and neglected,
while elaborate stone monuments offer men the double satisfaction
of getting rid of the real woman and celebrating their own false
idealization. The 'bas-relief' is half relief. When the women look, as
Swift did, at the Progress of Marriage, they too are apt to find images
of meanness, failure, folly, and greed, though they place the blame
slightly differently.

If the women writers share Swift's interest in marital failures and
courtship absurdities, they also share his sense of strong physicality.
Indeed, some of Swift's own imagery of intimate physical domestic
unpleasantness may have come to him not from a Latin-based satiric
tradition alone but also from some of women's own writings.
Everyone who has read Swift's 'The Lady's Dressing-Room' (that
violent irruption into woman's realm) has been struck with its
forceful imagery of matter in the wrong place, of contaminating
physical proximities:

> Now listen while he next produces,
> The various combs for various uses,
> Filled up with dirt so closely fixed,
> No brush could force a way betwixt. . . .
> But oh! it turn'd poor Strephon's bowels,
> When he beheld and smelt the towels;
> Begummed, bemattered, and beslimed;
> With dirt, and sweat, and ear-wax grimed.

No object Strephon's eye escapes,
Here, petticoats in frowzy heaps; . . .
The stockings why should I expose,
Stained with the moisture of her toes

(ll. 19–22; 43–48; 51–52)

Women writers have also occasionally been fascinated with sluttery
and produced rich imagery of feminine dirt. Swift's poem should be
compared with the fantasia of dirt and disorder created by Margaret
Cavendish, Duchess of Newcastle, in her play *The Matrimonial
Trouble*, published with her other plays in 1662. In the second scene
of *The Matrimonial Trouble* there is a dialogue between Master Thrifty
the Steward and Briget Greasy the Cook-maid. Thrifty accuses the
incompetent Briget of sending up puddings made of stinking guts
and fowls insufficiently drawn. This 'Slut' has other nasty habits:

Besides, your sluttery is such, as you will poyson all the House: for
in one place I find a piece of butter, and a greasie comb, full of
nitty hairs lying by it; and in another place flour and old-worn
stockings, the feet being rotted off with sweat; and in a third place,
a dish of cold meat cover'd with a foul smock, and your durty
shooes [*sic*] (for the most part) stand upon the Dresser-board,
where you lay the hot meat; besides, by your carelessness you do
waste and spoil so much, as it is unsufferable: for you will fling
whole ladlefuls of dripping into the fire, to make the fire blaze
underneath the pot.[21]

The maid is actually given a sexual reward for her sloppiness; crying
about the Steward's treatment of her she is discovered by her master,
and rapidly consoled by being made his mistress. The mix of body
dirt, sexuality, and kitchen stuff is very striking. Swift's lady's
dressing-room is also associated with the kitchen in his illustrative
imagery, drawn from cooking 'mutton cutlets':

If from adown the hopeful chops
The fat upon a cinder drops,
To stinking smoke it turns the flame
Poisoning the flesh from whence it came;
And up exhales a greasy stench,
For which you curse the careless wench:

(ll. 103–8)

Swift appears to be elaborating on Margaret Cavendish's Briget
Greasy, a 'careless Wench' indeed, whose spirit seems to pervade
Celia's chamber.

Swift seems especially fascinated with kitchen life, its accidents, squalor, and creativity. Although women novelists of the eighteenth century prefer to steer clear of the kitchen (perhaps determined not to cast their heroines into the pudding-making role), the women poets share Swift's fascination with kitchenry. In 'Crumble-Hall' Mary Leapor takes us through an old-fashioned stolid manor house, and includes a visit to the kitchen where 'The fires blaze; the greasy pavements fry; / And steaming odours from the kettles fly'. We return to the kitchen to see overeaten Roger snoring at table and the maid doing the washing up, a redeeming if comic domestic activity seldom described in literature: 'The greasy apron round her hips she ties, / And to each plate the scalding clout applies.' There is a touch of mock-georgic here, reminiscent of Swift's 'A Description of the Morning' (1709): 'Now Moll had whirled her mop with dexterous airs, / Prepared to scrub the entry and the stairs' (ll. 7–8).

Leapor's excursion through Crumble-Hall (an excursion which is a way of entertaining the visitor at this place where little happens) includes a trip to the lumber rooms at the very top of the house:

These rooms are furnish'd amiably and full;
Old shoes, and sheep-ticks bred in stacks of wool;
Grey Dobbin's gears, and drenching-horns enow;
Wheel-spokes – the irons of a tatter'd plough.[22]

The relaxed description of a visit neither brilliant nor unpleasant, paid to a place unglamorous but characteristic and insistently rich in particulars, is much in Swift's manner. He has written several descriptions of semi-boring or not-utterly-satisfactory visits, as, for instance, his account of the house-party in Gaulstown given in 'The Part of a Summer' (1721). The country woman 'Shows all her secrets of housekeeping, / For candles how she trucks her dripping' (ll. 81–82). The party pass their time in a desultory way, going fishing, playing backgammon. Nothing much happens until the advent of new guests brings changes unpleasant to visitors already in residence:

This grand event half broke our measures;
Their reign began with cruel seizures:
The Dean must with his quilt supply,
The bed in which these tyrants lie:
Nim lost his wig-block, Dan his jordan;
(My Lady says she can't afford one)
George is half scared out of his wits,
For Clem gets all the tiny bits.

(ll. 113–20)

Swift's work is rich in the kind of observed details (not necessarily satiric) that cannot be subsumed in or covered by some pretty literary convention. His minor grumbling, his attention to minute circumstances, create an odd sideways mock-heroic effect in such poems as 'The Part of a Summer'; masculine grandeur (which belongs to a grand historical world of Events, Seizures, and Tyrants) is turned into mere diurnal physical survival. (Gulliver, too, is of course the hero of unheroic diurnal physical survival, the man who experiences to an extreme degree the importance of quilts, tiny bits, and jordans.) This aspect of Swift shows him as very close not only to women's particular concerns, which he can describe seriously or mockingly (matters of candles and dripping), but to a view of the world that they can share. He acknowledges the vigorous presence of the mundane, the unliterary, which the women writers also wish to do, and must do if they are not to be swallowed up in literary conventions that ignore them and their lives, or turn them into lovely statues.

It seems, above all, the insistent unmarmoreal (or anti-marmoreal) physicality of Swift that attracted (and attracts) female writers. When Swift writes to and about Stella in his poems he writes of her as a physical human being, subject to pain and age. The talents and abilities she manifests are thus real human qualities, with all the credit of being exerted in the circumstances of life's constraints. Stella may be an Angel, or an hospitable entertainer, like the Angel-Inn, but the inn-sign, her face, shows the marks of age and wear: 'Now, this is Stella's case, in fact, / An angel's face, a little cracked' ('Stella's Birth-Day . . . 1720–21' (ll. 15–16)). This celebration of reality seems to have impressed the poet Mary Jones of Oxford (d. 1778), whom Thomas Warton praised as 'a very ingenious poetess . . . a most sensible, agreeable, and amiable woman'.[23] In a poem (published with Jones's other works in her *Miscellanies in Prose and Verse* (Oxford, 1750)) written to a woman friend who has suffered from the small-pox, Mary Jones borrows Swift's image of the sign, and the name of his lady:

> When skillful traders first set up,
> To draw the people to their shop,
> They strait hang out some gaudy sign,
> Expressive of the goods within. . . .
> So fares it with the Nymph divine;
> For what is Beauty but a Sign? . . .
>   What tho' some envious folks have said,
> That *Stella* now must hide her head,
> That all her stock of beauty's gone,

And ev'n the very sign took down: ...
For if you break a while, we know,
'Tis bankrupt like, more rich to grow.
A fairer sign you'll soon hang up, ...
Which all your neighbours shall out-shine,
And of your Mind remain the Sign.

('After the Small-pox', pp. 79–80)

Although often a Popean in her verse Mary Jones turns to the style of
Swift when she wishes to deal with harsh or humorous physical facts,
and she frequently does wish to deal with physical facts. Indeed, she
deals with the less salubrious matters alluded to in Swift's scatological
poems. In 'Holt Waters. A Tale. Extracted fom the *Natural* History of
Berkshire' (pp. 93–100) she tells a surprising fabliau. The story has a
decorous and polite beginning. 'Two nymphs of chaste *Diana*'s train,
/ Both fair, and tolerably vain' set out in a coach one morning with
'a brace' of 'well-dress'd Beaus'. The coach party proceeds, talking
'Of Queens and grottos, wars and Kings'. Soon Cloe feels uneasy;
she wishes for something, and the author comments defensively:
'Yet trust me, Prudes, it was no more / Than you or I have wish'd
before.' Cloe excuses herself from the coach, saying she must pay a
quick visit of condolence to a friend whose parrot has just died, and
shaking off the gallant offer of 'Sir Fopling' to attend her. She speeds
off alone, and comes to a little farm, but cannot see what she needs.
'What shall she do? Her wants are pressing / And speedily require
redressing.' Cloe finds the dairy, uninhabited, and there is no further
time to consider; the business must be done:

> The cream-pot first she filled with liquor,
> Fit for the thorax of the Vicar.
> Nay *Jove* himself, the skies protector,
> Would call such liquor heav'nly Nectar.
> So in a grot, I've seen enthron'd ⎤
> Some river goddess, osier-crown'd, ⎬
> Pour all her copious urns around, ⎦
> Hence plenteous crops our harvest yield,
> And *Ceres* laughs thro' all the field.
> A pan of milk, unskimm'd its cream,
> Did next receive the bounteous stream; ...
> Back to her company she flies,
> Quite unobserv'd by vulgar eyes.
> The muse indeed behind her stood,
> And heard the noise, and saw the flood.

The Muse, however, does not warn 'Goody Baucis', who returns unsuspiciously to the dairy; she is surprised at the full containers everywhere, and thinks they indicate magic assistance: 'How did she lift her hands, and stare! / And cry'd "What Fairy has been here?".' She immediately puts the magic gift to use:

> Now *Baucis*, who came hot from work,
> Was very dry, her dinner pork, . . .
> She drank, and down the liquor went;
> 'A little, and therewith content,
> We learn, says she, from good St. *Paul*:
> And sure Content is all in all!
> Our beer is dead, but no great matter,
> 'Tis better still than *common* water.'

Jones's country woman is obviously derived from the Ovidian 'Goody Baucis' of Swift's 'Baucis and Philemon' (1709) in which the cottagers are impressed with the miraculously filled jug, 'replenished to the top' (l. 33).

One may object that in Jones's tale the genteel Cloe's secret misdeed is paid for by the unsuspecting lower-class woman who mistakes the lady's piss for flat beer. The emphasis is on the physicality of both women, which they share with us. Cloe's wish is 'no more / Than you or I have wish'd before'. There are no pastoral nymphs, figures of the body without bodily needs, and the goddess as statue with dry stone urn is replaced by the living function of physical Cloe. Cloe's product is certainly not divine liquor, and she is no goddess who so desperately needs to find such relief. If Swift's Celia shits, Jones's Cloe pisses and pisses. We are reminded of some real '*Natural History*'. In 'Holt Waters' (the title seems a pun, as to hold the waters was what Cloe could not do) the female Muse presides knowingly over this female story of needs and liberations.

A still more surprising poem is Mary Jones's 'Epistle from Fern-Hill' (pp. 133–8). (It is a tribute to the robustness of this Age of Sensibility that both these poems were later included in *Poems by Eminent Ladies*.) Written jokingly about a visit to the author's close friend Charlot Clayton, the 'Epistle' is a complaint about the trials of such a visit with an over-complaisant hostess. The guest feels imprisoned, overstuffed with food, overheated with a scorching fire. 'But still in all I do, or say, / This nuisance *Breeding*'s in the way.' The author works out her dissatisfaction in an elaborate comparison to a particular kind of unease. Consider, she urges, the way the General permits himself to fart in company when disturbed with inward wind:

215

He wisely thinks the more 'tis pent
The more 'twill struggle for a vent:
So only begs you'll hold your nose,
And gently lifting up his clothes,
Away th' imprison'd vapour flies,
And mounts a zephyr to the skies.

This uncomfortable instance is the basis of a comparison; to our surprise we find it means that the visitor must be as uncomfortable to Charlot as the General's wind is to him. Like the unwelcome intestinal gas, the discontented visitor tumbles things about and proves a disturbance which the hostess is too polite to appear to notice: 'Yet, spite of all this rebel rout, / She's too well bred to let me out.' The speaker pleads for impolite release:

O *Charlot*! when alone we sit,
Laughing at all our own (no) wit,
You wisely with your Cat at play,
I reading *Swift*, and spilling tea;
How would it please my ravish'd ear,
To hear you from your easy chair,
With look serene, and brow uncurl'd,
Cry out, A – for all the world!
But You, a slave to too much breeding,
And I, a fool with too much reading,
Follow the hive, as bees their drone,
Without one purpose of our own:
Till tir'd with blund'ring and mistaking,
We die sad fools of others making.

It is hard to think of any other poetical work in which the poet is self-compared to a fart. The reference to 'reading *Swift*' points to influence and analogue. This is meant to be (and to be seen to be) a woman's original poem re-creating the Swiftian manner and subject-matter. In this piece, in a reversal of some of Swift's strictures, males prove unpleasantly physical (the General's fart) whereas the females are too proper, too restricted, too unkind to their physical and emotional desires. The poem is a striking plea for freedom from polite rules and lady-like squeamishness. Manners and reading are turning the women into 'fools of others making'. In following the proprieties they are acting inappropriately to themselves and to each other. Jones takes the Swiftian physical manner in order to reverse some of Swift's (and others') strictures of decorum, but Swift's manner and precedent allow for the discussion of such realities. The freedom from squeamish lady-like decorum is vividly acted out in a poem by one of the eighteenth century's 'Eminent Ladies' that still has the power to surprise and shock us.

It is not only the female verse writers who manifest the influence of Swift. The novelist Frances Burney (1752–1840) read both Pope and Swift in her youth, and on reading Pope's *Letters* in her teens she was moved at Pope's 'long friendship with Swift . . . the attachment of such eminent men to one another . . . almost awes me, and at the same time inexpressibly delights me'.[24] In 1774, four years before the publication of *Evelina*, in a conversation with her elderly Mentor Samuel Crisp and some uneducated ladies, Burney extemporized a mock-project, a book of etiquette:

> I told them I intended to write a *Treatise upon Politeness* for their edification. . . .
> 'Will it be like Swift's "Polite Conversation"?' said Mr. Crisp.
> 'I intend to dedicate it to Miss Notable', answered I; 'it will contain all the *newest fashioned* regulations. In the first place, you are never again to cough.'
> 'Not to cough?' exclaimed every one at once; 'but how are you to help it?'
> 'As to that,' answered I, 'I am not very clear about it myself, as I own I am guilty sometimes of doing it; but it is as much a mark of ill breeding, as it is to laugh, which is a thing that Lord Chesterfield has stigmatized.'
> (Early Diary, 1: 324–6)

After reprehending '*sneezing*, or *blowing the nose*' as impermissible, but admitting that breathing is 'not yet . . . quite exploded', Burney promises to send Crisp, who requires instruction, six copies of this important work. Burney shows her knowledge of Swift in immediately picking up Crisp's reference to *Polite Conversation* and alluding to the young 'heroine' of that work, the would-be-smart Miss in Swift's comic gallery of vulgarians. Once again a woman associates Swiftian material with the need to escape repressive rules of breeding, here parodied by being augmented to the point of impossibility. *Evelina* (1778) can be seen as Burney's shrewd 'Treatise upon Politeness'; it is also her version of *Polite Conversation*. Burney has an interest akin to Swift's in the clichés of public conversation and behaviour. Swift's characters in *Polite Conversation* speak in the pert clichés and old smart answers which he pretends to present as 'the Flowers of Wit, Fancy, Wisdom, Humour, and Politeness' (*PW*, 4: 111). Burney's characters often speak in similar hackneyed remarks, like the smart things and ugly faded compliments uttered by Mr Smith in *Evelina*. The climactic scene of that novel, in which the foppish Mr Lovel, confronted with his parodic counterpart the dressed-up monkey, attacks the beast and then is seized and bitten on the ear, has a Swiftian ring; it is reminiscent of the scene with the Brobdingnagian monkey and of episodes of Yahoo-encounters in *Gulliver's Travels*.[25]

Burney shares with Swift a violent imagination, and like him she makes us see the vulnerable living body beneath foppish disguise or constricting proprieties. Her fantasia upon a theme of a 'Treatise upon Politeness' points out the physical need which unheroically resists elaborate systems and refined pretences. For Frances Burney, as for Mary Jones, the Swiftian manner is associated with physical need, and with resistance to the social pressures that are so hard upon women, turning them into 'sad fools of others making'. It is little wonder that one of the first literary quotations we come upon in Burney's *Cecilia* (1782), that big satiric novel in which, as contemporaries noted, Burney wielded the lash, is that important couplet from *Cadenus and Vanessa*, misquoted slightly as 'For common rules were ne'er design'd / Directors of a noble mind'.[26] Burney's misquotation shows that she had rather challenge 'rules' than mere 'Forms', just as she imaginatively challenged through parody 'the *newest fashioned* regulations', those inanities that pinch women's lives and impede the exercise of both Sense and Wit.

Frances Burney's friend Hester Lynch Thrale (later Piozzi) was also an admirer of 'the admirable Swift'. Indeed, she was one of his female imitators. Her latest biographer, William McCarthy, notes that she had more Swift than Johnson in her library, and that in irony 'her chosen precursor' was not Pope or Johnson but Swift. McCarthy illustrates the point by quoting from one of Hester Lynch's earlier poems, 'Pompey, or a Doggrel Epistle from Pompey in the Shades – to his Master', in which the satire on Descartes is drawn from the Swift of *A Tale of a Tub*, and what McCarthy calls 'her bright-eyed octosyllables' from Swift's verse form: for example, 'So Brutes he wisely could maintain / Knew neither Pleasure, Fear nor Pain'.[27]

A more original use of Swift as precursor and influence can be found in Hester Lynch Thrale's 'Three Dialogues on the Death of Hester Lynch Thrale, Written in August 1779'. As she explains in her 'Preface', 'one of Dean Swift's happier Compositions is certainly the little poem on his own Death. My Death would be a slight Event indeed compared with his – it would I think just bear three Dialogues among the people I chiefly live with, and some of them are insignificant enough too.'[28] The morbidly witty dramatic scenes in prose fix for Hester Lynch Thrale her own position in the estimation of her friends, and of rivals like Elizabeth Montagu. Swift had offered

a valuable precedent in presenting himself, with some depression
and self-pity, in an ironic light, offering a realistic appraisal of his
own slight importance in the general social scheme of things. One
must not console oneself in imagining others' grief or lamentation:
' "The Dean is dead (*and what is trumps?*)"' ('Verses on the Death of
Dr. Swift' (1731), l. 228). So in Mrs Thrale's case her 'friends' of the
salons are imagined laughingly remembering her odd bearing with
Johnson ('Mrs. Thrale . . . had prodigious strong Nerves'), and Mrs
Montagu uses the occasion to display her talent in simile: 'She had
remarkable good Nerves, and yet – carried off suddenly – pounced
by Death like a Partridge upon the *Wing* – caught in one of her
Flights Mr. Pepys' ('First Dialogue', p. 27).

Swift is *the* model for ironic self-presentation, for the double-edged
view of the hard social perceptions forced on the helpless self. His
Dean of the poems is both mentally robust and physically and socially
vulnerable; if he maintains his independence it is sometimes at a cost
of gaucherie, uncertainty, social inadequacy. Swift had dared to
choose this unheroic persona, even though male writers could always
assume some grandeur, adopting the cloak of literary greatness of
the past. Pope, pretending modesty, merely refers himself to Horace;
his poetic persona is always strikingly competent, authoritative, and
virtuous. Women writers knew they could not make such claims,
at least not in such tones. The tropes of grandeur, of Virgilian or
Horatian power, of historical importance, were not for them. The
poet who had shown how to present the self as unglamorous, under-
appreciated (yet not faultless), vulnerable, and often absurd: this was
Swift. Of course, Swift's Swift is no mere victim; Swift presents
himself as having mundane unheroic qualities, not only in the
'Verses on the Death of Dr. Swift', where he admits to envy and
peevishness, but in countless other poems where he is a testy
interlocutor, or a busybody, or an uneasy guest.

To summarize the view of Swift generally held by women writers
of the eighteenth century, one can say that for them he was the
exciting poet of limitation. Swift above all other writers dealt with
cross-grained realities against the heroic mode. He made no grand
claims for human reason, and thus not for the rational, powerful, all-
controlling male. He was not in favour of conquests and systems. He
paid attention to the physical, and he acknowledged small as well
as large distresses. When women writers of his era think of dealing
with their domestic world in its hard detail, and often with some
ill humour as well as enjoyment, they tend to look to Swift as one
of their models. When they think of female physical needs, of the
irreducible demands of a body that stubbornly insists on its needs to
piss and fart, to cough and sneeze (and to live and die) they think, to

their comfort, of Swift. When they want to assert satiric energies
against a world that seems inclined to drain them through the
operation of politeness and duty, they turn to Swift again.

Middleton Murry would seem to have his horror to himself, or to
share it with a select circle, including Lord Orrery. In every century
exclamations over Swift's foul-mindedness have been much more
common among critics of Murry's sex. If Swift felt 'a particular
physical loathing of women' it was not reciprocated. Indeed, in
Cadenus and Vanessa he made the claim that he was loved. 'Fidelia'
of Lincoln thought him comically lovable; the persona of Swift has
its special kind of sexual appeal. That Swift won women's liking is
testified to by Orrery, who notes in jealous surprise Swift's power
'over all his females'. Orrery does not wish to regard the obvious
fact: that 'not the richest or most powerful lovers, no, not even
the Grand Seignior himself' can expect the kind of friendship and
affection from women that the man who is truly friendly to women
and values them will naturally receive. Swift liked women, and that
feeling was reciprocated. The relationship seems so unusual that
Orrery has to devalue it and degrade the women into passive
inmates of a 'seraglio'.

Swift's writings did not enclose women in conventions and
impossible stylizations. If, in his 'panegyrical descriptions' of women,
Swift, as Orrery complained, 'seldom descended lower than the center
of their hearts' the heart is worth acknowledging. Swift was not doing
what Orrery thought a poet dealing with women *should* be doing:
creating pleasing inanimate objects for men to enjoy, modelling 'that
delicacy of limb, and those pleasing and graceful attitudes which
have constituted the sex to be the most beautiful part of the creation'.
Orrery's imagery gives away himself and his whole culture: mention
of 'Woman' brings to mind something between an art gallery and a
strip show. Men are frightened of being robbed of the 'wholesome
lust' that Murry prefers. When Swift deals with the dirty or
disagreeable in females, or when his tone is scolding, he is still
urging self-respect, and he never imposes the injunctions to docility,
obedience, and mental lethargy so commonly repeated to women
throughout the century. He never tells woman that her whole aim
must be to charm, or that she rules best when she obeys. A 'seraglio'
was really what he did not want. He wanted Vanessas.

On the subject of Swift, women writers and critics of the twentieth
century seem very much in line with those of the eighteenth century.
Women praise Swift, even in considering those particular poems
which Murry assumes must make him most repellent to women.
Felicity A. Nussbaum, in *The Brink of All We Hate: English Satires on
Women, 1660–1750* (Lexington, KY, 1984), is inclined to defend the

Swift of the 'excremental' poems in which she sees Swift as trying 'to release men from passion and its attendant madness'. The mythology of love and courtship is itself a burden, and Swift can be a liberator: 'Swift seeks to destroy the misapprehensions in both sexes which lead to the folly of love.' Unlike Juvenal and others, Swift does not present women as responsible for the downfall of civilization; rather, he sees that 'woman like man, is not a rational animal, but only *rationis capax*' (pp. 122–23). In Stella he presents 'a positive ideal': 'The Stella of the poems is not praised primarily as the chaste guardian of moral values but as an able, alert companion who delights her friend because of her humanity. His ideal woman, fat, grey, and ill, is decidedly not a lady from romance' (p. 115).

In any modern comparison of Swift and Pope in relation to their views on women Swift is likely to come off much better: that is, if the person making the comparison be a woman. It is not just prim Sarah Green writing to her 'Favourite Niece' who finds Pope 'no friend to our sex'. Ellen Pollak, in *The Poetics of Sexual Myth*, has shown a decided preference for the values expressed in *Cadenus and Vanessa* over those expressed in *The Rape of the Lock*. In more lively and pugnacious vein the heroine of Erica Jong's mock-eighteenth-century novel *Fanny* expresses the same preference. Fanny finds Pope, the 'Divine Dwarf', a disappointment in every respect. When Fanny asks him, 'is it vain for a woman to wish to be a Poet?', Pope '[breaks] into a gale of unkind Laughter' and replies, 'Fanny, my Dear, the Answer is implied in the Query itself. Men are Poets; Women are meant to be their Muse upon Earth'. Waxing more eloquent in his words while warming in his sexual attempt upon her, Pope warns the girl that 'a Woman Poet is an Absurdity of Nature, a vile, despis'd Creature whose Fate must e'er be Loneliness, Melancholy, Despair and eventually Self-Slaughter'. Answering further objections with 'whate'er is, IS RIGHT', Jong's Pope discharges semen from 'his tiny pink Member' over Fanny's thighs and petticoats.[29]

The encounter with Swift is rather different: 'Just as I had rever'd Mr. Pope for his Poetical Works before I met him, and then grew disappointed with the Man himself, so 'twas the Reverse with Dean Swift: my Admiration grew, first from my knowing him, then from the Splendour of his Works' (p. 228). Swift's sexual tastes are, it is true, eccentric, for he wishes that Fanny could mate with a horse (or perhaps that the stallion would mate with him). Fanny and the Dean are, however, able to converse, and a friendship develops. Swift proves (unlike Pope) good to know. Even his personal misanthropy is sympathetic: 'He claim'd Mankind had no Pow'rs of Reason, and yet he fore'er tried to mend the World and bring it to its Senses. He was a slighted Lover of Mankind, one who lov'd not wisely but too well' (p. 235). The comically re-created and fantastic Swift of Erica Jong's *Fanny* is recognizably based on the Swift delineated by Laetitia Pilkington, the Swift who did walk a bit like a horse.

From the eighteenth century to the twentieth, women have tended to find Swift comic, sympathetic, and admirable; they do see 'the Splendour of his Works' and, like 'Fidelia', while 'charm'd with his writings' they 'admire his brave spirit'. The works seem more splendid the more they are looked at, and there are elements in them that are peculiarly helpful to women. Orrery was perhaps right to fear that Swift's view of women was a deep threat to the usual male definition and placement of the fair sex. Swift's very human and expressive voice, particularly in his poems, offered a useful and liberating model. Women writers have drawn Swift, and drawn upon him. He is worth arguing with, worth talking to. Moreover, he has provided a constant model and stimulus for women writers who have found themselves, like the Irish clergyman, Jonathan Swift, in a position of subjugation and supposed docility when they would rather speak out and vex the world a little as well as divert it.

Notes

1. JOHN MIDDLETON MURRY, *Jonathan Swift: A Critical Biography* (London, 1954), pp. 439, 441.

2. JOHN BOYLE, EARL OF ORRERY, *Remarks on the Life and Writings of Dr. Jonathan Swift . . . In a Series of Letters . . .* , third edition (London, 1752), pp. 78, 81.

3. LADY MARY WORTLEY MONTAGU, Letter to Lady Bute, 23 June 1754, in *The Complete Letters of Lady Mary Wortley Montagu*, ed. ROBERT HALSBAND, 3 vols (Oxford, 1967), 3: 56, 57.

4. See Halsband's second footnote to Montagu's letter of 23 June 1754, quoted above (*Letters*, 3: 56).

5. *Memoirs of Mrs Laetitia Pilkington . . . Written by Herself. Wherein are occasionally interspersed, All Her Poems; with Anecdotes of several eminent Persons*, 3 vols (Dublin and London, 1749–54; Garland reprint, New York and London, 1975), 1: 50–1.

6. MARY DAVYS, *The Merry Wanderer* (a revision of her novel of 1705, *The fugitive*), in *Works of Mrs. Mary Davys: Consisting of Plays, Novels, Poems and Familiar Letters*, 2 vols (London, 1725), 1: 161–2. SIOBHÀN KILFEATHER has suggested that *The fugitive* may have influenced *Gulliver's Travels*: 'Beyond the Pale: Sexual Identity and National Identity in Early Irish Fiction', *Critical Matrix*, 2 (Fall, 1986), 1–31.

7. 'The Statues: Or, The Trial of Constancy. A Tale. *For the* Ladies', in *Memoirs*, 1: 92–106. This poem was first published in 1739, after Pilkington's break with Swift, but she attributes the writing of it to an earlier period, and definitely links it to her acquaintance with him. See entry under 'Pilkington' in *A Dictionary of British and American Women Writers 1660–1800*, ed. JANET TODD (London, 1984), p. 251.

8. 'An Apology for not bringing an Exercise', *Poems on Several Occasions*, pp. 97–8.

9. 'Written for my Son, and Spoken by him at his first putting on Breeches', *Poems on Several Occasions*, pp. 13–14.

10. 'To the Right Honourable *John*, Earl of Orrery', 'Dedication' to Barber's *Poems on Several Occasions*, pp. vi–vii. See also *'Directions to Servants' and Miscellaneous Pieces 1733–1742*, PW, 13: 74.

11. Letter of February 1712, *Journal to Stella*, ed. HAROLD WILLIAMS, 2 vols (Oxford, 1948), 2: 482.

12. ELLEN POLLAK, *The Poetics of Sexual Myth: Gender and Ideology in the Verse of Swift and Pope* (Chicago and London, 1985).

13. Laetitia Pilkington was the daughter of a Dutch man-midwife, to whom Constantia Grierson was at one point apprenticed to learn midwifery. Grierson, who edited three major Latin authors before her death at age twenty-seven, was the daughter of an illiterate family, though she married a King's printer. Mary Davys, wife of a schoolmaster, was reduced to running a coffee-shop in Cambridge when she was widowed, and the divorced Pilkington was to try to run a book and print shop. Mary Barber was the wife of a clothier.

14. 'Sophia's Secret Sisters: Feminism in the *Gentleman's Magazine*', paper delivered at a conference of the Midwest American Society for Eighteenth-Century Studies, October 1986. I am grateful also to Phyllis Guskin for sending me references to poems referring to Swift.

15. 'Fidelia', 'To the GENTLEMAN who offer'd 50 Pounds . . .', *Gentleman's Magazine*, 4 (September 1734), 508.

16. 'Fidelia', 'To SYLVANUS URBAN, Gent.', *Gentleman's Magazine*, 4 (November 1734), 619.

17. Prize Epigram No. 2, 'On FIDELIA's Passion for D—n S——t', *Gentleman's Magazine*, 5 (January 1735), 45.

18. 'FIDELIA to SYLVANUS URBAN', *Gentleman's Magazine*, 5 (March 1735), 159.

19. MARY LEAPOR, *Poems upon Several Occasions* (London, 1748), pp. 81–90, 105–6.

20. ANN YEARSLEY, *Poems on Various Subjects* (London, 1787), pp. 129–30.

21. *The Matrimonial Trouble*, in *Playes Written by the Thrice Noble, Illustrious and Excellent Princess, The Lady Marchioness of Newcastle* (London, 1662), 1. 2 (p. 424).

22. *Poems by Eminent Ladies*, 2 vols (London, 1755), 2: 126–32.

23. See Warton's annotation, quoted by Boswell, to a letter of 1757 from Samuel Johnson to Thomas Warton containing a reference to 'Miss Jones'. Warton adds that since she was sister to the Chanter of Christ Church Cathedral 'Johnson used to call her the *Chantress*. I have heard him often address her in this passage from *Il Penseroso*: "Thee Chantress, oft the woods among / I woo, etc."' (Boswell, *The Life of Samuel Johnson, LL.D.*, edited by George Birkbeck Hill, 6 vols (Oxford, 1887), 1: 322–23).

24. *The Early Diary of Frances Burney*, ed. ANNIE RAINE ELLIS, 2 vols (London, 1907), 1: 146.

25. For Burney's monkey episode, see *Evelina, or the History of a Young Lady's Entrance into the World*, ed. EDWARD A. BLOOM (Oxford, 1970), pp. 400–1.

26. *Cecilia, or Memoirs of an Heiress*, 5 vols (London, 1782), 1: 20; and see SAMUEL HOOLE, *Aurelia; or The Contest* (London, 1783), p. 62: 'I stood, a favouring muse, at BURNEY's side, / To lash unfeeling Wealth and stubborn Pride.'

27. See WILLIAM McCARTHY, *Hester Thrale Piozzi: Portrait of a Literary Woman* (Chapel Hill, NC, 1985), p. 16. Despite her admiration for Swift, in her retrospective view of the eighteenth century Hester Lynch Piozzi finds fault with him for being too hard on a female ignorance socially caused. Women such as Swift's character who chats on about her candles and dripping have merely been 'disposed to keep in the sphere long assigned them'. Piozzi does not, however, object to the more notorious poems on women, only remarking that 'Swift tries to shock them [women] into cleanliness'. See PIOZZI, *Retrospection: or, A Review of the Most Striking and Important Events, Characters, Situations, and their Consequences, Which the Last Eighteen Hundred Years Have Presented to the View of Mankind*, 2 vols (London, 1801), 2: 352.

28. *Three Dialogues by Hester Lynch Thrale*, ed. M. ZAMICK (Manchester, 1932), p. 23.

29. ERICA JONG, *Fanny, being The True History of the Adventures of Fanny Hackabout-Jones* (London, 1980), Signet paperback edition (New York, 1981), pp. 34, 43–45.

12 Freud, Swift, and Narcissism: A Psychological Reading of 'Strephon and Chloe'*

THOMAS B. GILMORE, JR.

Many readers have doubted the wisdom of psychoanalytic criticism of Swift.[1] But even though such criticism usually has a weak basis in insufficient or conjectural biographical data, certain psychological concepts, used judiciously to interpret Swift's poems rather than their author, can help to illuminate them. These concepts may reveal that 'Strephon and Chloe' has a greater degree of thematic or didactic integrity than has generally been perceived.[2]

The urinary rouzer that Strephon lets fly in his bride's face on their wedding night is unquestionably the climactic shock of the poem. It may seem almost as shocking as the rouzer itself to maintain that its primary effect is pleasurable; yet Emrys Jones, in accounting for the appeal of Pope's characters in Book 2 of the *Dunciad*, affords support for this contention. Jones notes that the characters behave with the uninhibitedness of infants, and that to enter their world is 'to experience a primitive sense of liberation'.[3] Pope's childish dunces and Strephon's rouzer violate a sexual taboo, thus freeing the reader of these accounts to return vicariously to a state of polymorphous perversity and to recapture the undifferentiated sexual pleasure of infancy. As Freud and other psychologists have pointed out, coprophilia is among the most important components of this pleasure.[4] The reader's acceptance of the rouzer is probably further enhanced by two realizations: that any form of sexual expression is better for Strephon and Chloe than romantic sterility or Strephon's earlier awe of her; and that the particular form their expression takes is inevitable. In spite of their veneer of culture, Strephon and Chloe are so ignorant as to be sexual infants.

Jones understands, of course, that even as Pope conveys the appeal of the dunces in Book 2, he is judging them adversely. Swift's judgment of Strephon and Chloe, while not simultaneous with their

---

* Reprinted from *Contemporary Studies of Swift's Poetry* (Newark, DE: University of Delaware Press; London: Associated Universities Press, 1981), pp. 159–68.

wedding night, follows soon after and is extremely harsh.
Nevertheless, Swift's continuation of their story in lines 203–18 of
the poem is not only credible but psychologically consistent with
the rouzer scene. It is as if Swift is forcing us to do a double take:
what had seemed at first glance an innocent if infantile sexuality
is exposed in the later passage as a symptom of anal fixation or
eroticism resulting from narcissism. If this is a normal state in
infancy, Swift shows his disgust with it and its manifestations when
it completely determines the character of the relationship between
two immature adults. Obviously, Swift could not have been familiar
with the concept of narcissism as a neurosis (or with the other
psychological concepts used in this chapter); but especially in his
portrayal of Strephon he seems to have exposed that neurosis which
current critics like Christopher Lasch and Richard Sennett have
begun to regard as a major psychological ill of late twentieth-century
American society.[5]

Although Strephon lacks the development or complexity to be
seen as a victim of full-blown narcissism, he possesses several of its
most striking features. Even the Strephon of 'The Lady's Dressing-
Room' is a Narcissus figure: the legendary pool into which Narcissus
gazes, self-infatuated, becomes Celia's magnifying glass. Strephon
is 'frighted' (l. 61), not only by its enlargement of his visage but,
more important, by the fact that his discoveries about Celia in her
dressing-room, monstrously magnified as if by her glass, threaten
his narcissistic self-love, Celia being for him nothing more than
a projection and desired confirmation of his idealized self. His
namesake in 'Strephon and Chloe' may be less obviously a
descendant of Narcissus, partly because he goes through the social
rituals of courtship and matrimony. But as his wedding night
approaches, Strephon does not look forward to it with desire. The
absence of any thought of giving pleasure to Chloe or sharing it with
her seems attributable to something other than the understandable
nervousness of the sexually inexperienced Strephon. As Richard
Sennett observes, 'Narcissistic feelings often focus themselves on
obsessive questions of whether I am good enough, whether I am
adequate, and the like'.[6] These are just the sorts of questions running
through Strephon's head, especially in lines 71–94. Whatever he may
think, he is not in love with Chloe except in a narcissistic way; in his
worries about how she will receive his sexual advances, we are able
to see that his overriding concern is with using her, as an idealized
extension of himself, to affirm or validate a faltering self-image.

Freud wrote of the narcissist that he often chooses to love a person
with 'excellences which he never had' and cannot attain.[7] One
predictable outcome of this hope that someone else can supply inner

deficiencies is a disappointment that leaves the narcissist feeling empty or dead.[8] This is exactly the state of Swift's Cassinus (in 'Cassinus and Peter'), who not only feels dead but longs for death as a result of his dreadful discovery that Caelia, lovely Caelia, shits. But the passivity or resignation of Cassinus is only one type of narcissistic reaction to disillusionment in love, to the profound if usually unconscious 'conviction that other people . . . will never be good enough'.[9] There is often a further reaction, exemplified by Strephon in both 'The Lady's Dressing-Room' and 'Strephon and Chloe', which can be characterized as a desire for revenge. Vacillating 'between the extremes of overidealization and devaluation', narcissists may come 'to depreciate and treat with contempt those from whom they do not expect anything (often their former idols)'.[10] In 'The Lady's Dressing-Room', Strephon, having discovered the nastiness of his beloved Celia, generalizes his contempt for her to reach the conclusion that all women stink (ll. 121–28). His namesake in 'Strephon and Chloe' obtains his revenge and degrades his beloved by joining with her in a 'great society in stinking' (l. 210): not really a society at all, of course, but a kind of narcissism *à deux*, a form of sexual perversion 'involving primitive aggressive manifestations or primitive replacement of genital aims by eliminatory ones'.[11] The perversion also effectively fulfills Strephon's narcissistic desire to block the development of any genuine 'social dimension' in his sexuality.[12]

From another viewpoint the impasse of Strephon and Chloe may be explained as the result of their failure to sublimate, to engage in that process by which the sex drive is diverted into numerous channels whose end product is often called culture or civilization. According to Freud, society or community is the closest synonym to civilization; but the 'great society in stinking' established by Strephon and Chloe after their wedding night is only the noxious, unsublimated travesty of civilized society. Moreover, later in the poem, in a catalogue of female vices, the woman gossip who gives the impression of 'breaking wind' (l. 282) through her mouth may be another instance of anal fixation – and, if so, another travesty of healthy society.

Decency, a term much stressed in the last hundred lines of the poem, is perhaps Swift's equivalent to sublimation; and its result, disclosed in the poem's final paragraph, is friendship, the chief means, according to Freud, of strengthening 'the communal bond' and therefore the indispensable material of society or civilization.[13] For Norman O. Brown, 'Swift's ultimate horror' in the scatological poems is that 'sublimation – that is to say, all civilized behavior – is a lie and cannot survive confrontation with the truth'.[14] 'Strephon and Chloe' might seem to support this claim in its at times almost desperate insistence that women conceal their defecatory functions; this is perhaps one quality that Peter Schakel has in mind when he speaks of a 'fallible, uncertain, struggling Swift'.[15] Nevertheless, the poem may be credited with two major victories: it confronts the horror of anality, and Swift's recommendation of the civilizing virtue of friendship survives it.

One may still be dissatisfied with Swift's exclusive attention to anal fixation and friendship, with his neglect of the joys of mature sexuality. But although Freud is explicit on this subject where Swift is tacit, their attitudes are essentially similar. To explain his observation that there is 'something in the nature of the [sex] function itself which denies us full satisfaction', Freud advances a theory that is in line with Swift's implications. When man adopted an upright posture, Freud speculates, he began to develop a repugnance to genital odors and to the excremental odors physiologically inseparable from them that necessarily diminishes his sexual pleasures.[16] If Freud does not deny all possibility of sexual enjoyment, as Swift seems to, he agrees that the more civilized a person becomes, the more he will sacrifice or sublimate his sexual urges in favor of such goals as friendship.

Freud entertained no illusions about the bliss of civilization. Indeed, at least once in his writings he briefly considered the possibility that some or all civilizations are neurotic.[17] He was also aware that the renunciations required by civilization are painfully difficult for most people. Nevertheless, Freud would have regarded skeptically, if not with Swiftian derision, Norman O. Brown's idea that man's best hope is to give up civilization and restore his polymorphous perversity.[18] For Freud, the only alternative to civilization was not polymorphous perversity but the state of nature, in which men are inclined to 'satisfy their aggressiveness on . . . [their neighbor], to exploit his capacity for work without compensation, to use him sexually without his consent, to seize his possessions, to humiliate him, to cause him pain, to torture and to kill him'.[19] As Lady Macleod once murmured of Dr. Johnson, when he observed that man was inherently no more virtuous than a wolf, 'This is worse than Swift.'[20] If not worse, Freud's dark vision of man in a state of nature underscores his basic affinities with the greatest Augustan writers. And it suggests why, with them, he defended civilization for all its faults and frailties. If Freud's view of man is no more complete than that of the Augustans and if it tends toward Swift's pessimism about the possibilities of sexual delight, it is at least, like Swift's view, less insulting to man's complexity than the massages of *Playboy* magazine or the dream of Norman O. Brown.

Apart from the controversial Houyhnhnms, the closest Swift ever came to a positive vision or version of civilization was, perhaps, in some of the poems to Stella and in the last paragraph of 'Strephon and Chloe'. It is helpful to think of this paragraph as an abstract of a relationship more fully fleshed out in the Stella poems. Possibly because of the disenchantment with politics stemming from Swift's involvement in the Tory administration of Oxford and Bolingbroke, his model of civilization is a type of ideal relationship or friendship between a man and a woman. We can of course never fully know the realities of Swift's relationship with Esther Johnson; but through the Stella poems, the ending of 'Strephon and Chloe', and other sources, we do know what Swift thought or wanted it to be. And although we also know that Swift invested much effort in molding or educating Esther to fulfill his ideal of womanhood, we cannot fairly characterize his relationship with her, or with the Stella of the poems, as narcissistic. Whatever selfish gratification he may have derived from witnessing the success of his efforts, his primary satisfaction seems to have come from his helping to shape a woman of grace, probity, and intelligence, qualities that would make her worthy of the regard and friendship of equally estimable women and men. That is to say, Swift sought to form a woman possessing qualities very much like those named in the final paragraph of 'Strephon and Chloe'. If we look to classical myth for an analogue to Swift in his relations with Esther or Stella, the figure we are most likely to remember is not Narcissus but Pygmalion.

In spite of some real confusion and problems with tone in the last hundred lines of 'Strephon and Chloe', Swift firmly regains command in the two closing stanzas and neatly rounds off the poem in lines 307–14 by sharply contrasting a healthy relationship with the sick, burlesque 'society in stinking' of Strephon and Chloe. Since even in these lines he mentions passion and love (ll. 307, 310), Swift does not wholly ignore the element of physical or sexual attraction in a relationship between men and women. He emphasizes, however, the major drawback of this element – its lack of solidity or durability – as a foundation for any relationship by the dense architectural imagery in his next-to-last paragraph and by his contrast between the short-lived blaze or 'fire' (l. 222) of passional love and the 'mutual gentle fire' (l. 313) of friendship. Thus if a preoccupation with beauty or sexual attraction is likely to collapse into the fulsome society of Strephon and Chloe, the absence from a relationship of those virtues which Swift names near the end of the poem – sense, wit, decency, prudence, and good nature – is even more certain to produce misery and failure. To put Swift's 'message' in language familiar to the late twentieth century, he is suggesting not only at the end but throughout the poem that there are better alternatives than a relationship in which either the man or the woman treats the other as a sex object. If we doubt or reject Swift's priorities or values, we perhaps only demonstrate our disinclination to make those civilizing renunciations mentioned by Freud and our readiness to embrace the panaceas, *inter urinas et faeces*, of *Playboy* or Norman O. Brown.

Notes

1. See 'Forum', *PMLA*, 91 (1976), 465; also my essay 'The Comedy of Swift's Scatological Poems', *PMLA*, 91 (1976), 33–43. See also PHYLLIS GREENACRE's *Swift and Carroll: A Psychological Study of Two Lives* (New York, 1955).

2. JOHN M. ADEN, 'Those Gaudy Tulips: Swift's "Unprintables"', in *Quick Springs of Sense: Studies in the Eighteenth Century*, ed. LARRY S. CHAMPION (Athens, GA, 1974), p. 28. PETER SCHAKEL, 'Swift's Remedy for Love: The 'Scatological' Poems', *Papers on Language and Literature*, 14 (1978), 145, complains that 'the final ninety-six lines of heavy-handed sermonizing destroy the unity and, by not letting the situation speak for itself, the effectiveness of the poem'.

3. 'Pope and Dulness', Chatterton Lecture on an English Poet, *Proceedings of the British Academy*, 54 (1968), 254. Pope's bookseller Chetwood, engaged in a pissing contest with Curll, suffers a mishap similar to Strephon's:

   > A second effort brought but new disgrace,
   > For straining more, it flies in his own face;
   > Thus the small jett which hasty hands unlock,
   > Spirts in the gard'ner's eyes who turns the cock.
   >
   > (*Dunciad* (A), Twickenham edn, bk. 2, ll. 167–70)

   Swift, however, is characteristically more violent; Strephon's rouzer ends a verse paragraph, and its effect is not softened by any comic simile like Pope's in lines 169–70. Instead, the rouzer immediately disperses the frail images of romantic love ('little Cupids', 'Expiring shepherds', 'silver meads', ll. 193, 200–201), preparing the way for the 'great society in stinking' (l. 210), which succeeds romantic illusion for Strephon and Chloe.

4. Sigmund Freud, 'The Most Prevalent Form of Degradation in Erotic Life' (1912), in *On Creativity and the Unconscious: Papers on the Psychology of Art, Literature, Love, Religion*, ed. BENJAMIN NELSON (New York, 1958), p. 185; and KARL ABRAHAM, 'Contributions to the Theory of the Anal Character' (1921), in *Selected Papers of Karl Abraham M. D.*, trans. DOUGLAS BRYAN and ALIX STRACHEY (New York, 1960), p. 372.

5. See CHRISTOPHER LASCH, 'The Narcissist Society', *New York Review of Books*, 30 September 1976, pp. 5, 8, 10–13, and *Haven in a Heartless World: The Family Besieged* (New York, 1977), in which he claims (p. 156) that 'the narcissist, not the authoritarian, is the prevalent personality type' today. Two of Sennett's works are cited below.

6. RICHARD SENNETT, *The Fall of Public Man* (New York, 1977), p. 11.

7. SIGMUND FREUD, 'On Narcissism: An Introduction' (1914), in *The Standard Edition of the Complete Psychological Works of Sigmund Freud*, ed. JAMES STRACHEY, 34 vols (London, 1957), 14: 101.

8. Richard Sennett, 'Destructive Gemeinschaft', *Partisan Review*, 43 (1976), 348.

9. Sennett, *The Fall of Public Man*, p. 335.

10. Otto Kernberg, interviewed by Linda Wolfe, 'Why Some People Can't Love', *Psychology Today*, 12 (1978), 58; Kernberg, *Borderline Conditions and Pathological Narcissism* (New York, 1975), p. 17. I am indebted for these references to my friend James A. Glass. The publication of a lead article on narcissism in a popular journal is probably an indication of the rising interest in this subject in contemporary American society.

11. Kernberg, *Borderline Conditions and Pathological Narcissism*, p. 11. Significantly, this quotation appears in a section headed 'Polymorphous Perverse Sexual Trends'.

12. Sennett, *The Fall of Public Man*, p. 8.

13. Sigmund Freud, *Civilization and Its Discontents*, ed. and trans. James Strachey (New York, 1962), p. 56.

14. Norman O. Brown, *Life Against Death* (Middletown, CT, 1959), p. 188.

15. Peter Schakel, 'Swift's Remedy for Love', *Papers on Language and Literature*, 14 (1978), 147.

16. Freud, *Civilization and Its Discontents*, pp. 52, 53n. See also Freud's 'The Most Prevalent Form of Degradation in Erotic Life', in *On Creativity and the Unconscious*, pp. 185–6.

17. Freud, *Civilization and Its Discontents*, p. 91.

18. One expression of Freud's skepticism can be found in *The Future of an Illusion*, trans. W. D. Robson-Scott, The International Psycho-Analytical Library, ed. Ernest Jones (New York, 1953), p. 11. Defending civilization against the innate destructive, antisocial tendencies of man, Freud submits that the maintenance of every culture must probably involve 'coercion and instinctual renunciation' – including, surely, the renunciation of polymorphous perversity. Although more tactful and cautious than Swift would have been with dreams such as Brown's, Freud still treats them as visions of a 'golden age' and doubts that they can be realized.

19. Freud, *Civilization and Its Discontents*, p. 58. See also *The Future of an Illusion*, p. 26, where Freud asserts of nature that 'she destroys us, coldly, cruelly, callously', and that 'it is the principal task of culture, its real *raison d'être*, to defend us against nature'.

20. James Boswell, *The Journal of a Tour to the Hebrides, with Samuel Johnson, LL.D.*, in *Boswell's Life of Johnson*, ed. G. B. Hill and L. F. Powell, 6 vols (Oxford, 1950), 5: 211.

Part Four

Writing and Meaning

In linguistic philosophy one of the most tenacious areas of debate in semantics surrounds definitions of appropriate context. Words communicate in particular situations due to implications as well as primary meanings. For J. L. Austin, statements that do not simply state facts or describe states of affairs were *performative* speech-acts, that is, those statements that actually perform an action, such as the naming of either a ship at its launch or of an infant at baptism. Austin had in his sights a prevalent notion, the correspondence theory of truth, that regarded the validity of the communication transmitted by a sentence as dependent on its correspondence to known facts. What Austin noticed was that many speech-acts did not conform to such a theory and that the correspondence criterion of truth provided too broad a set of distinctions to enable any critical grasp on many kinds of statement. Truth could actually be a dimension of criticism, deduced from context, chosen discourse (plain, informal or aesthetic) or attitude of speaker:

> In order to explain what can go wrong with statements we cannot just concentrate on the proposition involved (whatever that is) as has been done traditionally. We must consider the total situation in which the utterance is issued – the total speech-act – if we are to see the parallel between statements and performative utterances. So the total speech-act in the total speech-situation is emerging from logic piecemeal as important in special cases . . .
> (J. L. Austin, *How To Do Things With Words* [Oxford, 1962], p. 52)

Indeed, so difficult does it eventually become for maintaining Austin's distinction between a performative utterance and a *constative* one (statements that could be deemed true or false) that he is driven to the conclusion that most statements that appear linguistically to conform to the constative are often performative but with qualifiers omitted, such as 'I hereby state that . . .'. A full critical view of context (for example, illocutionary items such as how you are stating something, to whom and on what occasion) is so much more revelatory than any exhaustive mapping of grammatical or locutionary features.

There are two aspects of Austin's perceptions that provide links to deconstructive readings: (a) what appears to be merely a statement of the obvious, of a fact or an evident state of affairs, is always an affirmation as well, which needs the additional evidence of illocutionary features in order to comprehend how and why the statement has been made; and (b) the description of context is potentially limitless. It is as if there is always the capacity to take more illocutionary features into account. This is especially true of writing where one cannot consult the original presence of speaker/writer, and it is a salient ingredient of language to depart from simple denotation to involve figuration. In all but the most programmatic allegories, language smuggles in images that exceed prose paraphrase; one could go further and point out that one's intentions may not be present to oneself, consciously, in simple language. Our thoughts may be organized around figures of expression rather than some unadorned calculus of language.

The three essays that conclude the volume are all in their own way indebted to the insights offered by Jacques Derrida, Geoffrey Hartman and Paul de Man. When Terry J. Castle examines the absence of script in Houyhnhnm culture it is a way of laying bare Swift's own fear of textual contamination: the assumption that mischievous writing is a fallen derivation from the purity of unadorned speech. This 'grammaphobia' invokes a sense of prior (spoken or intended) ideas that are unfortunately and inevitably translated in the passage to script. Swift constantly searches for the presence that should lie behind the marks on the page. The 'logocentric' hope that there may be some thought, reason or Word that would eventually serve as a non-linguistic foundation to underpin expression is, according to Derrida, a cultivation of a certain blindness to what we actually do when we interpret: project as well as infer, and often project *when* we think we merely deduce meaning (see his critique of Saussure in *Of Grammatology*, trans. GAYATRI CHAKRAVORTY SPIVAK [Baltimore, MD, 1977], pp. 27–73). Castle is aware of how this leads Swift into a paradox: 'the text is *inevitable*. It is already here. The evil text and human presence constitute an inseparable unit in the world' (p. 252).

What Derrida outlines in texts such as *Positions* (trans. ALAN BASS [Chicago, 1981]) is that the drive towards expressing positive propositions in language (and thus even of conceiving of them) depends on a passing off of the linguistic medium as in some way 'natural' or a transparent server of truth. The presumed gap between signifier and signified is, however, constantly eroded whenever we use language. Any opposing terms in philosophy, for example, are typically involved not in a 'peaceful coexistence' but a 'violent hierarchy': 'One of the two terms governs the other (axiologically, logically, etc.), or has the upper hand. To deconstruct the opposition, first of all, is to overturn the hierarchy at a given moment' (p. 41). The perversity of deconstructive readings stems from a radical insight about language, namely, that when we enter the linguistic realm in order to demonstrate or illustrate any proposition, covertly or not, we in effect have recourse to a governing metaphor which is necessary to organize not only the deployment of our thoughts on paper but the thoughts themselves.

For Swift, the Teller of *The Tale of a Tub* is an example of this surrender to language, which occasions the unravelling of sense and ordonnance to the point of madness. When is Gulliver in charge of his own account? Or when does it begin to take 'him' over? What Derrida terms *différance*, that constant play of items in thought merely different from each other, deferring full meaning, is the positive counterbalance to Swift's terror of limitless signification (see Derrida's analysis of Husserl's phenomenology in *Speech and Phenomena, and Other Essays on Husserl's Theory of Signs*, trans. DAVID B. ALLISON [Evanston, IL, 1973]). In literary interpretation one of the necessary aids to intelligibility is genre recognition, and, in Louise K. Barnett's approach to *Gulliver's Travels*, the constant defeating of easy assumptions about what type of writing is presented is regarded as very much part of Swift's overall strategy. The model of reading defined by E. D. Hirsch, that we gradually come to assimilate the type of writing we are reading by gradually coming to terms with the work's 'intrinsic genre', is made a contributory factor in the creation of meaning. For Hirsch, an 'intrinsic genre' is a more particularized description than those loose aesthetic categories from rhetoric, such as Tragedy or Comedy. The nearest he comes to a simple definition is when he addresses the temporality of reading, that divining of overall structure sentence by sentence until, by a process of trial and error, we can grasp the whole of the sequence-as-form:

> Because words follow one another sequentially, and because the words that will come later are not present to consciousness along with the words experienced here and now, the speaker or listener must have an anticipated sense of the whole by virtue of which the presently experienced words are understood in their capacity as parts functioning in a whole.
>
> (E. D. Hirsch, *Validity in Interpretation* [New Haven, 1967], p. 82)

As Barnett comes to realize, this sense of a whole is questioned root and branch by our reading experience of complex texts that change generic direction – or when these details are mixed. Rather like the innocent picaro, the reader is constantly introduced to situations and contexts that require both retrospective 're-reading' and a re-learning. The promise of full meaning (and adequate orientation) is constantly deferred (in Derrida's sense), and what positive terms we derive from the text of *Gulliver's Travels* are constantly under erasure.

There is a tendency of some deconstructive readings to convert most 'authorial' meanings into matters of hermeneutics. While texts may be 'about' many things, the rhetoric used in illustrating these subjects subverts easy mimesis and takes centre-stage. G. Douglas Atkins here follows the multiple suggestions of the Father's Will in the *Tale*: its authoritative function, announcing an apparently unequivocal set of prohibitions, but which progresses by way of metaphor whereby the reader as well as the Brothers cannot help but misread rebelliously. Reading, for Paul de Man, is not an easy entry into meaning; indeed, one must confront 'the impossibility of reading' (*Allegories of Reading: Figural Language in Rousseau, Nietzsche, Rilke, and Proust* [New Haven,

1979], p. 245), in that there is never a route to agreed meaning. We may try to separate the figural from the literal, but rhetoric always 'puts an insurmountable obstacle in the way of any reading or understanding' (p. 131). Insights can only arise from the cultivation of a certain blindness to other paths we may have taken or other options that could equally be the case. For Atkins, irony lies at the edge of however we read – with special relevance as regards the *Tale*. This chapter, the seventh of his *Reading Deconstruction/Deconstructive Reading* (Lexington, KY, 1983), follows immediately after one on John Dryden's poem *Religio Laici* (1682), which, in expounding a layman's faith, similarly finds its apparent thesis at odds with much of its expressive features: departing from the 'tyranny' of singular authority, it still contains a search for it. Swift's Teller sets out to manage a tale yet discovers that the needs of self-disclosure and the exigencies of narrative defeat him – and the reader.

13 Why the Houyhnhnms Don't Write: Swift, Satire and the Fear of the Text*

Terry J. Castle

The Houyhnhnms have no system of writing. When Gulliver transcribes Houyhnhnm words into English in his 'Master's Presence', the horse is puzzled. 'It cost me much Trouble to explain to him what I was doing; for the Inhabitants have not the least Idea of Books or Literature' (*PW*, 11: 235). This absence is not due, as one might expect, to the fact that the Houyhnhnms are hooved creatures. In Chapter 9, two paragraphs after noting again their lack of 'Letters', Gulliver is careful to tell us that the Houyhnhnms can 'do all the Work which requires Hands' (*PW*, 11: 274), including the threading of needles. Clearly a point is being made here. As on so many occasions in *Gulliver's Travels*, however, we may feel it is an enigmatic one. Is the Houyhnhnms' lack of writing, as Gulliver's chapter note suggests, part of a 'Defectiveness of their Language' (*PW*, 11: 271)? But Swift has severely undermined our sense of Gulliver's reliability by this point in Book 4: is the satirist really intending to present the absence of script as good? Is it a necessary feature of the Houyhnhnms' ideal community? Grammaphobia, or fear of the written word, is at least potential within the Swiftian text.

The Nambikwara have no system of writing. In *Tristes Tropiques* – a record, like *Gulliver's Travels*, of voyages to strange lands – Lévi-Strauss presents us with a transformation of the scene between Gulliver and his Master. When the Nambikwara chief first sees the anthropologist making field notes, he, too, is puzzled. Unlike the dispassionate Houyhnhnm, however, the chief immediately demands pencil and paper and begins to imitate this act of writing. Subsequently, he uses the scribbles he has made to mystify his fellow tribesmen: he threatens them with his own version of the anthropologist's magic. Lévi-Strauss, because he is a scientist and not a satirist, can make an explicit comment on all of this; he explicates the parable. It reminds us, he says, of the sinister ease with which

* Reprinted from *Essays in Literature*, 7, 1 (1980), 31–44.

writing can be alienated from its ostensible signification. Because of its incontrovertible presence as object, its semantic function may be co-opted by a sociological one. The written artifact, utterly voided of meaning, nevertheless retains an oppressive, disruptive effect on the human community. Writing 'had been borrowed as a symbol. . . . It had not been a question of acquiring knowledge, of remembering or understanding, but rather of increasing the authenticity and prestige of one individual – or function – at the expense of others.' The Nambikwara fall into the world of writing: with the discovery of the text in its most arbitrary and superstitious form, a kind of tyranny is instituted and natural personal relations are subverted. For the anthropologist, writing is thus always a pernicious addition to culture, precisely because its significatory function is so quickly betrayed by circumstance: 'the primary function of written communication is to facilitate slavery'.[1] Grammaphobia is more than potential in Lévi-Strauss's text.

The juxtaposition I have made is not an innocent one. Its consequences for Swift may be drawn out by the following digression. Commenting on the Lévi-Strauss anecdote in *Of Grammatology*, the French theorist of writing, Jacques Derrida, isolates in the anthropologist's assumptions a central myth of the written word. Lévi-Strauss's remarks epitomize for him the 'classical ideology' of language in Western culture. Briefly, Derrida suggests that 'from Plato to Rousseau to Hegel' an arbitrary relation has been enforced between speech and writing. In our mythic formulation, speech is primary and writing is secondary. We impute to speech a natural priority and purity: we identify it as the mode of signification appropriate to 'natural man'. Writing, by contrast, is traditionally imagined as an imitation of speech, as a belated development, as an unnatural superimposition upon the primal and exquisite purity of oral communication. The ideological separation soon modulates (following upon Plato) into a moral drama, a Fall: if speech preserves a pure relation between Nature and Word, writing interrupts, compromises, corrupts this relation. The medium of writing itself – because of its impoverished material status – breaches Nature and Word and lays open a ground for falsehood. The Text, as Devil, is 'the Father of Lies'. As such, it makes itself available in turn as an instrument of corrupt individuals. Thus the fantasy persists that writing is 'the dangerous supplement', the shoddy, distracting copy of original truth. Writing 'takes on the status of a tragic fatality come to prey upon natural innocence'.[2]

The operation of this myth of writing in Lévi-Strauss is patent: a pure (oral) society is disrupted by the intervention of writing, a writing, moreover, that points up, pathetically, its own radical shoddiness, its inauthenticity as signifier. I would like to claim that a similar myth may be seen working in Swift. Book 4 of *Gulliver's Travels* is, in one reading, a complex meditation on the problematic nature of writing and the possible corruption implied by the Text. But the theme reappears often in Swift's work. At these moments his obsessive apprehension of the philosophical and sociological dilemmas posed by writing suggests that he is influenced by a mythic structure of the kind Derrida describes. Swift, as we will see, confronts the Fallen Text in a number of works, and this text itself becomes, with varying degrees of explicitness, a satiric subject *par excellence*.

Swift, like Lévi-Strauss in *Tristes Tropiques*, makes the ideological assumption of a radical break between speech and writing. This point has played no part, really, in classic commentaries on Swift's work – those, for instance, of Ehrenpreis, Harth, Monk, Landa and others.[3] Indeed, Swift criticism has in general tended to leave aside both the question of the satirist's view of his own medium and the problem of the written artifact that his texts raise. In a well-known description of the rationalist utopia of Book 4 of *Gulliver's Travels*, Samuel H. Monk itemizes every feature of Houyhnhnm life except the one an anthropologist would be first to notice – that the horses have an exclusively oral culture. The omission here is typical of general inattention to the question of the written word.[4] Even in recent critical discussions that have focused especially on Swift's view of language, however, the mythic split – the fall of speech into writing – has been presupposed but unacknowledged.[5] Commentators on Swift's linguistic satire have tended to confine themselves to remarks of an unspecific kind – for instance, that the abuse of words satirized by Swift is linked to a larger satire of other kinds of abuse: political, religious, and the like. Thus William Koon writes, in an essay on language in *A Tale of a Tub*, that 'the *Tale's* corrupt language marks corrupt religion and learning as well as the fallen nature of man'. And again, 'man's sinful nature reveals itself in words as well as in thoughts and deeds'.[6]

However true these remarks, they tend to ignore the special force Swift applies in the *Tale* and elsewhere to a critique of textuality *per se*. The corrupt words are, in fact, written words. Speech retains all its natural priority in Swift. His fear, his satiric energy, is aroused by the blotted, besmeared copy of speech, by the perverse materiality of the printed page – by an 'excremental' vision of the script. The fallen nature of man is revealed most profoundly not in the fact that he speaks (Adam spoke with God in the Garden), but in the fact that he writes. Thus one must particularize the anxious element underlying Swift's work not simply as linguaphobic but as grammaphobic: his is

241

an exemplary examination of the paradoxes that obtain when words thicken, squirm, and breed before our eyes. Let us approach the enigma of the Houyhnhnms' missing script by placing it in a larger context. All of Swift's satiric pieces, to a greater or lesser extent, reflect upon the problematic status of the written word. The mode of reflection varies. Swift's revelation of the fallen nature of writing is primarily philosophic in *A Tale of a Tub*; sociological implications are drawn out in some of the smaller satires; and finally, *Gulliver's Travels* is regulated by an inclusive fiction of the text.

A Tale of a Tub, the most extensive early satire, is, one might claim, Swift's prototypical (and perhaps most complicated) diagnosis of the problem at the heart of the text. A duplicity, or doubleness, informs Swift's revelation: the *Tale* is simultaneously a history and an embodiment of the corruption potential in the scriptory. It is at once an hallucination of Text and an hallucinatory text. This doubleness has, of course, been noted by commentators.[7] Just as the three brothers puzzle over a text, their father's will, in the embedded history in the *Tale*, so Swift's readers must themselves enact a similar problematic process of textual interpretation as they confront the dark mysteries of his framing text – the prefaces, digressions, notes, addenda. We are made the mad interpreters of Swift's text; it invites us to engage in a *folie de texte* and replicate the process which is described anecdotally in the embedded parable of Peter and the rest. More critics than Wotton have fallen into Swift's trap. This formal complementary quality in the work is usually explained in relation to Swift's explicit satiric project noted in the Apology, the twofold exposure of 'gross Corruptions in Religion and Learning' (*PW*, 1: 1). Interpretation of text is the theme which conjoins Swift's satire of religious abuse in the allegorical portion of the *Tale* with his satire on pedagogic abuse, exemplified in the Modern editor's insane critical apparatus.

The theme of interpretation, however, suggests a deep structure in the Swiftian satire. The problem of meaning, raised everywhere on the surface of the *Tale*, points, it would seem, to an underlying, consistent fantasy of the Text itself. On the most profound level (the level of dream?), Swift's satire is motivated by a vision – potentially fearful – of the written artifact as a radically unstable object. This latent myth of the text conditions both the convoluted satiric strategy of a *Tale* and the passionate intensity with which this strategy is put into effect. But how might one specify the prototypical, anxious Text imagined in the *Tale*? How does the written word reveal itself to Swift – and to us – as a corrupt mode of signification? Swift's underlying critique of writing depends first of all, as I have already intimated by my own digression to the Derridean analysis, upon an

intuition of its compromised relation to speech. The model in Swift
is, in the most general application, Platonic – the written object is
a material rendering of something ideal, the pure world of speech.
Writing is a copy of a pre-existing, naturalized realm of discourse;
and for the satirist of the text, its very materiality attests to its
corruptness; and the copy, in this case, exemplifies a process of
degeneration. The solidification of speech into writing is, to use
a Derridean concept, a scandal; to use a Swiftian, a scatology.

Swift suggests much of this, of course, in the elaborate
bibliographic boondoggle with which the *Tale* begins. We learn in the
Apology prefixing the satire that the original version of the Modern's
manuscript has been lost, and that the primary text which we read is,
after all, that 'surreptitious Copy', 'with many Alterations', feared by
the 'Bookseller' in his own subsequent Preface. This would appear
to explain why the present manuscript is a pocked transcript, one
disrupted at all points by obscurities, typographical ellipses, holes.
Yet, the Apology blithely admits, the author's missing original itself
also held 'Chasms' though indeed, 'not so many' as the received text.
At this point an absurdity has intervened into Swift's potted history
of the text. This last information hints subtly at an epistemological
equivalence among all the texts; each is equally impure, even that
version which is described, oxymoronically, as the 'Original Copy'
(*PW*, 1: 9). Each is impure in regard to the world of spoken discourse,
which maintains here an assumed priority. What has been lost in the
process of transmission described in the Apology is not an originally
pure manuscript (no such thing exists), but truth itself, specifically
located in the voice, the words of a human speaker.

The *Tale* fictionalizes this loss most obviously in the mystery
attached to the Modern's identity and whereabouts. Again in the
Apology, Swift alludes to the rumor – though discounting it – that
the author of the manuscript we read is dead. In any case, the
Modern cannot be consulted directly regarding the cruxes in his text;
the authority of his voice – the voice of authorial intention – is absent.
The point here would seem to be that the Text cannot, ultimately,
be referred to the spoken discourse it purports to mirror: the point
of contact between speech and writing is breached by accident, by
history, by that very plunge into materiality that the written word
represents. Symbolically, a death, a disappearance, takes place
between oral and written modes. In the embedded allegory death
literally intervenes between speech and text: the appearance of the
disputed will in the world is here functionally dependent upon
the death of an authorial *voice*, the father. The will – an archetypal
version of Text – is thus compromised, de-natured, separated from
truth at its moment of origin. It is a deathly, parasitic artifact; it feeds

off an original, living form of discourse, and replaces it in the world. The Text falls into the world precisely as the voice, traumatically, leaves it – its frustrating, marred surface attests to its belated, unnatural, and ultimately dehumanized status.

The gap between speech and text fantasized in the symbolic fictions of a *Tale* is fearful because it occasions, necessarily, the breakdown of meaning. It brings about a hermeneutic catastrophe. The privileged, single meaning is abrogated by that death which mediates between the worlds of discourse and transcription. Because it cannot be referred back to the truth of the voice, the text's signification is unverifiable; its truth is always indeterminate. Once at large in the world, Swift suggests, the paradigmatic manuscript resolves immediately into an independent, free-floating structure of possible meanings – it constitutes its own infinitely expansive ideology. Yet this is the hermeneutic nightmare at the heart of the *Tale*, the source of the satirist's motivating phobia. Separated from the natural constraints of the voice, the text makes itself available for arbitrary, creative interpretation. Confronting, for instance, one of the famous hiatuses in Swift's own manuscript – the '*Hic multa desiderantur*' ('here much is left to be desired'; (*PW*. 1: 107)) – the reader can only conjecture what might fill the ellipsis. The text has lost its voice in the most radical way possible. Hence, like the three brothers of the allegory who encounter the '*altum silentium*' ('deep silence'; (*PW*, 1: 51)) of their father's will and fill the void as they wish, we are invited by the Modern's text to turn imaginists, to become creative readers. Noting his desire that 'every Prince in *Christendom*' assign to seven scholars the task of writing '*seven* ample Commentaries' on the *Tale*, the Modern asserts that 'whatever Difference may be found in their several Conjectures, they will all, without the least Distortion, be manifestly deduceable from the Text' (*PW*, 1: 117–18). No reading is disallowed by the pocked and whorish text.

It is worth noting in passing how close are Swift's insights regarding the problematic nature of textuality to certain discoveries formalized in modern linguistics and extended in contemporary structuralist literary theory. By raising questions about the interpretative process and the peculiar epistemological complexities that afflict any reader's relations to a text, Swift's work anticipates the concerns, in particular, of Continental theorists like Barthes and Kristeva. (The parallel refutes the notion, likewise, that it is only modernist texts of the twentieth century that expose the semantic variability of the literary sign.) To cite just one point of convergence: Swift's allusion to the 'Anagrammatick Method' of reading employed by Peter when he looks for the word 'SHOULDER' (*PW*, 1: 48–50) in the will suggests that it is possible to read the orthographic marks that make up the text in a non-sequential order. This graphemic way of reading, Swift knows, is not conventional; yet he also suspects, rightly, that there is nothing in the physical nature of the text *per se* to forbid it. Interpretation of a given text is based on arbitrary reading conventions – ways of arranging, conceptually, its visible marks – and these conventions may conceivably be broached by the innovative reader. Obviously deformed texts, those filled with typographical transpositions, shock us because they remind us precisely that the way we look at the text is arbitrary, and that we might, indeed, modify the process ourselves. Because its actual structure is always indeterminate, Swift seems to say, any text allows convention-free reading; any text might even be said to encourage such madness. The linguist Saussure, whose theory of signs underlies recent structuralist work on literary hermeneutics, made the same discovery in the early part of this century while studying anagrams in *De Rerum Natura*.[8] After positing the presence of anagrams of 'Aphrodite' in the opening lines of the Lucretian text, Saussure was forced to admit that he could not prove the anagrams had been intentionally placed there; the appeal to authority, the voice of the author, was impossible. Moreover, the linguist was left with the realization that just as the truth of his anagrammatic interpretation was indeterminate, so all textual exegesis might be equally indeterminate – shaped only by the desire of the interpreter. Writing, because of its hermeneutic instability, easily accommodates its own exploitation. Saussure was so disturbed by the hallucinatory text, the unconstrained text, that he never published his anagrammatic research. Swift attempts to protect himself from the same discovery by enclosing it within the context of satire, of derision. Yet the fantasy of the mercurial text persists.

The critique of writing implied at the deepest level of *A Tale of a Tub* enforces finally in that work a powerful and revealing troping of the text. The manuscript, with its spots and holes and blurs, becomes a demonic and ghastly material presence. It is a monster. Characteristically, Swift figures its monstrosity by way of an imagery of fertility, of breeding. The Text, for the satirist, is womb-like (might we say female?): it gives birth, in a process at once out of control and horrifying, to replicas of itself. The Modern's own text, with its offshoots and appendages, is our primary model of the oppressive text; it invites commentary, it seeks to generate new texts. It afflicts us with its apparatus – what Swift catalogues in another context as the innumerable, useless '*Prefaces, Epistles, Advertisements, Introductions, Prolegomena's, Apparatus's, To-the-Reader's*' (*PW*, 1: 81). But Swift shows everywhere, in explicit comment, the sickening ease with which any text may reproduce itself. Later we learn, for instance, that texts inspire in their readers '*Scholiastick* Midwifry' and that the readers deliver them 'of Meanings' which, the Modern notes by the by, 'the Authors themselves, perhaps, never conceived'. Written words, he continues, are like seed which 'will multiply far beyond either the Hopes or Imagination of the Sower' (*PW*, 1: 118). Human agency is thus excluded from the grotesque process of textual multiplication: the 'immense Bales of Paper' (*PW*, 1: 21) – which threaten ultimately to subsume Nature itself – begin to write themselves. The monstrous text Swift imagines is an utterly mindless entity, a mere physical automaton, endlessly replicating. The world is 'nauseated' says the satirist in his Apology, 'by endless Repetitions on every Subject' (*PW*, 1: 1).

The grotesque text troped in *A Tale of a Tub* may be redefined in Derridean fashion, summarily, as the guilty text. The text of *A Tale* itself exemplifies guilt: its truth status is compromised by its corrupt physical nature. Yet it is also guilty in the way that it compels us to construct our own guilty texts. It breeds us, its exegetes, as we read. One might argue at this point, however, that Swift may not necessarily mean to identify every version of Text as potentially corrupt. Do not texts remain somewhere which are in some fashion privileged? Can we not separate good texts from bad texts? Certain commonplace assumptions about satire – particularly, that it implicitly recommends to us an unstated, yet realizable mode of behavior – may mislead here. Viewed superficially, the satire on the evil text in *A Tale of a Tub* might indeed seem to predicate by indirection a good text. If the Modern's manuscript is a negative model of written discourse, it must be possible to extrapolate from it a positive model. Yet in the radical world of writing described in Swiftian satire, the innocent text ultimately does not, indeed cannot exist. So extreme is the anxiety surrounding the Text in the *Tale*, one is forced to conclude that the positive model invoked, paradoxically, is no writing at all. This would seem to be the import of Swift's obsessive returning, throughout the work, to the problem of Biblical interpretation. (The traumatic seventeenth-century discovery of the historical corruption of Biblical texts underlies Swift's work just as profoundly as it does a work like Dryden's *Religio Laici*.) No text is privileged in regard to truth; no text is scriptural. Swift would not have been surprised, one suspects, by the notorious 'Wicked Bible' printed in Leipzig in 1631, which – due to a typographical error – gave the Seventh Commandment as 'Thou shalt commit adultery'.[9] Such gross and shocking aberrations merely confirm once again, on the basic level of typography, the theme of the satire. Given its inescapably material status, every writing is a site for corruption, no matter what authority – natural, divine, or archetypal – we may wishfully invest in it. Because they constitute an earthly text, the Scriptures themselves pathetically and paradoxically make up part of the fallen world of writing. Is Swift's fiction of the text, then, a kind of blasphemy? Swift does not state so baldly that God's text itself is corrupt, but at the same time, the possibility is implicit everywhere in his satire. The text is to be feared, whatever its ostensible provenance.

I have dwelled at considerable length on *A Tale of a Tub* because it isolates powerfully the essential features of Swift's fantasy of the text. Its energy, I have tried to suggest, derives from what one might call an underlying phobic response to writing. That vision or hallucination of a fearful gap between speech and writing compels the satire, gives it an anxious, obsessive force. Turning to Swift's other satiric works, however – even those which might not seem at first glance to share an equal fascination with textuality – one finds, I think, evidence of the same theme, variants and elaborations of the same textual fiction.

How many of Swift's satiric pieces play off notions of the grotesquely physical text, the intrusive text, of that arrogant and monstrous text intimated by the *Tale*. *The Battle of the Books*, of course, depends upon the phantasmagoric troping of the text already seen in the earlier work. Swift's satire here, like Pope's in the *Dunciad*, is marked by a compelling sense of the materiality of the written artifact and of the pressure it exerts upon Nature. At the most reductive level, the satire hints, no book is free from these oppressive or guilty qualities. In 'The Bookseller to the Reader', for instance, Swift makes his characteristic schism between author and book, voice and text, and thus solidifies writing – as an *entity* – before our eyes: 'I must warn the Reader, to beware of applying to Persons what is here meant, only of Books in the most literal Sense. So, when *Virgil* is mentioned, we are not to understand the Person of a famous Poet call'd by that Name, but only certain Sheets of Paper, bound up in Leather, containing in Print, the Works of the said Poet, and so of the rest' (*PW*, 1: 139). Yet the Ancient text, once solidified in such a way as an artifact, is ready to breed a secondary text – the Modern text. The Ancient text itself supplies the necessary condition for the Battle: a world of violence is instituted with this primary materialization of the Word. Swift's overt purpose in his piece is to vindicate the works of the Ancients over those of the Moderns, but one may wonder how much this conscious project is complicated, even undermined, by the implicit fantasy of the text. In some sense, Virgil is responsible for Dryden: the primary text initiates the chain of replication. And both primary and secondary texts share the same compromised physical status in the end; both are equally present as sites for corruption. (This equivalence is suggested symbolically, perhaps, in the mystery surrounding the outcome of the Battle.) The Goddess Criticism, part

247

of Swift's fantastical mock-heroic machinery, must be seen, finally, as his inclusive model of the hallucinatory Text. She, an archetypal transmogrification of every text existing in the world, '. . . gathered up her Person into an *Octavo* Compass; Her Body grew white and arid, and split in pieces with Driness; the thick turned into Pastboard, and the thin into Paper, upon which, her Parents and Children artfully strowed a Black Juice, or Decoction of Gall and Soot, in Form of Letters; her Head, and Voice, and Spleen, kept their primitive Form, and that which before, was a Cover of Skin, did still continue so. In which Guise, she march'd on . . .' (*PW*, 1: 155). Even Virgil's writings, one must conclude, do not escape the universal reduction of text into paper and 'Black Juice'. In such a vision we contemplate the central image of Swiftian grammaphobia.

In works such as the *Bickerstaff Papers, A Modest Proposal*, the *Complete Collection of Genteel and Ingenious Conversation*, the satire of the text is given an analogous sociological expansion. Swift's vision of the physical corruptness of writing – likewise the condition of its hermeneutic guilt – modulates here into a vision of its social guilt. All the discoveries made about the text in *A Tale of a Tub* still apply, but the satirist's emphasis shifts to a consideration of its social effect. The intuitive leap made in these and similar works is easier to observe than to explicate, but one might brief it as follows. Just as writing is itself a dehumanized mode – physical yet mindless, separated at its moment of origin from the truth of the voice – so it works to enforce a larger pattern of dehumanization in society. Writing clogs the world: it mediates negatively between persons, imposes itself as object, as visible obstruction. The text Swift fears is not only materially corrupt, it is hypnotic, fetishistic. As we focus upon the impressive, yet false façade of truth it presents, we lose contact with human reality. While we read we cannot listen – the naturalized relations of the voice, of human connection, are breached. With the distraction of the text, moral chaos is made possible.

Thus, for instance, in the instructive pieces on conversation Swift shows us the text literally intruding upon the world of human relationships. Simon Wagstaff invites his readers to consult his book while entering into conversational situations; his text subsumes the voice directly, mediates the spontaneous oral interchange between persons. He recommends 'the following Treatise, to be carried about as a Pocket Companion, by all Gentlemen and Ladies, when they are going to visit, or dine, or drink Tea; or, where they happen to pass the Evening without Cards; . . . desiring they would read their several Parts in their Chairs and Coaches, to prepare themselves for every kind of Conversation that can possibly happen' (*PW*, 4: 105). But if the intrusive text is ludicrous and comical here – and likewise in

the Bickerstaff pieces – in *A Modest Proposal* it is less so. Swift's
greatest short satire models for us that dehumanized script which
encourages the dehumanization of the reader: its rhetoric is indeed
hypnotic. Swift's irony devastates precisely because it exploits our
conventional, even superstitious assumption about texts – that they
are authoritative signs. We imbue the text with authority because it
is a text: we fall immediately under its sinister mimetic spell. Yet, the
satirist warns, absorption in this dehumanized surface enforces our
own dehumanization. To accept the premise of *A Modest Proposal*
– the utility of cannibalism – is to divest ourselves, of course, of a
natural moral sense of things. The satire shocks and liberates because
it points up how easily the text distracts us, co-opts us, separates
us from human connections. Yet this effect, as I have tried to show,
depends upon those assumptions about the written artifact seen
elsewhere in Swift. Writing avails itself as an instrument of social
evil because its own nature is essentially evil to begin with. Thus
the Swiftian critique of Text – primarily framed upon philosophical
issues in the early satiric pieces – quickly takes on here a crucial and
profound pragmatic force. The epistemological exposé of writing
resolves into moral exposé as well.

The themes Swift associates with writing – its fallen aspect, its
hermeneutic indeterminacy, and physical and moral degeneracy –
all reappear, finally, within the fictional context of *Gulliver's Travels*.
One might even be tempted to claim that satire of the written word
is an underlying principle of organization in that work. No matter
how other perspectives shift from book to book (most notoriously
our view of the narrator himself), a critique of the written word
seems to remain a constant. It works as a symbolic reference point
against which other elements of the satire may be aligned.

Texts exert a different pressure on each of the societies Gulliver
visits, inviting the hypothesis that this pressure is a Swiftian index to
the nature of each place. In Book 1, for instance, when Swift satirizes
the pettiness and pomposity of the Lilliputians he shows us that their
society is pre-eminently text oriented. The Lilliputians are compulsive
writers: they organize their lives around significant texts – published
'Edicts' (such as the one which initiates the Big- and Little-Endian
controversy), the 'Proclamations' and 'Orders of State' of their
prince, treaties (which do not hold), and 'Articles' of behavior like
those presented to Gulliver on his arrival. The Lilliputians tend to
formalize all their experience – silly as it is – as text. Yet this process
of textualizing is, as elsewhere in Swift, a suspect one. Witness the
distortion that creeps in as the Lilliputians set out to describe, in
scientific discourse, the contents of Gulliver's pocket. Likewise,
Gulliver's plight in Book 1 worsens precisely as texts intervene. The

palace fire – the event that initiates Gulliver's fall from favor – starts because of the 'Carelessness of a Maid of Honour, who fell asleep while she was reading a Romance' (*PW*, 11: 55). The Englishman's fate is sealed by the 'Articles of Impeachment' ordered against him by corrupt Lilliputians. The text, the satirist suggests, disrupts both the physical and social order of things; it is the primary cause of Lilliputian error and the primary tool of their injustice. The Lilliputians are condemned by the intimacy they share with it.

The Brobdingnagians, in proportion to their greater magnanimity as a people, denigrate and restrict the influence of the text. Gulliver notes that they have printing, 'But their Libraries are not very large'. Similarly, 'they avoid nothing more than multiplying unnecessary Words', and institute – arbitrarily but as best they can – against the process of interpretation itself: 'No Law of that Country must exceed in Words the Number of Letters in their Alphabet; which consists only of two and twenty. But indeed, few of them extend even to that Length. They are expressed in the most plain and simple Terms, wherein those people are not Mercurial enough to discover above one Interpretation. And, to write a Comment upon any Law, is a capital Crime' (*PW*, 11: 136–37). Gulliver comments that as a result Brobdingnagian learning is very 'confined', but the joke is on him. We predicate Swift's satire on his narrator on a pre-existing satire of the text. Thus, when Gulliver's own pettiness is exposed in this book by the Brobdingnagian king, we find the king analogizing England and its inhabitants to a corrupted text: 'I observe among you some Lines of an Institution, which in its Original might have been tolerable; but these half erased, and the rest wholly blurred and blotted by Corruption' (*PW*, 11: 132). The immediate focus of Swiftian satire shifts, of course, between Books 1 and 2, but its underlying assumption remains the same: the 'little odious Vermin', whether Lilliputian or Gulliver himself, has pen in hand.

Again, in Book 3, the satire of the text underlies Swift's satire on the Academy of Projectors. Laputan writing is perhaps the most nightmarish in *Gulliver's Travels*. Among the various ridiculous inventions that Gulliver finds in Laputa, for example, is that implement 'for improving speculative Knowledge by practical and mechanical Operations' (*PW*, 11: 182) – the text-breeding machine. With this device 'the most ignorant Person . . . may write Books in Philosophy, Poetry, Politicks, Law, Mathematicks and Theology, without the least Assistance from Genius or Study' (*PW*, 11: 182–84). The invention generates arbitrary assortments of letters by mechanical rearrangement of bits of wood and paper, on which are written 'all the Words of their Language in their several Moods, Tenses, and Declensions, but without any Order' (*PW*, 11: 184). As in *A Tale of a Tub,* writing is figured as a non-intellectual process; it is automatic, mindless replication. 'The Pupils at his Command took each of them hold of an Iron Handle, whereof there were Forty fixed round the Edges of the Frame; and giving them a sudden Turn, the whole Disposition of the Words was entirely changed. He then commanded Six and Thirty of the Lads to read the several Lines softly as they appeared upon the Frame; and where they found three or four Words together that might make Part of a Sentence, they dictated to the four remaining Boys who were Scribes'. Already the texts created thus are many; 'several Volumes' exist of 'broken Sentences', and the inventor of the machine intends more. With the prospect of five hundred such devices in operation, the number of 'rich Materials' still to be produced is incalculable (*PW,* 11: 184). Swift here discovers, then, an appropriate physical model for meaningless, inhuman and infinitely reproducing writing. The text factory is the central locus for grammaphobia in Book 3, but one might note, too, the satirist's exposure again of the 'Anagrammatick Method' (*PW,* 11: 192) in the section on political projectors, and his dismissal of 'Commentary' (*PW,* 11: 197–98) and interpretation in the episode in which Gulliver calls back the Ancient writers from the dead. At all points in the Laputan scenes, even more so perhaps than in Lilliput, the reader encounters a world replete with writing, a world controlled by a technology of the text. In both societies, however, writing itself becomes the mark of an intrinsic intellectual and moral degeneracy.

And here we come back, of course, to the horses. As Gulliver has already told us, 'their Knowledge is all traditional' (*PW,* 11: 273). Unlike any other society in *Gulliver's Travels,* the Houyhnhnms have not taken the catastrophic fall into a world of letters. Their complete ignorance of books suggests an improvement even upon the relatively text-free Brobdingnagians.

The situation, however, is not without paradox. The pattern of grammaphobia in *Gulliver's Travels* conditions the appalling problem that confronts the reader in Book 4. Houyhnhnm society is indeed pure to the extent that it is free from textuality. It is a naturalized society. The Houyhnhnms are bound by a community of the voice; they are bound by a language of pure sound, the neigh. This is the sense in which Houyhnhnm society qualifies (as some critics would like to see it[10]) as a Swiftian version of the Platonic utopia. The secondary mode of signification is absent, along with its attendant corruption. No demonic texts here, getting in the way of the spoken discourse.

Swift queers the pleasant resolution of the grammaphobic situation – the escape to a Platonic Utopia – however, by one simple and ludicrous transformation. The residents in Utopia are not human. By virtue of the essential difference between Houyhnhnm and human, the naturalized society is not, and can never be, our own. Gulliver tries to imitate the gait and speech of the horses, but, most significantly, he is never able to stop writing. Already fallen, he cannot emulate the Houyhnhnms in this crucial respect. (Indeed, Swift hints everywhere of Gulliver's inescapable resemblance to the Yahoos – who, with their enthusiastic and decorative shit-smearing seem, anthropologically speaking, on the way to the discovery of a script.)[11] Thus the satirist's examination of textuality takes its most damning turn. The Houyhnhnms model that situation suggested at all points in Swift from *A Tale of a Tub* on as a good – no writing at all. But they are not we. For humankind, Swift suggests, the text is *inevitable*. It is already here. The evil text and human presence constitute an inseparable unit in the world.

This extension of the grammaphobic argument places the reader in an impossible position. Swift leaves us in Book 4 with confirmation of a logical tautology – because we are human, we are open to dehumanization. Indeed, we already possess the necessary tool. He infects us everywhere with the malignancy of the text, and then says there is nothing we can do about it. Attempted return to the innocence of the Houyhnhnm is doomed to be an incomplete gesture. Meanwhile, the Yahoos drop excrement upon us from the trees. They inscribe our very bodies with a text.

Gulliver's Travels ends, then, with a final implosion of the Swiftian fear of the text. It suspends with paradox, with the extra-logical confirmation of grammaphobia. Such anxiety is wholly appropriate to, and might be said to define, Swiftian satire; but on some level it also defines the author himself. In his own career, Swift lived out the identical paradox of the text figured in Book 4.[12] How, after all, can the writer not write? I have deliberately confined myself in this chapter to the mythology of writing revealed in Swift's satiric pieces, yet there is, biographically speaking, another side to the issue. The serious works on language reform – the *Proposal for Correcting, Improving, and Ascertaining the English Tongue* and others – suggest that at moments Swift did believe, or attempt to believe, in a resurrected text. The *Proposal*, for instance, argues that it is possible to reestablish a connection between writing and speech. Swift wishes here that the gap might be bridged nostalgically – that we might go back to the purity of speech when we write. The story, perhaps apocryphal, of Swift reading his works aloud to his servant in order to ensure their comprehensibility works mythically – Swift here resurrects his own text by referring it to the human contact of the voice. Obviously, Swift calls attention at times to a hope that his

own plain style – free of 'Corruptions' – will be a model for a new
purified English prose (*PW*, 4: 6).

Still, one may wonder, rightly I think, what the force of such
wishing is compared with the intensity and reductiveness of the
vision presented in Swiftian satire. My own inclination, as should
be apparent, has been to associate Swift's myth of the text – and
the world of satire itself – with unconscious forces, with underlying
traumatized modes of perception. Placed next to *A Tale of a Tub* and
the rest, the pieces on language reform look suspiciously like a kind
of reaction-formation; they respond, it would seem, to a prior, deeply
anxious experience of textuality. It appears questionable whether
Swift himself ever succeeded in domesticating – in the *Proposal*
or elsewhere – that hallucinatory material for which his satires
everywhere provide the evidence.

And finally, it is the hallucinatory perception in Swift that remains
with us, not his programmatic effort to resurrect the text. If Book 4 of
Gulliver's Travels shows that we, unlike Houyhnhnms, cannot be free
of writing, Swift's satires show what a problematic supplement this
is. Swift powerfully isolates for us the radical indeterminacy of the
very texts we allow to influence our lives. The critique is not always
logical; it is impelled by an energy that may remind us of the anxiety
dream. But its force is not undermined thereby. Particularizing
Swift's vision of the text in Derridean fashion, as a myth – as I have
tried to here – suggests how one might begin to analyze it, but even
this leaves its emotional impact unexplained. Swift's greatest works
make up together a Tale of a Text; and it is with this compelling text
itself that we, readers and writers all, ultimately fall.

Notes

1. Claude Lévi-Strauss, *Tristes Tropiques*, trans. John and Doreen Weightman (New York, 1974), pp. 335–6.

2. Jacques Derrida, *Of Grammatology*, trans. Gayatri Chakravorty Spivak (Baltimore, MD, 1976), p. 168.

3. In *Swift and Anglican Rationalism* (Chicago, 1961), for instance, Phillip Harth confines his description of the satire on interpretation in *A Tale of a Tub* to a theological issue – the perverse effect of 'zeal' (located in the interpreter) on Scriptural exegesis. Yet the 'zealous' exegete, Swift's own marred text suggests, is one who, among other things, exploits material flaws associated with textuality – *lacunae*, ellipses, visible obscurities and cruxes. It is difficult to escape the conclusion that for Swift the difficulty of interpretation derives as much from problematic elements in the object of interpretation itself, the written artifact, as from the deficiencies of interpreters. See in particular Phillip Harth, Chapter 2, 'Reason and Revelation'. Irvin Ehrenpreis's classic essay on Book 4 of *Gulliver's Travels*, 'The Meaning of Gulliver's Last

Voyage', *Review of English Literature*, 3 (1962), 18–38, while eloquently particularizing the dilemma Swift's reader faces (to emulate the virtuous Houyhnhnm is to deny one's own humanity) likewise leaves out the 'grammatological' dimension of this dilemma: it is impossible for Gulliver (and us) to imitate the purity of Houyhnhnm existence because it is impossible to unlearn the use of ciphers, and thus avoid, as they do, implication in a world of textuality.

4. SAMUEL H. MONK, 'The Pride of Lemuel Gulliver', *Sewanee Review*, 63 (1955), 48–71.

5. See, for example, CLAUDIA R. STILLMAN, 'The Theme of Language in the Prose Works of Jonthan Swift', Dissertation North Carolina, 1973; and JOHN R. CLARK's *Form and Frenzy in Swift's Tale of a Tub* (Ithaca, NY, 1970).

6. WILLIAM KOON, 'Swift on Language: An Approach to *A Tale of a Tub*', *Style*, 10 (1976), 28–40.

7. CLARK, *Form and Frenzy*, p. 178.

8. For a discussion of Saussure's work on anagrams, see JONATHAN CULLER, *Saussure* (Glasgow, 1976), pp. 106 ff. The 'Anagrammatick Method' of interpretation recurs in Book 3 of *Gulliver's Travels*, of course, when the Tribnian experts decipher '*Our Brother Tom has just got the Piles*' as '*Resist; a Plot is brought Home, The Tour*' (PW, 11: 191–92). ARTHUR E. CASE, in *Four Essays on Gulliver's Travels* (Gloucester, MA, 1958), pp. 91–2, identifies in this passage a satire on the Jacobites, who were alleged to use anagrammatic codes, and Bolingbroke, who went by the alias 'M. La Tour' while in France. Swift's political satire here does not exclude his satire on the malleable text; rather, as so often happens in his works, two targets are struck in a single satiric economy.

9. SIGMUND FREUD calls attention to the 'Wicked Bible' in *The Psychopathology of Everyday Life* in the section 'Mistakes in Reading and Writing'.

10. See, in particular, JOHN F. REICHERT, 'Plato, Swift, and the Houyhnhnms', *Philological Quarterly*, 47 (1968), 179–92.

11. FRANK BRADY makes a point of the Yahoos' approach to human behavior – and hence their transformation into satiric targets – in a note in his introduction to the collection *Twentieth-Century Interpretations of Gulliver's Travels* (Englewood Cliffs, NJ, 1968), p. 10: 'Strictly speaking, the Yahoos are satirized only to the extent they are assimilated to human beings. As Bergson pointed out, animal behavior is never comic.'

12. W. B. CARNOCHAN has suggested in *Lemuel Gulliver's Mirror for Man* (Berkeley, CA, 1968), pp. 92 ff., that Swift's satire modulates finally into 'self-satire', an illustration of the satirist's own 'self-critical ways'. A general paradox arises in that the greater 'satire on man' always points back to Swift himself. Carnochan writes of Gulliver: 'he embodies all Swift's doubts about his motives and his literary vocation'. Under this notion of vocation we may place our own topic – the paradoxical implication of the writer himself in the corrupt world of writing.

14 Deconstructing *Gulliver's Travels*: Modern Readers and the Problematic of Genre*

LOUISE K. BARNETT

I

Reading a literary text is a learned behavior applied to a recognized situation, an act that takes place within a particular cultural and individual context. As readers, we are no more monolithic entities than we are in other facets of our lives: we choose the role of reader for a variety of purposes and bring different frames of reference, degrees of attention, expectations, and evaluative standards to the texts that we encounter. At one end of the theoretical spectrum of reading behavior a casual frame of reference causes attention, expectation, and evaluation to be minimal; the experience is used to stave off insomnia, to relax on the beach, to pass time in the dentist's waiting room – the text is primarily a means to that end. At the other end of the spectrum, the critical reading of literature is a more demanding act: 'One must bring to it an implicit understanding of the operations of literary discourse which tells one what to look for.'[1] It further implies serious attention, well-formulated expectations, and a fairly complex set of evaluative determinations. Here the text as an aesthetic construct, an end-in-itself, is of major importance, and the experience of reading is a means to its comprehension and appreciation. To understand more fully an historical text that we wish to read critically, we often approach it by recreating ourselves as earlier readers, a process that means more than acquaintance with the kind of knowledge that provides basic intelligibility – vocabulary, literary conventions, and cultural context. Such re-creation seeks the specific goal of a meaning identified as the author's or the text's 'intentions', or an approximation of the original (not present) readers' experience of the work.

---

* Reprinted from FREDERIK N. SMITH (ed.), *The Genres of Gulliver's Travels* (Newark, DE: University of Delaware; London: Associated Universities Press, 1990), pp. 230–45.

If we forego this re-creation and read an early eighteenth-century
text from the vantage point of today, we will undoubtedly discover
that many of the responses of earlier readers are irrelevant to our
own. Reading *Gulliver's Travels*, for instance, we will not, as did one
reader in Swift's day, rush to a map in search of Lilliput; nor will
we react like the bishop Swift wrote to Pope about, who thought
the book to be 'full of improbable Lies, and for his part, he hardly
believed a word of it'.[2] We could not recover that kind of innocence
as readers even if it seemed desirable: much that struck earlier
readers as 'new and strange', according to Dr Johnson, will be neither
to us, any more than our own first glimpse of the Pacific Ocean will
be of the same order as Balboa's. Such earlier loci of critical attention
as the machinations of Augustan political factions and the satire on
scientific investigation will sustain our interest today little more than
will the geographical location of Lilliput. Similarly, we are less
inclined to attribute perceived peculiarities of the book to Swift's
'madness' or 'depravity'. The temper of our own age prefers other
theoretical bases. Yet in less obvious ways than is suggested by these
examples, modern critics stubbornly continue to recreate themselves
as earlier readers.

Genre is central to these interpretations since readers invariably
bring generic assumptions to texts.[3] Reading *Gulliver's Travels* as a
reader of the 1980s, however, requires that we abandon the long
history of categorizations that fit the book only partially or fit
according to the interests of another time; it also requires that we
relinquish the security of genre itself, its authority to confer and
name coherence. Jacques Derrida reminds us that the concept of
genre already contains its own antithesis, or the seeds of its own
deconstruction – the present and implicit assumption that genre
may be transgressed or transformed.[4] This is an established dialectic,
one that readily adapts to the tension between synchronic and
diachronic forces in a given genre. What is difficult to tolerate when
we approach a work through genre is plurality, a degree of latitude
that obliterates generic boundaries entirely rather than merely
emphasizing their existence by over-stepping them.

The present-day uncertainty about the genre of *Gulliver's Travels*
has its origin in the book's initial reception. In the words of Dr
Johnson, critics were 'lost in wonder; no rules of judgment were
applied to a book written in open defiance of truth and regularity'.[5]
This suspension of critical activity was only momentary, but it
reflects a problematic that has persisted. As Sir Walter Scott writes:
'Perhaps no work ever exhibited such general attractions to all
classes. It offered personal and political satire to the readers in high
life, low and coarse incident to the vulgar, marvels to the romantic,

wit to the young and lively lessons of morality and policy to the grave, and maxims of deep and bitter misanthropy to neglected age, and disappointed ambition.'[6] *Quot lectores tot genera*: every subgenre of fictive travel narrative has seemingly been applied to *Gulliver's Travels* by now, determining which aspects of the text are foregrounded and which ignored. It has been variously regarded as philosophical tale *à la Candide*, real-seeming adventure *à la Cyrano de Bergerac*, picaresque narrative *à la Lazarillo de Tormes*. It has also been included in such categories of contemporary interest and definition as children's literature and science fiction and even had the genre of Menippean satire revived more or less to accommodate it.[7] 'The history of genre theory', as Gérard Genette observes, 'is everywhere marked by these fascinating schemas that inform and deform the often irregular reality of the literary field and claim to discover a natural "system" when they construct a factitious symmetry with a great supply of blind windows.'[8] The history of reading *Gulliver's Travels* is a series of such genre decisions that attempt to cope with the text's polyvalence and indeterminacy by means of this principle – the implicit assumption that genre confers coherence and stability, that is, the text read monologically.[9]

Efforts to deal with the genre of *Gulliver's Travels* continue to appear, and I would like to place mine in the company of two recent readings in order to examine the problematic of genre from several different perspectives.

II

When a system is superimposed upon a text, there can never be a perfect match between the paradigm, which is abstract, and the text, which is real: 'The kinds are only *ideas* of form, established by custom and consensus . . . adumbrations of an idea of order, shapes for content, as well as the shadows cast by solid, individual works of literature.'[10] The delicate balance so well described by Rosalie Colie is especially subject to strain when a text is polyvalent: the better the fit achieved in one direction by imposing a monologic reading, the more troublesome aporias open in other directions.

As a case in point I should like to apply the idea that Gulliver is a picaro to the evidence that Frederick J. Keener presents for his interpretation of *Gulliver's Travels* as a philosophical tale, a reading that consists almost entirely of a critique of Gulliver as a philosophical protagonist intentionally manqué – inconsistent, self-centered, insensitive, superficial.[11] For Keener, Gulliver is a character who is always at fault: first, in not being as complicated a character as he should be, and then, in not being particularly likeable. If he were the ideal philosophical protagonist, Gulliver would remain at home devoting himself to family, country, and introspection. Instead, he shows 'a violent inclination not to stay put and examine what he is and the way he thinks . . .' (p. 126). Next best, Keener's remarks suggest, would be a reflective narration of his adventures, one that gave others 'credit for having a history of thought and feelings' (p. 103).

If, however, we approach *Gulliver's Travels* with another frame of reference, the picaresque, all of the above-mentioned qualities that make Gulliver a parodic philosophical hero contribute to defining him as a prototypical picaro.[12] The essential picaresque situation, as Ulrich Wickes defines it, 'is that of a protagonist, worse than we, caught up in a chaotic world, worse than ours, in which he is on an eternal journey of encounters that allow him to be alternately both victim of that world and its exploiter'. For Richard Bjornson, picaros are 'invariably confronted by a choice between social conformity (which is necessary for survival) and adherence to what they have learned to consider true or virtuous'. The ending of a picaresque narrative, according to Claudio Guillén, confirms the picaro's apartness by a 'final withdrawal from society'.[13]

Examples from picaresque criticism that suit *Gulliver's Travels* could be multiplied, and it is worth noting that those given above, taken as descriptions of what occurs in the text divorced from generic attribution, could readily be assimilated by Keener's reading. While Keener sees Gulliver's failure to examine his values as a fault in a philosophical character, the picaro is *properly* reactive and unanalytical, the passive experiencer of marvelous adventures. So, for example, when Gulliver says that the Lilliputian admiral Skyresh Bolgolam 'was pleased, without any Provocation, to be my mortal Enemy' (*PW*, 11: 42), Keener comments: 'It never occurs to Gulliver that the arrival of a superman would cause resentment in Lilliput or anywhere, especially resentment by those whose station and power the newcomer threatens' (p. 103). *Should* it occur to Gulliver? Not if he is a picaro, whose fictive role is simply to survive and record his experience with only the rudimentary evaluation appropriate to his naïveté. According to the requirements of one genre, Gulliver is a typical character, successfully realized; according to another, he is atypical, a parodic figure although no less successfully realized.

This does not mean that Gulliver can be both straightforward picaro and philosophical protagonist at the same time. In the larger terms of genre, 'that sense of the whole by means of which an interpreter can correctly understand any part of its determinacy', there can be no reconciliation.[14] Although Gulliver$_1$ and Gulliver$_2$ share some traits (naïveté and humorlessness, for example), they belong to systems, whether conceived of as prescriptive or descriptive, that resist intermingling. 'As soon as genre announces itself,' Derrida writes, 'one must respect a norm, one must not cross a line of demarcation, one must not risk impurity, anomaly, or monstrosity.'[15] This is the *law* of genre. To read *Gulliver's Travels* as picaresque narrative is to emphasize a series of adventures centered upon satiric interaction. To read it as philosophical tale is to emphasize a series of ideas that are embodied in these adventures and interactions.

Arriving here, we are apt to think of some version of a familiar refrain of *Gulliver* criticism: 'The most immediate problem is that of genre.' For Robert C. Elliott the issue is posed in a question and answer: 'Is *Gulliver* a novel? Probably not, although it is not easy to say (except by arbitrary stipulation) why it is not.'[16] This formula could serve for any number of genres and reader responses, including the two outlined above. It is easy enough to marshall evidence for a particular classification, yet the question and answer, with their attendant difficulties, remain. The text escapes encompassing rubrics and the kind of centering that such rubrics impose.

It is this sense of the text as elusive and indeterminate that governs the second reading I wish to examine, Robert W. Uphaus's reader-response approach.[17] Uphaus posits and rejects a reader whose commitment to 'objective' criticism obscures a basic affective response. Since his purpose is to explore this affective experience, he constantly eschews as its inimical antinomy any sort of classification: 'An obsession with generic distinctions and rules often blunts the powerful affective appeal of literature' (p. 7). Not surprisingly, Uphaus concludes: 'The variety of effects Swift's text produces . . . seems to me strong evidence that *Gulliver's Travels* is not written with any one effect in mind, other than to violate or vex the reader's expectations of coherent, rationally formulable meaning. Rather than reading *Gulliver's Travels* as if it were proceeding toward some one coherent and unifying goal, it may be truer to the reader's experience of the text to speak of a succession of moments that yield varying effects' (pp. 17–18). Thus, Uphaus feels that the very premise of genre, that of nameable form, is inappropriate. Instead of the homogeneous reading experience producing the stable, authoritative text necessary to a generic interpretation, Uphaus finds a diversity that resists the imposition of pattern and must simply be taken as a series of discrete moments.[18]

Neither this dynamic nor the concept of genre is necessarily at odds with the affective response Uphaus values, although 'an obsession with generic distinctions and rules' may very well be. But just as the danger of genre criticism is a monologic coercion of the text, so the danger of the genreless stance is a rejection of aesthetic form. In approaching one of the standard problems of *Gulliver's Travels*, the sequence of voyages, Uphaus writes: 'Book 3, we know, was written last, and yet Swift does not place it in this position. The fact that Swift does not place it last may tell us something about his attitude to formal coherence – namely, that there never was a developing pattern or an evolving plan which would explain the sequence of books 1–4, other than the general intention to vex the reader' (p. 19). Surely another possibility (which Uphaus does not consider) is that the departure from the order of composition expresses an artistic intention, one that has been confirmed over the centuries by the affective responses of readers who find the last voyage climactic.

Uphaus therefore acknowledges the problematic of genre, only to dismiss it as irrelevant to the reader-critic's real job or else beyond resolution, a determination that may leave as much to be desired as traditional readings that impose inadequate labels upon the text. Is *Gulliver* a genreless text? Probably not, although it is not easy to say (except by arbitrary stipulation) why it is not. Such literary institutions as genre transcend individual relation, and even the generic blind window that Genette refers to 'can on occasion let in a true light, and reveal the importance of a misapprehended term'.[19] We do not have to agree with E. D. Hirsch, Jr. that 'all understanding of verbal meaning is necessarily genre-bound' in order to feel the legitimacy of generic expectation, a shaping convention shared by writer and reader.[20]

III

There is a general consensus among interpreters of *Gulliver's Travels* that the book is puzzling in various ways but nevertheless a classic work of art. A satisfactory generic approach would speak to both of these attributes, neither ignoring the heterogeneity of the text as would a monologic reading nor embracing indeterminacy to the exclusion of formal meaning entirely. Such a reading can be attempted through deconstruction, for like all of Swift's greatest works, *Gulliver's Travels* proffers forthrightly the contradictory energies, marginal peculiarities, and generic aporias that characterize a text's own deconstructive potential.[21] Considering *Gulliver's Travels* as deconstructors *and* as modern readers leads to a dislodging of a number of earlier concerns: among them the literal voyage in whatever form – picaresque, fantastic, philosophical – and, in this post-Darwinian age, the idea that Yahoos are the shocking creatures they once seemed to be.

Now let us go back to Elliott's question, 'Is *Gulliver* a novel?' and this time answer it yes, in terms of our own experience as readers of postmodernist fiction, whose authors routinely abuse their characters more flagrantly than Swift does Gulliver. For critical readers of today there can be little doubt that any extended prose fiction with as much character and incident as *Gulliver's Travels* will be experienced as a novel; indeed by our standards it may even seem more conventional than experimental. That it is not a novel according to the conventions of Swift's time does not enter into our experience of the text when we are not pretending to be readers of that time or readers of Swift's mind.

Gulliver, the same ordinary Englishman that most interpretations agree upon, will continue to serve as the protagonist of a deconstructive reading, but it may seem that an abandonment of the 'earlier reader' posture has already ruled out a great deal for him to do. Deprived of those literal adventures, which I have already suggested cannot sustain the interest of contemporary readers, he must be translated to a metaphoric level where the text engages human experience in spiritual terms as valid now as when *Gulliver's Travels* was written. Generically, then, the work is a spiritual *Bildungsroman* in which humankind – Gulliver and the reader – must confront a reality that admits of only a pessimistic construction, a condition desperate enough to drive even a more intellectually resourceful person than Gulliver to the madness he ultimately exemplifies. The text may dissociate itself from Gulliver's final extremism, but it does not repudiate the dilemma that brings it about: namely, that the Houyhnhnms are an ideal that can never be realized by man, that the humanlike Yahoos are disgusting brutes, and that man, abusing his mere tincture of reason, is much worse than even a Yahoo.[22] For modern readers these propositions do not seem as extraordinary as they once did, but what remains puzzling is the ending – Gulliver's unbearable awareness of this condition without the possibility of salvation. Deconstruction can illuminate the way the text arrives at this denouement through an examination of Gulliver's apprenticeship to life/death, a typical Derridean opposition.

Given this almost cosmic sense of human inadequacy, religion would appear to be the great absence that haunts the text and calls to mind *Gulliver's* antitype, *The Pilgrim's Progress*. At the end of Gulliver's education there is awareness but no salvation. Far from being open-ended, *Gulliver's Travels* allows no way out of this impasse, whose unpalatable corollaries emerge in Swift's correspondence with close friends. To Pope he wrote that we are only *rationis capax*, analogous not only to Yahoos but to the kite that flew off with one of Swift's chickens and was later, to Swift's satisfaction, shot dead.[23] There is no reason to question the seriousness of his counsel to Sheridan: 'Expect no more from Man than such an Animal is capable of, and you will every day find my Description of Yahoes more resembling.' Or, his assertion to Pope: 'I hate and detest that animal called man.'[24] Like *Gulliver's Travels* itself, all of these pronouncements posit a flawed human nature ineluctably mired in its animal character. Swift's satire is hardly 'corrective', for, as John Traugott remarks, 'one cannot correct one's being'.[25]

We may further recall from Swift's letters that even the most excellent women were only 'bestes en juppes' (animals in skirts) compared to Vanessa, whom he could scarcely believe to be of the same species.[26] Although here the satire is turned to compliment, such animal imagery often recurs in Swift's writings as a standard satiric strategy given effective variation in the idea of the Yahoos. Additionally, as Roland M. Frye has pointed out, 'the very words used by Swift in describing the Yahoo are throughout strikingly like – and frequently identical with – those used by the theologians in treating "the flesh" and the sins to which it incites man'.[27] Flesh/ animal/man/sin: this conjunction, common in Swift's other writings, assumes its most effective form in the Yahoo, a creature both animal and man, whose flesh, because it is human rather than animal, is sinful.[28] Unreferred to and unacknowledged, sin is everywhere implicit in the exotic but still human or human-resembling worlds of *Gulliver's Travels*, either in the culpability of the beings Gulliver encounters or in his explanations of practices in his native land.

What is overtly inscribed in the text is death, the wages of sin. In a letter to Archbishop William King Swift once divided the world into 'two Sects, those that hope the best, and those that fear the worst. . . . [t]he former . . . is the wiser, the nobler, and most pious Principle; and although I endeavour to avoid being of the other, yet upon this Article I have sometimes strange Weaknesses.'[29] Death exposed the aporia of fearing the worst in its most intense form, the situation where religion and temperament clashed most poignantly and irreconcilably in Swift. In the first two books Gulliver moves from one adventure to another under the ever-present threat of sudden death, first as a helpless giant in Lilliput, subject to human treachery, then as a truly powerless homunculus, vulnerable to careless destruction. In the narrative paradigm Gulliver must always meet some test of survival in a strange and dangerous place, but in the first two books the pattern is simply repeated without any growth of insight on Gulliver's part. Meaning is deferred in keeping with Derrida's idea of *différance*.[30] The hierarchical opposition life/death seems to be affirmed by the voyages to Lilliput and Brobdingnag, for in spite of threats to his life Gulliver survives. Death emerges, startlingly for many readers, out of the fragmented and decentered episodes of the third voyage. By means of the Struldbruggs, the power relation of life/death is changed in keeping with Derrida's assertion that 'to deconstruct the opposition, first of all, is to overturn the hierarchy at a given moment'.[31]

The play of *différance* in the Struldbrugg episode can be located in an inconspicuous remark produced by Gulliver's innocence before the revelation that redefines the word *Struldbrugg* more accurately for him. When Gulliver's audience of knowledgeable Luggnuggians draws him out concerning what his own scheme of living should be were he a Struldbrugg, Gulliver prefaces his dizzying chronicle of lifetimes lived profitably and pleasurably with a clause given little syntactical weight: 'As soon as I could discover my own Happiness by understanding the Difference between Life and Death, I would first revolve . . .' (*PW*, 11: 209). The happiness that Gulliver thought to discover was to have been an affirmation of life through the absence of death, but in the first movement of *différance* the terms of the binary opposition life/death reveal that death is the desirable presence in the Struldbruggian, and by extension, the human economy. Learning the real condition of the Struldbruggs seems to bring about Gulliver's enlightenment as nothing else on his voyages has done. He writes: 'The Reader will easily believe, that from what I had heard and seen, my keen Appetite for Perpetuity of Life was much abated. I grew heartily ashamed of the pleasing Visions I had formed; and thought no Tyrant could invent a Death into which I would not run with Pleasure from such a Life' (*PW*, 11: 214). After his initial raptures over the imagined benefits of immortality, Gulliver now envisions death as a desideratum to be pursued actively ('run with Pleasure') in preference to a lifeless life.

At the moment this is only an intellectually apprehended horror. Gulliver himself is so far removed from a personal sense of menace that his next chapter eclipses the horror of the Struldbruggs with a matter-of-fact beginning: 'I thought this Account of the *Struldbruggs* might be some Entertainment to the Reader, because it seems to be a little out of the common Way . . .' (*PW*, 11: 215). 'Account', 'Entertainment': this uncharged language reflects Gulliver's desire to distance the trauma of his earlier reaction while at the same time it becomes charged with the anomaly of its inadequacy to the experience. Gulliver does not in fact come to understand the difference between life and death; the Struldbrugg exemplum is immediately turned into a text directed outward to the reader.

The play of *différance* continues in the fourth voyage where life/death is further deconstructed to elaborate upon the convertibility inherent on the periphery of the Struldbrugg episode. The text demythologizes death by overdetermining the web of relationship uniting the living and the dying so that there is no violent rupture between the two states. In the Houyhnhnm language 'to die' is 'to retire to his first Mother', the reinstatement of the primordial tie, with all of its accruing positive values. Similarly, the dying Houyhnhnm feels as if he were 'returning Home from a visit to one of his Neighbours'. The dying 'take a solemn Leave of their Friends, as if they were going to some remote Part of the Country, where they designed to pass the rest of their Lives' (*PW*, 11: 275). This controlling metaphor of the visit or interaction of the dying with relatives and friends is supported by an anecdote Gulliver tells:

> I remember, my Master having once made an Appointment with a Friend and his Family to come to his House upon some Affair of Importance; on the Day fixed, the Mistress and her two Children came very late. . . . Her Excuse for not coming sooner, was that her Husband dying late in the Morning, she was a good while consulting her Servants about a convenient Place where his Body should be laid; and I observed she behaved herself at our House, as chearfully as the rest . . .
>
> (*PW*, 11: 274–75)

Death, like life, is natural, appropriate, acceptable, even positive. The distinction between them is ultimately obliterated in terms of affect because Houyhnhnms have no different feelings about these two states. For humans, in contrast, only the horrific effects of life – the age and decay embodied in the Struldbruggs, for instance – can bring about an acceptance of death.[32]

Ties of affection are the chief vehicle of meaning, both metaphorically and literally, in Gulliver's account of the Houyhnhnms' attitude toward death since the death of loved ones would naturally be the most difficult test of acceptance. In his correspondence Swift remarks repeatedly that he cannot bear the death of friends.[33] When Lady Ashburnham died, he wrote to Stella, 'I hate Life, when I think it exposed to such Accidents and to see so many thousand wretches burthening the Earth while such as her dye, makes me think God did never intend Life for a Blessing'.[34] When he believed Stella herself to be dying, he confessed to Thomas Sheridan, 'All my Preparations will not suffice to make me bear it like a Philosopher, nor altogether like a Christian.'[35] Throughout Swift's writings 'nor altogether like' is the mark of *différance*, the undermining bent of temperament that deconstructs so many Swiftian positions.

What Gulliver finally comes to feel is that the life he is condemned to lead is a kind of death like that of the Struldbruggs, now that he knows what a life of perfect reason can be.[36] When his Houyhnhnm Master informs Gulliver that he must leave the country, his reaction is that 'death would have been too great an Happiness' (*PW*, 11: 280). Having experienced both enlightenment and bliss, Gulliver cannot willingly go back to a grossly imperfect existence in spite of the pressure exerted by the conventional human/equine hierarchy that the fourth voyage has so perversely deconstructed. But rather than dying, he goes mad: in England he clings to 'Houyhnhnm' in a context that recognizes only 'horse' and insists upon 'Yahoo' for his own species – substitutions that create conflicting demands in readers between their own (human) perspective and the involvement of first-person narration. Gulliver in the stable communing with his horses perfectly illustrates Diderot's definition of madness: 'To deviate from reason knowingly, in the grip of a violent passion, is to be weak, but to deviate from it confidently and with the firm conviction that one is following it, is to be what we call *mad*.'[37] The madman is engulfed by his own fiction, whereas Swift's fiction allows us to imagine ourselves through Gulliver in fantastic contexts without demanding that we actually experience or valorize these phenomena.

By continuing at home the disjunction between Gulliver and society that obtained in the lands he visited, the epilogue unexpectedly extends the by-now-familiar structure of the *Travels*. Yet the repetition entails *différance*. Gulliver is no longer the reassuring, earnest Englishman confronting a fantastic world; the world is now the familiar place and Gulliver fantastic. Once again, a hierarchical opposition has been subverted, not through a process of mechanical reversal but through a probing of its internal differences. 'Familiar' and 'foreign' lose their sharp polarity since the world Gulliver returns to – one of wives, children, and decent individuals like Pedro de Mendez – is also the world of the terrible list of book 4: 'Gipers, Censurers, Backbiters, Pickpockets, Highwaymen, House-breakers', etc. (*PW*, 11: 276–77) – a catalogue whose ruthless energy is authoritatively Swiftian. That powerful voice speaks the validity of Gulliver's realization that by a standard of *perfect* rationality man is without hope, and the weight of that message overshadows its vehicle, that is, Gulliver's madness. As Shoshana Felman writes, 'Every novel contains simultaneously the temptation of madness and the negation of this temptation, in a reflexive narrative system, where the "novelesque" at once discloses and denounces its own madness.'[38] Conventionally, the madness of a Gulliver reassures us of our own sanity, but a satirist is particularly apt to subvert these categories, to deconstruct sanity to reveal madness. Gulliver discloses the madness of accepting the unsavory world of the epilogue, yet his own behavior offers no viable alternative.

Gulliver's cloying speech on the virtues of British imperialism includes a mention of 'devout and able Pastors to propagate *Christianity*' (*PW*, 11: 296), but there is no evidence that religion is any solace to *him* for the loss of the secular paradise of Houyhnhnmland. We might remark that the world Gulliver returns to has need of Christian redemption, but within the boundaries of the text religion remains a felt absence, one that moves the work closer to a twentieth-century sensibility. Without establishing Christianity as explicit or implicit presence, *Gulliver's Travels* nevertheless partially deconstructs the binary opposition of life/death according to its tenets. Life is the sinful negative term, is in fact death, while death becomes positive.[39] Yet the essential part of the Christian transvaluation is obviously missing. Death loses its sting in the Christian belief-system because it opens the way to everlasting spiritual life; in *Gulliver's Travels* it contains no such promise. Fear of death is not mitigated by Christianity but by the perfect rationality of the Houyhnhnms, which strips it of pain, grief, and regret.

Since man cannot achieve this perspective on death, what Gulliver has learned among the Houyhnhnms is useless: the generic pattern of the *Bildungsroman*, the acquisition of wisdom, is thus deconstructed to produce, in Derridean terms, a critique of the *Bildungsroman* pattern undertaken within the work itself. As readers, we recognize this combination of fictive structure and its violation as postmodernist, a rubric that will readily accommodate *Gulliver's Travels*. Such an approach not only conforms to our present-day critical sensibility; it fits the shape of the text more accurately. The reader can hold opposing impulses without subjecting them either to the constraints of a monologic reading or to the amorphousness of an approach that denies generic validity completely. The (provisional) last word that describes this condition of simultaneous generic fulfilment and transgression belongs to Derrida: 'There is no genreless text ... yet such participation never amounts to belonging'.[40]

Notes

1. JONATHAN CULLER, *Structuralist Poetics: Structuralism, Linguistics, and the Study of Literature* (Ithaca, NY, 1975), p. 114.

2. John Arbuthnot to Swift, 5 November 1726, *Corr.* 3: 180; Swift to Alexander Pope, 27 November 1726, 3: 189.

3. RALPH W. RADER, 'The Concept of Genre and Eighteenth-Century Studies', in *New Approaches to Eighteenth-Century Literature, Selected Papers from the English*

Institute, ed. PHILLIP HARTH (New York, 1974), p. 90, states that 'readers are always aware to some degree of making generic assumptions', a process he traces back to the nature of mental activity itself.

4. JACQUES DERRIDA, 'The Law of Genre', trans. AVITAL RONELL, *Critical Inquiry*, 7 (1980), 57. Rpt. in *On Narrative*, ed. W. J. T. MITCHELL (Chicago, 1981), pp. 51–77.

5. *The Lives of the Most Eminent English Poets*, 2 vols (Charlestown, 1810), 2: 193.

6. WALTER SCOTT, *Life of Swift*, in *The Miscellaneous Prose Works of Sir Walter Scott*, 6 vols (Boston, MA, 1829), 2: 219.

7. NORTHROP FRYE, *The Anatomy of Criticism* (Princeton, NJ, 1957), pp. 308–12.

8. GÉRARD GENETTE, 'Genres, "types," modes', *Poétique*, 32 (1977), 408, my translation: 'L'histoire de la théorie des genres est toute marguée de ces schémas fascinants qui informent et déforment la réalité souvent hétéroclite du champ littéraire et prétendent découvrir un "système" naturel là où ils construisent une symétrie factice à grand renfort de fausses fenêtres.'

9. See MURRAY COHEN's pleas for the application of modern critical theory to eighteenth-century texts, 'Eighteenth-Century English Literature and Modern Critical Methodologies', *The Eighteenth Century*, 20 (1979), 5–23. He writes, 'In response to problems and complexities, we create more categories so that every assertion signifies a clear meaning; and at the evident inadequacy of the traditionally few genres, we invent new ones, for formalist critics abhor a text without a classification' (p. 5).

10. ROSALIE L. COLIE, *The Resources of Kind: Genre Theory in the Renaissance*, ed. BARBARA K. LEWALSKI (Berkeley, CA, 1973), pp. 127–8.

11. FREDERICK J. KEENER, *The Chain of Becoming: The Philosophical Tale, the Novel, and a Neglected Realism of the Enlightenment: Swift, Montesquieu, Voltaire, Johnson, and Austen* (New York, 1983), pp. 89–126. Further references will be given parenthetically in the text. It is not my purpose to take issue with Keener's reading; arguments against such an interpretation have long been in print. See EDWARD W. ROSENHEIM, JR, *Swift and the Satirist's Art* (Chicago, 1963), p. 157: 'Gulliver . . . is above all a *character* whose experiences – rather than postures, beliefs, or literary habits – constitute the major fiction of the work.' See also C. J. RAWSON, *Gulliver and the Gentle Reader: Studies in Swift and our Time* (Boston, MA, 1973), p. 27: 'The emphasis is so preponderantly on what can be shown through him (including what he says and thinks) than on his person in its own right, that we are never allowed to accustom ourselves to him as a real personality despite all the rudimentary local colour about his early career, family life and professional doings.'

12. The standard discussion of *Gulliver's Travels* as picaresque fiction can be found in RONALD PAULSON, *The Fictions of Satire* (Baltimore, MD, 1967), pp. 162–9.

13. ULRICH WICKES, 'The Nature of Picaresque Narrative: A Modal Approach', *PMLA*, 89 (1974), 242; RICHARD BJORNSON, *The Picaresque Hero in European Fiction* (Madison, WI, 1977), p. 11; CLAUDIO GUILLÉN, *Literature as System: Essays toward the Theory of Literary History* (Princeton, NJ, 1971), p. 88.

14. E. D. HIRSCH, Jr, *Validity in Interpretation* (New Haven, CT, 1967), p. 86.

15. DERRIDA, 'The Law of Genre', p. 57.

16. ROBERT C. ELLIOTT, *The Power of Satire: Magic, Ritual, Art* (Princeton, NJ, 1960), p. 184.

17. ROBERT W. UPHAUS, *The Impossible Observer: Reason and the Reader in Eighteenth-Century Prose* (Lexington, KY, 1979), pp. 9–27. Further references will be given parenthetically in my text.

18. What Uphaus finds to be true of reading Swift, the fragmentary nature of the process, WOLFGANG ISER finds to be true of reading in general. In *The Implied Reader: Patterns of Communication in Prose Fiction from Bunyan to Beckett* (Baltimore, MD, 1974), p. 288, he writes: 'We look forward, we look back, we decide, we change our decisions, we form expectations, we are shocked by their nonfulfillment, we question, we muse, we accept, we reject. . . .' While some texts will clearly require more of these operations than others, reading, Iser suggests, is always a spatial and temporal activity that demands constant readjustment – not an instantaneous mastery of an indivisible entity. It is always, in other words, a 'succession of moments that yield varying effects'.

19. GENETTE, 'Genres, "types", modes', p. 408, my translation: 'La fausse fenêtre peut en l'occurrence donner une vraie lumière, et révéler l'importance d'un terme méconnu. . . .'

20. HIRSCH, *Validity in Interpretation*, p. 76.

21. Most of what I draw on as theory comes from the writings of Jacques Derrida, from whom I take the basic assumption of deconstruction: 'The reading must always aim at a certain relationship, unperceived by the writer, between what he commands and what he does not command of the patterns of the language that he uses. This relationship is not a certain quantitative distribution of shadow and light, of weakness or of force, but a signifying structure that critical reading should *produce*.' JACQUES DERRIDA, *Of Grammatology*, trans. GAYATRI CHAKRAVORTY SPIVAK (Baltimore, MD, 1976), p. 158. For the idea of the text's self-deconstructive activity, see J. HILLIS MILLER, 'Deconstructing the Deconstructors', *Diacritics*, 5 (1975): 'The text performs on itself the act of deconstruction without any help from the critic' (p. 31).

22. A number of critics have already argued for these premises. See, among others, GEORGE SHERBURN, 'Errors Concerning the Houyhnhnms', *Modern Philology*, 56 (1958), 92–7; W. B. CARNOCHAN, 'The Complexity of Swift: Gulliver's Fourth Voyage', *Studies in Philology*, 60 (1963), 23–5; and ROSENHEIM, *Swift and the Satirist's Art*, p. 163.

23. Swift to Pope, 29 September 1725, *Corr.* 3: 103, and 26 November 1725, 3: 118.

24. Swift to Sheridan, 11 September 1725, *Corr.* 3: 94; Swift to Pope, 29 September 1725, 3: 103.

25. JOHN TRAUGOTT, '*A Tale of a Tub*', *Focus: Swift*, ed. C. J. RAWSON (London, 1971), p. 114.

26. Swift to Esther Vanhomrigh, 12 May 1719, *Corr.* 2: 326.

27. ROLAND M. FRYE, 'Swift's Yahoos and the Christian Symbols for Sin', *Journal of the History of Ideas*, 15 (1954), 215–16.

28. Swift often satirizes people in animal terms in his poetry. See, for example, 'The Salamander', 'The Legion Club', 'Wood, an Insect', 'The Character of Sir Robert Walpole', 'Dick, A Maggot', and 'Epistle to a Lady'.

29. Letter of 6 January 1709, *Corr.* 1: 117. Swift's admitted preoccupation with death is notable. He wrote to Bolingbroke, 31 October 1729, *Corr.* 3: 354: 'I was 47 years old when I began to think of death; and the reflections upon it now begin when I wake in the Morning, and end when I am going to Sleep.' SCOTT's anecdote, *Life of Swift*, may well be unreliable, but its existence suggests a propensity associated with Swift: 'For many years he used to bid

his friends adieu with these melancholy words: "God bless you, I hope we shall never meet again"' (p. 224).

30. JACQUES DERRIDA, 'Différance', *Margins of Philosophy*, trans. ALAN BASS (Chicago, 1982), p. 7. See also the definitions of *différance* in *Positions*, trans. ALAN BASS (Chicago, 1981), pp. 8–10, especially the following: 'The movement of *différance* . . . is the common root of all the oppositional concepts that mark our language, such as . . . sensible/intelligent, intuition/signification, nature/culture, etc.' (p. 9).

31. DERRIDA, *Positions*, p. 41.

32. As Swift wrote to John Gay, 10 November 1730, *Corr.* 3: 417–18: 'God hath taken care . . . to prevent any progress towards real happyness here, which would make life more desirable & death too dreadfull.' To Bolingbroke and Pope, 5 April 1729, 3: 329, he wrote: 'I never wake without finding life a more insignificant thing than it was the day before: which is one great advantage I get by living in this country, where there is nothing I shall be sorry to lose. . . .'

33. See, for example, Swift's letter to Rev. John Worrall, 15 July 1726, *Corr.*: 'I am of Opinion that there is not a greater Folly than to contract too great and intimate a Friendship, which must always leave the Survivor miserable' (3: 142). See also 3: 145, 234, 236, 311, and 435 for similar sentiments.

34. *Journal to Stella*, ed. HAROLD WILLIAMS, 2 vols (Oxford, 1948), 2: 595; letter of 27 July 1726.

35. Swift, *Corr.* 3: 147.

36. While human beings have passions that make it impossible for them to achieve perfect rationality, as CHARLES PEAKE discusses in 'Swift and the Passions', *Modern Language Review*, 55 (1960), 169–80, Swift tends to present the passions as a necessary evil, in need of subordination to reason and discipline, rather than as a desirable component of human nature. For example, Swift advises a young lady that what a husband wants is 'a reasonable Companion, and a true Friend'. Her match is one of 'Prudence and common Good-liking, without any Mixture of that ridiculous Passion which hath no Being, but in Play-Books and Romances' ('A Letter to a Young Lady, on her Marriage', *PW*, 9: 86, 89). In his sermon 'On the Trinity', in *PW*, 9: 166, Swift asserts: '*Reason* itself is true and just but the *Reason* of every particular man is weak and wavering, perpetually swayed and turned by his Interests, his Passions, and his Vices.' Writing to Reverend James Stopford, 20 July 1726, about Stella's approaching death, Swift claimed that 'violent friendship is much more lasting, and as much engaging, as violent love' (*Corr.* 3: 145). His poetry to Stella offers other evidence of an attempt to substitute a more rational form of attachment for a passionate one.

37. *Encyclopédie, ou dictionnaire raisonné des sciences, des arts et des métiers* (Lausanne and Berne, 1781), 14: 341–2, my translation.

38. SHOSHANA FELMAN, *Writing and Madness* (Ithaca, NY, 1986), p. 135.

39. JOHN WESLEY, *The Doctrine of Original Sin according to Scripture, Reason, & Experience* (1757), *The Works of John Wesley*, 14 vols (Grand Rapids, MI, n.d.), 9: 259, quotes another divine's reply to the assertion that death is a benefit: 'On the contrary, it is the king of terrors to them [men], the burden of their lives, and bane of their pleasures. To talk, therefore, of death's being a benefit . . . is to talk against the common sense and experience of the whole world.'

40. Derrida, 'The Law of Genre', p. 65.

15 Allegory of Blindness and Insight: Will and Will-ing in *A Tale of a Tub**

G. Douglas Atkins

Whatever Reader desires to have a thorow Comprehension of an Author's Thoughts, cannot take a better Method, than by putting himself into the Circumstances and Postures of Life, that the Writer was in, upon every important Passage as it flow'd from his Pen; For this will introduce a Parity and strict Correspondence of Idea's between the Reader and the Author.

(PW, 1: 26–27)

... they will furnish Plenty of noble Matter for such, whose converting Imaginations dispose them to reduce all Things into *Types*; who can make *Shadows*, no thanks to the Sun; and then mold them into Substances, no thanks to Philosophy; whose peculiar Talent lies in fixing Tropes and Allegories to the *Letter*, and refining what is Literal into Figure and Mystery.

(PW, 1: 121)

... the *true illuminated* (that is to say, the *Darkest* of all) have met with such numberless Commentators, whose *Scholiastick* Midwifry hath deliver'd them of Meanings, that the Authors themselves, perhaps, never conceived, and yet may very justly be allowed the Lawful Parents of them: The Words of such Writers being like Seed, which, however scattered at random, when they light upon a fruitful Ground, will multiply far beyond either the Hopes or Imagination of the Sower.

(PW, 1: 118)

... Whatever Difference may be found in [commentators'] several Conjectures, they will be all, without the least Distortion, manifestly deduceable from the Text.

(PW, 1: 118)

---

* Reprinted from *Reading Deconstruction/Deconstructive Reading* (Lexington, KY: University of Kentucky Press, 1983), pp. 105–17.

Allegory of Blindness and Insight: Will and Will-ing in A Tale of a Tub

These passages from throughout *A Tale of a Tub* illustrate a number of its characteristic features, including its complexity and sophistication and its central thematic concern with reading and interpretation.[1] They also suggest some of the ways in which this strange and discomfiting *écriture* ('book' hardly seems appropriate, though 'text' will perhaps do, for it is often impossible to decide who is writing here) resembles and anticipates several recent critical and theoretical positions. The first example I provided bears a striking affinity with the so-called criticism of consciousness of such 'Geneva critics' as Georges Poulet, which has also been called 'the tradition of identity'.[2] Indicative of the (mis)readings of their father's will in the Allegory of the Coats and the Three Brothers, my second example reminds one of both Harold Bloom's willful misprisions and the recent fascination, in structuralism and deconstruction alike, with rhetoric understood as the study of tropes. If a similar parallel suggests itself in my last example, the third one anticipates both Geoffrey Hartman's general call to return to allegoresis and exegetical modes of interpretation and his specific advice on 'how to reap a page' in *Saving the Text*.[3]

Even apart from these striking echoes, which tempt one to a metaleptical reversal of influence, thinking of the *Tale* as repeating what has recently been written, this puzzling and amazing text sounds themes now popular and often valorized. For example, when the *Tale* admits that 'how to analyze the *Tub*, was a Matter of difficulty', we are likely to read this as the self-reflexivity now often prized in 'primary' and 'secondary' texts alike as well as a direct reference to the Hack's attempt to deflect the 'Grandees of *Church* and *State*' from 'pick[ing] Holes in the weak sides of Religion and Government' (*PW*, 1: 24). Moreover, the *Tale*'s frequent contradictions of itself, or at least the Hack's contradictions of himself, will immediately suggest to the reader familiar with deconstruction 'the critical difference' that is inevitable in all texts, made of language and so bifurcated and dialogical.[4]

But if those given to 'hermeneutical highjinks'[5] are quick to value *A Tale of a Tub* as prescient and insightful, indeed as deconstructing the idea of the book as a totality, a more traditional critic will just as quickly object that these supposed insights are being satirized. Rather than Swift's own points, they are evidently part of the madness characteristic of the Hack, who intimates that his own imagination is 'exceedingly disposed to run away with his *Reason* . . . upon which Account, my Friends will never trust me alone, without a solemn Promise, to vent my Speculations in this, or the like manner, for the universal Benefit of Human kind' (*PW*, 1: 114). A deconstructionist like Paul de Man might retort, however, that Swift is of course blind to such insights as my opening quotations provide, his text precisely being most insightful in those areas in which the 'mad' Hack is most vigorously satirized.[6] Yet, because it ridicules such textual difference as deconstructive readings produce, *A Tale of a Tub* may complicate de Man's well-known account of the play of textual blindness and insight. Still, by means of close attention to both its declaration and its description of author–reader relations, I shall argue that the *Tale* is precisely an allegory of blindness and insight, telling the story of their crossing.

Though the *Tale* is frequently read as a satire on Modern writing, the Hack being, for example, unable to adhere to 'what is to the Purpose' (*PW*, 1: 90), ultimately admitting, in fact, that he is 'now trying an Experiment very frequent among Modern Authors; which is, to *write upon Nothing*; When the Subject is utterly exhausted, to let the Pen still move on' (*PW*, 1: 133), it is principally concerned with abuses in reading. Linking the satire on the 'numerous and gross Corruptions in Religion and Learning' (*PW*, 1: 1) and so the Allegory of the Coats and the Three Brothers with the digressions, in fact, is interpretation, the main issue treated in both 'parts' of the *Tale*. The *Tale* thus participates in that important but little-studied Augustan interest in reading and interpretation that Dryden makes the center of attention in *Religio Laici*, which can be read as a layman's approach to reading. The *Tale* may even be 'about' the effort to read and a satire on the perhaps inevitable desire to reduce and make comprehensible.[7]

In certain respects, the positions of Swift and his cousin Dryden are similar, even though the latter is lashed in the *Tale*: both worry about the disturbing and disrupting power of figurative language, and both desire as a supposed bulwark against figurality an unthreatening literalness. As we have seen, Swift opposes 'the converting Imagination', which 'fix[es] Tropes and Allegories to the *Letter*, and refin[es] what is Literal into Figure and Mystery'. Those who thus give rein to the fancy are among those who 'have spiritualized and refined [their writings] from the Dross and Grossness of *Sense* and *Human Reason*' (*PW*, 1: 37). Because then – so the argument goes – Swift values reason, 'the Senses, and common Understanding', which leads one to pass his 'life in the common Forms' (*PW*, 1: 108), he prefers the plain, literal sense, as in the father's directions concerning his will (about which more shortly) to the allegorical and 'mythological' readings produced by 'the converting Imagination'. Incidentally, this valorization of literal readings interestingly coincides with Swift's frequent literalizing of metaphors; characteristic of his writing generally, literalizing occurs in the *Tale* when, for example, Peter is said to value most 'a certain Set of *Bulls*' (*PW*, 1: 68, the reference is of course to Papal bulls), when the Hack describes his

'dissect[ion of] the Carcass of *Humane Nature*' (*PW*, 1: 77), and when
the Hack expatiates on his '*Histori-theo-physi-logical* Account of Zeal,
shewing how it first proceeded from a *Notion* into a *Word*, and from
thence in a hot Summer, ripned into a *tangible Substance*' (*PW*, 1: 86).
Common to Swift's preference of the literal and his frequent
literalizing of metaphors is de-mystification.

But unlike Dryden, who believes that Scripture at least is so
plain and clear as to require no interpretation, Swift nowhere in
the *Tale* suggests any hope that plain and clear language will yield
unequivocal meaning. Rather, he focuses on the ways by which even
supposedly plain meanings are abused, converted, and willfully
misread. Well aware of how texts can be, and frequently are, mauled
and used for one's own purposes, Swift urges final recourse to
authorial intention. He makes the point forcefully in the 'Apology'
(for example, *PW*, 1: 6, 10) and repeats it, generalized, as in the note
on *PW*, 1: 118: 'Nothing is more frequent than for Commentators to
force Interpretation, which the Author never meant.'

The point emerges most clearly in the Allegory of the Coats and
the Three Brothers (writing an allegory, Swift obviously distinguishes
between allegorized reading and the reading of allegory[8]). 'Once upon
a Time', the story begins, there was a certain man with three sons,
who on his deathbed bequeathed to them three coats, along with his
will containing 'full Instructions in every particular concerning the
Wearing and Management of your Coats' and commanding that they
'live together in one House like Brethren and Friends' (*PW*, 1: 44).
Though the brothers soon fall out with each other in a dispute over
the will, it is plain and clear. According to the Hack, 'it consisted', in
fact, 'wholly in certain plain, easy Directions about the management
and wearing of their Coats, with Legacies and Penalties, in case of
Obedience or Neglect' (*PW*, 1: 121). Influenced by Peter, the well-read
brother familiar with Aristotle's *de Interpretatione* (*PW*, 1: 51), the
brothers find it possible, because desirable, to read into and out
of the will whatever they decide upon. For one example of Peter's
willful misreading, consider the following passage, which describes
the brothers' allegorizing in order to authorize their desire for the
expressly forbidden silver fringe:

> Item, *I charge and command my said three Sons, to wear no sort of*
> Silver Fringe upon or about their said Coats, etc., with a Penalty in
> case of Disobedience, too long here to insert. However, after some
> Pause the Brother so often mentioned for his Erudition, who was
> well Skill'd in Criticisms, had found in a certain Author, which he
> said should be nameless, that the same Word which in the Will is
> called *Fringe*, does also signifie a *Broom-stick*; and doubtless ought

to have the same Interpretation in this Paragraph. This, another of the Brothers disliked, because of that Epithet, *Silver*, which could not, he humbly conceived, in Propriety of Speech be reasonably applied to a *Broom-stick*; but it was replied upon him, that this Epithet was understood in a *Mythological*, and *Allegorical* Sense. However, he objected again, why their Father should forbid them to wear a *Broom-stick* on their Coats, a Caution that seemed unnatural and impertinent; upon which he was taken up short, as one that spoke irreverently of a *Mystery*, which doubtless was very useful and significant, but ought not to be over-curiously pryed into, or nicely reasoned upon. And in short, their Father's Authority being now considerably sunk, this Expedient was allowed to serve as a lawful Dispensation, for wearing their full Proportion of *Silver Fringe*.

(PW, 1: 53–54)

Later, Peter's interpretive authority having been questioned and the other two brothers having gained complete access to the will, Jack, not so different from his learned brother after all, 'began to entertain a Fancy, that the Matter was *deeper* and *darker*, and therefore must needs have a great deal more of Mystery at the Bottom'. He sets out, therefore, to 'prove this very Skin of Parchment to be Meat, Drink, and Cloth, to be the Philosopher's Stone, and the Universal Medicine'. Having decided beforehand that the will is not what it plainly is, Jack finds it easy, as Peter did, to make that will into whatever he wills: 'He had a Way of working it into any Shape he pleased; so that it served him for a Night-cap when he went to Bed, and for an Umbrella in rainy Weather' (*PW*, 1: 121–22).

That the text at the center of this critical maelstrom is a will is another literalization of a metaphor and, I suggest, an example of Swift's insight (Dryden, as we saw, uses the same metaphor in *Religio Laici*); Swift's *Tale* literalizes the universal situation I described in 'The Story of Error' as 'a dialogue of questions that is a mutual coercion'. Indeed, in the Allegory of the Coats and the Three Brothers, between the father, on the one hand, and the three sons, on the other, and then later among the sons themselves occurs a battle of wills, and that representation becomes an allegory of the will and the will-ing involved in the reading of any text. Every textual field is, in fact, constituted as a battle of wills, claims of authority, and the force of desire. In Swift's Allegory, the text left to the sons is a will – in more than one sense – imposed by the authority of the father in an effort to coerce them to do what he desires; even after he leaves them, he *wills* to exercise authority over them. But the sons, like all other readers, have wills and desires of their own, and so the battle is joined. Another way to put this perhaps is to say that we witness in the Allegory a typical opposition between master and slave, authority being at stake. The father wills to be master, but the sons resist the slavery his authority would impose, restricting them to following the letter of his law, that is, to a simple execution of his 'plain and easy Directions'. As happens whenever such oppositions exist, first one and then the other side gains the upper hand, the slave eventually becoming master and repeating the tyranny. It is not long, therefore, before 'their father's Authority' is 'considerably sunk'. Of course, the *desire* of mastery, no matter in whom, represents precisely the *lack* of mastery, for 'it is not possible to desire that with which one coincides'.[9] To modify a well-known Derridean point, 'Without the possibility of difference, the desire of [mastery] as such would not find its breathing-space.' According to Derrida, that means that 'this desire carries in itself the destiny of its non-satisfaction. Difference produces what it forbids, makes possible the very thing that it makes impossible.'[10] If this begins to sound like the Hack's subversion of logic, that may be just the point.

Swift, of course, sides with the father, or the author, in this agonistic struggle for author-ity. Indeed, in terms of interpretive strategy, the reader, says Swift, should always seek the intentions – or authority – of the author in his quest to understand a text. Reading becomes, then, exactly that effort to achieve coincidence or harmony that is expressed, though in perhaps exaggerated fashion, in one of the quotations from the *Tale* I used as an epigraph: 'Whatever Reader desires to have a thorow Comprehension of an Author's Thoughts, cannot take a better Method, than by putting himself into the Circumstances and Postures of Life, that the Writer was in, upon every important Passage as it flow'd from his Pen; For this will introduce a Parity and strict Correspondence of Idea's between the Reader and the Author' (*PW*, 1: 26–27). Presented satirically, this passage nevertheless emerges as at least close to Swift's own desire that the reader seek and then adhere to authorial intention. But, it should be noted, the point concerning parity is misleading, for the reader is here being advised to submit himself or herself totally to the author, denying himself totally, emptying himself, as he occupies another's space, body, and mind.

A Tale of a Tub thus focuses on the relation of author and reader, insisting on the former's authority and pointing to the dangers when the reader 'usurps' that authority. So far, however, we have read only a part of the story the *Tale* tells, having attended to the text's declarations. We must try to be as rigorous as the text and so should attend as well to its figurative language. We have already seen, of course, that the *Tale* is built, despite Swift's preference for the literal, on word play: there is the play not only on will but also on author and author-ity.[11]

The *Tale* provides a chain of passages perhaps continuing this play of words (and sounds) but certainly relating writing to riding. Begin with this passage, which opens Section XI: 'in *Writing* it is as in *Travelling*: if a Man is in haste to be at home . . . if his Horse be tired with long Riding, and ill Ways, or be naturally Jade, I advise him clearly to make the straitest and the commonest Road, be it ever so dirty; But, then surely, we must own such a man to be a scurvy Companion at best' (*PW*, 1: 120). Other passages also employ the rider/horse analogy. First, a passage comparing the relationship of mind to its thoughts with that of rider to horse: 'And, whereas the mind of Man, when he gives the Spur and Bridle to his Thoughts, doth never stop, but naturally sallies out into both extreams of High and Low, of Good and Evil; His first Flight of Fancy, commonly transports Him to Idea's of what is most Perfect, finished, and exalted' (*PW*, 1: 99). Second, a passage presenting the relationship of reason to imagination as analogous to that of rider to horse: 'I my self . . . am a Person, whose Imaginations are hard-mouth'd, and exceedingly disposed to run away with his *Reason*, which I have observed from long Experience to be a very light Rider, and easily shook off' (*PW*, 1: 114). Third, the well-known passage that continues at least the imagery of mounting but inverts the (proper) relationship described in the previous quotation: 'But when a Man's Fancy gets *astride* on his Reason, when Imagination is at Cuffs with the Senses, and common Understanding, as well as common Sense, is Kickt out of Doors, the first Proselyte he makes is Himself' (*PW*, 1: 108). By means of the figures employed, Swift rigorously argues that the mind and the reason must not allow its thoughts and the imagination to have free rein, run away, and so usurp proper authority. Properly ordered, reason mounts and rides the imagination; madness occurs when that order is inverted and imagination takes the place of reason.

Now consider the following passage, in which the same figurative language we have been reading is used to present directly the relationship of reader to writer: 'Among these last [handles for catching hold of mankind], *Curiosity* is one, and of all others, affords the firmest Grasp: *Curiosity*, that Spur in the side, that Bridle in the Mouth, that Ring in the Nose, of a lazy, an impatient, and a grunting Reader. By this *Handle* it is, that an Author should seize upon his Readers; which as soon as he has once compast, all Resistance and struggling are in vain; and they become his Prisoners as close as he pleases, till Weariness or Dullness force him to let go his Gripe' (*PW*, 1: 130). There is no question here of the reader-horse running away with the writer-rider or of taking his place. The passage says, however, that the writer should hold fast the reader by means of the latter's curiosity. It says something else: though the reader, like the fancy or the imagination or the thoughts, must be governed, the reader is essential. In the terms of the passage quoted, reading is being mounted; if it is an act of being controlled by the author, it is also that author's means of conveyance along the journey that is writing. Without the reader, then, the writer cannot move. The writer needs the reader. The relationship of writer to reader may be one of master to slave, but it is at least complicated by the situation of need it describes.

The language Swift employs to present the writer-reader relationship is, of course, sexual. In 'mounting' the reader, the writer assumes the supposed sexual authority of the male, occupying the male's position in relation to the female position of the reader. The following passage, which opens with the paradoxical relationship of blindness to insight, raising again the question of Swift's own blindness and insight, explores most thoroughly the links among writer/reader, master/slave, and male/female:

> . . . wise Philosophers hold all Writings to be *fruitful* in the Proportion they are *dark*; And therefore, the *true illuminated* (that is to say, the *Darkest* of all) have met with such numberless Commentators, whose *Scholiastick* Midwifry hath deliver'd them of Meanings, that the Authors themselves, perhaps, never conceived, and yet may very justly be allowed the Lawful Parents of them: The Words of such Writers being like Seed, which, however scattered at random, when they light upon a fruitful Ground, will multiply far beyond either the Hopes or Imagination of the Sower.
>
> (*PW*, 1: 118)

We must read carefully this difficult passage. Though Swift desires that the natural parent have the authority, his language complicates the matter considerably. First, Swift concedes a good bit in turning immediately to the question of the 'lawful', that is, the merely conventional or socially established. Moreover, his figures carry him well beyond, and indeed counter to, his apparent intentions, for as with the previous passage we read, the writer no longer appears as independent, autonomous authority. According to this passage, indeed, the writer-male sows his seed, which requires for growth and development the fertile ground that is the reader-female. In this situation of partnership described by Swift's figurative language, the reader is just as important as the writer, the mother as the father. But the passage directly confronts another, related, and more immediate point, and that concerns the relation among writer, words, and meanings. A note following the word 'seed' in the passage claims that 'nothing is more frequent than for Commentators to force Interpretation, which the Author never meant'. Likewise, the main passage asserts that commentary 'delivers' texts of meanings 'the Authors themselves, perhaps, never conceived'. That is, commentary is creative, bringing out of the text what the author never put in. Yet the passage proceeds to grant that, even so, the author is the lawful parent because words are like seed. Here the passage obscures the crucial distinction between the author as male sowing his sperm-seed and author as sower of words as seed. But if words are like seed, and not just the male seed, they are no longer within the author's range of authority and control. Though the male may be said to have authored another being, no matter how scattered his seed was, what authority can seed, or words, claim? Surely not that of the sower, whose function is minimal. If the author is, then, like the sower of seed, rather than a father, his authority regarding the words sown or their meanings is negligible. If this is true, then contrary to Swift's claim, interpretations are not forced: words being free, freeplay reigns. Parentage is thus questioned, and so is the authority of the author. What we have here is evidently an example of what the text itself calls 'uncontroulable Demonstration' (*PW*, 1: 21).[12]

In 'A Digression concerning Critics' occurs another questioning of authority and a subversion of logic. According to the Hack, the Moderns 'have proved beyond contradiction, that the very finest Things *delivered* of old, have been long since invented, and brought to Light by much later *Pens*; and that the noblest Discoveries those Antients ever made, of Art or of Nature, have all been produced by the transcending Genius of the present Age' (*PW*, 1: 59, italics added). What was earlier delivered has recently been invented. The present has produced, that is, made, the discoveries past ages offered. The later pen (or penis) has authored what had been much earlier delivered. Is this satirized passage insightful or merely mad in its deconstruction of authority?

Logic is, of course, similarly flouted elsewhere in *A Tale of a Tub*. Homer, for example, that 'tolerable Genius', is blasted for his 'many gross Errors': not only did he 'read but very superficially, either *Sendivogius, Behmen*, or *Anthroposophia Theomagica*', but – 'a Fault far more notorious to tax this Author with' – Homer also reveals 'gross Ignorance in the *Common Laws of this Realm*, and in the Doctrine as well as Discipline of the Church of *England*' (*PW*, 1: 79–80). There is no denying the Hack's general madness, for as Swift presents him, his fancy has gotten astride his reason and has driven out the 'common Understanding'.

We can now see, however, thanks especially to the work of Derrida, de Man, and others, that what the Hack says, though presented as madness by the satirist, contains much insight. As Barbara Johnson puts it, a deconstructive reading shows 'the *necessity* with which what [an author] *does* see is systematically related to what he does *not* see'.[13] In the Hack, as in Swift's own declarations, appears a complex mixture of blindness and insight, which complicates the usual binary opposition. The supposedly insightful (i.e., satirical) text may then appear most blind in condemning the blind but insightful Hack. *A Tale of a Tub* itself makes the point when the Hack comments upon 'how near the Frontiers of Height and Depth border upon each other', how 'one who travels the *East* [eventually runs] into the *West*', and how 'a strait line [is eventually] drawn by its own Length into a Circle' (*PW*, 1: 99). Blindness and insight appear to relate to each other as do fancy and reason, slave and master, female and male, reader and writer, reading and writing. In this situation the will is a very complicated text.

Notes

1. I have discussed this issue, in somewhat similar but briefer terms, in 'Interpretation and Meaning in *A Tale of a Tub*', *Essays in Literature*, 8 (1981), 233–9. I have found the following studies particularly useful in threading my way through the maze of Swift's text: RONALD PAULSON, *Theme and Structure in Swift's 'A Tale of a Tub'* (New Haven, CT, 1960), and JOHN R. CLARK, *Form and Frenzy in 'A Tale of a Tub'* (Ithaca, NY, 1969).

2. See J. HILLIS MILLER, 'Georges Poulet's "Criticism of Identification"', in *The Quest for Imagination*, ed. O. B. HARDISON, JR. (Cleveland, OH, 1971), pp. 191–224, and his 'Tradition and Difference', *Diacritics*, 2 (1972), 6–13.

3. GEOFFREY HARTMAN, *Saving the Text: Literature/Derrida/Philosophy* (Baltimore, MD, 1981).

4 See, in this connection, BARBARA JOHNSON, *The Critical Difference: Essays in the Contemporary Rhetoric of Reading* (Baltimore, MD, 1980).

5. Hartman's term; see GEOFFREY HARTMAN, *Criticism in the Wilderness: The Study of Literature Today* (New Haven, CT, 1980), p. 226.

6. See PAUL DE MAN's *Blindness and Insight: Essays in the Rhetoric of Contemporary Criticism* (New York, 1971).

7. See the unpublished essay by my former student MICHAEL KILDUFF entitled 'Satire of Reading: Swift's *A Tale of a Tub*'.

8. On this point, as well as others relating to the *Tale*, see MAUREEN QUILLIGAN, *The Language of Allegory: Defining the Genre* (Ithaca, NY, 1979).

9. BARBARA JOHNSON, 'Translator's Introduction' to JACQUES DERRIDA, *Dissemination*, trans. BARBARA JOHNSON (Chicago, 1981), p. ix.

10. JACQUES DERRIDA, *Of Grammatology*, trans. GAYATRI CHAKRAVORTY SPIVAK (Baltimore, MD, 1976), p. 143.

11. See also QUILLIGAN, *Language of Allegory*, pp. 66–7, for such wordplay as that on 'textus' as both coat and text.

12. Swift does attempt to limit his points in the passage quoted to 'such writers' as 'the true illuminated'. I argue that the issue is not the degree of authorial 'sense' and control but language itself.

13. JOHNSON, 'Translator's Introduction', p. xv.

Notes on Authors

G. Douglas Atkins is Professor of English at the University of Kansas. He has written extensively on literary theory, especially deconstructive strategies: *Reading Deconstruction/Deconstructive Reading* (1983), *Geoffrey Hartman: Criticism as Answerable Style* (1990) and *Estranging the Familiar: Toward a Revitalized Critical Writing* (1992). He has also edited, with Laura Morrow, a conspectus of *Contemporary Literary Theory* (1987), and contributed two essays on the link between theory and the period: 'A(fter) D(econstruction): the Relations of Literature and Religion in the Wake of Deconstruction', *Studies in the Literary Imagination*, 18 (1985), 89–100, and 'A Matter of Difference: Deconstruction and Eighteenth-Century Studies', *The Eighteenth Century: Theory and Interpretation*, 28 (1987), 264–9. He has also put these theoretical concerns into practice in two studies, *The Faith of John Dryden: Change and Continuity* (1980) and *Quests of Difference: Reading Pope's Poems* (1986).

Louise K. Barnett is Associate Professor in English at Rutgers University, New Jersey. *Swift's Poetic Worlds* was published in 1981, and her study of 'Voyeurism in Swift's Poetry' appeared in *Studies in the Literary Imagination*, 17 (1984), 17–26. She also works extensively on American Literature. Her *Authority and Speech: Language, Society, and Self in the American Novel* appeared in 1993.

Terry J. Castle is Professor of English at Stanford University, California. Since her work on the deconstructive properties of *Gulliver's Travels* (1980) which is reproduced in this collection, she has written *Clarissa's Ciphers: Meaning and Disruption in Richardson's 'Clarissa'* (1982), *Masquerade and Civilization: The Carnivalesque in Eighteenth-Century English Culture and Fiction* (1986) and *The Female Thermometer: Eighteenth-Century Culture and the Invention of the Uncanny* (1995). Most recently, she has also worked on contemporary gay culture; see her *Noel Coward and Radclyffe Hall: Kindred Spirits* (1996). Her edition of Austen's *Northanger Abbey, Lady Susan, The Watsons and Sanditon* will appear in 1998.

Margaret Anne Doody is Professor of English and Comparative Literature at Vanderbilt University, Tennessee. Her revaluation of the period's verse, *The Daring Muse: Augustan Poetry Reconsidered* appeared in 1985. Since then she has worked on Samuel Richardson. Her edition (with Peter Sabor) of *Samuel Richardson: Tercentenary*

Essays appeared in 1989, and she was one of the editors of *The Clarissa Project* of 1990. She has edited Frances Burney's *Cecilia* (with Peter Sabor, 1988), *The Wanderer* (1991) and *Evelina* (1994), and also Jane Austen's juvenilia, *Catherine and Other Writings* (with Douglas Murray, 1993). Her *The True History of the Novel* appeared in 1997.

CAROLE FABRICANT is Professor of English at the University of California at Riverside. Her seminal study of *Swift's Landscape* first appeared in 1982, and was re-issued, with a new introduction, in 1995. She has explored the theoretical difficulties inherent in the evaluation of eighteenth-century writing in two essays: 'Pope's Moral, Political and Cultural Combat', *The Eighteenth Century: Theory and Interpretation*, 29 (1988), 165–87, and 'The Battle of the Ancients and (post) Moderns: Rethinking Swift through Contemporary Perspectives', *The Eighteenth Century*, 32 (1991), 256–73.

CAROL HOULIHAN FLYNN is Professor of English at Tufts University, Massachusetts. Her *Samuel Richardson: Man of Letters* was published in 1982 and *The Body in Swift and Defoe* in 1990. Her most recent work has been 'Closing Down the Theater and Other Critical Abuses', *The Eighteenth Century: Theory and Interpretation*, 37 (1996), 224–56.

THOMAS B. GILMORE, JR is an Emeritus Professor of English at Georgia State University. He has worked widely on the eighteenth century, especially Johnson and Boswell. He is the editor of *Early Eighteenth-Century Essays on Taste* (1972), and introduced the 1968 Augustan Reprint Society edition of Walter Harte's *An Essay on Satire, Particularly on The Dunciad*. His *Equivocal Spirits: Alcoholism and Drinking in Twentieth-Century Literature* came out in 1987.

BREAN S. HAMMOND is Pro Vice-Chancellor and Rendell Professor of English at the University of Wales at Aberystwyth. He has published widely on early eighteenth-century satire, and is editor of the *British Journal of Eighteenth-Century Studies*. His work on the Scriblerians has included *Pope and Bolingbroke: A Study of Friendship and Influence* (1984), a volume on *Pope* for the Harvester New Readings series (1986), an Open University Guide to *Gulliver's Travels* (1988) and the Longman Critical Reader on *Pope* (1996). His study of the cultural and economic contexts of *Professional Imaginative Writing in England, 1670–1740: 'Hackney for Bread'* appeared in 1997.

RICHARD H. RODINO was associate professor of English at the College of the Holy Cross until his early death in 1990. His work on Swift placed great emphasis not only on how he was actually read but also how he implicated the reader in his webs of irony. His major contributions were his edition of *Swift Studies, 1965–1980:*

An Annotated Bibliography (1984), followed by a supplement (co-edited with Hermann J. Real and Heinz J. Vienken) in 1987 and (posthumously) his edition (with Real) of *Reading Swift: Papers from the Second Münster Symposium on Jonathan Swift* (1993). He continues the themes announced in his *PMLA* essay included here in 'Canon and Hermeneutics in Eighteenth-Century Literary Studies', *Eighteenth-Century Life*, 16 (1992), 214–29.

EDWARD SAID is Professor of English and Comparative Literature at Columbia University. His most famous work has focused on the appropriation by the West of alternative modes of thinking, expressed most forcibly in his *Orientalism* (1978) and *Culture and Imperialism* (1993). The contribution reproduced here is from his collection of essays, *The World, the Text and the Critic* (1983; European edn, 1984), which traces the way any sense of original intention is always part of an intricate network of 'worldly' traces. Most recently, his 1993 Reith Lectures for the BBC have been published as *Representations of the Intellectual* (1994) and a set of explorations into the links between music and literary history as *From Silence to Sound and Back Again: Music, Literature and History* (1997).

PETER STALLYBRASS is Professor of English, Comparative Literature and Literary Theory at the University of Pennsylvania, and has mainly worked on Renaissance cultural representations. He co-authored *The Politics and Poetics of Transgression* (1984) with Allon White. With David S. Kastan he has edited *Staging the Renaissance: Reinterpretations of Elizabethan and Jacobean Drama* (1991), and, with Margreta de Grazia and Maureen Quilligan, *Subject and Object in Renaissance Culture* (1996). His most recent work is (co-edited with Jeffrey Masten) *Language Machines: Technologies of Literature and Cultural Production* (1997).

MARCUS WALSH is a Reader in English at the University of Birmingham. His valuable contribution to the theory of textual editing is best illustrated by his edition (with Ian Small) of *The Theory and Practice of Text-Editing: Essays in Honour of J. T. Boulton* (1991) and *Shakespeare, Milton and Eighteenth-Century Literary Editing: The Beginnings of Interpretative Scholarship* (1997). He has edited two volumes of the Clarendon Press edition of the Poetical Works of Christopher Smart: volume II (*Religious Poetry, 1763–1771* [with Karina Williamson, 1984]) and volume III (*A Translation of the Psalms of David* [1987]), and (with Karina Williamson) the Penguin *Selected Poems of Christopher Smart* (1991).

ALLON WHITE was Lecturer in English at the University of Sussex when he died tragically early in 1988. Besides his collaboration with

Peter Stallybrass, he wrote a wide-ranging account of *The Uses of Obscurity: The Fiction of Early Modernism* (1981). His autobiographical writings appeared first in the *London Review of Books*, and were published as *Too Close to the Bone* in 1991. John Barrell edited his collected essays and autobiography (with an Introduction by Stuart Hall) as *Carnival, Hysteria and Writing* (1992).

PENELOPE WILSON is Fellow of New Hall, Cambridge. Her essay on 'Feminism and the Augustans: Some Readings and Problems' first appeared in the *Critical Quarterly* in 1986. She has also edited Defoe's *Capt. Singleton* (1990).

DEBORAH BAKER WYRICK is Professor of English at Duke University, North Carolina. Her *Jonathan Swift and the Vested Word* was published in 1990.

EVERETT ZIMMERMAN is Professor of English at the University of California at Santa Barbara. Aside from *Swift's Narrative Satires* (1983), his interests in narratology can best be seen in his 'Tristram Shandy and Narrative Representation', *The Eighteenth Century: Theory and Interpretation*, 28 (1987), 127–47, and *The Boundaries of Fiction: History and the Eighteenth-Century Novel* (1996).

Further Reading

The following titles are to be consulted in addition to the sources for essays and extracts in the Reader. Headnotes to each section introduce these works.

Editions

The fullest is that used for the references in this collection, the Herbert Davis edition of the *Prose Works* and Pat Rogers's edition of the *Complete Poems*. In addition, the following selections offer helpful annotation:

1. McMINN, JOSEPH (ed.), *Swift's Pamphlets: An Introductory Selection* (Gerrards Cross, 1991).

Traces Swift's perennial Irish concerns throughout his writing career. The selection contains three of the *Drapier's Letters*, *A Modest Proposal* and his moving sermon, 'Causes of the Wretched Condition of Ireland'. An appendix provides a 'Checklist of Swift's writings on Irish affairs'. There then follows an up-to-date Select Bibliography on the Irish context.

2. ROSS, ANGUS and WOOLLEY, DAVID (eds), *A Tale of a Tub and Other Works* (Oxford, 1986).

This edition presents the works that accompanied the *Tale* in the 1704 edition, *The Battle of the Books* and *The Mechanical Operation of the Spirit*. The editors supply a lucid Introduction, a Chronology for the *Tale*, including events leading up to and after first publication. The annotation is informative, and is followed by a Glossary and Index. There are also sections on 'Additions' to the *Tale*, extracts from the literary context to the works and then one that examines the relationship of Thomas Swift to the *Tale*.

3. TURNER, PAUL (ed.), *Gulliver's Travels* (Oxford, 1971).

Concise but still very informative introduction. Detailed notes.

4. WILLIAMS, KATHLEEN (ed.), *A Tale of a Tub and Other Satires* (London and New York, 1975).

Further Reading

The contents of the 1704 volume plus (among others) *An Argument Against Abolishing Christianity* and *A Modest Proposal.*

Biographies

1. Downie, J. A., *Jonathan Swift: Political Writer* (London, 1984).

A critical biography that concentrates (although not exclusively) on Swift's political sensibilities, and much less on how he may be claimed for a Tory or Whig party. Informative chapters on the major works help the reader assess the interaction between text and author.

2. Ehrenpreis, Irvin, *Swift: The Man, His Works, and the Age*, 3 vols (London and Cambridge, MA, 1962–83).

A definitive achievement. Delivers on all that the title promises. Vol. 1: *Mr. Swift and His Contemporaries* (1962 – dealing in the main with the 1704 volume). Vol. 2: *Dr. Swift* (1967 – the political phase up to 1714). Vol. 3: *Dean Swift* (1983).

3. McMinn, Joseph, *Jonathan Swift: A Literary Life* (Basingstoke, (1991).

A compact account. Very perceptive on the later, Irish period.

4. Nokes, David, *Jonathan Swift: A Hypocrite Reversed. A Critical Biography* (Oxford, 1985).

A readable life, attempting to take Swift's own self-estimates alongside those of his contemporaries. Particularly helpful on the English political phase.

General Studies

1. Carnochan, W. B., *Lemuel Gulliver's Mirror for Man* (Berkeley, CA, 1968).

One of the first studies to emphasize how Swift played profound games with the reader. There are provocative sections on the philosophical background, definitions of Man and the satiric context.

2. Donoghue, Denis, *Jonathan Swift: A Critical Introduction* (Cambridge, 1969).

A sensitive examination of how Swift's *personae* initially hide but ultimately reveal his literary personality. One of the first studies to question the image of Swift merely as a master rhetorician.

3. DOWNIE, J. A., 'Swift and Jacobitism', *Journal of English Literary History*, 64 (1997), 887–902.

An unsparing look at the evidence for Swift's Jacobite links. Takes issue with Higgins's approach (see below) although there is also some common ground.

4. ELLIOTT, ROBERT C., *The Literary Persona* (Chicago, 1982).

Refuses to take the view that biographical accounts of Swift provide a master interpretation of his irony. Also casts doubt, however, on the New Critical bias on the text as the only reliable witness. Invaluable context on satiric traditions. Pp. 107–23 ('Swift's "I"') is an excellent survey of how Swift constructs an interpretative 'horizon' for the reader.

5. FABRICANT, CAROLE, 'The Battle of the Ancients and (Post)Moderns: Rethinking Swift through Contemporary Perspectives', *The Eighteenth Century: Theory and Interpretation*, 32 (1991), 256–73.

A survey of recent theoretical readings which manages to accomplish comprehensiveness as well as detail. Particularly enlightening on reader-response theories.

6. FERGUSON, OLIVER, *Jonathan Swift and Ireland* (Urbana, IL, 1962).

Still possibly the best account of how Swift's view of his heritage underwent at times radical change. An opening chapter on 'The "Singular Condition" of Eighteenth-Century Ireland' is alive to the complex nuances of the Irish cultural situation, and there then follow thematic sections, the most successful being that on 'The Drapier' and 'The Last Proposals', the latter of which shows how much his Irishness weighed heavily on Swift during his last attempts to make sense of his life.

7. GRIFFIN, DUSTIN, *Satire: An Introduction* (Lexington, KY, 1994).

Although a general generic study, Griffin's main clutch of examples are from classical and eighteenth-century literature. An excellent opening chapter, 'Theories of Satire in Polemical Context', moves the study of the form towards the theories of *heteroglossia* popularized by Bakhtin. Swift is referred to throughout.

8. GRIFFIN, DUSTIN, 'Swift and Patronage', *Studies in Eighteenth-Century Culture*, 21 (1992), 197–205.

A focused piece on the difficulties Swift faced in finding an audience for his work, and which he turned to advantage by means of his irony.

9. HIGGINS, IAN, *Swift's Politics: A Study in Disaffection* (Cambridge, 1994).

Reviewed as a defence of Swift's supposed Jacobite sympathies, but there is a great deal more than that in this study of his 'disaffection', which is as much a matter of temperament as conviction. Perhaps this lacks clinching evidence of Swift's Jacobitism in the last analysis but there is also excellent material on the ideologies available to Swift and succinct chapters on both the *Tale* and *Gulliver*. There is also a wide-ranging bibliography.

10. KROPF, CARL R. (ed.), *Reader Entrapment in Eighteenth-Century Literature* (New York, 1992).

Kropf's Introduction is an accessible study of ways to define the tendency of Swift, among others, to betray the reader (or have her/himself do it in the process of reading). G. Douglas Atkins ties it in with poststructuralism ('On the Critical Character: Reading and Writing in the Poststructuralist Age' [pp. 1–14]), Louise K. Barnett concentrates on 'Voyeurism as Entrapment in Swift's Poetry' (pp. 45–62) and Frederik N. Smith supplies a challenging chapter on 'The Danger of Reading Swift: The Double Binds of *Gulliver's Travels*' (pp. 109–30).

11. LEAVIS, F. R., *The Common Pursuit* (London, 1952).

Contains the influential 'The Irony of Swift' (pp. 73–87), which is the most negative verdict on the rhetoric, which it finds 'purely destructive'. A combative account which needs to be read alongside more indulgent perspectives.

12. MAHONY, ROBERT, *Jonathan Swift: The Irish Identity* (New Haven, CT, 1995).

An exhaustive trawl through Swift's critical heritage, examining his earliest critical stature at the hands of both Irish and English commentators. The last chapter on his reputation, 1930–1995, traces how Swift's patriot image was superseded by readings which stressed his personality.

13. MARTZ, LOUIS L. and WILLIAMS, AUBREY (eds), *The Author in his Work: Essays on a Problem in Criticism* (New Haven, CT, 1978).

Deserves to be read not just for its essay on Swift, 'The Mystery of Personal Identity: Swift's Verses on his Own Death' (pp. 245–62), but also for its general treatment of an authorial *ethos*.

14. MONTAG, WARREN, *The Unthinkable Swift: The Spontaneous Philosophy of a Church of England Man* (London, 1994).

Valuable for its detailed illustrations of Swift's religious and political ideas – or, to put it rather more accurately, how the state and belief were intermingled in current thinking. Montag perceives how Swift's impulses informed his faith, and there then follow perceptive sections on the major works, the most useful of which are those on the *Tale* (Chapter 3) and on Swift's own particular brand of Anglicanism (Chapter 2).

15. RAWSON, CLAUDE, *Gulliver and the Gentle Reader: Studies in Swift and our Time* (London, 1973).

The title essay is chapter one of this collection and has proved one of the most influential readings of Swift's irony (after Leavis). Rawson believes that the 'parodic intrusions of Swift's "authors"' carry a strength 'of personal charge'. The novelty of this strategy carries an attack on the reader as part of the overall thesis. Chapter two also bears on the *topoi* investigated in this collection, 'Order and Cruelty: Swift, Pope and Johnson', and in it Rawson answers (among others) Leavis's dismissal of the satire.

16. RAWSON, CLAUDE (ed.), *The Character of Swift's Satire: A Revised Focus* (Newark, DE, 1983).

Notable for its title essay by Rawson, which locates a dichotomy in the irony composed of the recognition of instinctual sin and also redemptive traditions. See also John Traugott's 'A Tale of a Tub' (pp. 83–126) which is full of information on where Swift took inspiration for his evil character sketches.

17. WOOD, NIGEL, *Swift* (Brighton, 1986).

A comparative attempt to read Swift's works from the perspectives of both 'mimetic' and 'textualist' criticism. Both 'Hard' and 'Soft' schools of thought where Swift's satire is concerned need to dwell more on the grounds (provided by Swift) for such disagreement.

Further Reading

Books and Articles on Particular Works

(a)   A Tale of a Tub

1. CONNERY, BRIAN A., 'The Persona as Pretender and the Reader as Constitutional Subject in Swift's *Tale*', in *Cutting Edges: Postmodern Critical Essays on Eighteenth-Century Satire*, ed. JAMES A. GILL (Knoxville, TN, 1995), pp. 159–80.

An astute piece that casts a cold eye on the premature distinction between 'mimetic' and 'textocentric' approaches. The latter are taken to be further divisible into those who aspire to absolute liberty and those who opt for 'limited monarchy', i.e., those who give themselves up to the game.

2. DE PORTE, MICHAEL, *Nightmares and Hobby Horses: Swift, Sterne, and Augustan Ideas of Madness* (San Marino, CA, 1974).

A study of contemporary theories of the imagination and madness. There is an ingenious deployment of these in an exploration of the Teller's deranged metaphors (see pp. 60–89).

3. KENNER, HUGH, *The Stoic Comedians* (London, 1964).

Treats the *Tale* (pp. 37–42) as a technocratic artefact, and shows Swift aware throughout of the new possibilities of print culture.

4. KORKOWSKI, EUGENE, 'With an Eye to the Bunghole: Figures of Containment in *A Tale of a Tub*', *Studies in English Literature*, 15 (1975), 391–408.

Swift's tub represents all types of containment for Korkowski, and it allows him to play with distinctions between inner/outer and real/false.

5. NASH, RICHARD, 'Entrapment and Ironic Modes in *A Tale of a Tub*', *Eighteenth-century Studies*, 24 (1991), 415–31.

A complex piece tracing the methods and also the compulsions of the *Tale* while reading it against Swift's apparent desire to ensnare the reader rather than to inform her/him.

6. SMITH, FREDERIK N., *Language and Reality in Swift's A Tale of a Tub* (Columbus, OH, 1979).

Argues for the proposition that it is style that creates meaning in the work. There is plentiful reference to the linguistic philosophies and theories that Swift parodied and also supported.

(b)   Gulliver's Travels

1. DAVIS, LENNARD J., *Factual Fictions: The Origins of the English Novel* (New York, 1983).

Explores the hybridity of the novel's genesis, the 'factual fiction', and how a requirement for journalistic style helped it become acceptable. The chapters on 'Theories of Fiction in Early English Novels' and 'The Language of Print' are valuable in providing a context for Swift's 'novel'.

2. HOLLY, GRANT, 'Travel and Translation: Textuality in *Gulliver's Travels*', *Criticism*, 21 (1979), 134–52.

Attempts to show how the process of signifying is actually the main subject of Swift's traveller's tale. Provocative, yet detailed, reading.

3. HUNTER, J. PAUL, *Before Novels: The Cultural Contexts of Eighteenth-century Fiction* (New York, 1990).

Not directly on *Gulliver's Travels* but excellent scene-setting on the form and an expected audience. There are three sections: 'Texts' (on the Novel form), 'Contexts' (readers) and 'Pre-Texts' (use made of non-fictional strategies), and each would aid a reading of Swift's irony.

4. KEENER, FREDERICK M., *The Chain of Becoming: The Philosophical Tale, the Novel, and a Neglected Realism of the Enlightenment: Swift, Montesquieu, Voltaire, Johnson and Austen* (New York, 1983).

Provides a genealogy of the philosophical tale. The chapter on *Gulliver's Travels* (pp. 89–126) associates the narrative with several 'print' prose forms – almanac, project and traveller's tale – that Swift officially found suspect.

5. LOCK, F. P., *The Politics of Gulliver's Travels* (Oxford, 1980).

A study that has been reviewed both very favourably and also with some animosity. Those who take issue with its approach find Lock's concentration on general philosophical and political scientific questions blind to Swift's own partisan outlook in the 1720s, yet, in general, its marshalling of political phraseology and literary allusion is a genuine contribution to a knowledge of Swift's reading.

6. SEIDEL, MICHAEL, '*Gulliver's Travels* and the Contracts of Fiction', in *The Cambridge Companion to the Eighteenth-Century Novel*, ed. JOHN RICHETTI (Cambridge, 1996), pp. 72–89.

An introductory essay reviewing the options taken by Swift in his manipulation of the form. The volume as a whole supports Seidel's work in this essay, and mention must be made of J. Paul Hunter's essay on 'The Novel and Social/Cultural History' (pp. 9–40).

7. TODD, DENNIS, 'The Hairy Maid at the Harpsichord: Some Speculations on the Meaning of *Gulliver's Travels*', *Texas Studies in Literature and Language*, 34 (1992), 239–83.

Uncovers many links with popular rituals, such as fairs and pageants, and applies this background to several of the grotesque features of the book.

(c) Poems

1. FISCHER, JOHN Irwin, *On Swift's Poetry* (Gainesville, FL, 1978).

A selective study of certain poems (most illuminating on 'Vanbrug's House'). Little to say about the scatological poems, but full of awareness of how Swift regarded the art of poetry itself.

2. FISCHER, JOHN IRWIN and MELL, DONALD C., Jr, (eds), *Contemporary Studies of Swift's Poetry* (Newark, DE, 1981).

A wide selection of essays on the poetry, most of which supply evidence towards the context of individual works. The following engage with some of the concerns explored in this collection: (a) RICHARD H. RODINO, 'Notes on the Developing Motives and Structures of Swift's Poetry', (b) LOUISE K. BARNETT, 'Fictive Self-portraiture in Swift's Poetry', and (c) ROBERT W. UPHAUS, 'Swift's Irony Reconsidered'.

3. NUSSBAUM, FELICITY, 'Juvenal, Swift and *The Folly of Love*', *Eighteenth-Century Studies*, 9 (1976), 540–52.

An extended reading of 'A Beautiful Young Nymph Going to Bed', wherein Nussbaum finally locates some sympathetic ingredients in Swift's version of a traditional *topos*. The intertextual nuances between Swift and Juvenal are sensitively explored.

4. Nussbaum, Felicity, *The Brink of All We Hate: English Satires on Women, 1660–1750* (Lexington, KY, 1984).

Particularly strong on the Restoration traditions that Swift inherited. Chapter VI (' "The Sex's Flight": Women and Time in Swift's Poetry' [pp. 94–116]) looks at Juvenal and, as a counterweight, the Stella poems.

5. Pollak, Ellen, *The Politics of Sexual Myth: Gender and Ideology in the Verse of Swift and Pope* (Chicago, 1985).

Concerned to identify the schism in Swift's representations of women between Angel and Whore. This fault-line went so deep that the integration in one person of spiritual and erotic qualities became impossible.

(d) Irish Tracts

1. Canning, Rick G., ' "Ignorant, Illiterate Creatures": Gender and Colonial Justification in Swift's *Injured Lady* and *The Answer to the Injured Lady*', *Journal of English Literary History*, 64 (1997), 77–98.

Traces the intersection of both racist and chauvinist models of thought in Swift's intended readership. To some extent, these work against each other, as the consequences of imaging the Irish nation as female has consequences that follow a figurative rather than a rational process.

2. Davis, Lloyd, 'Reading Irony: Dialogism in *A Modest Proposal*', *Journal of the Australasian Universities Language and Literature Association*, 77 (1992), 32–55.

Deploys Bakhtin's concept of the dialogic to capture the *Proposal*'s shifting perspectives, which in turn suggest genuine conflict in Swift.

3. Nokes, David, 'Swift and the Beggars', *Essays in Criticism*, 26 (1976), 218–35.

Draws on the sermons to demonstrate that Swift found economic hardship to be Man's lot. This position is modified when we come to the satires, where he could still target the English for Irish poverty.

4. Rawson, Claude, 'The Injured Lady and the Drapier: A Reading of Swift's Irish Tracts', *Prose Studies*, 3 (1980), 15–43.

Treats the Drapier as a rhetorical voice, which is devised only so as to be seen through. The self-revelations allowed the persona are carefully calculated to form an ideal of the Irish in response to the economically superior English.

5. REILLY, PATRICK, 'The Displaced Person: Swift and Ireland', *Swift Studies*, 8 (1993), 68–82.

Emphasizes the *anomie* in Swift's relationship with the Irish, where his own sense of loss of identity takes shape in a divided Anglo-Irish self.

(See also the volumes by Ferguson and Mahony above.)

Index

Index